The Art of
Instrument Flying

TAB
PRACTICAL
FLYING SERIES

Other Books in the TAB Practical Flying Series

The Art of
Instrument Flying

Third Edition

J.R. Williams

TAB Books

Imprint of McGraw-Hill

New York San Francisco Washington, D.C. Auckland Bogotá
Caracas Lisbon London Madrid Mexico City Milan
Montreal New Delhi San Juan Singapore
Sydney Tokyo Toronto

McGraw-Hill

A Division of The McGraw·Hill Companies

pbk   5 6 7 8 9 10 FGR/FGR   0 0
hc   3 4 5 6 7 8 9 FGR/FGR 9 0 0 9 8

Product or brand names used in this book may be trade names or trademarks. Where
we believe that there may be proprietary claims to such trade names or trademarks,
the name has been used with an initial capital or it has been capitalized in the style
used by the name claimant. Regardless of the capitalization used, all such names
have been used in an editorial manner without any intent to convey endorsement of
or other affiliation with the name claimant. Neither the author nor the publisher intends
to express any judgment as to the validity or legal status of any such proprietary
claims.

Library of Congress Cataloging-in-Publication Data
Williams, J. R., 1934–
     The art of instrument flying / by J.R. Williams.—3rd ed.
        p. cm.—(Tab practical flying series)
     Includes index.
     ISBN 0-07-070598-4 (h) ISBN 0-07-070599-2 (p)
     1. Instrument flying. I. Title. II. Series.
   TL711.B6W545 1995
   629.132'5214—dc20   95-39608
                                                        CIP

McGraw-Hill books are available at special quantity discounts to use as premiums
and sales promotions, or for use in corporate training programs. For more information,
please write to the Director of Special Sales, McGraw-Hill, 11 West 19th Street, New
York, NY 10011. Or contact your local bookstore.

Acquisitions editor: Shelley IC. Chevalier
Editorial team: Robert E. Ostrander, Executive Editor
                Norval G. Kennedy, Book Editor
                Jodi L. Tyler, Indexer
Production team: Katherine G. Brown, Director
                Wanda S. Ditch, Desktop Operator
                Nancy K. Mickley, Proofreading
                Jeffrey M. Hall, Computer Artist
                Janice Stottlemyer, Computer Artist
                Toya B. Warner, Computer Artist
Design team: Jaclyn J. Boone, Designer   0705992
             Katherine Lukaszewicz, Associate Designer   PFS

Contents

Acknowledgments

NO ONE JUST SITS DOWN AT A TYPEWRITER AND POUNDS OUT THIS TYPE OF book. It comes from years of experience and the help of numerous people; therefore, I would like to acknowledge as much of this help as the passage of years will allow me to remember. The list is by no means complete, and to those I have unintentionally omitted, I apologize.

In chronological order, none of this would have been possible without the help and support of my late mother and father, both of whom taught me that anything worth having is worth working for. They must have wondered many times if their number one son would ever settle down and amount to anything.

Then there was the late K. Russell Smith of the Smith Flying Service in Forty-Fort, Pennsylvania, who owned the J-3s, PA-11s, and the Cessna 150 and 172 that became my early classrooms. They were assigned to me by the late Ms. Gene Reynolds, who took care of her chicks like a mother hen, although they were ruled over by my primary and advanced flight instructor, the late John L. (Jack) Green with his ever-present cigar.

When I advanced into the instrument phase, I was tutored by the late Andy Perugino and Myrttyn Mack, both severe taskmasters who taught me to feel at home in a totally alien environment.

I will never forget my FAA friends at the Allentown, Pennsylvania, General Aviation District Office (GADO). Both John Doster, now retired, and the late Clarence Claybaugh not only flew check flights with me, but spent many additional hours answering questions both on the ground and in the air. Their patient reinforcement and improvement of techniques I had learned from my instructors plus their hammering on what seemed to be minor points certainly helped take off a lot of rough edges.

As an airline copilot (especially in an operation where you make a dozen landings a day and there are only about 50 captains) you learn something from everyone you fly with. Some of these things you accept as good practices and others you discard as not quite so good. But, if there is any semblance of professionalism in my flying, it was put there by watching and absorbing the styles of five fine gentlemen, now all retired: Captains Bruce S. MacBride, Emile J. Pepin, C.E. White, and the late Paul Hundsdorf, and Arthur Daegling. Art happened to be so close to me on the seniority list that I only flew with him once or twice, but we spent hours together discussing various flying philosophies and I learned a great deal. He was a long-time student of aeronautical history and a pilot par excellence.

After checking out as captain, I received an equal amount of help from many of the fine first and second officers I was proud to work with. Although the final decision has to rest with the pilot-in-command, it is augmented by the experience and inputs of everyone in the cockpit.

Throughout the book I mention the help I have received from Jeppesen Sanderson, Inc., but here I would like to specifically acknowledge the late Jack H. Davis, vice president, services, and his successor, James E. Terpstra, Senior Vice President, Flight Information and Technology, both of whom have personally given me every assistance I ever asked for. Thanks also must go to Williams B. King, Jr., flight information analyst, and all of the secretaries in their divisions who manage to get information to me seemingly the day after I ask for it.

For the second edition, Barbara Keepes, marketing communications manager at ARNAV Systems, Inc., was extremely helpful in providing me with all of the information I requested regarding their excellent Loran-C. Since that time, ARNAV has moved and I must thank Susan M. Hamner, Vice President Marketing, for her help in providing me with information concerning their fine GPS system.

I managed to locate an excellent modern instrument panel photograph at Raytheon/Beech Aircraft thanks to Mike Potts in public relations.

John Georg, public relations manager of Litton Aero Products, was very helpful in providing illustrations for the chapters on Omega and INS systems for the second edition. For this edition I must thank Mr. Newt Lesh, Division Counsel, and H. A. Baumach, Director Contracts and Subcontracts for their continued support.

I would also like to thank Tony L. Huebsch, public relations director at Collins Avionics, and all of his staff for being so kind as to provide illustrations for the flight director chapter in the second edition, and both Karen Tripp, public relations, and Mari Stark, marketing communications manager, for their continued support.

This project would never have gotten off the ground had it not been for my former editor (and now my very good friend) at *Private Pilot*, Dennis Shattuck, editorial director, who thought enough of my writing abilities to suggest a series of articles for his magazine and was magnanimous enough to subsequently release the rights to me so I could put everything together into a book form.

It was Howie Keefe, the world-famous unlimited racing pilot and past-owner of the modified P-51 *Miss America*, who suggested the chapter on the NOS charts. He then not only gave me the charts to use but showed me through his facilities at the Air Chart Co. in Venice, California, and spent a full day explaining how charts are developed. He also explained how he developed the concept for his simplified, time-saving method of chart revisions.

And I also want to acknowledge M. Gene Dow, at that time the owner/publisher of the General Aviation Press, who published the first volume, and Norval Kennedy, who edited it. In the "small-world department," Norval was subsequently the editor of the second edition and is the editor of this third edition.

Proofreading technical books, especially when the proofreader has no knowledge of the subject matter, has to be pure drudgery. I owe a lot to my wife, Jaslyn, for whom such a task was truly a labor of love.

I would like to thank Jeff Worsinger. Jeff was the aviation acquisitions editor of TAB Books, an imprint of McGraw-Hill, Inc., who was so helpful in breathing life into the first two editions of this book, and who contracted for this edition before beginning a new career.

For this third edition, thanks must go to Editor-in-Chief Kim Tabor, Aviation Acquisitions Administrator Sally Straight, and the new Aviation Acquisitions Editor Shelley IC. Chevalier, all of whom were most very helpful. I must also not forget all of the other aviation editors, secretaries, and proofreaders who worked so hard at perfecting the manuscript.

J.R. Williams

Introduction

THE ORIGINAL VERSION OF THIS BOOK WAS PRINTED IN MARCH 1980. IT MET with widespread approval and ended up winning the Best Technical Book Award for the Western Region of the Aviation/Space Writers Association in 1981. There were suggestions that we incorporate explanations of the National Ocean Service (NOS) approach charts along with those of the Jeppesen charts, and these were added to a subsequent edition in order to make it as useful as possible to the greatest number of people. A third version, TAB/McGraw-Hill's first edition, was improved further by the addition of a glossary containing terms of special interest to the instrument pilot. In turn, it won the 1989 Best Technical Book Award of the Western Region of the Aviation/Space Writers Association.

Review questions and answers were added to most of the chapters in the third edition. In addition, we incorporated chapters that would lead the readers into brief examples of what they can expect to work with as they move out of the simplest instrument cockpit, and into the esoteric world of flight directors, area navigation, and long-range navigation.

This edition adds an explanation of the newest state-of-the art navigational tool: the Global Positioning System (GPS).

I entered aviation after the lighted airways (beacons on mountain tops that were followed as airways—some were still in operation although not in use when I began flying) and just after the aural beams were being phased out. In fact, all of us in instrument training at the time had to suffer through endless hours in the original Link trainer attempting to "stay on the beam." If you were off to one side of the beam or other you would hear either an "N" (-.) or an "A" (.-) in Morse Code, depending on which side of the beam you were on. When on the beam, the signals would merge, resulting in a steady aural tone. Believe me, it was a maddening experience, but one that I am very happy to have attempted. Now, as I am leaving my aviation career, we are coming into a new age of exciting navigational performance, and that is the GPS system. Most of us feel that within a few more years the GPS system will replace all navigation that we are using now, including VOR, loran, Omega, and ILS. We are truly living in exciting times.

This book is the culmination of many years of work, study, and experience—most of which has been quite enjoyable.

The intent of this project is not to prime you to pass your instrument pilot written exam. The project contains no questions or answers that are connected with the FAA examinations. Nor is it intended to prepare you for a career as an instrument repair technician. Enough books are on the market that will do those things for you.

Instead, this text is intended to talk you through the actual "hands-on" flying of an aircraft, from the basics through the actual approaches, using only radios and instruments. In addition, I hope that you will be able to glean some of the nuances of the professional. To accomplish these goals I hope that as you read these pages you will be able to picture yourself at the controls of your own aircraft and that you can actually imagine that I am by your side talking you through the various maneuvers.

All of the chart formats and instrument procedures are based on U.S. Federal Aviation Regulations (FARs) and procedures, which can be quite different from the International Civil Aviation Organization (ICAO) terminologies and procedures used in other countries. If enough readers indicate an interest in ICAO procedures, perhaps they will be incorporated in a future edition.

There are many fine female pilots throughout aviation. Many of them are flying in the airline industry and perform as well or better than their male counterparts; therefore, efforts have been made to mix references toward men and women to reflect that fact.

For the instrument approaches, I have relied on material from Jeppesen Sanderson, Inc., because I feel that this material is the most frequently used in the aviation industry. I like the format as well as the method of revisions, although as I mentioned earlier, I will be explaining the various symbols shown on both the Jeppesen and NOS charts so that you will have no trouble making the transition from one format to the other.

Remember, however, that aviation is a rapidly changing industry, and regulations and chart formats keep changing in order to keep pace. What is in these pages was current when I wrote these words, but some of the regulatory or format information might be outdated by the time you read this, so it will be your responsibility to keep up with these changes as they come about.

Because there are more similarities in aircraft than differences, I have attempted to write this book in terms general enough that you will be able to easily adapt your flying skills to any aircraft you will be operating.

Abbreviations

ADF	automatic direction finder
ADI	attitude deviation indicator
A/FD	Airport/Facility Directory
AGL	above ground level
AI	attitude indicator
AIM	Airman's Information Manual
AIRMET	airman's meteorological information
ALS	approach light system
ALSF	ALS with sequential flashing lights
AMA	area minimum altitude
ARP	airport reference point
ARTCC	air route traffic control center
ASR	airport surveillance radar
ATC	air traffic control
ATIS	automatic terminal information service
ATP	airline transport pilot
BRG	bearing
CAS	calibrated airspeed
CAT II	ILS Category II
CATIII	AILS Category IIIA
CDI	course deviation indicator
CG	center of gravity
CTAF	common traffic advisory frequency
COP	changeover point
DA	decision altitude
DA (H)	decision altitude (Height)
DF	direction finder
DG	directional gyro
DH	decision height
DME	distance measuring equipment
DR	dead reckoning position
EAC	expected approach clearance time
EFC	expected further clearance time
ETA	expected time of arrival
ETD	expected time of departure
ETE	expected time en route
FAA	Federal Aviation Administration

ABBREVIATIONS

FAF	final approach fix
FAP	final approach point
FAR	Federal Aviation Regulation(s)
FAS	final approach segment
FL	flight level
FM	fan marker
FPM	feet per minute
FSS	flight service station
G	force of gravity
GADO	General Aviation District Office
GCA	ground-controlled approach
GPS	Global Positioning System
HAA	height above airport
HAT	height above touchdown
HDG	heading
HF	high frequency
HIRL	high intensity runway lights
hp	horsepower
HSI	horizontal deviation indicator
Hz	hertz; cycles per second
IAF	initial approach fix
IAP	instrument approach procedure
IAS	indicated airspeed
ICAO	International Civil Aviation Organization
IDENT	identify
IFR	instrument flight rules
ILS	instrument landing system
IM	inner marker
IMC	instrument meteorological conditions
INT	intersection
INS	inertial navigation system
IVSI	instantaneous vertical speed indicator
kHz	kilohertz; 1000 cycles per second
KIAS	knots indicated airspeed
KRM	instrument landing system used in eastern Europe
LAT	latitude
LDA	localizer- type directional aid
LF	low frequency
L/MF	low/medium frequency
LMM	middle compass locator
LOC	localizer
LOM	outer compass locator
LONG	longitude

MAA	maximum authorized altitude
MAP	missed approach point
MALSR	medium intensity approach lights with RAIL
MCA	minimum crossing altitude
MDA	minimum descent altitude
MEA	minimum en route IFR altitude
MHz	megahertz; one million cycles per second
MLS	microwave landing system
MM	middle marker
MOCA	minimum obstruction clearance altitude
MORA	minimum off route altitude
MPH	miles per hour
MRA	minimum reception altitude
MSA	minimum safe altitude/minimum sector altitude
MSL	mean sea level
MVA	minimum vectoring altitude
NA	not authorized
NDB	nondirectional beacon
NM	nautical miles
NoPT	no procedure turn
NOS	National Ocean Service
NOTAM	notice to airmen
OAT	outside air temperature
OBI	omni bearing indicator (same as CDI)
OBS	omni bearing selector
OCA	obstruction clearance altitude
OM	outer marker
omni	VOR
PAPI	precision approach path indicator
PAR	precision approach radar
PT	procedure turn
QFE	height above airport elevation (or runway threshold elevation) based on local station pressure
QNE	altimeter setting 29.92 inches Hg or 1013.2 Mb
QNH	altitude above sea level based on local station pressure
RAIL	runway alignment indicator lights
RCAG	remote center air/ground facility
RCL	runway centerline
RCLM	runway centerline markings
RCLS	runway centerline lighting system
RCO	remote communication outlet
REIL	runway end identification lights
RMI	radio magnetic indicator

ABBREVIATIONS

RNAV	area navigation
RVR	runway visual range
RVV	runway visual value
Rwy	runway
SDF	simplified directional facility
SFL	sequenced flashing lights
SID	standard instrument departure
SIGMET	significant meteorological information
SM	statute miles
SSALSR	simplified short approach light system with RAIL
STAR	standard terminal arrival route
SVFR	special visual flight rules
TACAN	tactical air navigation
TAS	true airspeed
TCH	threshold crossing height
TDZ	touchdown zone
TDZE	touchdown zone elevation
TDZL	touchdown zone lighting
TERPs	United States standard for terminal instrument procedure
TODA	takeoff distance available
TORA	takeoff run available
TWEB	transcribed weather broadcast
UHF	ultra high frequency
UTC	coordinated universal time; zulu time (Z); Greenwich mean time (GMT)
V_A	design maneuvering speed
VASI	visual approach slope indicator
VDP	visual descent point
VFR	visual flight rules
VHF	very high frequency
VIS	visibility
VMC	visual meteorological conditions
VNAV	vertical navigation
V_{NE}	never-exceed speed
VORTAC	VOR with TACAN
VOR	VOR test signal
VOT	VHF omnidirectional range
V_R	rotation speed
VSI	vertical speed indicator
W/P	waypoint
WX	weather
Z	zulu time; coordinated universal time (UTC); Greenwich mean time (GMT)

1
Instrument interpretation

INSTRUMENT FLIGHT IS AN EXCITING, PRECISE CHALLENGE BUT, MORE importantly, it is a psychological challenge. When you, as an instrument pilot, can psychologically accept two facts, you will have most of your problems licked.

Fact one is that your aircraft doesn't know the difference between day and night, or VFR and IFR conditions; it flies the same in all cases. From your first flight lesson you have learned that when you move the yoke or stick to the left, the left wing will roll away from you. If you push the left rudder pedal, the nose will yaw to the left. At slow speeds, such as when landing or taking off, this yaw will control your heading, while at higher speeds it will counteract the adverse yaw created by the drag of the aileron on the outside wing.

If you pull back on the stick or yoke, you pull the nose toward you. Opposite control forces will move the aircraft in the opposite directions.

Using power, your other control, only one thing is certain. If you reduce power sufficiently, your aircraft will descend, regardless of how you move the other controls.

I have intentionally avoided using the terms *up* and *down* as related to the horizon. When flying you can be in any attitude when you initiate a control input, and if you have enough speed and/or power, the aircraft will react as indicated above.

This becomes an important point to remember. Your aircraft will almost always re-act the same way to these control inputs, whether IFR or VFR, and whether single or multiengine, recip or jet, J-3 Cub or C5A. These are the physical facts of flight.

Fact two is simply that you must learn to believe your instruments. A few simple maneuvers are usually enough to prove to the most cynical pilot that seat-of-the-pants flying doesn't work too well when outside visual cues are obscured. It is not enough, though, to just look at one instrument and base your conclusions as to what the aircraft is doing on that one glance. To fly your aircraft accurately, you must be able to look at each of your instruments in a systematic fashion and interpret them properly. To inter-pret properly, you look for trends, which are explained in depth later.

Once you put your mind at ease, you will be able to proceed much more efficiently with the proper scan and interpretation of the instruments and to quickly initiate the proper corrective responses.

Because of the wide range of flight and navigational instruments available, this discussion will have to be made in generalities. The points will be basic in nature. There might be some slight variations depending upon the equipment in the aircraft you'll be flying. But in the majority of cases, the principle explored here will work for everyone.

These discussions will not tell you how to read each instrument. That in itself would take a book. There are at least three different types of altimeters, two types of vertical speed indicators, plus many variations of attitude indicators and other instruments.

TRIM, PRESSURE, AND CONTROL DISPLACEMENT

When learning to fly, every student has a difficult time with two techniques: separat-ing control pressure from control displacement and the proper use of trim tabs.

Trim is the easier of the two to explain. An explanation of trim: The proper use of trim, in each trim-equipped control axis, is to remove the existing pressure from the as-sociated cockpit flight control in such a manner that the aircraft will continue in the de-sired flight path or attitude with little or no assistance from the pilot.

It is also easy to explain how to trim to accomplish this. Manipulate the cockpit controls to elicit the desired flight path or attitude from the aircraft. Then operate the trim control for each trim-equipped axis, one at a time, until the pressure being exerted on the control is eliminated. To double check, remove your hand or foot from the con-trol. If the aircraft continues as desired, the trim is proper. Note that you do not fly the aircraft with the trim; you merely use it to remove the pressure from the controls; to try and fly the aircraft with the trim will usually result in the trim and the aircraft ending up 180 degrees out of phase. The proper use of trim is very important to good instru-ment flight.

Differentiation of control pressure and control displacement is difficult to explain and to teach, and I have found that many people never actually learn it. Properly learned and executed, this differentiation is what separates the aircraft drivers from the aircraft pilots. Many times, control pressure will not result in any noticeable control displacement; it is merely a light touch in the direction you want the control to move.

You cannot feel these pressures if you're gripping the yoke tightly. If you do grip tightly, you deaden some of the nerve endings that are necessary for this sense of feel: RELAX. That's one of the most important words for any pilot. Turn loose of the yoke and flex your hand a few times to restore the blood circulation, then place your hand—lightly—back on the wheel. Don't clamp it tightly; allow some space between your hand and the yoke all the way around. That way, if the aircraft is out of trim, you will feel the pressure immediately.

Although many times the aircraft "driver" will deliver a very precise flight, the aircraft "pilot" will give the smoothest flight, with precision as well: RELAX—that's the word. Remember, everyone reading this has carried passengers or will someday. When you do, although your primary consideration has to be safety, your secondary consideration should be passenger comfort. Your passengers should not know when your aircraft leaves the blocks and should have minimal sense of taxiing to the runway, braking, takeoff, cruise, descent, landing, taxiing onto the ramp, and stopping on the blocks. This goes for J-3 Cubs as well as 747s. It's the mark of a good pilot.

This is not to say that you don't displace the controls, for you certainly do. The slower you fly, the more displacement is necessary to achieve the same pressure, and when recovering from unusual attitudes, you use a lot of displacement and throw pressure out the window.

Although some of your instruments have lags related to them, a good instrument pilot should imagine that he has a string connected between the controls and the instrument he wants to move and that proper control pressure will move the instrument in concert with the pressure, even eliminating the inherent lag.

VISUAL AND INSTRUMENT CORRELATION

A current, and ongoing, question among instructor pilots is how much instrument integration instruction a student pilot should receive, and how soon it should be integrated.

My personal feeling on this is that the student pilot should be taught to use the instruments and to correlate them with his or her external visual references from the first lesson. At no time, however, should the necessity of adequate head-up flying be minimized. I have always felt that no student should be soloed until he or she can take off, fly the pattern, and land with a simulated blockage of the airplane's pitot-static system. As much stress should be placed on the full use of a pilot's senses (sound of wind and engine, and visual height separation) as in the days of open-cockpit biplane trainers.

From the beginning, though, the student should be shown the similarities between the instrument and the visual cues, such cues as the attitude indicator showing wings level, the outside horizon being level, and the like.

He or she should also be shown how to interpret this information. For example, if your aircraft is flying wings-level with the nose on the horizon, and your attitude indicator shows the same, does this mean that you are actually flying straight and level? The answer is "Of course not." If you encounter an updraft or downdraft (*wind shear*), or if your power is too high or too low, your aircraft can climb or descend accordingly and still be in a level flight attitude. Visually, the ground will appear to come nearer or farther away. On instruments you will notice the vertical speed indicator deflect up or down, with a corresponding change in the altimeter. If the instrument changes are due to changes in power setting, you will also notice improper airspeeds and a change in engine sound, and the power instruments will show a difference in RPM and/or manifold pressure.

Here's another example. Does a nose-high attitude indicate a climb? Not unless you have added sufficient power. In slow flight the aircraft has to assume a nose-high attitude to maintain altitude.

All of these relationships should be pointed out to the student from the beginning. What we should be pointing out to the students, in other words, is that one visual cue, or the indication of one instrument, is not enough. You must derive information from as many sources as possible in order to accurately interpret the flight path and attitude of the aircraft.

INSTRUMENT SCAN AND INTERPRETATION

If you were able to see the flight path of an aircraft, you would see that it is maintained by a series of corrections to the controls to make the aircraft follow the desired track. The smaller and more frequent these corrections are, the closer the aircraft will conform to the desired path.

In order to make small corrections, you must receive a large input of information in a short period of time, interpret it correctly, and then make the desired control response in a timely fashion.

How do you do this? You learn to scan the instruments and to interpret what you see. As you practice this procedure, you learn to give bare notice to those instruments with a proper indication, while devoting most of your attention to those instruments that have deviated because they will stand out like a soldier out of step.

The two major errors most commonly made in instrument scanning are omitting necessary instruments from the scan and spending too much time looking at one instrument. An instrument is omitted from the scan because the pilot is spending too much time worrying about another one, so these errors are usually interrelated.

At one time or other, we are all guilty of having unwanted heading changes of 15–20 degrees or unwanted altitude deviations of ±100–150 feet. How much time would such inadvertent changes take? Unless your aircraft encounters exceptional trim changes, wind shears, updrafts, downdrafts, or power changes, the normal rate of climb (or descent) in an unpressurized aircraft is rarely more than 500 fpm. At this rate, it would take 10–12 seconds for your altimeter to change by 100–150 feet. This means that for 10–12 seconds you have omitted the vertical speed indicator, altimeter, and attitude indicator from your scan. Ten to 12 seconds of daydreaming is a long time, but we all do it. How can we avoid it? By practice and hard work, of course. Keep your eyes constantly moving over the instruments: SCAN.

PROPER INSTRUMENT SCANNING

You must have a systematic approach to your scan. In most IFR situations the attitude indicator will be your prime instrument, just as in most VFR situations the outside horizon will be your prime visual aid. Some people will argue with this idea, but I feel it's easier to learn to fly on instruments by keeping one of the instruments as a primary one that you can always fall back on.

Your scan will almost always begin with the attitude indicator and proceed to the supporting instruments for the aspect of flight that you're focusing on. You will scan the other instruments as well, but your major concern will be those that support the flight characteristics that you are most interested in at the time.

For example, in level flight your scan would begin with the attitude indicator, and then, while attempting to hold a constant attitude, you would glance at the altimeter, the vertical speed indicator, the airspeed indicator, the power setting, and back to the attitude indicator. Hopefully, by the time you get back to the attitude indicator, it will still be indicating the same as the first time you glanced at it. You will then repeat the scan of the instruments mentioned above.

Provided that your attitude and power have remained constant, one of three trends will have been established: descent, level flight, or climb. One cue that you will look for is the airspeed. Is it higher, lower, or normal for your power setting? Notice that the position of the attitude indicator has not been mentioned; it is enough that you hold the attitude indicator constant. At this point a lower airspeed at a given power setting would indicate a climb (or flight through a strong downdraft). This will be confirmed by the second scan of the vertical speed indicator and the altimeter. The second and third scans determine the trend. If the trend indicates a climb or descent when you want level flight, you will have to correct it. This correction should be accomplished in two *smooth* steps (notice the stressed word). The first step is to stop the unwanted trend. The second step is to begin a trend back to the desired flight situation.

In the example above, you began to climb slightly. If your power setting is proper for level flight, you will stop your climb by a slight change of the pitch attitude shown on the attitude indicator. You do this by relaxing enough back pressure (or by adding enough forward pressure) on the yoke to cause the imaginary string leading to the vertical speed indicator and altimeter to move the needles to a level-flight indication.

Although an experienced pilot would actually be doing all of these things simultaneously, as a student you will have to try to control one instrument at a time while learning. Because the attitude indicator has the least lag, it is the easiest instrument to control.

After you have made your slight change, you again try to hold the attitude indicator constant at the desired attitude and scan the other instruments again. Your change will have accompanied one of three things:

- If you did not change the pitch attitude sufficiently, you will continue climbing, but at a reduced rate.

- If you made an overcorrection, you will descend and your airspeed will increase.
- If you have changed the pitch the proper amount, your altimeter and vertical speed indicator should indicate level flight, and your airspeed will begin to increase. After you have stopped the unwanted trend, you can apply another small correction to reverse the previous trend and get your aircraft back to its desired flight path or attitude.

As you learn to control the vertical speed better through smooth corrections, and to coordinate that with the changes made to the attitude indicator, you will find that more of your corrections will be of the latter type.

The smaller and smoother you can make your corrections, the less chance you will have of developing *vertigo* (spatial disorientation), the smoother ride you will afford your passengers, and the more accurately you will fly your aircraft.

INSTRUMENT ERRORS

Earlier explanations intentionally made no mention about the initial attitude indication. This is because you must think of the attitude indicator as a *relative* instrument rather than as an absolute indicator of the aircraft performance. Your aircraft (and its attitude indicator) can be nose-low or nose-high, and depending on loading (center of gravity) and speed, still be in normal flight.

The attitude indication on instruments will also change due to precession of the gyro as well as from acceleration and deceleration errors. For example, if you have been climbing for a long while, the attitude indicator gets used to indicating a nose-high attitude, and it will continue to indicate slightly more nose-high than normal for a few minutes after you have leveled off and established cruise airspeed; therefore, all attitude corrections are made to the previous indication, not to the actual attitude.

Gyro precession and acceleration errors are inherent gyro instrument errors that you learn to live with, and with proper scanning procedures, they become relatively unimportant. Nongyro instruments are also subject to errors. You have all undoubtedly heard of altimeter and vertical speed instrument lag. By horsing the controls abruptly you can get a momentary instrument reaction opposite to the aircraft's reaction, but if you make slow, smooth corrections as mentioned earlier, this lag becomes barely noticeable.

Many good books thoroughly explain instruments and their construction and the reasons for their errors. My purpose is only to tell you how to live with them.

AIRSPEED CONTROL

The remainder of this chapter concentrates on changing airspeed while maintaining level flight. The purpose of this is to teach the relationships among power setting, pitch attitude, airspeed, and trim.

One nice thing that you will learn about trim is that it is closely related to airspeed, and that once trimmed for a given speed and center of gravity (CG), the aircraft will tend to remain at the same airspeed regardless of the power setting. When you reduce the power, the airspeed will want to decrease, but if you are trimmed for the higher speed, the nose will lower instead and you will begin to lose altitude. If your plane is fairly stable, it will porpoise a few times, and eventually the speed and the rate of descent should stabilize.

From this point on in these discussions you will be attempting to maintain exact altitudes, airspeeds, headings, and rates of climb or descent. Here the allowable margin of error will be ±0. I realize that the FAA Practical Test Standards are more lenient, but you will not achieve a high level of competence by training for minimum performance. You should be striving for perfection from the start. You'll never achieve it, but you should try.

Let's begin with this thought. In level flight, any given power setting should result in a specific airspeed and corresponding pitch attitude (instrument error disregarded). Ideally then, at cruise power and airspeed, your attitude indicator should show precisely level flight.

Because the four forces working on an aircraft (lift, thrust, drag, and gravity) must always be in balance, anytime one of them varies, the other three will change to bring all four back into equilibrium.

If you increase power and maintain pitch, the thrust will overcome drag and your speed will increase until the drag and thrust balance each other out. At the same time, the increased speed (with no deliberate change of attitude) will increase lift. This, in turn, will cause your aircraft to climb until the lift is balanced out by gravity again.

To counteract this climbing effect, as the airspeed increases, you must slowly lower your pitch attitude to maintain level flight. To do this you will apply forward pressure on the yoke: enough pressure to keep the vertical speed indicator at zero and the altimeter at the required altitude. The more the speed increases, the more forward pressure you will have to exert on the yoke. The opposite occurs if you reduce power while trying to maintain altitude.

John Doster, past director of the FAA GADO at Allentown-Bethlehem-Easton Airport in Pennsylvania, has always felt that the level turn was the best training maneuver to teach aircraft control. He would begin by asking each of his thousands of students and flight certificate candidates what caused an aircraft to turn. There was and is only one correct answer: lift.

As the ailerons deflect to roll into a turn, the lowered aileron on the up-wing causes increased drag, which turns the nose of the plane slightly in the direction opposite the turn. Rudder pressure has to be added to counteract this yawing tendency.

As the aircraft banks, part of the lift that up to now has balanced out gravity (to maintain level flight) is vectored to the inside of the bank, *lifting* the aircraft into the turn.

Inertia is a factor for a little while. The aircraft maintains level flight until the vertical component of lift decreases enough to allow gravity to take over, causing the aircraft to descend. As this occurs, back pressure has to be applied to the yoke to increase the angle of attack on the wing, thereby inducing enough added lift to maintain the desired altitude. Unfortunately, this added lift also increases drag, and the plane begins to slow down unless enough thrust is applied to overcome the increased drag and keep all four forces in balance.

The opposite situation occurs when rolling out of the turn. First, the rudder has to be applied again to counteract yaw. As the aircraft rolls to a wings-level attitude, inertia again works on it momentarily. Then the plane wants to begin climbing, due to the increased vertical component of lift.

This climbing tendency can be overcome by forward pressure on the yoke (decreasing the angle of attack) but when you do this, the power you added previously begins to overcome drag, and your airspeed increases unless you reduce power again.

John Doster feels that the best training maneuvers for any pilot are turns of various degrees of bank and duration, with zero permissible altitude and airspeed fluctuation.

As mentioned above, when your airspeed changes, so will the control pressures, and here's where it's very important to retrim the aircraft. Remember that the goal is to have the aircraft trimmed in such a manner that it will maintain its desired path and attitude if you momentarily take your hands off the controls.

By learning how to maintain level flight while varying pitch and power settings, you also learn how to slow down to approach speed before beginning your descent. This will be of importance when you get into the approach phase of instrument flight.

During all phases of instrument flight, try to keep changes as simple as possible. When beginning an approach, try not to go from cruise speed/attitude/power to approach speed/attitude/power all at once. You can control your aircraft easier if you first slow to approach speed/attitude while still maintaining level flight and then begin a descent by easing off a little power, lowering some flaps, or extending the landing gear.

For practice, try flying level, with and without the hood, varying the airspeed from 5 knots above stall speed to 5 knots above cruise speed. Trim the aircraft as the speed changes so that once your speed has stabilized, the aircraft will fly practically hands-off. When you do this without the hood, compare your aircraft's nose and wing tip positions (their relationship with the horizon) to what is presented on the attitude indicator. Naturally, you should have an instructor or safety pilot with you to scan outside at all times.

Develop your instrument scan by covering one pitch instrument at a time and flying with the remaining pitch instruments to learn their interrelationship. With the attitude indicator covered, try to develop a touch and smoothness on the yoke that will minimize the instrument lag inherent in the vertical speed indicator and the altimeter.

CHAPTER QUIZ

1. An aircraft requires different control techniques when operating in an instrument environment than it does when in a visual environment.

   True _____ False _____

2. Fill in the blanks. In order to set the elevator trim properly, you must first _____, then _____, and finally _____.

3. In level flight, the attitude indicator will indicate:

   a. Nose down   c. Nose up

   b. Level flight   d. Any of the above

4. The attitude indicator always indicates the actual attitude of the aircraft.

   True _____ False _____

5. The two steps to take to correct an unwanted flight path are:

   1. _____.

   2. _____.

6. Which of the following instruments is subject to the least amount of instrument lag?

   a. Airspeed   c. Attitude indicator

   b. Altimeter   d. Vertical velocity

7. If your aircraft is trimmed properly for level flight, and the thrust is reduced slightly, the aircraft will have a tendency to:

   a. Continue in level flight as it is trimmed for it.

   b. Begin a descent at the speed it is trimmed for.

   c. Stall due to lack of thrust.

   d. Slow down due to the lack of thrust.

8. What turns an aircraft when it is in flight?

   a. Aileron   d. Lift

   b. Rudder   e. Thrust

   c. Drag

9. If no power is added in a turn and the altitude is kept constant, the airspeed will decrease. Why?

Answers are in the appendix.

2
Vertigo awareness

THERE ARE ONLY TWO TYPES OF INSTRUMENT PILOTS. THOSE WHO HAVE suffered from vertigo and those who will. Your eyes are a most important factor in maintaining equilibrium in flight. You will have a tendency to lose your orientation if your supporting senses conflict with what you see.

One source of this conflict (known as *flicker vertigo*) during night and instrument conditions is the reflections of anticollision or strobe lights on clouds or on the aircraft's wings and canopy. These flickers make you feel as if you are turning. You can even be bothered by the airplane's shadow projected onto clouds in an otherwise dark night sky. The easiest way to correct this problem is to turn off the rotating beacon and/or strobe lights until you get over the feeling.

Climbing or descending through an area of broken clouds, either IFR or VFR, can give you the impression that your airspeed and altitude are changing rapidly. This is especially prevalent when flying over water on a bright hazy day or through areas of heavy haze when you lose the horizon. Your best bet in such situations is to go on instruments immediately.

Many times when banking soon after takeoff on a dark night, or when leaving a bright area and proceeding over dark water, desert, mountains, or forests, you will get the impression that the stars are actually lights on the ground. Other times, ground lights that you know are lower than your altitude will appear to be higher.

Both of these impressions will cause you to develop symptoms of vertigo that can be overcome only by going on the gauges at once. (I have long felt that for this very reason, an instrument ticket should be a prerequisite for night flying. There is a long list of night accidents in which the probable cause was listed as the pilot's inability to maintain orientation due to a loss of visual landmarks.)

In addition to sight, we possess the postural senses of touch, pressure, and tension, and the motion-sensing organs of the inner ear. The postural senses cannot detect an unchanging velocity; there must be acceleration or deceleration. Without the sense of sight to help us, the +2G centrifugal force of a steep turn feels identical to a +2G pull-up from a dive, and a wing load of ±1–2Gs often feels the same whether caused by in-flight turbulence or by rough control pressures related to leveling off, climbing, or beginning descents. Most complications with spatial disorientation begin in the inner ear.

THE INNER EAR

Basically, the inner ear consists of a reservoir, called the *common sac*, to which are fitted three hollow rings called the *semicircular canals*. These semicircular canals are orientated in each of three planes, and the entire unit is filled with fluid. Very fine hairs, called *sensory hairs*, project into the fluid within the semicircular canals.

Picture yourself holding a glass of water. If you twist the glass, the water will tend to stay where it is at first. If you were to tape a few threads to the inside of the glass (similar to the sensory hairs of the semicircular canals) and then twist it, the water would stand still at first, and the threads would drag backwards in the water.

The same thing happens in the inner ear. If you begin turning, the semicircular canals begin turning with you, but because of the laws of inertia, the fluid in the canal (in the plane of rotation associated with your motion) resists moving at first, and the sensory hairs are deflected as they drag in the fluid. The hairs send a signal to the brain, telling the brain that you are moving.

If you continue turning (or accelerating, or decelerating) at the same rate, the fluid will begin moving, and after a while it will move at the same rate as the canal. At this time, the sensory hairs will return to their static position and your brain will sense that your turn, and the like, has stopped, even though your aircraft and your body are still turning.

Then, when you begin to roll out of the turn, the opposite will happen. The semicircular canal will move in the opposite direction, and the hairs will deflect to tell the brain that you are moving in the opposite direction. In the case of rolling in and out of a turn, this will work out fine as long as you roll smoothly. But, if you roll out abruptly, when you stop the roll the fluid will continue moving, carrying the hairs in the opposite direction again. Even though you are flying straight and level, your brain will think that you are in another turn.

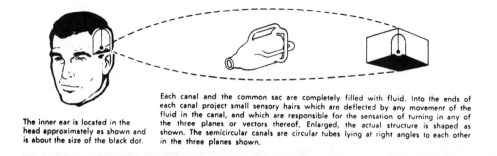

The inner ear is located in the head approximately as shown and is about the size of the black dot.

Each canal and the common sac are completely filled with fluid. Into the ends of each canal project small sensory hairs which are deflected by any movement of the fluid in the canal, and which are responsible for the sensation of turning in any of the three planes or vectors thereof. Enlarged, the actual structure is shaped as shown. The semicircular canals are circular tubes lying at right angles to each other in the three planes shown.

MECHANICS OF THE INNER EAR

As the head is rotated, the canal in that plane of rotation will move with respect to the fluid in it. Since this fluid has inertia, the resulting deflection of the sensory hairs will cause a sensation of turning.

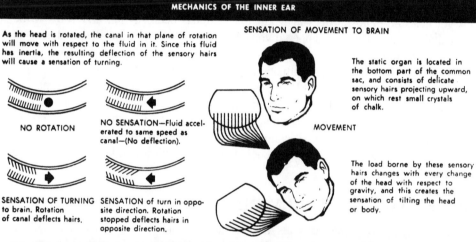

NO ROTATION

NO SENSATION—Fluid accelerated to same speed as canal—(No deflection).

SENSATION OF TURNING to brain. Rotation of canal deflects hairs.

SENSATION of turn in opposite direction. Rotation stopped deflects hairs in opposite direction.

SENSATION OF MOVEMENT TO BRAIN

The static organ is located in the bottom part of the common sac, and consists of delicate sensory hairs projecting upward, on which rest small crystals of chalk.

MOVEMENT

The load borne by these sensory hairs changes with every change of the head with respect to gravity, and this creates the sensation of tilting the head or body.

SEMI-CIRCULAR CANALS CAN PRODUCE FALSE SENSATIONS

IN A SLOW STEADY TURN YOUR SEMICIRCULAR CANALS CAN FOOL YOU

Straight flight

Beginning of turn. Only canals move.

Continuing turn fluid begins to move.

Still in turn fluid catches up with walls. Illusion created.

WHEN YOU STOP TURNING, YOUR SEMICIRCULAR CANALS CAN FOOL YOU

Start of right turn. Canal moves. Fluid stationary.

Continuing turn. Fluid catches up with walls.

Stopping turn. Canals stop. Fluid continues.

Beginning of left turn.

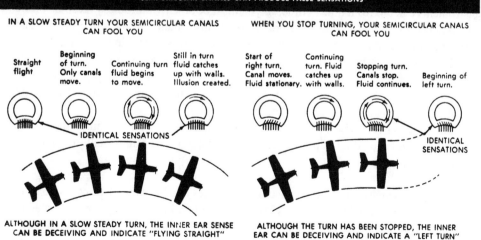

IDENTICAL SENSATIONS

IDENTICAL SENSATIONS

ALTHOUGH IN A SLOW STEADY TURN, THE INNER EAR SENSE CAN BE DECEIVING AND INDICATE "FLYING STRAIGHT"

ALTHOUGH THE TURN HAS BEEN STOPPED, THE INNER EAR CAN BE DECEIVING AND INDICATE A "LEFT TURN"

Fig. 2-1

As long as you can see the outside horizon, or the attitude indicator and the directional gyro, you will not be too confused. Under visual conditions, the outside horizon alone will suffice to tell you that you are turning; you will see objects on the horizon or on the ground as they pass across your view.

When you're on instruments, you need two gauges to give you the same information. The attitude indicator or the turn-and-bank indicator will tell you if you are in a bank, and the directional gyro will confirm that you are actually turning; the numbers rotating past the lubber line will take the place of the objects going by on the outside horizon.

If you close your eyes while making a smooth entry into the turn, roll out suddenly, and then open your eyes and look only at the instruments, the instruments will tell you just the opposite of what your inner ear has been saying, and you will be primed for vertigo. This can happen if you allow yourself to bank too steeply during an instrument turn, then notice your error and overcontrol, snapping quickly back to the desired angle of bank. In such a situation, if you doubt the instruments, you will find that you become dizzy and unable to control your muscle functions. By the time you realize that the attitude indicator is telling you the true attitude, it might be too late. One part of your brain is trying to tell your muscles to roll out of the turn, but another part of your brain has become so confused that it refuses to allow the muscles to respond. In this situation, you are experiencing extreme vertigo, and you are set up for a catastrophe.

BELIEVING THE INSTRUMENTS

The only way to overcome vertigo is to understand it, catch it at its outset, and believe the instruments. You must train yourself to disregard all of the false senses and try to rely solely on the instruments. This takes patience and practice. You must also remember that instruments can fail from time to time, so you must be able to reinforce what some of the instruments are telling you by interpreting other instruments in the same group. The more experience you have, the less chance you'll have of succumbing to vertigo.

There are some specific maneuvers designed to induce vertigo, and though each is designed to produce a specific sensation, any sensation at all will help you learn that you can't trust your senses. Be certain that these maneuvers are only undertaken with an instructor or qualified safety pilot on board.

These maneuvers will show you the absolute need to rely on your instruments and give you an understanding of how head movements, in various aircraft attitudes, cause disorientation:

- While flying straight and level, close your eyes and have the instructor skid right or left while holding the wings level. You will feel as though your body is actually tilting in the direction opposite the skid. As soon as you feel that you are tilting, tell the instructor what direction you're tilting in and open your eyes to see what the aircraft is doing.

- While flying straight and level with the aircraft slowed down to approach airspeed, close your eyes. Have the instructor increase the speed to climb speed while maintaining a straight-and-level attitude. You'll feel as though you're climbing. This is important to remember when executing a missed approach from low airspeeds, especially if you have to divert your head from the instruments to reset a radio or to check a chart for a procedural point.

- From a straight-and-level attitude, close your eyes and have the instructor execute a slow roll into a well-coordinated 45-degree banked turn. Hold this 1.5G turn for 90 degrees. Because of the gravity forces in the turn, you will feel as though the aircraft is climbing. Keep your eyes closed and have the instructor roll out of the turn slowly and with coordinated pressures. Because of the decrease in gravity forces, by the time you have rolled halfway out, you will feel as though you are descending.

The reason for these sensations is that with a lack of visual reference, if the rate of angular acceleration is less than 2 degrees per sec./sec., the body is unable to detect a change of direction in any one of the three planes of motion; therefore, the change of gravity forces, usually associated with climbing or diving, is all that will be felt.

You can experience a false sense of reversal in motion by using the following maneuver:

- With your eyes closed while straight and level, have your instructor smoothly and positively roll into a 45-degree bank while using opposite rudder pressure to keep the nose in a point. If the roll rate is suddenly stopped, you will feel as though you are actually rotating in the opposite direction, and a recovery based solely on your senses could be fatal. This demonstration, when properly executed, will drive home the need for smooth, well-coordinated control usage, and a firm need for a belief only in your instruments.

The next two demonstrations can also be shown by strapping the student in a rotating chair. Whether done in a rotating chair or in flight, the results will be extreme disorientation, causing a quick and forceable, almost violent, movement of the head and body, upward and backward, and to the side opposite the rotation. Naturally if this reaction were applied to the controls of an aircraft in flight, you could get into a lot of trouble:

- From straight-and-level flight, either close your eyes or look down at the floor. The instructor should roll positively into a coordinated bank of 45 degrees (or begin spinning the chair). As the aircraft is rolling into the bank, bend your head and body down and look to either side, and then immediately straighten up and sit normally. The instructor should stop the bank (or stop the chair rotation) just as you reach the normally seated position.

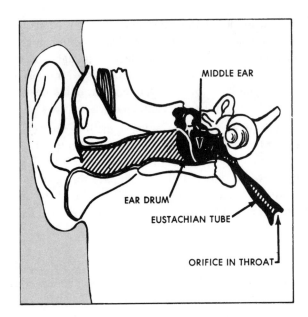

MIDDLE EAR

EAR DRUM

EUSTACHIAN TUBE

ORIFICE IN THROAT

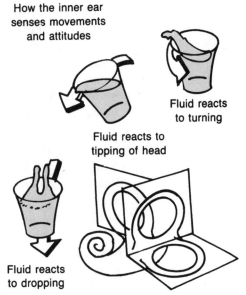

How the inner ear senses movements and attitudes

Fluid reacts to turning

Fluid reacts to tipping of head

Fluid reacts to dropping

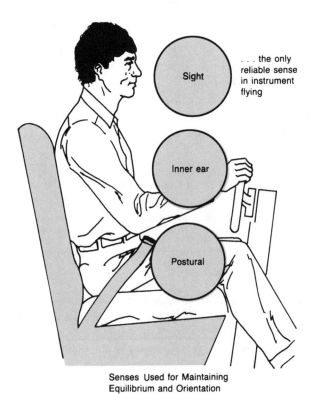

Sight

. . . the only reliable sense in instrument flying

Inner ear

Postural

Senses Used for Maintaining Equilibrium and Orientation

Fig. 2-2

• Watch as the plane is rolled into a steep, descending spiral. After 15 seconds or so, bend your head and body down and look to either side as you did in the first maneuver, and again immediately resume the normal seated position.

The disorientation might be severe. You might even become nauseated. This could easily happen in a real-life situation if the aircraft begins turning as you are looking for a chart or book in your flight case. The reaction is usually more severe when you are forced to look down and to the rear. This is one of the reasons for placing all of the charts and paperwork in some handy location such as on top of the glareshield where you can reach them without turning your head and body.

Normal vertigo can only be overcome by familiarity with your instruments, belief in them, and continuous practice. The more you fly on instruments, the less susceptible you will be to false sensations.

CHAPTER QUIZ

1. What is flicker vertigo?

2. What can be done to overcome the effects of flicker vertigo if it occurs?

3. In order for the postural senses to detect velocity, either _____ or _____ must be present.

4. The reservoir within the inner ear is called the _____.

5. The other parts of the inner ear are the _____ and the _____.

6. Sudden, jerky control inputs during instrument flight can lead to _____.

Answers are in the appendix.

3
Physiological factors

COMBINING WHAT YOU'VE LEARNED SO FAR, WE'LL INCORPORATE ALL OF the flight instruments into your scan to enable you to maintain altitude, speed, and heading, and to establish climbs and descents.

Before getting into that, however, let's discuss a few more physiological factors that will affect your flight performance in general and affect your instrument capabilities in particular.

The effects of pressure changes on pilots are well known, and we have all been advised not to fly with a cold or when we have ear or sinus blockage. We must also take care after scuba diving because we can set ourselves up for the bends if we fly at too high a cabin altitude too soon after diving.

LEGAL DRUGS

A second problem when flying with a slight cold deals with the effect of medication in your system. Drugs, even the over-the-counter variety, which would have little or no effect on you on the ground, can end up having disastrous results when you fly. This is especially true when you're on instruments.

Antihistamines might cause dizziness, drowsiness, headaches, and/or nausea, and they usually also affect vision.

Barbiturates, as they wear off, bring about sleepiness that often goes unrecognized. They also affect motor and thinking functions.

Diet pills are responsible for nervousness and impaired judgment.

Muscle relaxants, by their nature, cause weakness as well as sleepiness and vertigo.

Stimulants, like diet pills, cause nervousness and impaired judgment as well as blurred vision.

Tranquilizers also cause blurred vision and sleepiness.

Some of these pills can be bought without a prescription, and many times your family doctor will prescribe medication containing these or other ingredients detrimental to the safe operation of aircraft. Ask your doctor about the effects that the medication might have on your ability to fly. If you have any doubt, or if you're thinking of taking an over-the-counter pill in some part of the country where you don't have a doctor, contact the local FAA medical examiner for advice. If, for some reason, you're unable to get medical advice, stay away from the pilot's seat of an aircraft for at least 24 hours after taking any medication.

ALCOHOL, CIGARETTES, AND HYPOXIA

Another serious physiological problem stems from the consumption of alcoholic beverages. It takes only 25 percent as much alcohol to impair flying skills as it does to impair driving skills. One or two drinks will decrease your flying ability below safe standards, and in instrument conditions this danger is multiplied. Alcohol, which is readily absorbed into the bloodstream, interferes with the normal use of oxygen by the tissues. As you climb, it causes you to suffer effects similar to *hypoxia* (oxygen starvation). Hypoxia is caused by foreign or toxic substances in the blood and is also caused by reduced atmospheric pressure.

Oxygen is carried through the bloodstream by *hemoglobin*. A certain amount of pressure in the lungs is required to combine the hemoglobin with the oxygen. The higher you go, the lower the pressure, and the less oxygen is absorbed. Not only that, the higher you go, the less oxygen is available in any given volume of air that you inhale.

For all practical purposes, you can consider 10,000 feet MSL as the upper limit for safe, long-range flight for a normal, healthy body without supplemental oxygen. The FAA allows you to fly at 12,500 feet MSL without any supplemental oxygen at all. If you have any physiological problems at all, you might not be able to even handle 10,000 feet safely, and I have already mentioned that alcohol will interfere with your body's normal use of oxygen and this will affect your susceptibility to hypoxia.

What is it about smoking that affects your body? *Carbon monoxide*, that colorless, odorless, tasteless killer chemical. It is absorbed by the hemoglobin in the bloodstream 200 times easier than oxygen. Every bit of carbon monoxide that is absorbed by the hemoglobin takes the place of that much needed oxygen; in the bloodstream, it cannot be cleared out by just a little suck on the oxygen mask. It is more difficult to *remove* carbon monoxide from the bloodstream than it is to absorb it.

Carbon monoxide can be absorbed into the bloodstream from sources other than cigarettes. One prevalent source is exhaust gas from a cracked exhaust pipe. Another is the smoke from a passenger's cigarette. In fact, recent findings tend to support the contention that the nonsmoker suffers more from this passive smoke in a confined area than does the smoker.

The greatest danger of hypoxia, from whatever source, is the way it numbs the brain so the person suffering from it can black out, recover, and have no recollection of the experience, except for a possible headache. In fact, unless you have some definite proof, a victim of hypoxia will argue about ever being unconscious. United Airlines made an interesting training film showing some of their personnel in a decompression chamber. It is a sobering and frightening experience to watch the film, and you subsequently develop a healthy respect for the dangers of hypoxia.

Hypoxia brings about the following symptoms, although not necessarily in the following order:

- Dizziness: not always apparent because it is more often just a little lightheadedness.
- Tingling: again not always noticed because the person sometimes feels as though that part of the body is "falling asleep."
- Blurry vision: often confused with fatigue or tired eyes.
- Feeling of warmth: "who turned on the heater?"
- Euphoria: a feeling of well-being (here's where the brain remains for some reason, feeling nothing else).
- Mental confusion.
- Inability to concentrate.
- Loss of judgment.
- Slow reflexes.
- Clumsiness.
- Loss of consciousness and eventually death, unless oxygen is administered.

Even after recovery, some irreparable damage might have been suffered by the brain. Naturally, through all of the adverse symptoms mentioned above, the person is very susceptible to vertigo.

Another physiological problem, in which many symptoms are the same as hypoxia, is *hyperventilation*. This occurs when you get excited and begin breathing quickly and heavily. In so doing, your body gets rid of too much *carbon dioxide*, a waste product of muscular exertion. A body requires a certain balance between the oxygen and carbon dioxide in the blood. Too much oxygen in relation to the carbon dioxide will cause dizziness and faintness. Take a few fast deep breaths and see for yourself.

People tend to hyperventilate when they get into tight situations involving stress and fear. The best protection against this problem is to learn to relax, calmly appraise the situation, don't allow yourself to panic, don't fall for "sucker holes," don't try flying when conditions are minimal, practice your instrument skills, know your aircraft, know your own capabilities, and calmly force yourself to breathe slowly and steadily.

The red-light-at-night idea is also something that we should think about.

If you're in combat situations, where night vision could mean the difference between life and death, then it is important to maintain your night vision; however, in today's civil aircraft environment, you are constantly encountering white lights from cities, from airports, and from aircraft strobe lights.

Each time your eyes see white lights at night, your night vision will be affected for up to 15 minutes. In the military you're taught to close the same eye immediately so as to preserve at least part of your night vision. This is impractical at best and certainly unnecessary in today's flight environment.

Your eyes are made up of rods and cones. The cones react to white lights and give you the ability to see colors. The rods see only different shades of gray. This is why the night vision is so important in combat. You want to be able to discern movement.

Still and all, if a laser could burn out all of the cones in your eyes, leaving only the rods, you would be left with 20/200 vision. In other words, you would be legally blind.

Finally, with all of the colors and hues on modern day charts, it is imperative to keep your color vision. For this reason, it is recommended that you keep at least some white light in your cockpit. It shouldn't be so bright as to prevent you from seeing outside, but it should be good enough to allow you to see your important charts and flight documents. Remember, as soon as you see those approach lights at the airport, your night vision is canceled.

Another thing regarding night vision. At night we become relatively nearsighted. This tends to change the runway configuration somewhat, causing the far end to tilt forward. This is another good reason to stay on the glide slope, monitor your rate of descent, and watch the VASI.

ILLEGAL DRUGS

Before closing this chapter, it is important that you look at the effects of illegal drugs on the body. There isn't room to cover them all, but the most prevalent today seems to be cocaine and its derivative crack.

Recall the tragic death of college basketball star Len Bias. The news media reported that he died of a heart attack *the first time he used cocaine*. Some people said that was impossible, but recent studies are pointing to the very distinct possibility.

Cocaine is a constrictor. It clamps down on your blood vessels. If nothing else, it restricts the blood flow to your brain, causing the same loss of oxygen as smoke. But it also does far worse.

Cocaine has been used in surgery, especially nose surgery, for years. Besides reducing pain, it also constricts the small veins, stopping bleeding. But, a recent study, conducted by doctors at the University of Texas Southwestern Medical Center in Dallas, and published in the *New England Journal of Medicine*, has determined that cocaine is worse than anyone imagined.

The doctors studied the effects on 45 volunteers. They received between 150 and 180 milligrams of cocaine. This is only about two-thirds as much as they would get from normal anesthesia. The results: "Even that small dose caused coronary blood flow to fall by 15 to 20 percent," according to Dr. L. David Hillis, who conducted the test.

When you realize that cocaine users use many times that amount, it is easy to see how some die of heart attacks. By shutting off the flow of blood to the heart, the heart dies.

Hillis said that cocaine stimulates the body's production of adrenaline and other hormones. These trigger the blood vessels to narrow so that less oxygen-carrying blood can get through. At the same time, the drug increases the heart's need for oxygen by boosting the heart rate.

In short, if you've never used cocaine, don't. If you know of someone who does, don't get into any vehicle with him or her, especially an aircraft.

CHAPTER QUIZ

1. You're laying over in a strange town and feel flulike symptoms. You're not sure of the effects of medication in your suitcase. You should:

   a. Ask a pharmacist

   b. Ask a doctor

   c. Check with an FAA flight surgeon

   d. Don't fly for at least 24 hours after taking them

   e. Any of the above

2. You have a sore back and your doctor has prescribed muscle relaxants. You're scheduled to fly the next day. Should you fly or call in sick? Why?

3. How does alcohol affect your system?

4. The substance that transports oxygen through the bloodstream is _____.

5. Carbon monoxide is easily absorbed into the bloodstream.

   True _____ False _____

6. It is quite easy to notice the onset of hypoxia and take steps to avoid it.

   True _____ False _____

7. Hyperventilation brings about many of the symptoms of _____. It is caused by breathing _____ and _____.

8. The use of cocaine can bring about sudden heart attacks by _____ the blood vessels. This decreases the _____ supply to the heart and _____.

Answers are in the appendix.

4
Attitude instrument flying

PSYCHOLOGICAL AND PHYSIOLOGICAL FACTORS ASIDE, IT IS TIME TO get back to instrument flying. Let's take a look at controlling the heading. To start off with, we'll work with just the heading instruments and concentrate on making turns at standard rates without worrying too much about altitudes. We'll tie everything together later.

HEADING CONTROL

The heading instruments consist of the *attitude indicator, needle/ball* (sometimes called the *turn/slip* or *slip/skid*) or *turn coordinator*, and the *heading indicators*. The heading indicators will consist of at least the *magnetic compass* and the *directional gyro*. Sometimes you'll find *slaved* gyros, *flux gate* compasses, and/or *automatic sensing azimuths* for the automatic direction finders.

The primary turn instrument will still be the attitude indicator because the aircraft can't turn unless it is banking. (This isn't exactly true because rudder pressure might cause the aircraft to skid, and this will cause the heading to change somewhat, but for the most part, it is the sideways lift vector of the banked wing that lifts you through the turn.)

Remember that you set your attitude by relative pitch indications on the attitude indicator. When you turn, you also use the attitude indicator as the prime instrument, only now you set a relative bank indication on it.

The amount of bank you will use will depend on the number of degrees you have to turn, the amount of airspace you have to work in, the time you have to spend in the turn, and the speed of the aircraft. The greater the speed, the steeper you will have to bank to get the same rate of turn. A good rule of thumb to use for most aircraft is one degree of bank for each degree you want to turn, up to the angle of bank necessary for a standard-rate turn.

You should practice rolling into and out of your banks at the same roll rate. This will be helpful in rolling out on the proper headings so that you can expedite your turns and at the same time prevent overshooting desired headings. For example, if your roll rate is such that you turn through 10 degrees before the bank is established, you should use the same roll rate when rolling out of the turn and begin the rollout 10 degrees prior to the intended heading. So the key to this is a consistent roll rate.

OVERCOMING COMPASS ERRORS

Directional gyros, slaved gyros, and flux gate compasses are, for the most part, direct-reading indicators. The only error you have to be concerned with is the precessional error of the directional gyro. To eliminate that, merely reset the directional gyro to the magnetic indication every 10 minutes or so. To do this accurately, your aircraft must be flying straight and level and at a constant airspeed; otherwise, the magnetic compass might be inaccurate.

Magnetic compasses are prone to two errors: *northerly turning* error and *acceleration* error. Both errors result from magnetic dip, which is greatest near the poles and least near the equator. This dip is caused by the needle trying to align itself parallel to the magnetic force field of the Earth.

When you decide to turn, you roll the aircraft into a bank, and as you do so, the magnetic compass card tilts also. When it does, the north-seeking end of the compass tends to dip to the low side of the bank. This error is greatest when you are heading north or south, and least when heading east or west.

The effect on the compass, when heading north, is to cause an initial apparent turn opposite to the direction of the actual turn. When heading south this error will show the airplane to be turning in the proper direction, but it will cause the magnetic compass to indicate a faster turn than you are making. When heading north or south, the magnitude of this error will approximate the degree of latitude. As mentioned above, it will be minimal when you are heading east or west. Through practice and interpolation, you should be able to roll out right on course when you apply your roll-rate lead, plus the amount of error, for the desired heading.

The acceleration error is most noticeable when accelerating or decelerating on an east or west heading. It also occurs when climbing and descending on these headings.

Raytheon Aircraft Co.

Fig. 4-1. *The complete IFR panel of a Baron 58P.*

(There should be no appreciable acceleration error on a north or south heading.) When accelerating or descending, the compass card will turn to the north, and when decelerating or climbing it will turn to the south. You can remember the errors easier by thinking of the acronym ANDS, which means *A*ccelerate, *N*orth; *D*ecelerate, *S*outh.

To keep all of these errors consistent you must make smooth, coordinated turns. If the errors are constant, you will be able to compensate for them. In addition, the bank should be limited to less than 18 degrees to prevent the magnetic compass card from binding. You should practice flying to specific headings using only the magnetic compass. After awhile, you will find that you can roll out consistently on course with an accuracy of ±2½ degrees.

STANDARD-RATE TURNS

After you perfect this technique, you should develop the ability to execute standard-rate turns. A standard-rate turn for normal general aviation aircraft is 3 degrees per second. This means that it will require 2 minutes (120 seconds) to execute a 360-degree circle. For slower aircraft this turn rate will require a bank angle of 10–25 degrees. High-performance aircraft require steeper banks. High speeds can even require a 4-minute (or half-standard-rate) turn in order to keep the bank angle from becoming excessive. The maximum bank angle you'll want to make on instruments is 30 degrees, and most flight command systems will limit the aircraft to 27 degrees.

One instrument that will help maintain a constant standard-rate turn is the turn coordinator or its equivalent. Most general aviation aircraft use a 2-minute turn indicator. Because all instruments have certain errors, it becomes necessary to determine the exact needle position on your turn coordinator that will result in a standard-rate turn.

Roll smoothly into a turn and place the low wing of the airplane figure on the turn index mark. Check the bank angle on the attitude indicator. Fly through 360 degrees, timing your turn as you pass through a few of the cardinal headings; continue through another 360 degrees or so, readjusting the angle of bank as necessary to complete a 360-degree turn in 2 minutes at your normal cruising airspeed.

Once you have established the exact needle position and attitude indicator position for your aircraft, you should be able to execute a 3-degree-per-second turn every time. Time the turn coordinator in both directions.

Timing the turn through a few cardinal headings can be explained. If you are turning at a rate of 3 degrees per second, you should turn through 30 degrees in 10 seconds, 45 degrees in 15 seconds, and 60 degrees in 20 seconds; so, as you are turning, you won't have to fly the entire 360 degrees to see if your angle of bank is resulting in the desired rate of turn. But once you have adjusted and readjusted your bank angle to get the desired results, it is still necessary to go through a complete 360-degree turn to ascertain that it is correct.

Once you have accomplished this experiment, you should be able to establish a standard-rate turn by using either the turn coordinator or the attitude indicator. Naturally, when both instruments are working, you will constantly use one as a cross-check against the other, but if one fails, you should still be able to complete the turn. Not only that, but by rolling into and out of turns smoothly and slowly, always at the same roll rate, you should be able to roll out on any heading—or be able to make a turn of any number of degrees—without reference to the heading indicators, just by timing the turns. This ability has saved many pilots when their respective magnetic compasses have sprung a leak.

To execute a timed turn properly, begin timing just as you begin rolling into the turn, and begin rolling out again at the end of the timing period.

The ball on the turn coordinator will help you keep the turn coordinated. It should always be centered. If the ball is on the high side of the turn, it indicates a *skid*. If it is on the low side, it indicates a *slip*. In either case, "step on the ball" to center it. First, take all pressure off the rudder pedals, which will usually eliminate 70 percent of the skid. Then apply just enough rudder pressure to center the ball, pressing the rudder pedal on the same side to which the ball is deflected.

As explained in chapter 1, apply smooth pressure to the aileron and rudder to roll slowly into a coordinated turn. As the aircraft reaches the desired angle of bank as indicated both by the turn coordinator and the attitude indicator, the speed will decay somewhat due to some of the lift being used to turn the aircraft. As it occurs, the nose will begin to drop as evidenced by the attitude indicator. About this time, the vertical speed indicator will indicate a descent, and if you wait much longer, the altimeter will begin unwinding.

Apply back pressure to the yoke to hold the proper nose attitude on the attitude indicator and then trim off the back pressure, cross-checking the compass and heading indicator, turn coordinator, and attitude indicator for the proper rate of turn. It will be necessary to add a small amount of power to maintain the desired speed due to the increased drag produced by the increased angle-of-attack.

As you approach the desired heading, apply smooth, coordinated pressure to the opposite aileron and rudder to roll out of the turn on the proper heading. As you near a wings-level attitude, the upward lift vector will increase and the nose attitude will tend to rise. Stop this by applying forward pressure on the yoke and then by trimming off the pressure. It will also be necessary to ease off the extra power applied when entering the turn.

The most common errors committed while rolling into and out of turns are:

- Rolling in and out of turns at varying roll rates.
- Omitting the attitude indicator from the scan, allowing the nose to lower after entering the turns or rise after rolling out.
- Anticipating an altitude loss entering turns or a gain when rolling out and reacting too soon, causing the opposite results.

Practice should consist of perfecting turns using the magnetic compass, perfecting timed turns, and rolling in and out of turns smoothly and at a consistent roll rate.

STRAIGHT-AND-LEVEL FLIGHT

Combine the pitch instruments with the heading instruments and try to fly straight and level.

The first thing to do is to get the attitude indicator (AI) to show a wings-level, nose-level attitude with the power set for cruise. You must program both a heading and an altitude in your mind. As you scan the instruments, if you find the airspeed is higher or lower than normal for the power you have set, check the altimeter and vertical speed indicator (VSI) for any deviation. If none is noted, check your power control to determine if it has slipped in or out.

If you do have a change of altitude, make a slight pitch change, referencing the AI, to try to stop the unwanted trend. It will be important to remember the new pitch position of the AI. After making the slight pitch change, you should scan the directional gyro (DG) and needle/ball (or turn coordinator, as the case might be). If the needle is upright (or the airplane figure is wings-level), the ball is centered, and the AI indicates wings-level, you should have no change in the heading.

If your heading has changed and is still changing, the turn needle will be deflected and the ball will probably be off center. To stop the turn, apply aileron pressure opposite the direction of the turn needle deflection, and use pressure on the rudder pedals to keep the ball centered.

If you apply slow, smooth pressures, you might imagine that the turn needle (or airplane figure) is directly connected to the yoke or stick, and you can almost "will" it to the center by the light pressure you are exerting on the yoke. When the needle centers, glance at the AI to note the wing position. That will be your new wings-level reference for straight flight, at least momentarily, until any precession has worked out of the gyro.

Now, return your scan to the pitch instruments. The altitude deviation should have stopped due to your corrective pitch change, and now you can make another pitch change to bring the aircraft back to your desired altitude. This pitch change should result in a vertical speed equal to twice the altitude change required, up to a maximum of 500 fpm. In other words, if the altitude is off by 100 feet, you should climb or descend by 200 fpm until you return to the desired altitude. This 100-foot climb or descent will take 30 seconds, during which time you will go back to the heading indicators and begin a slight correction back to the desired heading.

Straight-and-level flight is probably the hardest to master, perhaps because most pilots become complacent and feel that it's too easy. Once you're able to fly fairly straight and level at cruise power and speed, start varying your speed as you did before, only this time keep your heading by scanning the heading instruments.

From straight-and-level flight at cruise power, reduce to approach speed, maintaining both heading and altitude. Slowly and smoothly reduce the power to slightly less than required for approach speed. As the airspeed begins to decrease, you will notice a tendency for the pitch attitude to lower, accompanied by the VSI showing a descent. You should apply back pressure smoothly, raising the pitch attitude on the AI at a rate necessary to maintain a zero indication on the VSI and altimeter. This back pressure should be trimmed off as necessary.

At the same time, the ball will tend to move to the left and the nose will tend to yaw to the right. This can be corrected by either easing the pressure off the right rudder pedal or by applying sufficient pressure to the left rudder pedal, as the case might be, to keep the ball centered. Properly executed, this maneuver should result in no change of heading.

When the airspeed reads 3–5 knots above the approach speed, the power should be advanced smoothly to the approach speed power that you learned earlier. The pitch attitude and power setting will be a close approximation and might have to be adjusted slightly to maintain the proper airspeed and altitude.

Now, increase airspeed back up to cruise, while at the same time maintaining heading and altitude. To do this, increase the power smoothly to the climb power setting and reverse the previous procedures. Keep the ball centered by using slight right rudder pressure as the power is increased. When the airspeed reaches cruise, smoothly reset cruise power.

CLIMBS AND DESCENTS

Once you are able to do these maneuvers fairly well, try a climb, straight ahead. To initiate a climb, apply slight back pressure to set a climb attitude indication on the AI. As the airspeed decreases, the increasing back pressure on the yoke should be trimmed off. When the airspeed reads 5 knots above climb airspeed, slowly and smoothly advance the power lever to the climb power setting. This procedure will result in a smooth transition from level flight to a climb attitude.

Throughout this maneuver, the right rudder pressure will have to be slowly increased to keep the ball centered and to hold the desired heading. If the aircraft has a rudder trim tab, this pressure should be trimmed out. Pitch attitude should be readjusted as necessary to establish and maintain a 500-fpm rate of climb on the VSI.

During the last 100 feet of climb, the pitch attitude should be gradually changed to level off at the desired altitude. As the airspeed increases, the pitch control pressure should be removed through the use of trim. When the airspeed reaches cruise speed, the power should be smoothly reduced to cruise power, and the rudder pressure should be removed to keep the ball centered.

So far, so good. Now for descents. There are at least three different airspeeds commonly used during descents. You should learn to use them all.

The first and easiest is merely to lower the pitch attitude and retrim as needed to establish a 500-fpm rate of descent on the VSI, allowing the airspeed to increase, and reducing power only if the airspeed approaches the redline V_{NE}. This is a good descent procedure to use in calm air. But instrument flight is seldom conducted in calm air, so a slower descent, your second choice, is made by merely reducing the power sufficiently to establish a 500-fpm descent at cruise airspeed. In this case, very little pitch trim will be necessary. Close to the desired altitude, slight nose-up pressure (trimmed out) and reestablishment of cruise power should hold the airspeed constant.

The last type of descent is made at approach speed. From level flight and approach speed/power, you can lower the gear and/or flaps and retrim to establish the required descent rate, reduce power as you did in the preceding method, or use a combination of these methods. The important thing is to first reduce to approach speed and level flight. The fewer attitude, speed, and configuration changes you have to make at one time, the easier it becomes to do it correctly.

If you have to use drag devices (gear and/or flaps) to establish the descent, when the aircraft is close to the desired altitude, maintain the altitude by retracting the drag devices or increasing power. Establishing the new altitude by the retraction of drag devices requires a longer lead time than by establishing the altitude with power changes, and usually tends to confuse or alarm passengers.

All of these procedures should be practiced first in straight flight and then combined with turns to specific headings until they can be accomplished smoothly with little or no noticeable changes of gravity forces and with minimum instrument deviation. The turns should be practiced using the directional gyro, the magnetic compass, and time, separately and in combination. Altitude changes should be practiced using altimeter and time.

In short, practice, practice, practice, until the procedures become second nature and your instrument scan becomes automatic, avoiding the most common errors:

- Omission of one or more instruments from the scan.
- Gazing too long at one instrument, called *instrument fixation*. This is sometimes caused by staring at the instrument while waiting for a change to take place.

- Anticipating the need for corrective pressures and applying them before they are needed. This is especially prevalent when rolling into or out of turns.
- Misinterpreting the instruments, resulting in such errors as unnecessary power changes. For example, you see the airspeed is too high, so you reduce power without noticing that the increased airspeed is due to a loss of altitude and that simply leveling off by applying back pressure will slow the airspeed.
- Muscle tension on the controls that hampers your ability to sense unwanted control pressures. From time to time, flex your hands and feet to maintain sensitivity and blood circulation.
- Erratic and excessive control displacement, resulting in excessive instrument deflections, instrument lag, and gravity forces, leading to vertigo.
- Improper trim techniques.

CHAPTER QUIZ

1. Directional gyro precession can be corrected by the pilot.

   True _____ False _____

2. If the answer to question 1 is True, how does the pilot correct for it?

3. Attitude indicator precession can be corrected by the pilot.

   True _____ False _____

4. If the answer to question 3 is True, how does the pilot correct for it?

5. Northerly turning error of the magnetic compass is caused by _____.
   It becomes greater _____.

6. The acronym ANDS stands for _____.

7. By taking the _____ and _____ into consideration, a pilot can consistently make accurate turns to specific headings using the _____.

8. Timed turns to specific headings can be accomplished with great accuracy by using a clock, the _____, and/or the _____.

9. To accomplish both questions 7 and 8, it is necessary to have a _____ and _____.

10. The smoothest climb is accomplished by not _____ until the airspeed is within _____.

Answers are in the appendix.

5
Airspeed/altitude control

SOME YEARS BACK, MAYBE BACK IN THE BEGINNING OF TIME AS FAR AS airplanes are concerned, someone thinking about flight in general, or instrument flight in particular, came up with the idea that the elevator controlled the airspeed, while the power controlled the altitude. This started a controversy that has lasted ever since, sort of like "Which came first, the chicken or the egg?"

This concept was widely taught throughout the industry and has created a lot of confusion. One young instructor, so the story goes, was hired by an airline for the express purpose of teaching this new idea to the airline's pilots. He was busy transitioning a grizzled, 20,000-hour DC-3 captain into a DC-6 while at the same time teaching the captain this new instrument technique.

After the first landing and while taxiing back for another takeoff, the disgruntled captain turned to the instructor and said, "OK, Sonny, let me make sure of this. This yoke's supposed to control my airspeed, while the throttles will control the altitude, is that right?"

"That's it, Captain," the instructor beamed, "Now you're getting the point."

Being cleared for takeoff, the captain maneuvered onto the active runway and began pumping the yoke back and forth with the throttles at idle.

"What are you doing, Captain?" the young instructor asked.

"Well, Sonny," the gray-beard muttered with a sly smile, "I'm pumping up some airspeed, and when I get to V_R, I want you to grab them four throttles and jam in a little altitude."

Well, we've all laughed at the joke, but most of us accepted the theory and became proficient at it. Then along came the *flight director*, the device that not only told us that we were above or below the glide slope but also how much of a pitch correction to make to intercept it again.

All of a sudden our altitude was controlled by the elevator again, and the throttles, quite naturally, handled the airspeed. Sure, the logical answer is that they're interrelated and that you can seldom change one without also changing the other.

Finally, and at long last, the FAA has come out with a very logical breakdown that should do a lot to eliminate the confusion and controversy. Basically, the "new correct premise" is this: When power is variable and available, the power controls the speed and the elevators control the altitude or rate of altitude change. This means that in level flight, rate-climbs or rate-descents, and instrument approaches, the power will control the speed.

When the power is fixed or not available, the elevator will control either speed or rate of altitude change, such as full-throttle takeoffs or during descents when the engine(s) have failed or are at zero thrust (idle descents).

Hopefully this will end most of the controversy. Try it out, you'll like it, and it's logical.

FLYING THE PARTIAL PANEL

What will you do if the AI and DG both quit? You will be left within the basic panel, which is called by many people the *partial panel*, or the *needle-ball-and-airspeed* group. For many years these were all the instruments that were available to pilots; now a partial panel is used as part of the instrument flight test.

I can remember when I learned to fly. (Sounds like an old man, doesn't it?) I took my primary training in a Piper PA-11, which was basically a J-3 Cub with a 90-hp engine. One day, my instructor told me that we would learn to fly on instruments. He briefed me very quickly on the then-current (1962) method of partial-panel flying, called the one-two-three method. In this method, the pilot would:

1. Use only the rudder to center the needle.
2. Use only the ailerons to center the ball.
3. Use only the elevator to maintain the proper airspeed.

The altitude would be controlled by the power, but for some reason it was never considered as step 4. Maybe it was thought to be so obvious that it didn't need to be made part of the method.

In any event, this method resulted in the most uncomfortable, uncoordinated, mechanical, vertigo-inducing type of flight you can imagine, and the first time I tried it, I was all over the sky.

One day it came to me—perhaps after reading it in a book, although I don't remember—that the turn needle looked like the stick in the PA-11, and I would try to make the needle move in relation to the movement of the stick. That part worked fine, and so did the advice to "step on the ball" to center it.

From then on, I had no more trouble controlling an aircraft on instruments. Things just seemed to fall naturally into place, and I found the procedure resulted in well-coordinated, smooth flight, even in the PA-11.

When I progressed to aircraft that used yokes instead of sticks, I pretended that when I moved the wheel, I was really moving a stick and the procedure still worked well. Now that so many aircraft are equipped with turn coordinators, it's easy to visualize in a direct manner again. If you picture the sides of the wheel as being connected to the wings of the turn coordinator (or to the AI for that matter), it becomes a simple matter of "pushing" downward on the left side of the yoke to force the left side of the turn coordinator (or the AI) down.

What all of this really boils down to is that it makes no difference where your visual clues concerning the attitude of the aircraft come from. Whether it's VFR, IFR on a full panel, or IFR on a partial panel, you should always fly the aircraft the same way. For the best results and smoothest flight, this way should be a smooth and coordinated manipulation of all of the controls, with a minimum of aircraft attitude change.

Previous chapters examine the instruments that support the AI. Now assume that due to severe turbulence or other factors the AI has tumbled or has otherwise become disabled, the DG has packed up, and you are all alone in a big sky filled with soft, white fluffy clouds that you can't see through. You are on partial panel. Here's where the gentle pressures and proper scanning techniques that you have been practicing become very important.

Think back to the earlier lessons where you became so good at applying smooth control pressure that you were able to make the VSI act as a direct extension of the yoke. Now, under partial panel, use the same techniques to control altitude, climb, and descent. In level flight, you will control airspeed by power and altitude by pressure exerted on the elevator. All of your turns will be timed turns, based on the needle and ball, backed up with the magnetic compass.

UNUSUAL ATTITUDES

There might be times when, due to inattention or turbulence, you might end up in an unusual attitude, normally the *power-on spiral* (Fig. 5-1), or the *climbing approach to a stall* (Fig. 5-2). In either case, the cause, or the result, might leave you with an unreliable AI, so recovery should be based on the partial panel.

The indications of a power-on spiral would be obvious:

- An extreme deflection of the turn needle (The ball might end up being almost anywhere, but it will usually be near the center.)
- High and usually increasing airspeed

- Altimeter unwinding at a rapid rate
- VSI indicating a high rate of descent, perhaps even pegged-out

The recovery must be smooth and coordinated, but it will usually be somewhat mechanical. The first step should be to reduce the power. This will flatten the blades of a constant-speed propeller, producing some drag, and it will either pull the fixed-pitch propeller out of the redline area or prevent it from going in.

The second step should be to roll out to wings-level. To do this, apply aileron opposite to the deflection of the turn needle (in other words, push the needle back to an upright position or the wings of a turn coordinator to a level position), and smoothly apply rudder pressure as necessary to center the ball and to keep it centered.

Fig. 5-1. *Unusual attitude: power-on spiral.*

Fig. 5-2. *Unusual attitude: approach to a stall.*

As the wings roll level, the upward lift coefficient of the wings will increase, tending to make the nose pitch up, thereby reducing the dive angle. The increased airspeed might cause the nose to pitch high enough to cause a rapid climb and resultant stall. If the aircraft had been trimmed for level flight before the spiral and the trim had not been changed, you would not have to use any back pressure at all to level off. Until the airspeed drops down to cruise, you will very possibly need slight forward pressure to prevent a pitch-up. Be very careful that you do not allow the G forces to get too great during the pullout, whether the aircraft is recovering itself or you have had to apply some back pressure.

As you pull level, check the airspeed indicator. When it first reverses its trend (when it stops increasing and just begins to decrease), the aircraft is for all practical purposes in a level-flight attitude *for that airspeed.* At this point, the altimeter will have stopped unwinding. Hold that attitude (hold the yoke in that specific position regardless of pressure) for a few moments and then begin controlling the altitude with the elevator, cross-checking the VSI and airspeed. This part of the recovery will be mostly mechanical. When the airspeed slows down to within 10 mph of cruise speed, increase the power smoothly to the cruise power setting.

After the aircraft is back under control and trimmed out properly, begin a smooth climb back to the desired altitude. To do this, apply smooth back pressure to the yoke to bring the VSI to the desired rate of climb. When the airspeed slows down to about 5 mph above climb speed, add power smoothly to the climb power setting, and fly the airspeed indicator or VSI, depending on which instrument is the most desirable based on the aircraft capabilities at that altitude.

In the initial recovery for this unusual attitude, follow three steps:

1. Power reduction
2. Roll (bank) recovery
3. Pitch recovery

If you try to pull out of the dive without first rolling the wings level, you will tighten the spiral. This will increase the speed, the rate of descent, and the wing loading and will greatly increase the chances of folding the wings.

Sometimes, when the wings are level, you might have a tendency to try to level out faster by applying excessive back pressure, which might result in another unusual attitude, an *approach to a stall.* This can be recognized by a rapidly decreasing airspeed, a high rate of climb, and an increasing altitude (both of which might be leveling off if you're close to or in a stall), and possibly a turn indication on the needle/ball.

To initiate the recovery, you should shove the throttle(s) in rapidly but smoothly to the full-power setting while at the same time pushing forward slightly on the yoke, or by relaxing back pressure as the case might be. Finally, center the needle/ball with smooth, coordinated control pressures.

How much pitch control displacement is necessary? As in the spiral, only enough to stop the airspeed indication from decreasing or make it begin increasing, in case it has stopped decreasing. In other words, just enough to make a perceptible change in the airspeed. When this change occurs, you'll be roughly in a level-flight attitude.

If you've waited too long to notice the approach to a stall and the stall break has occurred, you must lower the nose a little more to hasten the recovery and to prevent a secondary stall. When near stall speed, it's very important to keep the ball centered to avoid entering a spin.

Again, and this must be reemphasized, just as in a spiral, when the airspeed has shown a definite change of trend, you are near level flight *for that specific airspeed,* and you should fly the altimeter and VSI until the airspeed approaches cruise, at which time you should readjust your throttle(s) to cruise power and retrim. Once under control, you should return smoothly to the desired altitude.

The recovery from a stall or from an approach to a stall can then be summed up in three steps:

1. Maximum thrust (power)
2. Pitch recovery
3. Roll wings level

Although pitch and power changes are mentioned as two separate steps in the recovery from an approach to a stall, these two steps are normally combined into one smooth but largely mechanical action. The same holds true for the recovery from a power-on spiral. You really make the recovery the same as if you're in visual conditions.

In both recoveries demonstrated, the altitude gained or lost should be recovered (or at least the recovery attempt should be initiated) before you worry too much about the heading. In most cases, the altitude will be the most critical problem. If you try to do too many things at one time, especially on a partial panel, you can very easily end up doing more harm than good and might create confusion, vertigo, and more unusual attitudes.

Remember, *during unusual attitudes treat the AI and DG as if they have tumbled because chances are that they have*. You must base the recovery on the primary instruments, adding the AI and DG to your scan only when you are absolutely certain that they have regained their reliability.

INSTRUMENT TAKEOFFS

The instrument takeoff is basically a training maneuver. If the weather is really zero/zero, not even the birds will take off, let alone intelligent pilots. After all, where could you go if you had to make an emergency landing shortly after takeoff?

A pilot would be justified in making an actual ITO in only a few instances, perhaps if the airport is socked in by a strictly local condition, such as a ground fog where the tops are only a few hundred feet high and there's another field nearby that is open. Even then you'd be taking a chance, but at least it would be well calculated.

In making an ITO, taxi onto the runway, line up with the centerline, and let the plane roll a few feet to make sure that the nosewheel or the tailwheel is rolling straight, then stop. Set the DG to the painted runway heading, even though the magnetic compass might be reading differently. You can and will always reset the DG later, but on takeoff it's easier to steer to a specific mark on the face of the DG.

Next, set the attitude indicator to the proper aircraft attitude, which is approximately nose level with a tricycle gear but nose high (near the normal climb attitude) in a taildragger.

Be sure that the gyros are uncaged and up to speed. Remember that it takes up to 5 minutes for gyros to spin up to a reliable speed.

Finally, advance the throttle(s) smoothly to maximum allowable power (takeoff power) while keeping all pressure off the brakes. Do not attempt to steer with the brakes. As in visual takeoffs, you will be correcting the heading with rudder pressure. There will be a psychological tendency to overcontrol your heading at first because you will think that you are about to tear out all of the runway lights. Pay more attention to the action of the DG on your next visual takeoff to see the normal reactions and to help you understand them better during an ITO.

As your airspeed approaches climb speed, establish a climb attitude on the AI. This will be about the same attitude whether you are in a tailwheel or nosewheel aircraft. In a taildragger, you will have to lift the tailwheel off the ground first, but just bring it off slightly, nowhere near the amount you do on a normal visual takeoff. For this reason, you should practice this technique a few times under visual conditions to see what it feels like and looks like before trying it under the hood.

Remember, as the aircraft lifts off, the AI will precess and show a slightly higher nose attitude. Scanning the AI and VSI should be quick because you're holding the heading with the DG and the needle/ball. Improper interpretation of the AI at liftoff can result in touching back down. The first 150 feet of altitude will be fairly critical. Above that, you will be well out of ground effect and the instrument precession and lag should have pretty much recovered.

ITOs are a lot of fun, and while they might not be the most practical maneuver, they do a lot of good toward teaching good instrument scanning techniques. They also help pilots build confidence.

CHAPTER QUIZ

1. The _____ controls the speed when power is variable and available.

2. When power is variable and available, the _____ controls the altitude, or the rate of altitude change.

3. What controls the altitude, or the rate of altitude change when power is fixed, or not available?

4. What controls the airspeed when the power is fixed or unavailable?

5. If recovery from a power-on spiral under instruments was broken down into steps, the first thing you would do would be to _____.

6. The next two steps in question 5 would be _____ and _____.

7. The three steps in recovering from a stall while on instruments are:

   a. _____,

   b. _____, and

   c _____.

8. When recovering from either a power-on spiral, or a stall, you know you are in a level attitude for that specific airspeed when there is a _____ in the _____ of the___ _____.

9. When recovering from unusual attitudes under instrument conditions you should rely specifically on the attitude indicator and the directional gyro.

   True _____ False _____

10. When lifting off during an instrument takeoff, the attitude indicator has a tendency to _____.

Answers are in the appendix.

6
Practice, practice, practice

NOW THAT WE'VE WORKED THROUGH MOST OF THE BASICS, ONE BY ONE, let's combine them in some practice problems to make use of all the basic flying skills you'll need to keep the aircraft in the air. In addition, let's begin adding the clock to your scan. The clock is quite necessary in an actual IFR flight, and it is one of the culprits that greatly interferes with the scan of many pilots who tend to stare at it waiting for it to move while flying a timed portion of a flight.

The problems you will be working with in this chapter are designed to make aircraft control and instrument scan second nature, while the use of the clock will add some external pressure to prepare you for the more advanced portion of instrument flight.

At the end of this chapter you will be working with a problem that utilizes a VOR. This is designed to get your mind working rapidly on factors away from the instrument panel.

The first problem is fairly simple, incorporating airspeed control, level turns, descents, and climbs. You should fly each of these patterns visually the first time to get an idea of what's happening. Then fly them with a full panel until you are very good at them, and finally finish up using only a partial panel.

A BASIC MANEUVER

We begin flying the problem illustrated in Fig. 6-1 from a cruise power, cruise airspeed, straight-and-level configuration. If there is any appreciable wind, you should begin the problem by flying crosswind so that the initial turn will be made upwind. The reason you do this is to remain in the same relative practice area. Look at Fig. 6-1 and follow along.

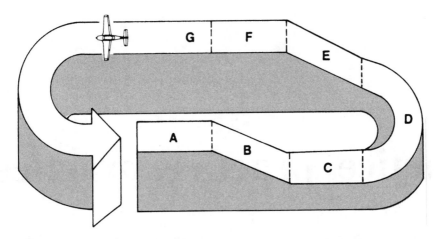

Fig. 6-1

Segment A. Slow to approach airspeed, and fly straight and level for 1 minute.

Segment B. Begin a descent for 1 minute at approach airspeed and a 500-fpm rate of descent.

Segment C. Level off, and fly 1 minute at approach airspeed. Here you should be 500 feet lower than when you began the maneuver at A.

Segment D. Make a level, standard-rate turn. Remember that a standard-rate turn is 3 degrees per second. Make this turn for 1 minute, which should result in a turn of 180 degrees.

Segment E. Climb for 1 minute at climb airspeed and a 500-fpm rate of climb.

Segment F. Here you should be at your initial altitude. At this point, accelerate to cruise airspeed and cruise power.

Segment G. Make a standard-rate level turn for 1 minute, rolling out on your initial heading.

When you fly this pattern the second time, you should make the turns in the opposite direction and alternate the directions of the turns from then on, not only for the practice of different turns, but also to remain in the same practice area.

During the descent segment (B), you should use as many different aircraft configurations as you can. In other words, make one simulated approach in the clean configuration, using only power to adjust the rate of descent. Then, if the aircraft has retractable gear, make a descent by lowering the gear, adjusting power as necessary to maintain a 500-fpm descent. Finally, use various flap settings, with and without the gear, paying attention to the specific pitch attitude and the approximate power setting needed for each type of descent.

If the aircraft has retractable gear, try flying the level turn segment (D) with the gear down and the flaps in the clean and the proper maneuvering positions. No matter what configuration you are using in segment D, you have to remember to clean up the aircraft when you begin the climb in segment E.

Learn the aircraft thoroughly. It's necessary to practice this pattern of maneuvers until controlling the aircraft on instruments becomes second nature, until:

- You can change the gear and flap configurations without gaining or losing any altitude.
- The airspeed remains nailed where you want it.
- One minute of descent results in a loss of exactly 500 feet; 1 minute of climb results in a gain of exactly 500 feet; 1-minute turns come out to exactly 180 degrees.

Once you have mastered this basic pattern, you can make one change in it that will turn it into a procedure that at one time was part of all ATP flight tests. The *canyon approach* was and is an excellent test of aircraft control.

The premise is that as the captain of an aircraft you have been cleared for an approach to an airport located in a canyon. (Refer back to Fig. 6-1.) You reduce power to approach airspeed in segment A. At the beginning of segment B, you cross the initial approach fix (a radio beacon theoretically located on the rim of the canyon), lower gear and flaps, and descend to a minimum descent altitude that is 500 feet below your cruising altitude.

Once down to minimum descent altitude, you fly out the allotted time, which in this pattern is depicted as segment C (1 minute at approach speed), and when you don't see the airport, you initiate the missed approach procedure. In this case, the missed approach procedure calls for an immediate 180-degree climbing turn, as depicted in segment D, which will take you back to the initial altitude. Naturally, the gear and flaps must be retracted during the wave-off.

The one change you have made to the original practice pattern is that you no longer make that nice level turn at D. Instead, you have combined segments D and E into a climbing turn. Still, it's necessary to be at the initial altitude and the reciprocal heading as you complete the 1-minute climbing turn.

If you are flying a multiengine aircraft, have the instructor pilot cut the inside engine (by retarding the throttle) while beginning the climbout. With most light twins you won't be able to make the 500-fpm climb, but if you are really on the ball, you will get the turn timed correctly and also keep from descending below the minimum descent altitude. This is not only a great instrument practice problem, but it sharpens your engine-out procedures as well.

PUTTING IT ALL TOGETHER

Another interesting sequence of maneuvers can be seen in Fig. 6-2. It is broken down into 22 1-minute segments that will review every aspect of aircraft control under instruments with the exception of unusual attitudes.

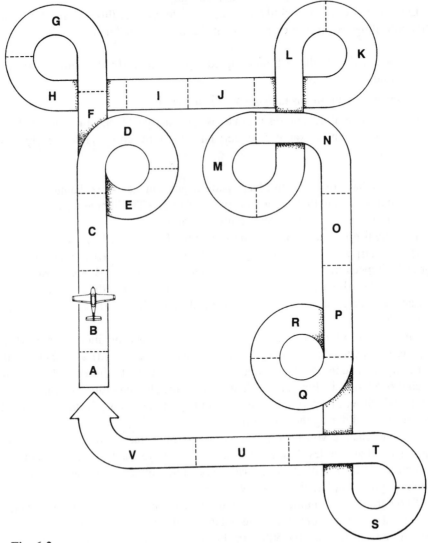

Fig. 6-2

In this series, you will probably need to have the safety pilot review the procedure step-by-step as you go along, which is also good training for the day you will be flying in a two-pilot cockpit where the pilot not at the controls reviews the procedures for the person doing the flying.

One thing should be noted. There is nothing sacred about this series of patterns; you can always make up a series of your own. As with the other pattern, fly this one through visually at first to get an idea of what it's like. Then fly it on a full panel and finally with a partial panel. Try to be extremely precise with timing, as well as with the airspeeds, altitudes, and headings. Remember that each segment should be 1 minute in duration:

Segment A. Begin at 5,000 feet AGL, cruise power, and cruise speed. Use any heading, though it's easier if you start on a cardinal point: north, south, east, or west.

Segment B. While maintaining the heading and altitude, smoothly reduce your airspeed to approach speed.

Segment C. Begin a 500-fpm rate of descent while still maintaining the original heading.

Segment D. Continue the 500-fpm rate of descent, and initiate a standard-rate 360-degree turn to the right.

Segment E. After 180 degrees of the turn, level off (you should now be at 4,000 feet AGL) and maintain the approach airspeed. Continue the turn, and roll out on the initial heading.

Segment F. Reestablish a descent of 500 fpm.

Segment G. While continuing the descent, roll into a standard-rate 270-degree turn to the left, and after 1 minute, level off at 3,000 feet AGL, maintaining approach airspeed.

Segment H. Continue the turn for 30 seconds, rolling out on the initial heading plus 90 degrees.

Segment I. Accelerate to cruise airspeed. Maintain the new heading and an altitude of 3,000 feet AGL.

Segment J. Initiate a 1-minute 500-fpm climb while maintaining the heading.

Segment K. Continue the climb, and begin a standard-rate 270-degree turn to the left.

Segment L. After 180 degrees of turn, continue the climbing turn for another 30 seconds (for a total of 90 seconds), and then, while maintaining the climb, roll into the first 90 degrees of a standard-rate 360-degree turn to the right.

Segment M. Continue the climbing turn, leveling off at 5,000 feet AGL.

Segment N. Continue to turn for 30 seconds (for a total of 2 minutes) while accelerating to cruise speed, finally rolling out on the reciprocal of the original heading in Segment A.

Segment O. Reduce power to approach airspeed.

Segment P. Initiate a 500-fpm descent, and if the aircraft has retractable gear, extend the gear.

Segment Q. While descending, begin a 360-degree standard-rate turn to the right and extend approach flaps.

Segment R. Continue the descending right turn with gear and flaps extended. At the end of this second minute of the turn, you should once again be on the reciprocal of the initial heading and at 3,500 feet AGL.

Segment S. Here you will initiate a climbing, 270-degree standard-rate left turn to simulate a missed approach, retracting the gear (if applicable) and flaps while climbing at 500 fpm.

Segment T. Continue the climbing standard-rate left turn for 30 seconds (a total of 90 seconds), rolling out at the original heading plus 90 degrees, all the while continuing the climb.

Segment U. Continue the climb, leveling off after 1 minute of straight flight. The altitude should be 4,750 feet AGL.

Segment V. Continue climbing and begin a 30-second, 90-degree standard-rate turn to the right roll out and accelerate to cruise airspeed. You will then be in position to begin segment A at the original altitude, heading, and airspeed.

This maneuver, properly executed, will go a long way toward preparing you to handle an aircraft with the precision necessary for instrument flight. During the procedure, you will have simulated all aspects of a normal instrument flight: level flight, speed control, turns (climbing, descending, and level), approach configurations, and missed approach.

You can devise other patterns of your own, of course, but a pattern similar to the one depicted here will get all of the necessary maneuvers in without wandering all over the countryside.

VOR TRACKING AND TIME/DISTANCE PROBLEMS

You have one last area to work on before departing on your first cross-country instrument flight. This is a procedure that will cover VOR tracking, radial intercepts, and time-and-distance problems. You can usually accomplish this problem successfully in one practice session using a single VOR facility (Fig. 6-3).

To begin with, cross the VOR and proceed outbound on the 135-degree radial for a period of 5 minutes, then turn right to a heading of 270 degrees. The problem now will be to intercept and track inbound on the 180-degree radial.

In addition, you will need to figure the time to the station from the point of intercept. This problem is primarily one of mental computation, devised to get your thought processes working independently of the motor processes that are actually flying the aircraft.

Once again, the pattern has been set up to keep you within a reasonable amount of airspace. You can set up any headings and intercepts you want, though the ones depicted here are easy to follow and will suffice to teach what you will need to know in actual instrument conditions.

A simple solution to a time/distance problem on an intercept is to position the aircraft 90 degrees to the inbound radial. When 20 degrees from the radial, begin timing through the next 10 degrees of bearing change, converting the time to seconds. Ten percent of the resulting time in seconds (just place the decimal point one digit in from the right) will provide the approximate time to the station in minutes.

For example, if you have flown through 10 degrees in 2 minutes (or 120 seconds), time to the station (in minutes) would be 10 percent of that, or 120 seconds × 10 percent = 12.0 minutes. Distance from the station would then be the ground speed (in nautical miles per minute) times the time to the station. So if you have a ground speed of 120 knots (or 2 nm per minute), you would be 24 nm from the station. Easy? You bet, but it seems much more difficult in a moving aircraft when you are trying to control it on instruments alone or with a partial panel.

You can then add one other step to the problem. In order to allow adequate time to pin down the inbound course before entering the cone of confusion around the VOR, you should make it a practice to turn inbound only if you are more than 3 minutes from the station. This means that it must take more than 30 seconds to cross that 10 degrees of bearing change that you timed.

If you find that you are 3 minutes or fewer from the station, you should turn 30 degrees away from the reciprocal of the inbound course, fly outbound for 1.5 minutes, and make a standard-rate 180-degree turn (in the direction away from the station) back toward the course. Once you intercept the course, fly inbound to the station. Take another look at the diagram in Fig. 6-3. You can see how this resembles a procedure turn. In addition to everything else, this pattern should also give you practice in procedure turns.

Returning to the explanation of the problem depicted in Fig. 6-3: You are heading 270 degrees, which is 90 degrees to your inbound course (the 180-degree radial of the VOR). To orientate the *omni bearing indicator* (OBI), or *needle*, properly, you should have it set to your inbound course, which will be 360 degrees TO. In this example then, the OBI should be deflected to the left, showing that you have not reached the course.

(Before everyone jumps on me for using the term *omni bearing indicator* instead of *course deviation indicator* (CDI), I prefer to use the term CDI in relation to flight directors, and OBI in relation to the simple VOR receiver. If you prefer the term CDI, feel free to substitute it whenever you see OBI.)

In order to time yourself through 10 degrees of bearing change and still have time to make decisions as to whether to fly inbound or to fly a procedure turn first, you should back up the omni bearing selector (OBS) 20 degrees from the inbound course. That means that in this example, you should set it to 340 degrees TO. Once again, the needle should be deflected to the left side of the indicator.

Before long the needle will move off its peg. When it centers, you should check the clock, noting both the minute hand and sweep-second hand positions or the indication of minutes and seconds on a digital clock. Reset the OBS to 350 degrees TO. When the needle centers again, take the time in seconds and compute the time and distance. For the first 30 seconds of time from 340 degrees TO through 350 degrees TO, it's useful to keep saying "procedure turn." After 30 seconds have passed, if I have not yet made it through the 10-degree bearing change, I automatically start saying "direct inbound."

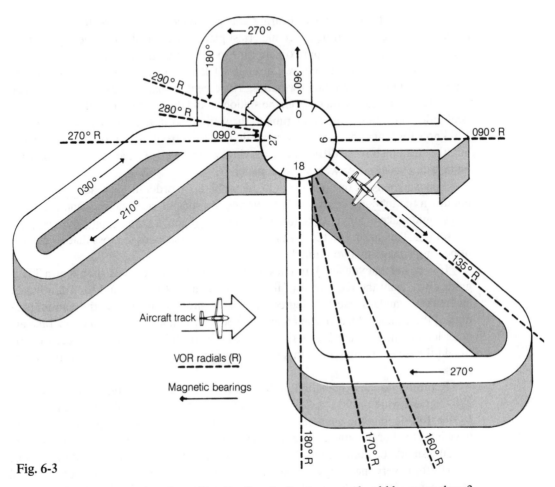

Fig. 6-3

If you flew the initial outbound leg for 5 or 6 minutes, you should be more than 3 minutes from the station, and you will make a right turn inbound when you get to the course. Naturally, after crossing the 350-degree course that was set on the OBS, you should immediately reset it to the desired inbound course of 360 degrees. All this time, you should be maintaining the proper heading, airspeed, and altitude.

A strong wind will play havoc with this procedure because it might screw up your estimates, but for the most part, the estimates should work out pretty close.

Now turn inbound, track to the VOR, and continue on the same course outbound for 1 minute. As you cross the VOR, you should make a simulated position report to ATC. Your new problem is to track inbound on the 270-degree radial.

In order to track that radial inbound, you must first be positioned on the proper side of the station; therefore, after flying the 1-minute outbound leg from the station, you should turn left to a heading of 270 degrees and fly outbound for 1 minute. Then turn south, which will be 90 degrees to your inbound course again.

Once again, set the inbound course on the OBS. This time it will be 090 degrees TO. The OBI should be deflected to the right. If it is, reset the OBS to 110 degrees TO, which is 20 degrees from the desired inbound track. When the needle centers, check the time, and advance the OBS 10 degrees at 100 degrees TO. In this case, assuming that your time is less than 30 seconds (it should be), you should fly a procedure turn as depicted, and while turning outbound, you should once again set the inbound course on the OBS.

As you can see, you can set up many problems using this simple pattern, although with the exception of the procedure turn, it might not be of much use on an actual IFR flight. Still, it is an excellent pattern for building up mental prowess and your command of reciprocal bearings, while at the same time teaching you to fly the aircraft on instruments almost automatically.

Once you feel that you have mastered the instruments and are quite comfortable doing these problems, you will be ready for the first actual cross-country IFR flight.

CHAPTER QUIZ

To determine the answers to the following questions, assume that you are flying southbound, somewhat to the southwest of a specific VOR. You are instructed to intercept the 215-degree radial of the VOR, track inbound to the station on that radial, and forward an ETA over the station as soon as practicable.

1. What will the inbound course be when established inbound on the 215-degree radial?
2. What heading should you turn to in order to intercept the 215-degree radial at 90 degrees?
3. What course would you set first on the OBI?
4. Why would you set this course?
5. Where should the OBI needle be if you have not yet crossed the 215-degree radial?
6. What is the next course to set in the OBI?
7. Why?
8. Where should the OBI needle be once the course in question 6 is set?
9. What is the next course to set in the OBI?
10. The OBI needle centers in 65 seconds. How long will it take you to cross the station after turning inbound?
11. At a cruise speed of 90 knots, how far will you be from the station when intercepting the inbound course?
12. Should you turn inbound or outbound when intercepting the 215-degree radial?

13. Should you turn inbound or outbound if the time in question 10 is 20 seconds?

14. If you turn inbound, how long will it take you to reach the station? If you turn outbound, what would the first outbound heading be?

15. After 1½ minutes, you turn to the _____ to a heading of _____ to reintercept the inbound course.

16. How long should it take you to cross the station after first crossing the inbound course in question 14?

17. How did you arrive at that figure?

Answers are in the appendix.

7
Planning the IFR flight

PREFLIGHT PLANNING TO MANY PEOPLE MEANS NOTHING MORE THAN scanning the charts, making a quick call to the weather service or flight service to see if it's still VFR, and a cursory glance at the aircraft with perhaps a perfunctory kick at a tire.

Instrument pilots cannot afford this degree of nonchalance. Murphy's well-known law states that, "Anything that can go wrong, will go wrong." When we combine that with the fact that emergencies always seem to snowball, we tend to become a little more careful, or at least we should.

At least 50 percent of effective instrument flying is psychological; thus, a proper and careful preflight procedure will put us in a mental condition to properly handle the flight. In addition, this proper preflight procedure is required by the regulations. FAR 91.103 says:

Each pilot in command shall, before beginning a flight, familiarize himself with all available information concerning that flight. This information must include:
(a) For a flight under IFR . . . weather reports and forecasts, fuel requirements, alternatives available if the planned flight cannot be completed, and any known traffic delays of which the pilot in command has been advised by ATC. . . .

THE FLIGHT KIT

A fairly good place to begin this discussion is with the pilot's personal flight kit. Every instrument-rated pilot eventually puts together a flight kit that seems to work best for him or her. The items listed below make up a fairly comprehensive kit. As you gain more experience, you may add to it or subtract from it to suit individual desires. You'll notice that I have recommended more than one of some of the items; these are inexpensive items that don't take up space or add much weight to your flight kit. Believe me, you'll be willing to pay a king's ransom should one fail or wear out in flight and you end up without a spare.

- Airway charts, SIDs, STARs, and approach plates for the section of the country you'll be flying in. For most light aircraft, the enroute low altitude charts will suffice for the airway charts.

- Sectional charts to cover the same area, and/or WAC charts, depending on the speed of your aircraft. These charts will better enable you to visualize the terrain you'll be flying over. There are many times when you'll get enough of a break in the clouds to catch a glimpse of the ground, and in many cases, the sectional will enable you to confirm your position. (One other use of the sectional shall be discussed later.)

- Two or more flashlights, with fresh spare batteries and extra bulbs, in case of an electrical power failure at night. If you, like some other pilots, prefer to put a red lens on one of the flashlights, you'll have to remember that red lines and markings on your charts will be invisible under the red light.

- Two or more pens; the felt tips work best. They write heavily and dark enough to show up well in both dim lighting conditions and in turbulence, and they are excellent for copying clearances. Black is the best color for maximum visibility.

- Six or so sharpened pencils (#2 lead seems to be the best) for working up flight plans and other miscellaneous figuring. Dull points are difficult to write with and read later, so you should carry a small hand-held pencil sharpener, like you'd find in a child's pencil box. In fact, a child's pencil box is a great container for all of these small items. And don't forget a good eraser. The erasers on the pencils wear out a lot faster than the pencils do, so it's a good idea to have spares.

- One pocket calculator, at least. There are many good computers on the market today; I happen to prefer the Jeppesen CR-2, which fits in a shirt pocket.

- Two or more plotters, one for sectional and WAC charts, and one for the IFR enroute charts. Remember, unlike the WAC or sectional charts, the enroute charts can be almost any scale. Always check the chart's scale so you will use the proper plotter scale.

- A pad or two of the latest FAA flight plan forms.

- Scratch pads or note paper. Here I find that the backsides of the small telephone message forms work just fine for clearances and miscellaneous figuring. They'll fit right in your shirt pocket along with your computer so they're always close at hand.
- You'll be working with at least two different times: local time for everyday life and UTC (Zulu) for filing flight plans and flying. Two inexpensive dual-time watches are ideal; wear one and leave the spare in the flight bag. The two watches permit easily shifting from local to UTC and from 12- to 24-hour time-keeping. These watches are available in all drugstores as well as catalogues.

IFR AIRCRAFT REQUIREMENTS

Just as you need special charts, your aircraft will need special instrumentation for IFR flight. Part 91.205 lists what you need on board to operate in all environments. The instruments and equipment required for IFR flight are, in addition to those required for VFR flight:

- A two-way radio communications system and navigational equipment appropriate to the ground facilities to be used
- Gyroscopic rate-of-turn indicator
- Slip/skid indicator
- Sensitive altimeter
- Clock showing hours, minutes, and seconds with a sweep-second pointer or digital presentation
- A generator or alternator of adequate capacity
- Artificial horizon (attitude indicator)
- Directional gyro or equivalent
- For flight above 24,000 feet MSL, distance measuring equipment (DME).

There are also special requirements for VOR receivers. Part 91.171 says this:

(a) No person may operate a civil aircraft under IFR using the VOR system of radio navigation unless the VOR equipment of that aircraft—
(1) Is maintained, checked, and inspected under an approved procedure; or
(2) Has been operationally checked within the preceding 30 days, and was found to be within the limits of the permissible indicated bearing error. . . .

These permissible errors are ±4 degrees when using an FAA-operated or approved VOR *test signal* (VOT), or designated (usually by paint marks) surface VOR receiver checkpoint, or if dual VORs are checked against each other. The permissible error is ±6 degrees if monitored on an approved in-flight check.

An aircraft logbook entry must be made for each VOR check; however, it is not necessary to have a mechanic do the check. You can do your own check as the pilot, but don't forget to make the logbook entry according to FARs.

Other required items for IFR flight deal with external items such as lighting and won't be covered in this discussion.

ICING AND THUNDERSTORM HAZARDS

After ascertaining that the aircraft and personal flight kit are in order, you should move to the weather briefing. After all, if the weather's too bad, you won't go. Remember, an instrument ticket is not a license to fly in any and all weather. Rather, it's proof that you've been taught to recognize which weather not to fly into, as well as which weather conditions you can handle.

For example, the regulations prevent you from flying into most icing conditions. Part 91.527, which concerns large and turbine-powered multiengine aircraft, states:

(a) No pilot may take off in an airplane that has—
(1) Frost, snow, or ice adhering to any propeller, windshield, or powerplant installation, or to an airspeed, altimeter, rate of climb, or flight attitude instrument system;
(2) Snow or ice adhering to the wings or stabilizing or control surfaces; or
(3) Any frost adhering to the wings, or stabilizing or control surfaces, unless that frost has been polished to make it smooth.
(b) Except for an airplane that has ice protection provisions that meet the requirements in [a regulation setting forth anti-ice and deice requirements not applicable to most light aircraft] no pilot may fly—
(1) Under IFR into known or forecast moderate icing conditions.

Although these restrictions are specifically written to apply to large and turbine-powered multiengine aircraft and there are no restrictions specifically written concerning light aircraft, it would be foolish to fly lightplanes where the heavies have been restricted. It could be considered a violation of FAR 91.13 (careless or reckless operation) to do so.

Ice is one of the greatest hazards a pilot can face, short of a wing falling off. It can add weight to the aircraft very quickly, which will increase the stalling speed. Additionally, it might build up to the point that the engine is no longer capable of carrying the load. It can build up in such a manner as to put the aircraft outside of CG limits, and especially with *rime ice*, it builds in such a nonuniform shape as to completely destroy the lift of the wings. The worst icing conditions that you can encounter are freezing rain and freezing drizzle, both of which are capable of pulling you out of the sky in just a few minutes.

Though rime ice can form at temperatures as low as −40°F (−40°C), the very hazardous *glaze* or *clear ice* is usually confined to temperatures of 14–32°F (−10–0°C).

Check the weather carefully for reports of icing, and avoid flying into IFR conditions when the outside air temperature (OAT) is in the range of 10–32°F. Find a different altitude that will result in a higher or lower OAT.

Even following these hints, you will eventually find yourself in icing conditions. You must remember that ice does increase the stalling speed, so be prepared to land at a higher speed than normal should you have ice on the aircraft.

One of the most insidious forms of icing is *carburetor ice*. If the humidity is high enough, this can form at any OAT from 14–70°F. A functioning carburetor heat control will usually melt the ice, provided it is used in the early stages of formation. Pulling the carburetor heat out for a few minutes every 10 or 15 minutes will usually prevent major carburetor icing.

The reason that carburetor ice will form at high temperatures is that as the intake air passes through the venturi of the carburetor, the air cools rapidly, and any moisture in the air can frost up the throat of the carburetor as well as the fuel nozzles. (I have had carburetor icing even over Hawaii.) This is why carburetor heat is pulled out on many aircraft when you close the throttle during power-off landings.

Another hazard to avoid like the plague is the thunderstorm. In addition to the icing hazard always associated with these awesome phenomena, you can be subjected to hail that can damage windshields and the leading edges of airfoils. They are also associated with severe *wind shears* that literally break an aircraft into pieces, and with *microbursts* that have even forced high-powered jet aircraft into the ground.

The thunderstorms usually associated with fast-moving cold fronts can normally be seen and avoided, but if they're hidden (*embedded*) inside the solid blanket of clouds associated with warm fronts, stationary fronts, or the warm side of occlusions, stay on the ground and fly another day.

AIRWAYS AND ALTITUDES

After checking the weather, you will have to check any NOTAMs that might apply to your flight, and, if you are flying into or out of large terminal areas, you will be looking for the possibility of preferred routes that have been established for the most orderly flow of traffic in and around those busy areas. These routes are listed in the back of the *Airport/Facility Directory (A/FD)*; the routes are either one-way or two-way.

Now, with all of this in mind, check your charts for a routing, using preferred routes if possible, that will avoid the thunderstorms and icing conditions. You might still have other restrictions to your choice of routes, such as altitude restrictions and obstructions that are beyond the operational limits of the aircraft.

It might be a good idea to review some of the terminology and definitions that you will run across. The lowest altitude you can ever fly on airways under instrument conditions will be determined from one of the following four restrictions as spelled out in the glossary section of the *Air Traffic Control Manual*:

- **Minimum Enroute IFR Altitude.** The lowest published altitude between radio fixes which assures acceptable navigational signal coverage and meets obstacle clearance requirements between those fixes. The MEA prescribed for a Federal Airway or segment thereof, area navigation low or high route, or other direct route, applies to the entire width of the airway, segment, or route.

- **Minimum Crossing Altitude.** The lowest altitude at certain fixes at which an aircraft must cross when proceeding in the direction of a higher minimum enroute IFR altitude (MEA).

- **Minimum Obstruction Clearance Altitude.** The lowest published altitude in effect between radio fixes on VOR airways, off-airway routes, or route segments which meets obstacle clearance requirements for the entire route segment and which assures acceptable navigational signal coverage only within 25 statute (22 nautical) miles of a VOR.

- **Minimum Reception Altitude.** The lowest altitude at which an intersection can be determined.

If a specific route lists both MEA and MOCA, the pilot may operate below the MEA down to but not below the MOCA only when within 25 statute miles of the VOR concerned. This can be helpful when you have to descend to avoid or get out of icing conditions.

It is legal, and sometimes necessary, to operate off the airways. When the pilot decides to do so, the *ATC Handbook* states:

> Pilots are reminded that they are responsible for adhering to obstruction clearance requirements on those segments of direct routes that are outside of controlled airspace. The MEAs and other altitudes shown on low altitude IFR enroute charts pertain to those route segments within controlled airspace, and those altitudes may not meet obstruction clearance criteria when operating off those routes. When planning a direct flight, check your sectional or other VFR charts, too.

Aha, there is the other use of the sectional charts previously mentioned in this chapter. Sectionals are a necessary part of your IFR flight kit.

Another reason to be concerned about MEAs and MOCAs is that in some sections of the country you have to cross high terrain and might run into the need for supplemental oxygen that might not be on board. The regulations stipulate that all required crewmembers be on oxygen for all flight time exceeding 30 minutes that the aircraft is above 12,500 feet MSL cabin altitude, up to and including 14,000 feet MSL. For flight at *cabin altitudes* above 14,000 feet MSL, crewmembers must be on oxygen for the entire period of time. In unpressurized aircraft, *aircraft altitude* and *cabin pressure altitude* are one and the same. Perhaps you will have to consider the alternative of roundabout routings if you do not carry oxygen.

When making up a tentative route, study the charts carefully to be familiar with all other routes that will be nearly parallel because it is not unusual to be cleared for a routing other than what you file for, or to have the routing suddenly changed after becoming airborne.

FUEL AND ALTERNATE AIRPORT REQUIREMENTS

With all of this in mind, you can now prepare the flight plan. This should be done as accurately as possible, using all available wind and weather information. Even though you know that the conditions will seldom be exactly as forecast, especially in the lower altitudes, it's a lot easier in flight to make small corrections rather than major corrections. Besides, you base the required fuel load on the information on the flight plan. In order to see exactly what's figured in, in the way of IFR fuel, take another look at the regulations. You can find the fuel requirements in Part 91.167:

> (a) . . . No person may operate a civil aircraft in IFR conditions unless it carries enough fuel (considering weather reports and forecasts, and weather conditions) to—
> (1) Complete the flight to the first airport of intended landing;
> (2) Fly from that airport to the alternate airport; and
> (3) Fly after that for 45 minutes at normal cruising speed. . . .
> (b) Paragraph (a)(2) of this section does not apply if—
> (1) Part 97 of this subchapter prescribes a standard instrument approach procedure for the first airport of intended landing; and
> (2) For at least 1 hour before and 1 hour after the estimated time of arrival at the airport, the weather reports or forecasts or any combination of them indicate—
> (i) The ceiling will be at least 2,000 feet above the airport elevation; and
> (ii) Visibility will be at least three miles.

Although part (b) might sound a little confusing at first, all it really means is that if the intended airport has an instrument approach procedure that has been approved, and if the weather is forecast to be VFR (actually, with the 2,000-foot ceiling, a little higher than VFR), you won't need to file an alternate airport, and your VFR fuel will suffice.

There is a built-in safety margin here if you look at it again. The fact that the field has an instrument approach should allow you to get in. The chances are quite remote that the weather will go from VFR all the way down to below IFR minimums without being forecast. On the other hand, if the weather is below VFR minimums or forecast to go below VFR minimums within the previously mentioned two-hour time period, you must file an alternate airport just in case the weather really does go down fast and closes the destination airport.

Under IFR alternate airport weather minimums, FAR 91.169:

> (c) . . . Unless otherwise authorized by the Administrator, no person may include an alternate airport in an IFR flight plan unless current weather forecasts indicate that, at the estimated time of arrival at the alternate airport, the ceiling and visibility at that airport will be at or above the following alternate airport weather minimums:
> (1) If an instrument approach procedure has been published in Part 97 of this chapter for that airport, the alternate airport minimums specified in that procedure, or, if none are so specified, the following minimums:
> (i) Precision approach procedure: ceiling 600 feet and visibility 2 statute miles.
> (ii) Nonprecision approach procedures: ceiling 800 feet and visibility 2 statute miles.
> (2) If no instrument approach procedure has been published in Part 97 of this chapter for that airport, the ceiling and visibility minimums are those allowing descent from the MEA, approach, and landing under VFR.

The alternate minimums are normally well above the primary landing minimums for the airport. This additional safety margin is thrown in because if the weather at the intended airport goes below IFR minimums and you have to divert to the alternate, chances are that the weather will still be above landing minimums at the alternate airport. But at the moment you divert, the alternate airport becomes your new airport of intended landing, and the published landing minimums are applicable for what is now your new destination, utilizing the facilities that are appropriate for the procedure.

Be aware that in determining your alternate airport and fuel loading requirements, even if the forecast for the intended destination airport indicates that conditions will only be "occasionally" (or "chance of") below the minimums specified in 91.167(b)(2) and 91.169(b), an alternate is still required.

Similarly, you cannot select an alternate that is forecast to be "occasionally" (etc.) below the minimums in 91.169(c).

ATC advises filing a flight plan at least 30 minutes prior to estimated time of departure; otherwise, expect a delay up to 30 minutes long. If you file before the aircraft preflight check, you should have the clearance in hand and be ready for departure by the time you're finished with the preflight and the runup.

CHAPTER QUIZ

1. For a flight under IFR, the pilot must consider:

   a. Weather reports

   b. Weather forecasts

   c. Fuel requirements

   d. Alternatives

   e. Known traffic delays reported by ATC

   f. All of the above

2. Sectional charts are not a required part of an instrument flight kit.

   True _____ False _____

3. To be usable for IFR flight, VOR equipment must be checked for accuracy within every _____ days.

4. A qualified technician must make the required VOR equipment checks.

   True _____ False _____

5. The regulations prohibit general aviation pilots from flying in icing conditions.

   True _____ False _____

6. Clear ice usually forms in the temperature range of from _____.

7. Carburetor ice can form in any outside air temperature from _____.

8. What is the difference between MEA, MOCA, and MRA?

9. The basic fuel requirements for IFR are: enough fuel to land at the destination airport, plus enough fuel to fly from there to an alternate airport, plus enough fuel to fly for an additional _____ minutes at normal cruise speed.

10. The alternate airport (and its fuel requirement) mentioned in question 9 is not required, provided that the destination airport has a standard instrument approach procedure, and that for a period of _____ the estimated time of arrival at the airport, the weather reports or forecasts or any combination of them, indicate that the ceiling will be at least _____, and the visibility will be _____.

11. The basic alternate airport minimums for an airport with a published instrument approach procedure are a ceiling of _____ and visibility of _____ for a precision approach, and a ceiling of _____ and visibility of _____ for a nonprecision approach.

12. An airport cannot be used as an alternate IFR airport unless it has either a precision, or nonprecision instrument approach procedure published for it.

    True _____ False _____

Answers are in the appendix.

8
Departure helpers

TAKEOFF: YOU ARE PERCHED EXPECTANTLY AT THE EDGE OF THE RUNWAY, awaiting your clearance. If this is like most small fields, you might have filed a flight plan something like this:

> IFR to Big Lake Airport via Lost Deer VOR, V16, V3, Fish, V22, Tuway intersection, V5, 8,000 feet.

If you are departing from a typical large airport, you will find that the same clearance will be quite a bit more complicated because many times ATC will add departure instructions. For example, if you filed the same flight plan from a large airport, you might receive a clearance something like:

> Speedy 50X is cleared to Big Lake Airport as filed, except, after takeoff turn right to a heading of 150 degrees until intercepting the 262-degree radial of Trout VOR, turn left via the 262-degree radial of Trout VOR until intercepting the 180-degree radial of Lost Deer VOR, direct. Maintain 2,000 feet until intercepting the 262-degree radial of Trout VOR, then climb to and maintain 4,000 feet to Lost Deer VOR, as filed, maintain 8,000.

SIDs

You could have simplified the entire process by using a SID *(standard instrument departure)*. If you had used a SID in the flight plan above, you might have received a simplified clearance:

> Speedy 50X is cleared to Big Lake Airport, Holiday 1 Departure, Fish Transition, as filed, maintain 8,000 feet.

All of the rest of the complicated departure instructions would have been included in the SID.

SIDs, STARs (see chapter 10), and other abbreviated clearances have been developed because of the need to put as many aircraft as possible into and through the ATC system. To accomplish this, it becomes necessary to keep the radio transmissions as brief as possible; hence, the use of abbreviations like "as filed," and the use of SIDs and STARs.

Another reason for these SIDs, and such, is to put them down on paper in such a manner as to simplify what otherwise could be a difficult clearance to copy, read back, understand, and comply with. In order for this to work, however, pilots have the responsibility to thoroughly understand the restrictions involved.

The *Jeppesen Airway Manual* introduction has this to say about SIDs:

> Pilots of IFR civil aircraft operating from locations where SID procedures are effective may expect ATC clearances containing a SID. Use of a SID requires possession of at least the textual description of the SID. Pilots not desiring to use the SID are expected to advise ATC. Notification may be accomplished by filing "NO SID" in the remarks section of the filed flight plan or by the less desirable method of verbally advising ATC.

I can't see any reason to turn down a SID as long as you have the required textual portion in your possession and your aircraft can meet the various restrictions, which are explained later. Turning it down will only make more work for everyone involved. If you filed "NO SID," the only difference is that you will get the complete textual portion read to you, and you'll have to copy it down and read it back, which is sometimes very complicated and time-consuming. After all, ATC has devised the departure routings to expedite traffic and to give adequate separation between inbound and outbound flights, so it stands to reason that as long as you will be departing on that route anyway, you might as well make it easy on all concerned by having the SIDs in your possession and reviewing them before flight.

OBSTACLE CLEARANCE CONCERNS

It might be a good idea here to take a look at how the FAA devises obstacle clearance specifications, explained by Jeppesen:

Obstacle clearance is based on the aircraft climbing at 200 feet per nautical mile, crossing the end of the runway at 35 feet AGL, and climbing to 400 feet above the airport elevation before turning unless otherwise specified in the procedure. *[This is the basic obstacle clearance specification.]* A slope of 152 feet per mile, starting no higher than 35 feet above the departure end of the runway, is assessed for obstacles. A minimum of 48 feet of obstacle clearance is provided for each mile of flight. If no obstacles penetrate the 152 feet per mile slope, IFR departure procedures are not published. *[So far so good. If nothing is specified on the SID or in the takeoff section of the airport plan chart (more on that in chapter 16), then all you need do is meet the above climb criteria.]* If obstacles penetrate the slope, obstacle avoidance procedures are specified. These procedures may be: a ceiling and visibility to allow the obstacles to be seen and avoided; a climb gradient greater than 200 feet per mile; detailed flight maneuvers; or a combination of the above. In extreme cases, IFR takeoff may not be authorized for some runways. *[Unless you have some really bad problems, any aircraft capable of IFR flight is able to meet the standard obstacle climb gradient.]*

Climb gradients are specified when required for obstacle clearance. Crossing restrictions in the SIDs may be established for traffic separation or obstacle clearance. When no gradient is specified, the pilot is expected to climb at least 200 feet per mile to MEA unless required to level off by a crossing restriction. *[Perhaps we should get our heads together here. We are used to thinking in terms of climbing and descending at a certain feet per minute rate. These climb gradients are based on climbing so many feet per mile. To meet these restrictions, the rate of climb will be a function of both airspeed **and groundspeed**. The faster you fly across the ground, the higher your rate of climb will have to be to meet the climb gradient.]* Climb gradients may be specified to an altitude/fix, above which the normal gradient applies. Some procedures require a climb in visual conditions to cross the airport (or an on-airport NAVAID) at or above an altitude. The specified ceiling and visibility minimums will be enough to allow the pilot to see and avoid obstacles near the airport. Obstacle avoidance is not guaranteed if the pilot maneuvers farther from the airport than the visibility minimum. *[This is a very important point. If you are given an IFR clearance with a two-mile visibility restriction, it is your responsibility to stay within two miles of the airport until above the ceiling specified in the same clearance. You must remain in visual conditions to see and avoid any obstacles.]* That segment of the procedure which requires the pilot to see and avoid obstacles ends when the aircraft crosses the specified point at the required altitude. Thereafter, standard obstacle protection is provided.

Take a look at an actual SID. Figure 8-1 is the DUMBARTON FIVE DEPARTURE from San Francisco, California. You can see that it is labeled SID in the upper right hand corner so as not to be confused with an approach plate or a STAR (*standard terminal arrival route*). As a further identification aid, Jeppesen assigns SIDs the code number of 10-3 followed by an alphabetical suffix if there is more than one SID for the airport, as opposed to the code number 10-2 for STARs, and 10-1 for area charts.

As procedures are changed, ATC changes the numerical suffix of the SID. In this case, the Dumbarton Five Departure has updated the Dumbarton Four Departure, so

JEPPESEN 31 DEC 93 (10-3) Eff 6 Jan SID SAN FRANCISCO, CALIF
SAN FRANCISCO INTL

BAY Departure (R) 120.9

DUMBARTON FIVE DEPARTURE (DUMB5.BARTN) (PILOT NAV)
(RWYS 10L/R and 19L/R)

This SID requires the following minimum climb gradients for obstacle clearance:
Rwy 19L: 480' per NM to 1400'.
Rwy 19R: CAT A & B, 480' per NM to 1400', CAT C & D, 530' per NM to 1800'.

Gnd speed-Kts	75	100	150	200	250	300
480' per NM	600	800	1200	1600	2000	2400
530' per NM	663	883	1325	1767	2208	2650

TAKE-OFF
Rwys 10L/R and 19L/R: Turn LEFT (Rwys 19L/R departures turn LEFT as soon as practicable due to steeply rising terrain to 2000' immediately south of airport) and climb via SFO R-090 to Bartn Int. Thence via (transition) or (assigned route). Expect further clearance to filed altitude 10 minutes after departure.

TRANSITIONS
Linden (DUMB5.LIN): From Bartn Int to **LIN VOR:** Via OSI R-028 and LIN R-229. Cross OSI R-028 D24 at or above 11000'. **MAINTAIN** assigned altitude.
Red Bluff (DUMB5.RBL): From Bartn Int to **RBL VOR:** Via OSI R-028 and RBL R-152. Cross OSI R-028 D24 at or above 11000'. **MAINTAIN** assigned altitude.
Sacramento (DUMB5.SAC): From Bartn Int to **SAC VOR:** Via OSI R-028 and SAC R-177. Cross OSI R-028 D24 at or above 11000'. **MAINTAIN** assigned altitude.
Woodside (DUMB5.OSI): From Bartn Int to **OSI VOR:** Via OSI R-028.

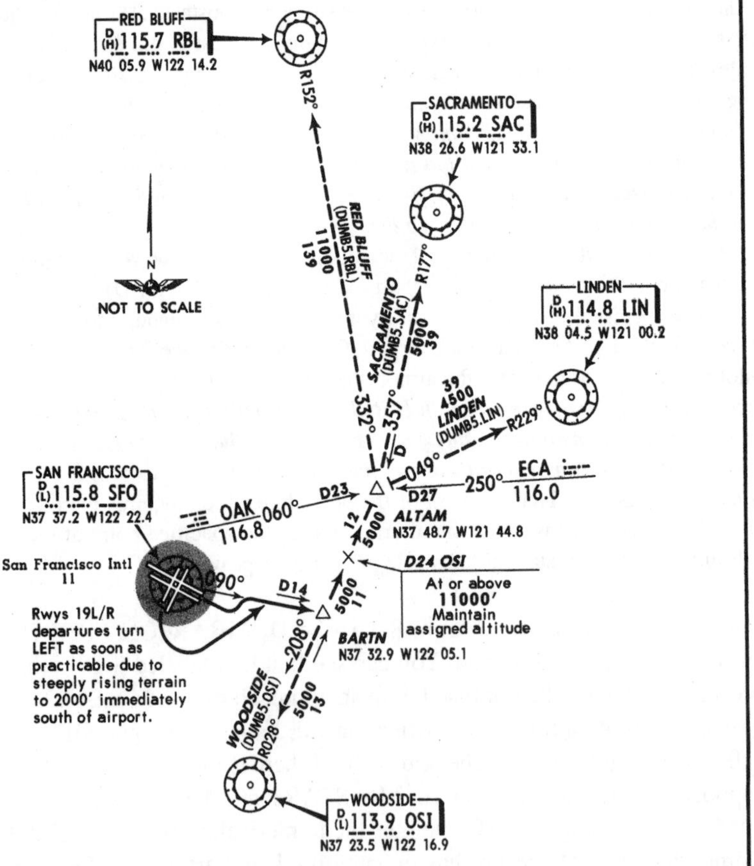

RED BLUFF
D(H) 115.7 RBL
N40 05.9 W122 14.2
R152°

SACRAMENTO
D(H) 115.2 SAC
N38 26.6 W121 33.1
R177°

RED BLUFF (DUMB5.RBL) 11000 139

N NOT TO SCALE

SACRAMENTO (DUMB5.SAC) 5000 39 332° 357°

LINDEN
D(H) 114.8 LIN
N38 04.5 W121 00.2
R229°

39 4500 LINDEN (DUMB5.LIN)

049° 250° ECA 116.0
D27

SAN FRANCISCO
D(L) 115.8 SFO
N37 37.2 W122 22.4

OAK 116.8 060° D23 12 5000 ALTAM
N37 48.7 W121 44.8

San Francisco Intl 11

Rwys 19L/R departures turn LEFT as soon as practicable due to steeply rising terrain to 2000' immediately south of airport.

090° D14 5000 11

D24 OSI
At or above 11000' Maintain assigned altitude

208° 5000 13 BARTN
N37 32.9 W122 05.1

WOODSIDE (DUMB5.OSI) R028°

WOODSIDE
D(L) 113.9 OSI
N37 23.5 W122 16.9

CHANGES: Alcoa, Bebop, & Clukk Ints deleted.

Fig. 8-1 Reproduced with permission of Jeppesen Sanderson, Inc. Not for use in navigation.

you must make sure that you have the correct numerical suffix for the SID that is specified in the clearance.

(Reminder: By the time you read these words, many of the charts appearing in this book will be obsolete. *Do not attempt to use any chart in this book for actual navigation.* It is your responsibility to obtain the current charts for the routes you plan to fly.)

The Jeppesen SID shows the SID both textually and pictorially so you can follow it more easily. Remember that you must have at least the textual portion in your possession.

The text of the SID is self-explanatory, giving headings and altitudes as well as the direction of all turns for each takeoff runway that you might use. If there is a runway at the airport that is not mentioned in the SID, you are not allowed to use it for an instrument takeoff when using that specified SID.

Following along with the Dumbarton Five SID, you can see that, after following the takeoff instructions for the runway you are using, you fly to the Bartn Intersection, and then fly whatever transition has been assigned. That will get you on your way in good shape. You can see that on two of the runways, 19L and 19R, you have to climb as soon as practicable because of the steeply rising terrain immediately south of the airport. Departures from these runways will require specific climb gradients as mentioned earlier. The climb gradient chart at the upper left of the SID illustrates how ground speed affects the rate of climb in order to achieve these specific gradients.

An important point to learn that should be reiterated: There will be much less radio congestion and much less chance of error in copying, reading back, and complying when you receive a simple clearance using a SID. In this case you might hear something such as:

> Speedy 50X is cleared to the Lake Tahoe Airport, Dumbarton Five Departure, Sacramento Transition, then as filed, maintain 11,000 feet.

Isn't this a lot better than the clearance you'd receive if you didn't use the SID? Without the SID, the same clearance would be complicated:

> Wordy 20F is cleared to the Lake Tahoe Airport as filed, maintain 11,000 feet. After takeoff, climb via the San Francisco 090-degree radial to Bartn Intersection. Then via the Woodside 028-degree radial and the Sacramento 177-degree radial. Cross the 24-mile DME on the Woodside 028-degree radial at 11,000 feet.

Filing for a specific SID is straightforward. The computerized world of the ATC system has codes for all of its intersections, fixes, SIDs, STARs, approaches, and the like. If you look again at the DUMBARTON FIVE DEPARTURE, you will notice that the computerized code is (DUMB5.BARTN).

When you file your flight plan, you will use this code if you use the SID and don't care about which transition you fly. On the other hand, if you look down at the transitions listed, you will see that each one has its own specific code. The Sacramento Transition mentioned earlier has the specific code (DUMB5.SAC), and if you wanted to file that specific SID and transition, it would be filed as that code. Computers work better when they're given specifics, and it eases the workload on an already over-worked ATC system.

AIRCRAFT PERFORMANCE RESTRICTIONS

You won't always be able to use a specific SID due to operating limitations of your air-craft. An obvious example can be seen in the SID we have been examining. Although this is not calculated on the chart, the SID requires a rate of climb that will average out to about 400 feet per mile or greater in order to cross the Woodside R-028/24 DME fix at or above 11,000 feet because that fix is only 25 miles from the airport.

If you are heavy or have a low-performance aircraft, you might not be able to make it. For example, if your best-rate-of-climb airspeed will average out at 90 knots groundspeed, you will need an average rate of climb of about 650 feet per minute all the way to 11,000 feet. Will your low-powered aircraft be able to sustain that rate of climb up to 11,000 feet? If your best-rate-of-climb airspeed averaged out at a ground-speed of 120 knots, you would need an average rate of climb of 915 feet per minute. It is something to contemplate because the faster your airspeed in climb, the less time you will have to make the altitude, so the higher your rate of climb will have to be. If you are unable to comply with the requirements of a SID, you naturally cannot accept it, and most of the time you are the only one who knows the performance capabilities of the aircraft. ATC might give you a clearance utilizing a SID you can't conform with and it's up to you to advise them of the appropriate capabilities.

I might as well explain what the Woodside R-028/24 DME fix is. Although it looks a little complicated at first, it is simply identifying the fix by giving the VOR involved (Woodside), the radial off of Woodside (028-degree radial), and the distance away from the VOR on that radial (24 DME). It really shouldn't be necessary to mention this, but as Murphy's Law is always lurking just around the corner, remember that the radial mentioned is just that, a radial *from* the VOR.

In some cases it's quite obvious that the SID has been designed for high-perfor-mance aircraft. A good example of this is the 10-3G SID for San Francisco, SHORE-LINE NINE DEPARTURE. It isn't necessary to show the actual SID to get a point across. The Melts Transition for this departure calls for crossing the Linden R-240/18 DME fix at or above 16,000 feet, crossing the Linden VORTAC at or above Flight Level 200 (approximately 20,000 feet; above 18,000 feet altimeters are set to 29.92 inches and the altitude is referred to as a flight level, which is the altitude reading sans the last two zeros), and then crossing Melts Intersection at FL 230. Those last two re-quirements, high altitudes, put all but transport and very-high-performance general aviation aircraft out of the picture.

Because of mountains to the west of SFO, there is also a note on the SHORE-LINE NINE DEPARTURE that says, in part, when departing Runway 28 L/R, the weather conditions must be 2,000-foot ceiling and 3 miles prevailing visibility with

5 miles to the west and northwest, so here you see another form of obstruction-clearance instructions.

Refer back to the climb gradient chart in the illustration. It is laid out to comply with the climb restrictions off Runway 19 L/R. The note says climb is required at a minimum of 480 feet *per nautical mile* to 1,400 feet, if you are taking off from Runway 19L. If you are taking off from Runway 19R and are operating a CAT A or B aircraft, climb is required at a rate of 480 feet per nautical mile to 1,400 feet; a CAT B or D aircraft rate of climb must be 530 feet per nautical mile to 1,800 feet. Notice the high rate of climb required for high-performance aircraft.

The climb gradient chart has ground speeds across the top and the required rates of climb listed below. It would appear that many general aviation aircraft might be hard pressed to comply with the 480 feet-per-nautical-mile gradient required off Runway 19 L/R, especially with strong south winds dumping down off the mountains.

This points out again the need to study all of the information available before you file a flight plan. As a rule, the people at ATC have no concept of the operational capabilities of your aircraft. ATC is trying to help you out, and by trying to do so, it might issue a clearance that you have asked for; however, you could very well find yourself in the air, IFR, and unable to comply with the limitations of the SID or some other part of the clearance. You have to study it all beforehand because you won't have much time once you're in the air.

If you are unable to comply with the requirements of one SID, you might still be able to find one that will be compatible with the operating capabilities of your aircraft. If you can't find one that you can use, or if you don't feel comfortable with any, simply file, "NO SID" in the remarks section of the flight plan. It's really much easier for all concerned to use the SIDs. Remember the old saying, "A picture is worth a thousand words."

There's another phrase in your clearance that you need to look at: cleared as filed. This is an abbreviation that is used by ATC when the route is essentially the same as what you filed. If only one small portion has been changed, you might get a complete readout, or you might receive, "Cleared as filed, *except . . .*" with a readout of only the portion that has been changed.

One very important point that must be emphasized here is that the cleared-as-filed clearance does not include the altitude filed for. Examine earlier examples in this chapter to see what I mean. The altitude must be given to you in addition to the cleared-as-filed portion.

If the original clearance has been substantially changed by you, your company, or ATC, you will definitely receive a full readout of the new clearance. If you don't receive it automatically, then you should request it.

For an example of an abbreviated clearance with a slight change, suppose that you have filed to Lake Tahoe from San Francisco, and have asked for a "Dumbarton Five Departure, Direct . . . FL 180." You might get a clearance that reads:

> Speedy 50X is cleared to the Lake Tahoe Airport, Bartn Transition, then as filed; maintain flight level 180, except, climb on runway heading to 2,000 feet before turning intersecting the San Francisco 090-degree radial.

In order to ensure the success of the program, as well as the accurate relaying of information, you should:

- Include specific SID/transitions and preferred routes in your flight plans whenever possible.
- Avoid making changes to a filed flight plan just prior to departure.
- Most especially, *request route/altitude verification or clarification from ATC if any portion of the clearance is not clearly understood.* You should never be put in a position to have to say, "Well I thought you meant. . . ."

FILING THE FLIGHT PLAN

The preceding chapter mentioned filing a flight plan at least 30 minutes prior to departure to give ATC ample time to process the clearance and to fit it into the system. Once a flight plan has been filed, how do you go about getting your clearance?

This will depend upon which type of airport you are operating from. You will normally find yourself in one of three situations:

- At an airport with a tower and a *discrete clearance delivery* frequency, you will simply call clearance delivery directly prior to calling *ground control* for taxi clearance; at airports where pretaxi clearance procedures are in effect (as indicated in the *Airport/Facility Directory*), you will get the clearance not more than 10 minutes prior to taxi; at airports where this procedure is in effect, you will then know if you are to expect a flight delay prior to starting the engine(s).
- At an airport with or without a tower or flight service station, but at least within radio range of one of the above, you will get the clearance over the radio from whichever facility you are able to contact, the tower being the first choice. One exception to this rule is when you are unable to contact any of the above, but are able to establish contact with an *air route traffic control center* (ARTCC) frequency, in which case you can call them directly.
- At an airport with no ATC facilities, and one from which you are unable to contact a control facility by radio while on the ground, you may take off in VFR conditions and pick up the IFR clearance once airborne (and still VFR) and within radio range of a facility. If you are unable to take off in VFR conditions, you will have to telephone the facility with which you filed your flight plan. He or she will normally ask what time you expect to depart, and you will usually be given a clearance containing a "clearance void" time, which means that if you are not airborne by that time, your clearance will be voided and you will have to call for a new one. If something happens that makes it look as if you won't be able to make it off by the clearance void time, your best bet is to get on the horn again and ask for an extension of the void time. In any case, you must let ATC know within 30 minutes that you will not be able to comply. This will help pre-

vent further delays as well as costly reroutes to other traffic that have been issued clearances based on your departure.

You should have a good working knowledge of all of the facilities and basic airways in the vicinity of the departure airport. This is because it isn't unusual to receive a change to the clearance shortly after becoming airborne. If you know the primary airways and the VOR frequencies, it will enable you to comply with the changes at once, double-checking the charts as time permits, rather than trying to fumble with the charts while still trying to get the gear up or maintaining control in turbulence.

These course changes are especially prevalent in radar environments. You will be advised of any expected radar vectors prior to takeoff, normally advised of the initial heading and the reasons for the vectors. By listening to the instructions, you merely fly basic instrument maneuvers (climbs, turns, etc.) until you are established on course and told to "resume normal navigation."

Sometimes, *departure control* will hand you off to a center frequency where you will receive further vectors. You must not allow yourself to become too complacent when following these simple directions. You must still monitor the navigation receivers and be continuously aware of the aircraft position with respect to your requested route of flight. You never know when the radios might decide to take a holiday and leave you with no air/ground communications.

Before going any further, an emphatic statement: *You should read back every clearance you receive.* If the controller read it wrong or if you copied it wrong, this will be your last chance to correct the error. This holds true for all clearances, including taxi, takeoff, climb, descent, approach, landing, or whatever. Also, don't try to be a speed reader because the faster you read back the clearance, the more chance there is for an error to go undetected. Be sure that you include your complete aircraft number or flight number in the read back. *EVERY clearance.*

LOSS OF RADIO COMMUNICATION

If you do lose radio contact, what will you do? We'll look into this subject much more deeply during the *enroute* discussion in chapter 10, but if it happens during the departure phase of your flight, you will find yourself in one of three situations:

- Flying the clearance as received, in which case you keep right on complying with the clearance
- Flying an amended clearance
- Flying a radar vector

When flying either an amended clearance or a radar vector, you will have been issued instructions as to where the change of heading is taking you. The amended clearance might be explained:

50X, amendment to your clearance, now climb on the 030-degree radial until 8,000 feet and then turn left on course.

If you lose communications capability while climbing through 3,000 feet on the 030-degree radial, just comply with the clearance as it was given. Continue climbing to 8,000 feet, and then turn left to get on the flight planned route.

If you were on a westbound radar vector, you might have been told something like:

50X, radar contact, turn left now, heading 240 degrees to intercept the Spartan 276-degree radial.

If you were to lose communications at that point, you should turn farther left to intercept the radial at a 90-degree angle in order to comply with Part 91.185(c)(1)(ii):

If being radar vectored, [fly] by the direct route from the point of radio failure to the fix, route, or airway specified in the vector clearance.

We'll talk more about loss of communications in later chapters.

During taxi to the active runway, give the instruments a good check. Prior to taxiing, you should have set the directional gyro to the magnetic compass heading. Then during turns while taxiing, you are able to check for proper movement of the DG.

The same thing holds true for the needle/ball, turn/slip, slip/skid indicator, or turn coordinator, whichever term is the vogue for this instrument at the time you read this. (I prefer to call it the needle/ball.) In any event, watch it while turning. The needle should deflect to the same direction the aircraft is turning.

Remember that the attitude indicator, needle/ball and DG are all gyro-driven, and should have at least five minutes to come up to speed to prevent excessive precession and bearing wear.

COCKPIT ORGANIZATION

There's one thing that we have to talk about before you shove the throttle in and set off on the flight. You have to figure out what to do with all of the charts, flight plans, and assorted papers that are in the cockpit.

As time goes by, everyone develops a personal method of cockpit organization. I'll tell you how and why I operate in a light aircraft and let you take it from there.

In the first place, although I have used several types of kneeboards, I have never found one that I have liked. Besides getting in the way of the yoke, they cause me to bend my head down more than I like to, and I hate to take a chance at getting my middle ear confused (vertigo) when I'm the only pilot on board.

So, I take the SIDs, STARs, approach plates, and airway charts that I am most likely to use out of my flight kit. I have found that in most light aircraft they fit nicely in the corner formed by the windshield and the glareshield. Here they are both handy and out of my normal line of vision, and I don't have to bend my head down to look at them. The remainder of my flight kit is stowed close at hand if I need it, but out of my way.

I keep the flight plan with my charts; holding it against a chart or two gives me a stiff enough surface to write on so that I don't need a clipboard, especially if I'm using the felt pens mentioned earlier because they do not require very much pressure. If you do decide to use a clipboard, remember to keep the metal part of it away from the magnetic compass. This is the reason I don't even use a paper clip to hold my charts together.

My plotters stay in my flight kit because I should have no more use for them if I have done my preflight work properly. My computer fits in my shirt pocket, along with a felt-tip pen, a few sharp pencils, and one of those small telephone-message note pads, which are just the right size to jot down clearances and still fit in a shirt pocket where they're always close at hand. I tear off the old sheet of paper and store it out of the way when I get a new clearance; it's a good idea to keep all of your clearances in the event any questions ever arise as to the conduct of the flight.

These procedures have worked just fine for me. As for yourself, a system of your own should evolve as time goes by.

CHAPTER QUIZ

1. If you don't have the graphic view of a SID in your possession, you're not allowed to use it.

   True _____ False _____

2. The basic IFR obstacle clearance climb requires an aircraft to climb at a rate of _____ feet per _____, crossing the end of the runway at _____ AGL, and climbing to _____ above the airport elevation before turning, unless otherwise specified in the procedure.

3. If no climb gradient is specified in the SID, the pilot is expected to climb at a rate of at least _____ to the _____ unless required to level off by a crossing restriction.

4. The proper computer code to use to file a DUMBARTON FIVE DEPARTURE with a Red Bluff Transition is _____.

5. Referring to the DUMBARTON FIVE DEPARTURE, when departing Runway 19L, what would the rate of climb need to be in order to climb at 480 feet per nautical mile with a ground speed of 120 knots?

6. If you receive a "cleared as filed" clearance, it means that you are to fly the routing you filed for, but it does not include the altitude you filed for.

   True _____ False _____

7. After takeoff you enter the clouds and intercept the course, then lose air-to-ground communications. You should:

   a. Descend to VFR conditions and return to the field

   b. Fly the ATC clearance as you received it

    c. Fly directly to the initial approach fix of your departure airport to return to the field

    d. Fly two, 360-degree turns to alert ATC, and then fly as in answer "c"

8. Gyro instruments will require at least _____ to stabilize after starting the engines.

9. It is not necessary to do anything to the gyro instruments other than allow them to get up to speed and then to set them.

    True _____ False _____

Answers are in the appendix.

9
Stay on top of things

ONCE AIRBORNE AND NEAR THE LIMITS OF THE DEPARTURE CONTROL jurisdiction, you will be handed over to the appropriate ARTCC controller. Even though the departure controller has coordinated your handoff with the center, there are three things the center controller wants to know:

- Who you are
- Your present altitude
- Your final assigned altitude

Proper radiotelephone techniques are covered in the *AIM* and the *ATC Handbook*, but some will be repeated here because far too many pilots flying today don't use the correct phraseology and cause frequency congestion.

In the above case, your initial call to the center would be something like:

New York Center, Cessna One Seven Two Zero Zulu, out of 5,000 for 7,000.

This says it all in just a few words. You have told ATC that you are on the frequency, who you are, what altitude you are passing through, and what altitude you are climbing to, which is the altitude you have been assigned. This is not necessarily your final altitude. Departure might have given you 7,000 feet for some reason, usually because of other traffic, and before she's sure you are clear she's handed you off to center. In this case, you may call center with the following terminology:

> New York Center, Cessna One Seven Two Zero Zulu, out of 5,000 for 7,000, looking for 9,000.

This has told the center that you are going to level off at an intermediate altitude for some reason. Perhaps he doesn't know it, or perhaps departure control got busy and forgot to clear you out of it. In any case, it's only four additional words and it might save an entire exchange of transmissions later. You might find that the center controller will clear you to your final altitude when he acknowledges your original call-up.

You'd be surprised how many people omit this information on their initial call; even seasoned airline captains are guilty of the omission. Many times I've heard, "Center, Air Carrier Six Sixteen, over." Then center has to come back with something like, "Roger, Air Carrier Six Sixteen, confirm you're climbing to assigned flight level of 250." This requires another response from the air carrier, which becomes a needless transmission.

If the previous controller has given you a specific heading to fly, you should include that in your initial call-up also:

> New York Center, Cessna One Seven Two Zero Zulu, out of 5,000 for 7,000, looking for 9,000, heading 070.

Once again, this is a safety call in the event the first controller has forgotten to pass on the information.

You have made the radio calls and have climbed to the cruising altitude where you have set up cruise power and cruise configuration. Now you can sit back and relax, right? Wrong. Your job is just beginning.

Numerous tasks still must be accomplished. For example, in addition to the basic aircraft control, you have flight plans to keep up to date, reporting points to keep track of, communications, fuel management, and weather changes in-flight, as well as at your destination, to monitor and interpret.

I don't know what it is that makes perfectly good pilots grip the yoke and turn white knuckled when they enter a cloud, but they do. It's happened to me and it will happen to you. Do we expect the aircraft to fly differently just because we can no longer see outside? Well, remember that the aircraft doesn't know the difference, so we must learn to relax. Don't grab the yoke in a death grip.

Remember when your primary instructor tried to teach how to differentiate control pressure from control displacement? He'd usually have you grip a pencil tightly, right? And then he'd apply pressure against it and ask you which way the pressure was being applied. If you were like I was, you couldn't tell him, proving that a gripping hand can't differentiate pressure.

The same thing holds true in instrument flight. If you're having a difficult time controlling the plane, remove one hand from the yoke and shake it a bit to get the blood circulating. This will allow the nerve endings to be sensitive to pressure again. Put your hand back on the yoke lightly, and do the same with your other hand. Then do the same thing with your feet. You'll notice quite a difference in the control of the aircraft; then, and only then, will you be able to properly trim the control pressure with the trim tabs.

"OK," you say, "so much for aircraft control, but what's this about flight plans? Didn't I use all the available information during flight planning to come up with an accurate flight plan?"

The answer, of course, is yes, you did use all available information when you made up and filed the flight plan, but weather conditions change and actual in-flight wind conditions are usually different from those forecast, especially at the lower altitudes; therefore, keeping a running fix of position and an accurate update on ground speed will take up a lot of your time. You will also be working in-flight problems (mentally) to come up with a good wind correction angle so you will have an idea of the wind direction and velocity. This is a most important in-flight task.

ESTIMATING YOUR POSITION

Although you are under radar most of the time, there are still times when you won't be. When this happens, the controller will call you in the following manner:

> Cessna 20Z, radar contact lost, what is your [next compulsory reporting point] estimate?

Normally the estimate she's asking for is to the next compulsory reporting point along the route of flight. This will be part of the flight plan unless you have had a route change since filing. If this is the case, or if the winds aloft have changed sufficiently from those forecast to change your ground speed, you will have to come up with a new estimated time from the last fix to the next reporting point. If all factors have remained the same, you will be able to read the estimate from the flight plan. In any case, the controller wants an estimated time as soon as you can possibly give it to her because she has a lot of traffic to sequence through the area.

You might have to "guesstimate." You can do this easily and quite accurately by taking the indicated airspeed in knots and dividing it by 60 to come out to the nearest half-mile per minute. If you are indicating 120 knots, you will come out with a speed of two nautical miles per minute. If you are indicating 145 knots, you can use a speed of two-and-a-half miles per minute. This is actually the speed for 150 knots, but it will be close enough.

If there is a strong headwind/tailwind factor, you can apply that as well. And if you are at an altitude above 5,000 feet MSL, you will have to work in the true-airspeed factor. These factors should be applied to indicated airspeed before dividing by 60. In any case, take the resulting miles-per-minute figure, divide it into the miles-to-go to your fix, add the result to the current time, and you will have a good estimate to start with. You can always update it later, but at least ATC will have something to work with.

How accurate is this system? Well, let's figure that the airway you are on has a midpoint of 40 miles. The chart in Fig. 9-1 shows that, generally, the faster the aircraft, the more accuracy you will have (accuracy also improves with shorter distances), but you'd need an unusual wind condition, or an error in your true airspeed, to make much of an error in your guesstimates.

The *AIM* says that you are allowed an error of ±3 minutes and that you must contact ATC and revise the estimated time to a reporting point if it becomes apparent that your previous estimate will be off by more than 3 minutes.

Because there is always the chance of radar failure and/or winds that are other than those forecast, you should work out the actual ground speed as soon as possible after reaching cruising altitude.

As mentioned before, I feel very strongly about eliminating unnecessary head movements while flying on instruments, especially when I am the only pilot on board. (You remember that this decreases the possibility of suffering from vertigo, and these head movements tend to aggravate such a condition.) So, you should use as many mental tricks as you can in order to avoid the need to look around the cockpit for computers, calculators, and the like. At the same time, these tricks should maintain a high degree of accuracy.

If you have DME or GPS on board, it is a simple matter to figure ground speed. Many units have ground speed built in, but for those that don't, merely check the miles covered in 1 minute (measuring to the nearest half-mile) and use that. Estimates based on these figures will be well within limits.

With no DME or GPS on board, you will have to check ground speed between two fixes shown on the enroute chart. If no convenient fixes are shown, you can make your own by drawing radials from VORs that will cross the airway you are on. The closer the VORs are to the aircraft (as long as the aircraft is outside the cone of confusion), and the more perpendicular the radial is to the airway, the more accurate the results will be. In most of these cases, however, you will need the computer to work out the ground speed.

THE WEATHER'S ALWAYS CHANGING

Don't just compute the ground speed once and forget it because the winds might change drastically as the flight progresses, especially during a frontal passage. Refigure or reconfirm the ground speed whenever time permits. You should always try to remain ahead of the aircraft.

How much these winds can vary from those forecast can be very surprising. I remember a flight from Burlington, Vermont, to Wilkes-Barre, Pennsylvania, one winter day some 25 years ago. I was flying a Cessna 205 without DME. The winds at my altitude, 6,000 feet, were forecast to be light, about a 10-knot headwind component. These winds were just about as forecast on my outward flight, so I used them on the

Indicated airspeed (knots)	nm/minute (round to nearest .5)		Est. time to reporting point (to nearest minute)	Actual time to reporting point (minutes)	Error (minutes)
90	1.5		27	26.7	.3
100	1.5		27	24.0	3.0
110	2.0		20	21.8	1.8
120	2.0		20	20.0	—
130	2.0		20	18.5	1.5
140	2.5		16	17.1	1.1
150	2.5		16	16.0	—
160	2.5		16	15.0	1.0
170	3.0	Distance	13	14.1	1.1
180 ÷ 60 =	3.0	40 nm ÷ =	13	13.3	.3
190	3.0		13	12.6	.4
200	3.5		11	12	1.0
210	3.5		11	11.4	.4
220	3.5		11	10.9	.1
230	4.0		10	10.4	.4
240	4.0		10	10	—
250	4.0		10	9.6	.4
260	4.5		9	9.2	.2
270	4.5		9	8.9	.1
280	4.5		9	8.6	.4

Fig. 9-1. *The accuracy of this estimation method increases with airspeed.*

return flight plan to Pennsylvania and elected not to refuel because I had more than my legal requirements on board, based on all contingencies.

I was to cross a fix shortly after reaching cruising altitude, and when I didn't get to it right away, I became suspicious. I worked out a ground-speed estimate as soon as I could and came up with a 65-knot headwind component, which left me with only a 65-knot ground speed. When I reported this to ATC, the controller didn't believe me at first, although it was confirmed about 15 minutes later by a Mohawk Airlines flight. I had to make an unscheduled refueling stop in Albany, New York.

On the subject of changes in forecast weather, maybe we should take a look at how accurate a weather forecast should be. Here are a few figures from the National Weather Service:

- In a 12-hour forecast, a forecast of good weather (VFR) is more likely to be correct than an IFR forecast.
- Three to four hours in advance there's an 80-percent chance of accuracy when forecasting conditions below VFR.
- The tendency is to forecast too little bad weather when distinct weather can be plotted.

- Surface visibility is difficult to forecast due to changes in snow or rainfall, fog density, and the like.

The following forecasts have a 75-percent chance of accuracy:

- Passage of warm fronts or slow-moving cold fronts, within ±2 hours, when forecast as much as 10 hours in advance.
- Rapid lowering of ceiling below 1,000 feet in prewarm-front conditions, within ±200 feet and within ±4 hours.
- Onset of a thunderstorm 1 or 2 hours in advance, if radar is available.
- The time rain or snow will begin, within ±5 hours.

By the same token, forecasters cannot accurately predict:

- The time freezing rain will occur.
- Location and occurrence of heavy icing.
- Location and occurrence of a tornado.
- Ceilings of 100 feet or zero.
- Thunderstorms not yet formed.
- Ice fog.

It is up to the pilot-in-command to keep updated about changes in weather conditions both on the proposed route of flight and at the destination and alternate airports. The easiest way to do this is to keep the volume up on the VOR receiver. Even though the identifier becomes monotonous, it will tell you that the station is still on the air, and you will automatically get the sequence, AIRMET, and SIGMET reports. Additionally, you might lose the communications receiver and not know it, and ATC might try to contact you through VOR voice.

Recall the discussion on airframe and carburetor icing. The most insidious of the two, in my opinion, is carburetor ice. After all, you can see the airframe begin to ice up and you can initiate precautionary measures, but you can't see inside the carburetor. Carburetor icing usually occurs at much higher outside air temperatures than airframe ice. Not only that, its adverse effects build up so gradually that you do not realize it; therefore, at least once every 10 minutes, use the carburetor heat momentarily. When using it, pull the control all the way out. Partial carburetor heat can actually cause icing by heating up otherwise too-cold air to the icing temperature.

If ice has been building up inside the carburetor, the engine will run rough for awhile after the carburetor heat has been pulled out. You might have to work hard to maintain airspeed and altitude. Because carburetor ice builds faster during low power settings, it might even build up during taxi to the active runway. You should always experience a manifold-pressure or RPM drop when you check the carburetor heat, but if unusual roughness is detected as well, before you begin the takeoff roll, keep the carburetor heat out until the roughness goes away.

Carburetor ice is especially prevalent in areas of high outside air temperature, 50–80°F, combined with high humidity; as the air flows through the carburetor venturi, the air cools, and its moisture condenses. As mentioned earlier, it was even a problem when I was flying in Hawaii.

If you are a victim of carburetor ice, you will notice that you will have to add more and more throttle to maintain cruising speed. This is why the first action you are taught in trying to find the cause of engine failure is to pull out the carburetor heat. By all means though, consult the aircraft operating manual about the use of carburetor heat in the engine you are operating.

Fuel-injected engines also experience icing in the intake system, although this is usually ice over the air cleaner. In this case, the use of an alternate-air source will usually clear up the problem, but again, consult the flight manual.

Other factors to consider are temperature and atmospheric pressure changes, both of which can cause erroneous altimeter readings. Pressure changes can be compensated for by resetting the altimeter whenever you are given an updated setting. Remember that the altimeter must be set to a station within 100 nautical miles. The old saying, "When moving from hot to cold or a high to a low look out graveyard down below," still holds true. As the barometric pressure and/or temperature lowers, the altimeter will read higher than the actual altitude. These errors will be especially prevalent near mountains, which is why the regs require 2,000 feet of ground clearance in mountainous areas.

When you received the weather briefing, if you remember, you looked at the past weather sequence reports as well as the current one. This was to give you an idea of the trend and the rate of change of the weather. As you cruise toward the destination, you will receive weather updates on the VOR voice and should be correlating them with the previous weather trend. If it appears that the weather is changing for the worse, then you should start directing your thinking toward diverting to the alternate. The sooner you make the actual decision to divert, the more fuel you will have to play with, and the more time you will have. If the weather at your intended destination is going down faster than forecast, then the same will probably hold true for the weather at the alternate.

AIRWAYS AND ALTITUDES

While you are cruising, you will also have to pay close attention to your position as far as the airway centerline is concerned. FAR 91.181 requires that you operate on the centerline of airways, and the only time you can deviate is if you deliberately turn before or after a turning fix to avoid flying outside the airway while in the turn. Most of us in general aviation aircraft don't have to worry about flying outside the airway in a turn. After all, it's 8 miles wide (4 miles each side of the centerline), but some high-performance, high-altitude business aircraft must take this factor into consideration.

You can also deviate from the centerline to avoid heavy weather buildups, but only after first advising ATC of your intentions and receiving permission to deviate.

The FAA has established guidelines to use during climb or descent. There are two basic climb or descent clearances.

If the controller includes the words "at pilot's discretion" in the clearance, he has offered you the option to begin climb or descent when you desire. You are also able to climb or descend at any rate desired, and even to level off at any intermediate altitude. The only restriction ATC applies to this clearance is that once you leave an altitude you cannot return to it. In other words, once you begin a descent, you must continue the descent (except for leveling off at an intermediate altitude). You cannot climb again at any time. The same holds true for a climb. The only time you could vary the altitude by climbing, descending, and then climbing again, or vice versa, is when you have been given a "block" altitude.

If ATC does not add the words "at pilot's discretion" to the clearance, you should begin the maneuver promptly. ATC also expects you to climb or descend at the "optimum rate consistent with the operating characteristics of the aircraft." Continue the climb or descent at this optimum rate until 1,000 feet before reaching the new altitude, and then attempt to climb or descend at a rate of 500 fpm. At anytime the ability to climb or descend at the rate of at least 500 fpm is lost, you should notify ATC.

The key phrase is the "optimum rate" for the aircraft. In an unpressurized aircraft, any rate exceeding 700 fpm would not be practicable, especially on descent. A climb or descent at 400–500 fpm would be best for passenger comfort. Naturally, in pressurized aircraft, you can climb or descend quite a bit faster than that.

The 500-fpm suggestion for the final 1,000 feet of altitude change is to allow stabilization of the climb/descent and to approach the assigned altitude at a slow enough rate to be able to level off without flying through the altitude.

Two other points concerning altitude changes: First, you are expected to initiate the changes as soon as you acknowledge the clearance, unless it contains a restriction such as, "after crossing . . . descend/climb to. . . ." If for some reason the controller wants you to vacate the altitude immediately, she will add the word "now" to the clearance:

Cessna 20Z, descend to 4000. Begin descent now.

The second point is that if for any reason you have to level off at an intermediate altitude (say, a passenger develops a bad earache), unless you are descending at pilot's discretion, you must notify ATC immediately.

VOR transmitters and airborne receivers have allowable errors. The farther you fly from the transmitter, the farther you'll be off course if you hold a constant heading. Remember that one degree of error equals one nautical mile off course for each 60 nm flown. If the airborne equipment error is 4 degrees and you fly an indicated centerline, when you get 60 miles from the VOR, you will be at the outside limit of the airway.

To prevent this from happening, ATC attempts to set the airways up so that aircraft are always within 45 miles of the transmitters. On long route segments, when the distance between the VORs is more than 45 miles, *specific changeover points* (COPs) are indicated on the enroute charts by this symbol:

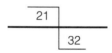

The numbers show the distance (in nautical miles) to the COP from each of two navigational facilities.

CHAPTER QUIZ

1. While in a radar environment, what information should you give on the initial radio call-up when handed off from one controller to another?

2. If the previously estimated time to a required reporting point changes by more than _____ minutes, you are required to give a revised estimated time of arrival to that reporting point.

3. How often should you refigure ground speed?

4. Three good reasons to keep the volume turned up on the VOR receiver are:

   1. _____;

   2. _____; and

   3. _____.

5. How will temperature and/or barometric changes affect the altimeter?

6. Why should you check the past weather reports as well as the current reports?

7. If the weather report at the destination airport is changing for the worse faster than forecast, you should consider _____.

8. While conducting an IFR flight in the United States, always fly to the right of the route centerline.

   True _____False _____

9. When you are given a new altitude by ATC, what rate of climb or descent should be flown?

10. When are specific changeover points indicated on enroute charts?

Answers are in the appendix.

10
Radio rhetoric
and holding patterns

BEFORE RADAR COVERAGE WAS AVAILABLE, RADIO COMMUNICATIONS played a much greater role in the progress of an aircraft from point A to point B. Two major types of radio contacts were initiated by the pilot back then. The first was merely a radio contact, such as when a plane was handed off from one controller to the next. The second was the position report that was given when the aircraft crossed a fix that required such a report.

The use of radar has caused the position report to almost become extinct. Because of this, pilots tend to become sloppy in the procedure. (They have the same problem with flying ADF approaches and holding patterns because these maneuvers are becoming more and more scarce in most parts of the country. Actually, this is the time when you should practice these things more.)

The day will come when the center's radar will be down, and you will be forced to make these position reports. In order to cut down on radio frequency congestion, you should be well versed in their use.

Let's take a look at some of these basic communications procedures. Recall the discussion about a radio contact when changing from departure control to center. The same holds true whenever you change from any controller to the next, whether departure, another center sector, or approach. If you are in a radar environment, you will merely state whom you are calling, who you are, your altitude or flight level, and whether you're climbing, descending, or flying level. If climbing or descending, you must also add the assigned altitude or flight level you're flying toward:

> Cleveland Center, Cessna 1720Z, out of 5,000 for 8,000.

If you are not in a radar environment, and you do not have to give a *full* position report, your initial contact would include whom you're calling; who you are; your estimated time to the next compulsory reporting point; current altitude or flight level; whether climbing, descending, or in level flight; and again, if climbing or descending, the assigned altitude or flight level that the aircraft is climbing or descending toward:

> Cleveland Center, Cessna 1720Z estimating Big Lake intersection at one five [past the hour], level at 8,000.

PROPER POSITION REPORTS

In a nonradar environment, a full position report would have to be made whenever you cross a *compulsory reporting point*. A compulsory reporting point is indicated on the enroute chart by a solid triangle.

If you were not in a radar environment and were told to make the frequency change when crossing a compulsory reporting point, the initial call, and all subsequent calls when crossing compulsory reporting points, would be simply whom you're calling, who you are, and where you are:

> Cleveland Center, Cessna 1720Z, Big Lake intersection.

This will alert the center that a full position report will be forthcoming, and the controller will merely answer:

> Cessna 20Z, Cleveland Center, go ahead.

Reply with a complete position report, which will consist of:

1. Who you are.
2. Where you are, which will be the fix you just crossed.
3. The time you were there, in universal coordinated time (UTC) based on a 24-hour clock.
4. The altitude or flight level (and, if necessary, whether you're climbing or descending: if you are, the assigned altitude or flight level you're climbing or descending to).

5. The estimated time you'll cross the next compulsory reporting point.

6. The name of the next compulsory point following that estimated in #5.

Naturally, if numbers 5 or 6 were your clearance limit, you would state that also.

Example: You were to contact Cleveland Center when crossing Big Lake intersection. You crossed it at 10 minutes after the hour and you were climbing to a cruising altitude of 8,000 feet. The next compulsory reporting point on your route is Frosty VOR, which is 40 miles ahead. Your ground speed has been averaging 120 knots. The next compulsory reporting point past Frosty VOR is Smokey Intersection. Smokey Intersection happens to be the clearance limit.

The initial contact would be unchanged, but after Cleveland Center responds, you would give the remainder of your report:

Cessna 20Z, Big Lake at two zero one zero, leaving five thousand to maintain eight thousand, estimating Frosty at three zero (if the hour is going to be the same hour, just like in the first part of the position report you give only the minutes), Smokey next, clearance limit.

As you can see, this is a simple procedure that condenses a lot of information into just a few short words, but it requires a lot of practice to perform it properly and professionally, especially when it's used so seldom within the radar-coverage environment.

Once back in radar contact, you will discontinue making the position reports unless you are informed that radar contact has been lost again or that for some reason radar service has been discontinued.

REQUIRED REPORTS TO ATC

Additional reports must be made to ATC or an FSS without request:

- When leaving any previously assigned altitude or flight level for a newly assigned altitude or flight level.
- When an altitude change will be made while operating "VFR on top."
- When unable to climb/descend at least 500 fpm.
- When you have missed an approach, in which case you must request a specific action, such as clearance for another approach or to your alternate or perhaps to hold for awhile to try another approach when and if the weather improves. (This would be the case if visibility had been restricted by one of a series of rain or snow showers, and you are trying to get in between them.)
- When the average true airspeed at cruise altitude varies by 5 percent or 10 knots (whichever is greater) from what you filed on the flight plan.
- The time and altitude or flight level when reaching a holding fix or the point that you have been cleared to.

- When leaving any assigned holding fix or point.
- When any VOR, TACAN, ADF, LF, ILS, or air/ground communications capability is lost.
- When leaving the final approach fix (or outer marker) inbound on final approach. (Only required when *not* in radar contact.)
- A corrected estimate whenever you realize that a previously submitted estimate is in error in excess of three minutes. (Only required when *not* in radar contact.)

You must also report any weather conditions that have not been forecast and any other hazards to flight, including icing, snow, clear air turbulence, and even flocks of migrating birds.

COMMUNICATIONS CONFUSION

The airspace is becoming more congested every day. The ATC system is being overworked in some sectors, and there are many new controllers who are not full performance level. Because of this, we cannot be too careful in what we say when we communicate with them. Although we know enough to repeat all clearances we receive, in the hope that it will provide a second chance to correct any errors in reception or understanding, records now indicate that many clearances that have been read back wrong will be accepted as having been read back correctly by an overworked controller. This means that anytime you have any question regarding a clearance, ask for a specific confirmation. If there is any chance that you made a mistake or the transmission was a little garbled, double check. Don't just assume that you received it correctly.

Many questions exist regarding semantics, as well as different phraseologies between different countries. For example, in the United States, when cleared to taxi to a runway, you might be told "Taxi to Runway 8L, hold short." In Jamaica, "Taxi to position Runway 8."

They both mean the same thing, but if you didn't know any better, you might taxi into position on Runway 8 in Jamaica. Why is that? Because in the United States, when cleared onto the active runway, you would be told to "Taxi into position and hold."

Hear how that sounds like the Jamaican instruction to position the aircraft at the taxiway hold line? In Jamaica, the instruction to taxi onto the active runway would be "Line up and wait."

An airline accident in New York emphasized problems with semantics and various countries' phraseologies. An Avianca 707 ran out of fuel and crashed. On a number of occasions, the pilot told ATC that he was low on fuel and asked for *priority* handling. Because he didn't use the word *emergency*, ATC merely took him out of a holding pattern and put him into a line for approach. If he had said that he had a low-fuel emergency, they would have put him ahead of everyone on approach. I can't help but wonder if the word *priority* in Colombia means the same as *emergency* in the United States.

No matter how cool, confident, and in control we like to sound when the chips are down, I'm sure that the flight would have had more expeditious handling if the pilot had said "I'm just about out of fuel and if you don't put me ahead of everyone else I'm going to crash. Pan Pan, Mayday, Mayday, Priority, Emergency."

In other words, use as many different phrases as you can think of to alert everyone that you do have a very serious situation aboard the aircraft. Don't ever let the survivors say "Well, I thought the pilot meant. . . ."

MORE COMMUNICATION FAILURE PROCEDURES

The situation will become rather sticky though, if you suddenly lose two-way communications capabilities. The regulations are set up to guide you as best as they can in such a situation, even though emergencies rarely follow a set pattern, and it's hard to write a set of rules telling you how to handle them. The following has been set up as a guide, remembering that FAR 91.3, "Responsibility and Authority of the Pilot in Command," says:

> (a) The pilot in command of an aircraft is directly responsible for, and is the final authority as to, the operation of that aircraft.
>
> (b) In an emergency requiring immediate action, the pilot in command may deviate from any rule of this subpart or of Subpart B to the extent required to meet that emergency. . . .

Unless you see fit to exercise your emergency authority as outlined above, FAR 91.185 sets up specific actions to follow if two-way communications capability is lost.

As with many FAA rules, this section begins with the words, "Unless otherwise authorized by ATC, each pilot . . . shall comply with the rules of this section."

The rule goes on to say that if flying in VFR conditions, or if VFR conditions are encountered afterwards, continue VFR and land as soon as practicable. Notify ATC as soon as possible that you are on the ground safely. If you're at a controlled airport, this is a simple trip to the tower, but if it's a noncontrolled field, you'll have to find a phone.

If you are in IFR conditions, however, continue by specific routes and altitudes as follows:

- If already on an airway, you should fly the route as assigned in the last clearance.
- If you were being radar vectored to a route or fix, fly as directly as possible to the route or fix you were being vectored toward. Of course, beware of obstacles, such as high mountains, that you were being vectored around.
- If recleared during flight to a specific point, and told to expect further clearance via a specified route, fly the route you have been told to expect.
- If you haven't been told to expect a specific routing, fly what you filed in the flight plan.

- Your altitude must be the highest of: the altitude last assigned by ATC, the altitude ATC has advised you to expect in a later clearance, or the minimum enroute altitude for each segment of the route.

A good example is the situation in Fig. 10-1. A pilot has been cleared via A, B, C, and D to E. While flying between A and B her assigned altitude is 6,000 feet, and she is told to expect a clearance to 8,000 feet at B. Prior to receiving the higher altitude assignment, she experiences two-way radio failure. The pilot would maintain 6,000 feet to B, then climb to 8,000 feet (the altitude she was advised to expect). She would maintain 8,000 feet, then climb to 11,000 at C, or prior to C, if necessary, to comply with a minimum crossing altitude at C. Upon reaching D, the pilot would descend to 8,000 feet (even though the MEA is 7,000) because 8,000 is the highest of the altitude situations stated in the rule.

So far, everything's pretty straightforward, and although the actual wording of the FARs sometimes sounds complicated, if we sit and reason the regs out with an example or two and try to see what the FAA's author(s) had in mind, the FARs tend to simplify themselves.

The only other question would be when to leave a clearance limit, which is answered in FAR 91.185 (c) (3):

(i) When the clearance limit is a fix from which an approach begins, commence descent or descent and approach as close as possible to the expected further clearance time if one has been received, or if one has not been received, as close as possible to the estimated time of arrival as calculated from the filed or amended (with ATC) estimated time en route.

(ii) If the clearance limit is not a fix from which an approach begins, leave the clearance limit at the expected further clearance time if one has been received, or if none has been received, upon arrival over the clearance limit, and proceed to a fix from which an approach begins and commence descent or descent and approach as close as possible to the estimated time of arrival as calculated from the filed or amended (with ATC) estimated time en route.

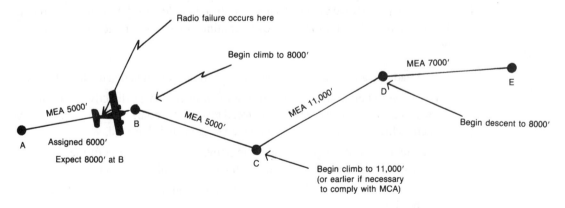

Fig. 10-1

If you have not received holding instructions and are ahead of the flight plan ETA, you should hold at the fix so that you land as close to the ETA as possible. If there is more than one approach at the destination, make the approach of your choice, based on weather forecasts. ATC will have cleared the airspace on all of the approaches.

In the event that two-way communication is lost, ATC will provide service on the basis that you are operating in accordance with the above rules. Naturally, during all of this, you will be monitoring the navaid voice facilities and will follow any instructions you might receive. Try to establish radio contact on the last frequency over which you had two-way communications, which is why you should always write down each assigned frequency, perhaps on the telephone-message notepad, rather than just switch the radio to the new frequency.

Failing to make contact on the last frequency, you should try to make contact on FSS frequencies, and on 121.5 MHz. Squawk code 7600 for the remainder of the flight.

THE HOLDING PATTERN

Back to normal flight operations: As you proceed, ATC might find it necessary to slow you down or stop you to properly sequence all of the flights in the area. Because you cannot actually stop in midair, they will have you fly a racetrack flight path called a *holding pattern*, which serves the purpose. You will enter a holding pattern automatically if, when you come to a clearance limit, you have received no further clearance.

Most holding patterns are depicted on the appropriate charts for the area. If you are required to hold at a fix where no pattern is depicted, you will receive specific information:

- The direction to hold in relation to the holding fix: north, northeast, east, and the like.
- The fix itself.
- The radial, course, magnetic bearing, or airway.
- The length of the outbound leg, if the hold is based on DME distances.
- Instructions to make the turns to the left, if the holding pattern is nonstandard.
- The time to expect a further clearance.

Figure 10-2 shows the terminology used in a standard (right turns) holding pattern. The maximum holding airspeeds are 175 knots IAS for prop-driven aircraft and 200 knots IAS for civil jets under 6,000 feet. Civil jets are also restricted to 210 knots IAS between 6,000 feet and 14,000 feet and 265 knots IAS above 14,000 feet.

If an airspeed reduction is necessary to comply with these maximum speeds, you must begin the reduction within 3 minutes of the ETA over the holding fix.

Time the pattern so that the time of the inbound leg will be 1 minute if at or below 14,000 MSL; above 14,000 feet, the inbound leg should be 1½ minutes long. In order to establish this, you should fly the initial outbound leg for these durations and then ad-

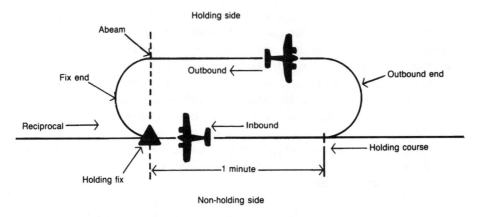

Fig. 10-2. *Standard (right-hand) holding pattern in no-wind condition.*

just the outbound leg time to get the proper inbound time. Timing is commenced abeam the fix. There might be times when ATC will designate a different inbound time, and if the holding fix is predicated on a DME distance, you don't worry about the time other than to note what the inbound and outbound times are so that you can cross the fix inbound at any time specified by ATC.

Holding pattern turns should be made at the least bank angle of the following:

- 3 degrees per second (compass/DG).
- 30-degree bank angle (attitude indicator).
- 25-degree bank angle (flight director).

HOLDING PATTERN ENTRIES

The hardest thing for most pilots to figure out is how to enter a holding pattern. There are only three correct ways to enter a pattern, and you determine which one to use depending on the arrival heading with relation to the inbound leg.

As a guide, the FAA has established one line at 70 degrees to the inbound leg on the holding side and another line at 110 degrees from the inbound leg on the nonholding side.

If you enter the holding pattern from within this sector (Area 3 in Fig. 10-3), merely fly to the fix and turn outbound in the same direction of the hold—turn right for right patterns and left for left patterns: a *direct entry*.

If you enter from Area 1 in Fig. 10-3, cross the fix, make a turn opposite the direction of the holding turns, and then fly the first outbound leg on the nonholding side. At the end of the outbound leg, make another turn opposite the holding turns, intercept the inbound leg, cross the fix, and enter the normal pattern: a *parallel entry*, or a parallel entry on the nonholding side.

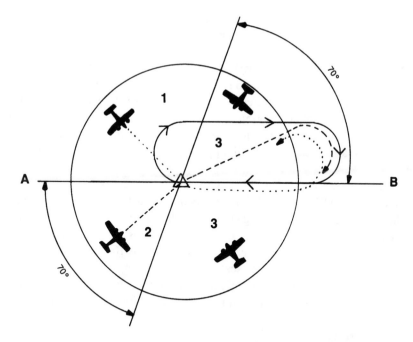

Fig. 10-3. *Entry procedures for standard (right-hand) holding pattern. Aircraft approaching from Zone 1 use a parallel entry; aircraft in Zone 2 use a teardrop entry; and aircraft in Zone 3 enter directly.*

Finally, if you enter from Area 2 in Fig. 10-3, cross the fix and turn to fly a heading 30 degrees to the outbound leg on the holding side. Fly this heading for 1 minute and then turn in the same direction as the holding turns to intercept the inbound leg: a *teardrop entry.*

In all of these entries, you should make the necessary corrections to compensate for the known wind. Although reams have been written to explain how to know which entry to use, I have found that 90 percent of the time the easiest entry to make from your position is the correct one.

If you're flying an aircraft with a full-faced DG, you might try this idea: Take a piece of thin, stiff, clear plastic, and a felt-tip pen. Trace Fig. 10-3, which depicts the entries for a standard right-hand holding pattern. Lay the line A-B over the face of the DG, with A on the inbound heading, B on its reciprocal, and the fix in the center, and read your entry directly from the pattern. For left-hand patterns, turn the plastic over. Simple? Try it.

STARs

Close to the destination, the ATC clearance might include a STAR *(standard instrument arrival route)*: a preplanned instrument flight rule (IFR) air traffic control arrival procedure published for pilot use in graphic and/or textual form. STARs provide transition from the enroute structure to an outer fix or an instrument approach fix/approval waypoint in the terminal area.

STARs are usually made for airports in high-density areas, and similarly to the SIDs that are used in departures, the STARs's main purpose is to simplify clearance procedures and cut down on radio frequency congestion. As with a SID, the pilot must possess at least the textual description. The final decision to accept or reject a STAR rests with the pilot, and it simplifies matters a great deal if she makes the remark "NO STAR" in the remarks section of the flight plan if she doesn't want to avail herself of this aid.

Figure 10-4 shows the Downe Four Arrival to Los Angeles International Airport. The chart resembles a SID, except for the letters in the black box in the upper right corner and the "2" in the numerical listing (10-2), which is used for STARs. Remember, 10-1 is for area charts, 10-2 is for STARs, and 10-3 is for SIDs. Multiple SIDs and STARs at a single airport will have a letter after the numeral such as 10-2B, 10-2C, and the like.

Again, this is a schematic, not to scale, but it does show, in pictorial form, the altitude restrictions enroute for each transition to the approach and, in textual form, the exact routes to be flown. It also shows all runway restrictions that are pertinent.

CHAPTER QUIZ

1. A compulsory reporting point is indicated on the charts by:
   a. A circle with a dot in the center
   b. A solid circle
   c. A triangle inside a circle
   d. A solid triangle
   e. A circle inside a triangle

2. When giving a position report in a nonradar environment, two times are necessary. These times are:
   1. _____; and
   2. _____.

   There are certain reports that must be given to ATC without a request, mark questions 3 through 5 as true or false.

3. When leaving any previously assigned altitude or flight level for a newly assigned altitude or flight level. True _____False _____

4. When reaching an assigned altitude or flight level.

   True _____False _____

5. When you have missed an approach. True _____ False _____

   Questions 6 and 7 assume that you are on an IFR flight plan and two-way communication is lost.

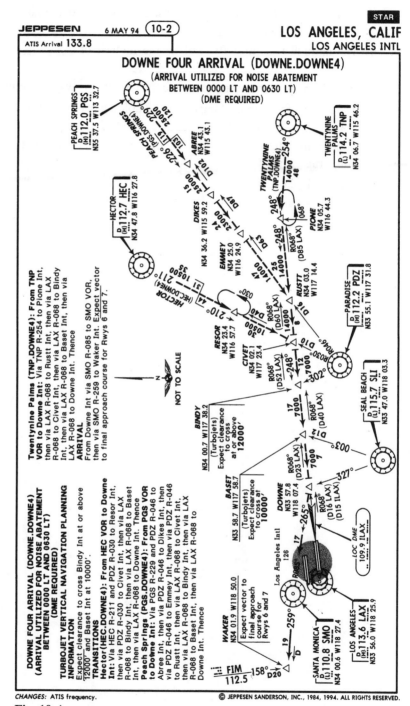

Fig. 10-4 Reproduced with permission of Jeppesen Sanderson, Inc. Not for use in navigation.

6. You are in VFR conditions. You must continue on your flight-planned route. True _____ False _____

7. The altitude you must fly will be the highest of _____, _____, or the _____.

8. What is the proper transponder code for loss of two-way communications?

9. The length of the inbound leg in a timed holding pattern should be _____ below _____ feet, and _____ above _____ feet.

10. In order to utilize a STAR, the PIC must possess at least the textual description. True _____ False _____

Answers are in the appendix.

11
Approach angles

MANY PILOTS THINK THAT INSTRUMENT FLIGHT IS THE ULTIMATE TEST OF an airman's skill. If this is so, then flying a good instrument approach has to be the epitome of the craft of flying.

Before we get into the actual approaches, let's take a look at some background information, basic concepts, and definitions of terms. Then I shall elaborate on certain pertinent regulations concerning instrument approaches.

The *Air Traffic Control Handbook* explains the purpose of instrument approach procedures:

> Instrument approach procedures are designed so as to ensure a safe descent from the en route environment to a point where a safe landing can be made.

> A pilot adhering to the altitudes, flight paths, and weather minimums depicted on the Instrument Approach Procedure (IAP) chart or vectors and altitudes issued by the radar controller, is assured of terrain and obstruction clearance and runway or airport alignment during approach for landing.

Sounds simple, yes?
You say no?
Well, it really is; however, just like learning to take off and land, it is first

necessary to establish a firm background to build upon. If at this time you are not proficient in straight-and-level flight, level turns, climbs and descents (both straight ahead and while turning), slow flight, speed control, and emergency procedures—all under the hood—you're not ready for approach work. In addition to the maneuvers mentioned previously, you should also be fairly proficient in flying airways, procedure turns, and holding patterns.

GETTING IT DOWN SAFELY

I suspect that you are asking, "Why? What's so different? Instruments are instruments." It's simply that when you get on an approach, your mind will be so filled with procedures and figures that aircraft control will have to be almost automatic. Not only that, but when you're on the approach, your margin of error becomes progressively smaller and smaller.

You can equate instrument flight with two cones lying on their sides with the large ends connected. The airports are at each small end; one end is the departure field and the other end is the destination. After takeoff, you point the nose skyward and begin to climb. The higher you get, the larger the sphere of allowable error becomes. If your attention wavers, you can go to a full-needle-width deflection of the OBI before you get outside of the airway, which extends 4 nautical miles each side of the centerline.

Sure, the regs say that you should be on the centerline, but if you drift off, you are still in protected airspace. Also, if the altitude starts drifting off and you go up or down 300 feet, it's probably not dangerous, but it's poor airmanship and subject to a citation or a violation. The chances of hitting something up there will be rare, unless someone else is also doing a sloppy job of holding an assigned altitude.

The sphere of allowable error gets smaller each second while on the approach. Close to minimums, the allowable error becomes very small. At this point, a full deflection of the needle isn't 4 miles off, but the width of the airport environment (if flying a VOR or NDB approach) or the width of the runway (if flying an ILS/MLS or localizer approach).

Tall structures can be found outside of this protected area, and running into one of them is not the right way to end a flight. Altitude becomes more critical down here also, and a 300-foot error could mean sudden and serious disaster.

It is assumed that you're fairly good at the basic hood work and that you practice from time to time with a safety pilot. You're ready to begin working on instrument approaches. But first, maybe you should know how the instrument approach procedure charts came about.

IN THE BEGINNING

Way back in 1930, a 23-year-old barnstormer by the name of Elroy B. ("Jepp") Jeppesen was offered a job as an airmail captain for Boeing Air Transportation Company, which is now known as United Air Lines. This promised a steadier income than that provided by barnstorming his World War I surplus Jenny, so he took the job.

He was flying the rugged mountain terrain between Cheyenne and Salt Lake City. It was a dangerous route with or without the navigational aids, which ranged from few to none. The route claimed many planes and pilots.

One day, Jepp bought a small 10-cent notebook and began jotting down all of the pertinent information regarding his routes. In addition to field lengths, obstructions, and altitudes, he even compiled a list of phone numbers of farmers along his route whom he could call for weather information. Some of this information would be very informative, while some might amount to no more than, "Well, I can see the barn through the snow." It was not unusual on his days off to find Jepp with a pocket altimeter climbing mountains, trees, water tanks and other obstructions to ascertain their correct heights.

Before long, pilots began talking both of his longevity and his "little black book," and he gave a few copies to his friends. The demand grew so great that he started publishing them in the cellar of his rooming house and selling copies to interested airmen. Business was so good that it was taking all of his time, so he tried to sell it to United Airlines for $5,000. The airline management turned the offer down, a move that ended up making Jepp a millionaire. He took an early retirement from United in 1954.

He opened a facility in Frankfurt, Germany, in 1957 due to the international demand, and in 1958 he opened an office in Washington, D.C., to interface with the government. He sold his publishing firm to the Times/Mirror Publishing Company in 1961. Times Mirror bought Sanderson Films, Inc., in 1968, and in 1970, when Times Mirror took Sanderson Films to Denver, the two company names were merged into today's Jeppesen Sanderson, Inc.

Jepp's "little black book" has grown to volumes of charts and procedures that cover airways worldwide and approaches to more than 16,000 airports. Revisions are issued weekly. Jeppesen manuals are used by all United States commercial airlines and many foreign carriers, as well as by a great majority of private and business pilots.

(I am indebted to Jeppesen Sanderson, Inc., and to the Times/Mirror Publishing Company for the permission they have granted me to use excerpts from the firm's manuals and copies of Jepp approach charts for illustrations.)

The government also publishes a set of charts, but because the airlines in the United States all use Jepps and many instrument students have aspirations to fly for the airlines, I have elected to use the Jepps during most of these discussions. I will, however, devote a chapter to explaining the NOS charts so you will be aware of the similarities and differences between the two.

PRECISION AND NONPRECISION APPROACHES

There are two basic types of approach procedures: precision and nonprecision. Simply stated, the nonprecision approach is a standard instrument procedure that does not use an electronic glide slope. Three precision approaches use a glide slope: instrument landing system (ILS), microwave landing system (MLS), and the precision approach radar (PAR). Implementation of the MLS has stagnated as a disappointment and will be disregarded in this discussion. PAR approaches are few and far between; they will also be disregarded because the ground controller talks the pilot in, and about all the pilot can do is listen and do what the controller says.

Several components are necessary for an approach to be classified as an ILS. The ground components are a *localizer, glide slope, outer marker, middle marker*, and *approach lights*. If a procedure specifies a visibility minimum based on *runway visual range* (RVR), it will also need *high intensity runway lights* (HIRL), *touchdown zone lighting* (TDZL), *centerline lighting* (RCLS) and markings, and, naturally, the RVR transmissometers for that runway. Of course, before the pilot can accept an ILS approach, her aircraft must have the airborne equipment necessary to receive the ground components.

A few variations exist. The regulations do allow a compass locator or a precision radar to be substituted for the outer marker (OM) or middle marker (MM), and an *airport surveillance radar* (ASR) can usually be substituted for the outer marker.

All other approaches are nonprecision. These primarily consist of the *localizer, back course, VOR, NDB* (ADF), ASR, and the newest of all, GPS approaches—although before long you will see both precision and nonprecision GPS approaches. The VOR and NDB (ADF) approaches are, in effect, designed to bring the aircraft down to the overall airport environment, while all other approaches will bring you right down to the runway.

APPROACH MINIMUMS

One of the most important terms used in conjunction with the instrument approach procedure charts is *minimums*. The minimums are comprised of two factors, the *minimum descent altitude* (MDA)—in the case of a precision approach, the *decision height* (DH)—and visibility. Each approach has its basic minimums that are modified for different airports depending on many factors, including obstacle clearances and terrain.

Visibility is the factor that governs whether or not airliners can *initiate* the approach. When we speak of a field being closed due to weather, the visibility is lower than that allowed by the available approaches. Under Part 91, you can start an approach regardless of visibility, which is discussed later. Prudent pilots, however, would not try to begin an approach when visibility is below minimums. The MDA or DH specified is merely the lowest altitude to which you can descend on the approach unless you have the runway environment in sight and are in a position to make a safe landing. If the airport is reporting a lower ceiling than the MDA/DH specified for the approach, you would still be allowed to commence the approach, although you would not normally expect to see the runway environment when the aircraft arrived at minimums.

The minimums are modified further if certain navigational aids on the ground or in flight are inoperative. These modifications are all specifically spelled out on the instrument approach charts.

On ILS approaches, if the localizer is out, the approach is not authorized. If the glide slope is out, the approach becomes a nonprecision approach and the DH turns into an MDA as specified in the procedure. If the outer or middle marker is out, the DH is increased by 50 feet and the visibility increase will depend on the *aircraft approach category*, which is discussed later in this chapter. On ILS and PAR approaches, if the ALS *(approach light system)* is out, the DH goes up by 50 feet and the visibility increases by ¼ mile. If the SSALSR *(simplified short approach light system* with *RAIL)* or MALSR *(medium intensity approach light system* with *RAIL)* is out, the DH for category A, B, and C increases by 50 feet and the visibility requirements go up by ¼ mile. RAIL stands for *runway alignment indicator lights,* which are the sequenced flashing lights seen on approach light systems that many pilots have nicknamed the *rabbit,* because they tend to run quickly toward the runway threshold.

If you are flying on an ILS approach with a visibility minimum of 1,800 or 2,000 feet RVR, the localizer and glide slope requirements are the same as above. But if the outer or middle marker is out, you must increase the DH by 50 feet for all categories, and for category A, B, and C, the visibility goes up to ½ mile, while in category D, it increases to ¾ mile. If the ALS is out, the DH goes up 50 feet and the visibility goes to ¾ mile. With the HIRL, TDZL, RCLS, or RVR out, there is no change in the DH, but the visibility goes to ½ mile. If only the RCLMs *(runway centerline markings)* are missing, there is no visibility increase, but the DH will change according to the procedure.

In VOR, LOC, LDA *(localizer type directional aid)*, and ASR, if the ALS, SS-MALSR, or the MALSR is out, the visibility increases ½ mile in category A, B, and C. It will increase ¼ mile in category A, B, and C if the SSALS, MALS, HIRL, or REIL *(runway end identification lights)* is out.

In NDB (ADF), with the ALS, SSALSR, or MALSR out, the visibility increases by ¼ mile in category A, B, and C.

The differences are confusing, but no one expects you to memorize the information. I only brought it up to show you that there are many times when the basic minimums might change, and you should be aware of them and know that you can find the new minimums in the appropriate blocks in the category/minimum section of the IAP chart that you'll be using.

AIRCRAFT CATEGORIES AND DESCENT MINIMUMS

The FAA established categories based upon aircraft approach speeds to make primary minima as safe as possible. Here are the actual definitions according to the pilot/controller glossary:

> AIRCRAFT APPROACH CATEGORY—A grouping of aircraft based on a speed of 1.3 times the stall speed in the landing configuration at maximum gross landing weight. An aircraft shall fit in only one category. If it is necessary to maneuver at speeds in excess of the upper limit of a speed range for a category, the minimum for the next higher category should be used. For example, an aircraft [that fits] in Category A, but is circling to land at a speed in excess of 91 knots, should use the approach

Category B minimums when circling to land. The categories are as follows:
1. Category A—speed less than 91 knots.
2. Category B—speed 91 knots or more, but less than 121 knots.
3. Category C—speed 121 knots or more, but less than 141 knots.
4. Category D—speed 141 knots or more but less than 166 knots.
5. Category E—speed 166 knots or more.

You'll notice the visibility requirements increase as the category speeds increase. That is because the turn radius is greater at the higher speeds and the aircraft will need more room and consequently more visibility to maneuver in.

Two descent minimums, the DH and the MDA, should be defined:

DECISION HEIGHT/DH—With respect to the operation of aircraft, means the height at which a decision must be made during an ILS, MLS, or PAR instrument approach to either continue the approach or to execute a missed approach.

MINIMUM DESCENT ALTITUDE/MDA—The lowest altitude, expressed in feet above mean sea level, to which descent is authorized on final approach or during circle-to-land maneuvering in execution of a standard instrument approach procedure where no electronic glide slope is provided.

The DH is a go-no-go altitude, and you have absolutely no choice in the matter. If you can see enough of the runway environment upon reaching the DH to continue and land *safely*, you do so. If you don't see the runway environment you go around—*immediately*. What constitutes the runway environment is explained in FAR 91.175 below.

The MDA affords a little more time to sort things out. With no electronic glide slope, you will reach the MDA at an uncertain distance from the runway. Once at the MDA, you may fly out the time to the MAP (*missed approach point*). You cannot descend below the MDA until the aircraft is in a position to make a normal approach to the runway. This is spelled out quite clearly in FAR 91.175, Takeoff and landing under IFR (in part):

(c) *Operation below DH or MDA.* Where a DH or MDA is applicable, no pilot may operate an aircraft . . . at any airport below the authorized MDA or continue an approach below the authorized DH unless—

(1) The aircraft is continuously in a position from which a descent to a landing on the intended runway can be made at a normal rate of descent using normal maneuvers. . . .

(2) The flight visibility is not less than the visibility prescribed in the standard instrument approach procedure being used;

(3) . . . At least one of the following visual references for the intended runway is distinctly visible and identifiable to the pilot:

(i) The approach light system, except that the pilot may not descend below 100 feet above the touchdown zone elevation using the approach lights as a reference unless the red terminating bars or the red side row bars are also distinctly visible and identifiable.

(ii) The threshold.

(iii) The threshold markings.

(iv) The threshold lights.

(v) The runway end identifier lights.

(vi) The visual approach slope indicator.

(vii) The touchdown zone or touchdown zone markings.

(viii) The touchdown zone lights.

(ix) The runway or runway markings.

(x) The runway lights; and

(d) *Landing.* No pilot operating an aircraft . . . may land that aircraft when the flight visibility is less than the visibility prescribed in the standard instrument approach procedure being used.

(e) *Missed approach procedures.* Each pilot operating an aircraft . . . shall immediately execute an appropriate missed approach procedure when either of the following conditions exist:

(1) Whenever the requirements of paragraph (c) of this section are not met at either of the following times:

(i) When the aircraft is being operated below MDA; or

(ii) Upon arrival at the missed approach point, including a DH where a DH is specified and its use is required, and at any time after that until touchdown.

(2) Whenever an identifiable part of the airport is not distinctly visible to the pilot during a circling maneuver at or above MDA, unless the inability to see an identifiable part of the airport results only from a normal bank of the aircraft during the circling approach.

That certainly spells things out clearly enough. Sometimes it might take a few readings to get it all set in your mind, but these are some of the most important things to remember about an instrument approach. Failure to comply with these paragraphs has cost us a lot of lives and a lot of aircraft.

CHAPTER QUIZ

1. How can a pilot be assured of terrain and obstruction clearance as well as runway or airport alignment when flying on instruments?

2. Who was the father of our modern day instrument approach procedure charts?

3. What is the main difference between a precision and a nonprecision approach?

4. What is the difference between DH and MDA?

5. The aircraft approach category is a grouping of aircraft based on a speed of _____ times _____ in the _____ at _____.

6. Is it ever necessary for an aircraft to use a different approach category than that determined by the definition in question 5?

7. What are the three basic conditions that must be met in order for a pilot to descend below the DH or MDA?

8. If you lose sight of the landing runway environment while executing a circling approach, you must immediately execute a missed approach, unless _____.

Answers are in the appendix.

12
Mastering minimums

BEFORE WE CONTINUE LEAFING THROUGH THE MANUALS, THERE ARE TWO general definitions to review: *visibility* and *visual approach*. Additionally, there is a difference between *ground* and *in-flight* visibility.

VISIBILITY

Visibility on the ground is determined by the human eye or by an instrument known as a *transmissometer*, which is a device that measures the visibility by determining the amount of light that passes through the atmosphere.

The prevailing visibility is recorded by a trained observer at or near ground level. He looks at objects that are at known distances from his vantage point: trees, buildings, smokestacks, mountains, and radio and TV broadcast antennas; at night the observer looks at lights in the same manner. Prevailing visibility is reported in miles and fractions of miles:

Prevailing Visibility—The greatest horizontal visibility equaled or exceeded throughout at least half the horizon circle which need not necessarily be continuous.

A transmissometer measures two types of visibility:

Runway Visibility Value/RVV—The visibility determined for a particular runway by a transmissometer. A meter provides a continuous indication of the visibility (reported in miles or fractions of miles) for the runway. RVV is used in lieu of prevailing visibility in determining minimums for a particular runway.

Runway Visual Range/RVR—An instrumentally derived value, based on standard calibrations, that represents the horizontal distance a pilot will see down the runway from the approach end. It is based on the sighting of either high-intensity runway lights or on the visual contrast of other targets, whichever yields the greater visual range. RVR, in contrast to prevailing or runway visibility, is based on what a pilot in a moving aircraft should see looking down the runway. RVR is horizontal visual range, not slant visual range. It is based on the measurement of a transmissometer made near the touchdown point of the instrument runway and is reported in hundreds of feet. RVR is used in lieu of RVV and/or prevailing visibility in determining minimums for a particular runway.

A very important thing to note here is that both RVV and RVR values are for specific runways, and it is sometimes possible to make an approach to another runway when the prevailing visibility is higher. You will find this occurring at airports near the coast, where fog might roll in and cover only part of one runway, and that might be the runway with the transmissometer(s).

It's important for you to know that because the RVR and the human visibility measurements are horizontal range, the visibility might be more or less than what you'll see using slant range from the cockpit. Normally the visibility reported from the ground will be slightly better than what you'll find looking from the windshield on approach.

VISUAL APPROACH

Occasionally, while under radar control, you might be cleared for a visual approach. Be careful. A visual approach is defined in the pilot/controller glossary:

Visual Approach—An approach conducted on an instrument flight rules (IFR) flight plan which authorizes the pilot to proceed visually and clear of clouds to the airport. The pilot must, at all times, have either the airport or the preceding aircraft in sight. This approach must be authorized, and under the control of the appropriate air traffic control facility. Reported weather at the airport must be ceiling at or above 1,000 feet and visibility of 3 miles or greater.

The trap is the phrase "to proceed visually and clear of clouds." If you enter a cloud, or an area where the conditions revert to IMC *(instrument meteorological conditions)*, you are in violation. So, it pays to look well ahead before you accept a visual approach. You might be able to see and identify the aircraft you are instructed to follow, but look all the way along the approach path, and if there are clouds that must be penetrated, you cannot legally accept the visual approach clearance. It is a useful tool, though, in helping avoid long drawn-out approaches, and it eases the burden on ATC. There is one other possible trap. The *ATC Handbook* amplifies the visual approach:

a. When it will be operationally beneficial, ATC may authorize an aircraft to conduct a visual approach to an airport or to follow another aircraft when flight to, and landing at, the airport can be accomplished in VFR weather. The aircraft must have the airport or the identified preceding aircraft in sight before the clearance is issued. If the pilot has the airport in sight but cannot see the aircraft he is following, ATC may still clear the aircraft for a visual approach; however, ATC retains both separation and wake vortex separation responsibility. When visually following a preceding aircraft, acceptance of the visual approach clearance, constitutes acceptance of pilot responsibility for maintaining a safe approach interval and adequate wake turbulence separation.

Consider this example. Approach control is working four other aircraft. You are told that you are following a Hawaiian Airlines L-1011 at 12 o'clock, 6 miles. You see traffic at your 12 o'clock position, or perhaps 1 o'clock, and it seems to be about the right distance. But before you say, "Cessna 20Z has the L-1011," are you actually sure that it is an L-1011? Is it actually inbound? Is it a Hawaiian plane? Are there any clouds in the vicinity that might block it from your view before you land? You should only acknowledge the traffic if you can identify it positively without a doubt in your mind and be able to keep it in sight from then on until you land. Remember, once you are cleared for a visual approach based on your identifying a preceding aircraft, are told to follow it, and you accept the clearance, you will be responsible for your own wake turbulence separation. Be careful.

I think this is one of the most common mistakes of pilots with whom I used to fly. They seem to be in such a hurry to please ATC that they supposedly positively identify preceding aircraft, even at night, when a dozen other aircraft or lights surround the airport area. When a DC-9 collided with a Cessna approaching San Diego airport some years ago, one of the last sentences on the voice recorder of the DC-9 was that they had been looking at the wrong plane. Don't let this happen to you, no matter how big a hurry you are in to get to the field and no matter how much you'd like to please ATC.

DON'T SAY YOU HAVE A PRECEDING AIRCRAFT IN SIGHT UNLESS YOU CAN IDENTIFY IT POSITIVELY.

Recently the *ATC Handbook* has further amplified these procedures. Sections d and g are identical. One of them is probably an oversight by the authors, but then again, ATC might consider it as being so important that it bears repeating.

These sections state: "Authorization to conduct a visual approach is an IFR authorization and does not alter IFR flight plan cancellation responsibility. . . ." So, be sure to remember to cancel your IFR flight plan after you land. ATC will not do it for you automatically.

There are a few more amplifications to the rules, so you should be cognizant of them. Section e. says:

A visual approach is not an IAP and therefore has no missed approach segment. If a go-around is necessary for any reason, aircraft operating at controlled airports will be issued an appropriate advisory/clearance/instruction by the tower. At uncontrolled airports, aircraft are expected to remain clear of clouds and complete a landing as soon as possible. If a landing cannot be accomplished, the aircraft is expected to remain clear of clouds and contact ATC as soon as possible for further clearance. Separation from other IFR aircraft will be maintained under these circumstances.

This really gives us another reason to be very careful about accepting a visual approach. Even though IFR separation will be provided if you cannot land, the responsibility to remain clear of clouds while maneuvering remains with you.

CONTACT APPROACH

In addition to the visual approach, there is one other time that you can deviate from the published approach procedure. Perhaps you are executing an approach that has a 1½-mile minimum visibility requirement. The tower informs you that the visibility has just dropped to 1 mile. Also suppose that you are below the base of the clouds and can see a highway below. You identify the highway and know that it runs alongside the runway.

Because the field has just dropped below minimums, you may either execute a missed approach when you reach the MAP or you may request a *contact approach*. From the *ATC Handbook*:

> a. Pilots operating in accordance with an IFR flight plan, provided they are clear of clouds and have at least 1 mile flight visibility and can reasonably expect to continue to the destination airport in those conditions, may request ATC authorization for a contact approach.
>
> b. Controllers may authorize a contact approach provided:
>
> (1) The contact approach is specifically requested by the pilot. ATC cannot initiate this approach.
>
> (2) The reported ground visibility at the destination airport is at least 1 statute mile.
>
> (3) The contact approach will be made to an airport having a standard or special instrument approach procedure.
>
> (4) Approved separation is applied between aircraft so cleared and between these aircraft and other IFR or special VFR aircraft.
>
> c. A contact approach is an approach procedure that may be used by a pilot (with prior authorization from ATC) in lieu of conducting a standard or special IAP to an airport. It is not intended for use by a pilot on an IFR flight clearance to operate to an airport not having an authorized IAP. Nor is it intended for an aircraft to conduct an instrument approach to one airport and then, when "in the clear," to discontinue that approach and proceed to another airport. In the execution of a contact approach, the pilot assumes the responsibility for obstruction clearance. If radar service is being received, it will automatically terminate when the pilot is told to contact the tower.

The contact approach can be very helpful to the instrument pilot. Remember, though, that in order to execute a contact approach, you must be on an IFR flight plan, you can only use the approach to fly to the destination airport as filed on the flight plan, you cannot use it without ATC authorization, and you are fully responsible for obstruction clearance.

Many airports also have DF *(direction finding)* instrument procedures, but these are only for use when the pilot has declared a distress or urgency condition, such as would happen when navigational capabilities are lost.

STRAIGHT-IN AND CIRCLING MINIMUMS

Straight-in and/or circling minimums are published for most runways; circling minimums are always higher than the straight-in minimums. What constitutes a straight-in or circling approach presents a problem at times. I have had a number of students ask me why a certain airport will have circling minimums when the final approach course is on the same heading as the runway (from the *ATC Handbook*):

(b) Straight-in minimums—Straight-in minimums are shown on IAP charts when the final approach course of the IAP is within 30 degrees of the runway alignment and a normal descent can be made from the IFR altitude shown on the IAPs to the runway surface. When either the normal rate of descent or the runway alignment factor of 30 degrees is exceeded, a straight-in minimum is not published and a circling minimum applies. The fact that a straight-in minimum is not published does not preclude the pilot from landing straight-in if he has the active runway in sight and has sufficient time to make a normal approach for landing. Under such conditions and when ATC has cleared him for landing on that runway, he is not expected to circle even though only circling minimums are published. If he desires to circle he should advise ATC.

(d) Circling Minimums—The circling minimums . . . provide adequate obstruction clearance and the pilot should not descend below the circling altitude until the aircraft is in a position to make final descent for landing. . . .

(1) Maneuver the shortest path to the base or downwind leg as appropriate, under minimum weather conditions. There is no restriction from passing over the airport or other runways.

(2) It should be recognized that many circling maneuvers may be made while VFR or other flying is in progress at the airport. Standard left turns or specific instructions from the controller for maneuvering must be considered when circling to land.

(3) At airports without a control tower, it may be desirable to fly over the airport to determine wind and turn indicators, and to observe other traffic. . . .

CIRCLING APPROACH

It is important to recognize that if you sight the runway too late to make a normal descent to landing, you are required to circle. When circling, you cannot descend below the circling altitude until you are in position to make a normal landing, usually when you turn final. A lot of good pilots have crashed while executing a circling approach because they went too low and hit one of the many obstructions found in the vicinity of most airports, or they developed vertigo when making a tight turn close to the ground and stalled or spun in.

Remember the exception to the aircraft category that puts the aircraft in a higher than normal category if the maneuvering speed in a circling approach is higher than the $1.3 V_{SO}$ stall speed normally used on a straight-in approach because the radius of turn will be greater with the higher speed. The obstruction clearance at the slower speed and tighter radius might not be adequate for the higher speed; selected visibility requirements increase dramatically as the category of the aircraft increases.

I remember watching a Convair 440 break out of the clouds years ago. He was just over the end of a 6,000-foot runway. The pilot, not wanting to take a wave-off and being below circling minimums, tried to land. The descent was too steep and the airspeed was too high. He was using up way too much runway, and he was determined to get it on the ground, so he pushed the nose over. Halfway down the runway the nosewheel hit and collapsed, and the aircraft slid to a stop about 50 feet from a 300-foot dropoff. Fortunately no one was injured, but the aircraft suffered considerable damage, the field was closed for two days, and an 18-year veteran pilot lost a job. Instrument flying is no time to cut corners.

Figures 12-1 through 12-4 are examples of circling maneuvers. In these maneuvers, the turns are executed using outside visual references and instruments. Keep a close eye on altitude, airspeed, and angle of bank.

RUNWAY NOT IN SIGHT

This brings us down, so to speak, to the *missed approach*. There are three situations in which a missed approach is mandatory. The first is when you reach the DH or MAP de-

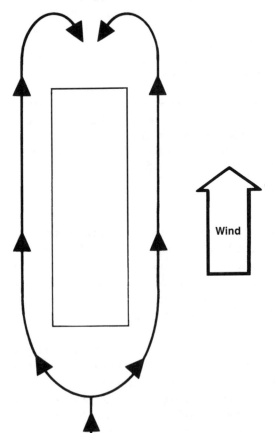

Fig. 12-1. *You are making an approach downwind and must circle to land into the wind. Once you sight the airport, you break right or left to make a standard downwind leg. This way you should never lose sight of the field.*

Wind

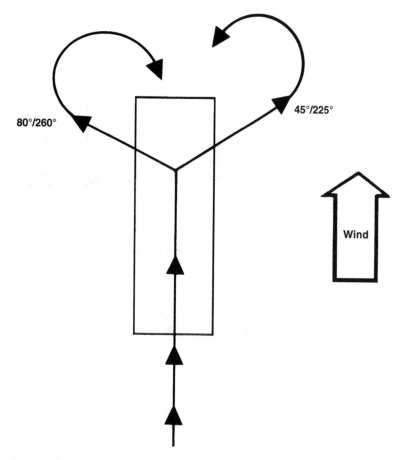

80°/260°

45°/225°

Wind

Fig. 12-2. *In this approach, you either sight the field too late to maneuver as shown in Fig. 12-1, or the weather conditions along the normal downwind legs will not allow you the latitude to circle in that manner. In this case, fly directly down the runway (at the circling MDA), and upon reaching the approach end, execute any type of procedure turn that will keep you from losing visual reference with the runway (except when banking).*

picted on the IAP chart and do not have sufficient visual reference to complete the landing. The second is any time that visual reference to the airport is lost after reaching the DH or MDA. The third is when visual reference to the airport is lost while executing a circling approach.

Whenever you execute a missed approach, you must either comply with the published missed approach procedure as printed on the chart or follow directions from ATC if directed to deviate from the published procedure. If you lose visual reference while executing a circling approach, initiate the missed approach by making a climb-

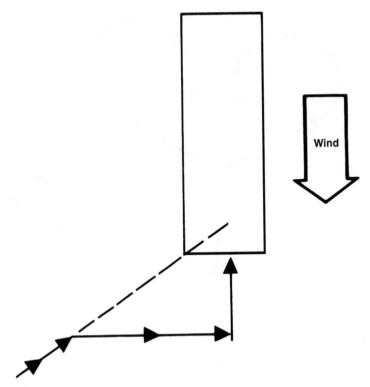

Fig. 12-3. *This shows your most desired break-off from a circling approach. You must sight the runway in time to maneuver normally onto the extended centerline and execute a normal landing.*

ing turn toward the landing runway. Continue the turn until established on the proper missed approach procedure.

You should have noticed by now that, as mentioned in chapter 11, you'll be pretty busy flying the procedure, and the actual mechanics of flying the aircraft must be practically automatic.

It will be a good idea to practice the maneuvers suggested before—straight and level, climbs, and descents—with and without turns and at normal speeds and slow or maneuvering speeds. This time, special emphasis should be placed on the proper use of trim.

Anytime the aircraft is established in a new attitude, all possible control pressures should be relieved by proper trim. Remember that to use trim properly, you must first apply control pressure to establish the new attitude, then use the trim tabs so that the aircraft will maintain the required flight path practically hands off. This will create time to take quick looks at approach plates, retrieve an errant plate off the floor, or jot down a new clearance without the aircraft wandering around. It will also allow you to

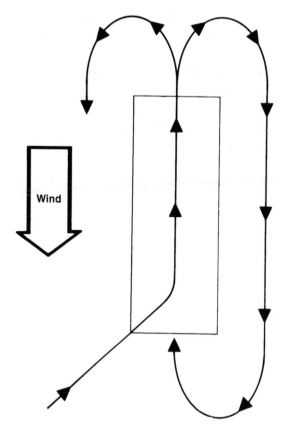

Fig. 12-4. *If you do not see the runway in time, but are approaching into the wind, you should fly down the runway to the departure end, and turn left or right to execute normal downwind and base legs.*

change attitudes quickly, such as going from descent to a missed approach climb without having to impart excessive pressures to the controls.

CHAPTER QUIZ

1. What two methods are used to determine visibility?

2. When cleared for a visual approach, ATC assures the pilot of safe approach intervals and adequate wake turbulence separation? True _____False _____

3. What three conditions must be met in order for a pilot to request a contact approach?

4. What is the main advantage to a pilot in a contact approach as opposed to a visual approach?

5. The two things a contact approach is not intended to do is to be used by a pilot to _____, _____ nor _____ "_____," _____.

6. During a contact approach, although ATC is still providing separation between your aircraft and other IFR and special VFR traffic, you are still responsible for _____.

7. When will a straight-in approach to an airport not be furnished?

8. When is a pilot expected to land straight-in, even though cleared for a circling approach and only circling minimums are listed?

9. While executing a circling approach to a runway, descend just enough below the MDA to assure that you won't penetrate clouds while circling.
   True _____ False _____

10. How would you execute a missed approach if you lost sight of the runway while circling to land?

Answers are in the appendix.

13
Enroute charts

LET'S TURN OUR ATTENTION NOW TO THE ENROUTE CHARTS. WE'LL ONLY BE working with Jeppesen charts; National Ocean Service (NOS) charts will be easy to transition to when necessary. The low-altitude (LO) charts in the continental United States and Canada are effective up to but not including 18,000 feet MSL. If you intend to fly higher, use either the high (HI) or high/low (H/L) charts.

Look at the index map on the cover of the chart (Fig. 13-1), and note the gray squares and rectangles. These are found around some very large cities where the airway/facility congestion is so bad that a lot of information has to be omitted. To solve this problem, Jeppesen has larger-scale area charts that should be used whenever you are flying into or out of these specific areas. The area charts are referenced on the enroute charts by a heavy dashed line with the identifier and location name.

Many of the symbols that are found on the area charts are shown on the enroute charts in reduced scale so that pilots who are overflying the area can do so without having to open an area chart. But remember, if you are going to land or take off within that area, you need to use the area chart. Many important intersections and other features are shown on the area charts.

The LO and H/L Jeppesen charts have a unique feature that Jeppesen calls a Zigdex. You know how much of a problem it is to fold and unfold large charts in the

◀ 20 US (LO) JEPPESEN US (LO) **19 ▶**
1 INCH = 20 NM   1 INCH = 20 NM

UNITED STATES
LOW ALTITUDE ENROUTE CHARTS
© JEPPESEN SANDERSON, INC., 1978, 1994. ALL RIGHTS RESERVED.

MEETS FAA REQUIREMENTS FOR AERONAUTICAL CHARTS

Within the continental U.S., the airways shown on these charts are effective up to but not including 18,000' MSL. At 14,500' MSL and above, all airspace is controlled Class E airspace. Shaded blue areas shown on the face of enroute charts designate airspace that is not controlled (Class G) below 14,500' MSL. The Jet Route structure is superimposed to show its relationship with the low altitude airways. For operational detail for Jet Routes at or above 18,000' MSL, use US(HI) charts.

REVISION DATA

CHART US(LO)19 2 DEC 94 Stevens Point, Wisc VORTAC station declination changed. Red Wing, Minn NDB freq changed. Mason City, Iowa VOR holding desig. Plugs Int formation bearing changed (Gopher, Minn R-333). Wetly Int renamed Apnel (Wiarton, Ont R-316).

CHART US(LO)20 2 DEC 94 Manchester, NY VORTAC shutdown. Picaa Int renamed Buker (Berlin, NH R-178). Alert Area CY(A)-611(T) revoked (NE of Montreal, Que VOR).

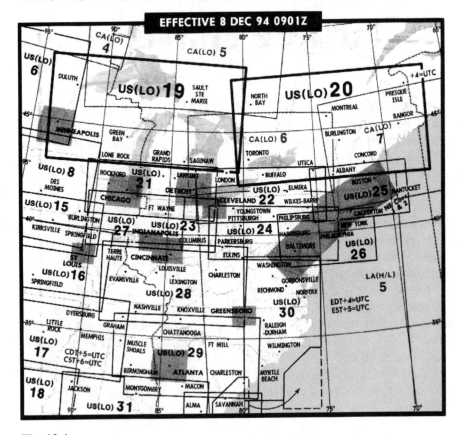

Fig. 13-1 Reproduced with permission of Jeppesen Sanderson, Inc. Not for use in navigation.

confined space of small cockpits. This is even more difficult when you are trying to control a plane under IFR conditions. On the back of the chart (Fig. 13-2), note that the upper edge has been trimmed off at an angle so that when it is folded up, it zigzags back and forth like the switchbacks of a mountain trail. These folds divide the face of the chart into three sections. Each fold is designated by a major city found within that specific section. To find a specific area on the chart, it is only necessary to open it up at the correct fold. For example, if you're going to be operating around Green Bay, you would open chart 19 at fold 2. From then on, all you have to do is open and close the folds like the pages in a book, which is a lot easier than trying to open and refold the entire chart.

Most elevations on the enroute chart are in feet above mean sea level (MSL), although some are in flight levels, in which case they will be noted as such.

Enroute communications are shown in two places on the chart: on the face of the chart and on the end folds (Fig. 13-2) for convenience when planning a flight. Except on the high-altitude charts, terminal communications are also shown in the tabulations on the end folds.

The lower part of the facing page of the chart (Fig. 13-3) also describes the restricted airspace found on the chart. A circle explaining the hemispherical rule altitudes is on the bottom of the page, with a note below it to add 500 feet for VFR altitudes.

ROAD MAPS IN THE SKY

The charts are not all drawn to the same scale, so check the scale printed along the upper or side margin of the chart face before measuring anything on it. Jeppesen manufactures navigation chart plotters that have a compass rose as well as all of the various scales marked on them. These plotters come in very handy when measuring distances and bearings.

Let's take a look at some of the symbols to be found on the enroute chart. Radio identification and communications can be seen in Fig. 13-4.

All navaid facilities that form an airway or a route component are enclosed in shadow boxes. If they are not collocated, they will be so noted in parentheses below the box. The name of the facility, its frequency, three-letter identification, and Morse code identifier will be found inside the box, and if it has DME capability that is frequency-paired, a small D will be included preceding the frequency.

There are still quite a few TACAN stations operating throughout the country. Some of these have frequency pairing, which means that the VOR frequency is also the DME frequency. In this case, the frequency is shown with the three-letter ID. If it is not frequency-paired, the ghost VOR frequency will be shown in parentheses below the TACAN information.

To facilitate aircraft using area navigation such as *loran-C, inertial navigation system* (INS), *GPS*, and *Omega*, the H/L and HI altitude charts also show the geographical coordinates below the code ID for all navaids forming airways and routes.

◀19US (LO)   **COMMUNICATIONS**   US (LO)**20▶**

BOLD NAME—Voice call. Light Names/Abbreviations —Identifying names/abbreviations not used in radio call. T—Transmit only. G—Guard only. *—Part-time operation. X—On-request. **(R)**—Radar Capability. **C**—Clearance Delivery. **Cpt**—Clearance (Pre-taxi Proc). KDEN p6D— Charted location is shown by Area chart initials and/or by quarter panel number-letter combination. Common EMERGENCY 121.5 is not listed. Refer to Glossary and Abbreviations in Introduction pages for further explanations.

A.━	G━━.	M━━	S...	Y━.━━	5.....
B━...	H....	N━.	T━	Z━━..	6━....
C━.━.	I..	O━━━	U..━	1.━━━━	7━━...
D━..	J.━━━	P.━━.	V...━	2..━━━	8━━━..
E.	K━.━	Q━━.━	W.━━	3...━━	9━━━━.
F..━.	L.━..	R.━.	X━..━	4....━	0━━━━━

ALBANY, NY   p5C
Albany ATIS 120.45. **Albany App(R & Class (C))/Dep(R & Class (C))** 194°-011° 118.05, 011°-194° 125.0 124.7 127.15. **Twr** 119.5. **Gnd** 121.7. **C** 127.5.

ALMA, MICH.   p3C
Gratiot. **Saginaw** *App/*Dep 118.45.

ALPENA, MICH.   p3C
Alpena Co Regl. **Wurtsmith App(R)/Dep(R)** 134.8 128.6. **Alpena** *Twr 121.35 127.75. **Gnd** 121.9.

APPLETON, WISC.   p2C
Outagamie. *ATIS 127.15. **Green Bay** *App(R)/ *Dep(R) 126.3. **Appleton** *Twr 119.6. **Gnd** 121.7.

AUBURN, MAINE   p6C
Auburn-Lewiston. **Portland** *App 125.5 124.05. *Dep 125.5. *Cpt 124.05.

AUGUSTA, MAINE   p6C
Augusta State. **Brunswick** *App(R)/ *Dep(R) 128.35 **C** 119.95.

AUSTIN, MINN.   p1C
Austin. **Rochester** *App(R)/*Dep(R) 119.8.

BANGOR, MAINE   p6D
Bangor Int'l ATIS 127.75. **Bangor App(R&Class (C))/Dep(R&Class (C))** (335°-154° 124.5, 155°-334° 125.3). **Twr** 120.7. **Gnd** 121.9. **C** 135.9.

BAR HARBOR, MAINE   p6D
Hancock-Bar Harbor. **Bangor App(R)/Dep(R)** 124.5. **C** 119.9.

BARRIE, ONTARIO   p4C
Barrie Executive. **Toronto/Buttonville Rdo** Arr/Dep 126.7.

BAY CITY, MICH.   p3C
Clements. **Saginaw** *App(R)/*Dep(R) 126.45.

BELFAST, MAINE   p6D
Belfast. **Bangor App/Dep** 125.3.

GRIFFISS AFB, NY   p5C
Griffiss AFB. **Griffiss App(R)** 329°-157° 126.65, 158°-328° 118.5. **Dep(R)** 120.9. **Twr** 126.25. **Gnd** 121.8. GCA.

HARTFORD, WISC.   p2C
Hartford. **Milwaukee App(R)/Dep(R)** 124.75.

HIBBING, MINN.   p1A
Chisholm-Hibbing. **Duluth App(R)/Dep(R)** 125.45 **C** 127.4.

HIGHGATE, VT.   p5D
Franklin. **Burlington App(R)/Dep(R)** 121.1 (East), 126.3 (West).

JUNEAU, WISC.   p2C
Dodge. **Madison** *App(R)/*Dep(R) 119.15.

K.I. SAWYER AFB, MICH.   p2A
K.I. Sawyer AFB. **Sawyer App(R)** 119.1 116.3T. **Dep(R)** 119.1. **Twr** 126.8 116.3T.

KITCHENER, ONTARIO   p4C
Kitchener/Waterloo-Guelph Regl *ATIS 125.1. **Waterloo** *Twr ATF 126.0. **Gnd** 121.8.

LACONIA, NH   p6C
Laconia. **Manchester** *App(R)/*Dep(R) 134.75. **C** 119.85.

LA CROSSE, WISC.   p1D
La Crosse. *ATIS 124.95. **La Crosse** *Twr 124.3. **Gnd** 121.8. **La Crosse Rdo** (LAA) 124.3 121.8 when Twr inop.

LEBANON, NH   p5D
Lebanon *ATIS 118.65. **Lebanon** *Twr 125.95. **Gnd** 121.6.

LINCOLN, MAINE   p6B
Lincoln. **Bangor App(R)/Dep(R)** 124.5.

MANCHESTER, NH   p6C
Manchester *ATIS 119.55. **Manchester** *App (Class (C)) S124.9, N 127.35 134.75. *Dep 124.9 134.75. *Twr 121.3. **Gnd** 121.9. **C** 135.9.

PALMYRA, NY   p4D
Palmyra. **Rochester App(R)/Dep(R)** 119.55.

PEMBROKE, ONTARIO   p4B
Pembroke. **Ottawa** *Tml Ctl(R) (Arr/ Dep) 135.2. **Petawawa** *Adv 126.4.

PITTSFIELD, MAINE   p6C
Pittsfield. **Bangor App** 125.3. **Dep** 126.85.

PLATTSBURGH, NY   p5D
Clinton. **Burlington App(R)/Dep(R)** 121.1 (East), 126.3 (West). **C** 121.7. Plattsburgh AFB. **Burlington App (R)/Dep(R)** 121.1 (East), 126.3 (West). **Plattsburgh Twr** 120.7. **Gnd** 121.8. GCA.

PORTAGE, WISC.   p1D
Madison *App(R)/*Dep(R) 124.0 120.1.

PORTLAND, MAINE   p6C
Portland Int'l *ATIS 119.05. **Portland** *App(R & Class (C))/*Dep(R & Class (C)) (N 125.5, S 119.75, 132.4). *Twr 120.9. **Gnd** 121.9. **C** 121.65.

PORTSMOUTH, (NE CORR 1p3B) p6C
NH
Pease Intl Tradeport. *ATIS 132.05. **Manchester** *App(R)/*Dep (R) 118.8. **Pease Twr** 128.4. **Gnd** 120.95. Boston Center 128.2 when Manchester App/Dep inop.

PRESQUE ISLE, MAINE   p6B
Northern Maine Regional. **Bangor App(R)/Dep(R)** 124.7. **C** 121.6

PULASKI, WISC.   p2C
Carter. **Green Bay** *App(R) 119.4. *Dep(R) 126.55

QUEBEC, QUEBEC   p5B
Quebec/Lesage Intl ATIS (Eng 119.8, Fr 128.3). **Quebec** *Arr/*Dep 127.85. **Twr** 120.3. **Gnd** 121.9.

Fig. 13-2 Reproduced with permission of Jeppesen Sanderson, Inc. Not for use in navigation.

When landing aids perform enroute functions, they are identified by round-cornered boxes. As in the navaid shadow box, the frequency is provided in the box, as well as the DME if it is available and frequency-paired. These facilities include LOC, SDF,

AIRSPACE RESTRICTED AREAS
LEGEND

CY-Canada
(Canadian Alert Areas additionally coded as   (A) Acrobatic   (H) Hang Gliding
(P) Parachute Dropping   (S) Soaring   (T) Training)

22 APR 94

R-4201A
GND-23000
0800-1600 LT
TUE-SAT
O/T BY NOTAM
MINNEAPOLIS ARTCC

R-4201B
GND-9000
0001 LT SAT-
2359 LT SUN
O/T BY NOTAM
MINNEAPOLIS ARTCC

R-4202
GND-8200
NOTAM
MINNEAPOLIS ARTCC

R-5201
GND-23000
CONT 4/1-9/30
GND-20000
0600-1800 LT
10/1-3/31
& BY NOTAM
BOSTON ARTCC

R-5207
GND-2000
0730-1815 LT
MON-FRI

R-6501A
GND-4000
0700-2300 LT
MON-FRI
0000-2359 LT
SAT-SUN
O/T BY NOTAM
BURLINGTON APP

R-6501B
4000-13600
INTERMITTENT
BURLINGTON APP

R-6901A
GND-20000
CONTINUOUS
5/1-9/30
0800-2200 LT
MON-THUR
0800 LT FRI-
2200 LT SUN
O/T BY NOTAM
10/1-4/30
MINNEAPOLIS ARTCC

R-6901B
GND-20000
NOTAM
MINNEAPOLIS ARTCC

CY(R)-508
GND-1400
DAYLIGHT

CY(A)-520(T)
GND-4000
DAYLIGHT

CY(R)-604
GND-1500

CY(R)-613
GND-800

CY(R)-614
GND-1300

CY(A)-622(F)
GND-2000
DAYLIGHT
MON-FRI
4/1-11/30
NOTAM

CY(R)-624
GND-1300
DAYLIGHT
BELL HELICOPTER/
TEXTRON

CHIPPEWA MOA
7000-FL 180
TUE-SAT
0930-1130 &
1330-1530 EST
O/T BY. NOTAM
MINNEAPOLIS ARTCC
EXCLUDES FL 180

FALLS 1/2 MOAs
500 AGL-FL 180
1200-2000 LT TUE
0800-1600 LT
WED-SAT
O/T BY NOTAM
MINNEAPOLIS ARTCC
EXCLUDES FL 180

VOLK EAST MOA
8000'-FL180
1200-2000 LT TUE
0800-1600 LT
WED-SAT
O/T BY NOTAM
CHICAGO ARTCC
EXLUDES FL 180

VOLK SOUTH MOA
500 AGL-FL 180
1200-2000 LT TUE
0800-1600 LT
WED-SAT
O/T BY NOTAM
CHICAGO ARTCC
EXCLUDES FL 180

VOLK WEST MOA
500 AGL-FL 180
1200-2000 LT TUE
0800-1600 LT
WED-SAT
O/T BY NOTAM
MINNEAPOLIS ARTCC
EXCLUDES FL 180 &
R-6904A/B when active

CRUISING ALTITUDES

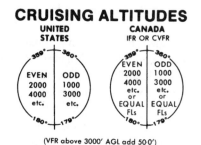

(VFR above 3000' AGL add 500')

Fig. 13-3 Reproduced with permission of Jeppesen Sanderson, Inc. Not for use in navigation.

LDA, MLS, and KRM. Certain facilities have not been previously defined in this book; Jeppesen defines them as:

Simplified Directional Facility (SDF)—A navaid used for nonprecision instrument approaches. The final approach course is similar to that of an ILS localizer except that the SDF course may be offset from the runway, generally not more than 3 degrees, and the course may be wider than the localizer, resulting in a lower degree of accuracy.

Microwave Landing System (MLS)—An instrument landing system operating in the microwave spectrum which provides lateral and vectored guidance to aircraft having compatible avionics equipment.

KRM—A system which provides three-axis position indication, similar to ILS, used in eastern Europe.

Flight service station (FSS) VHF frequencies in the United States and Canada will be found above the navaid names. Frequencies shown are usually all in the 120-MHz range and are shown with the first two digits (12) omitted; 3.6 denotes 123.6 MHz.

Figure 13-4 has five samples of how FSS River Radio operates. In the first example, you will see that River VOR is on frequency 114.6, with the identification RIV. It has DME and will transmit and receive on 122.2 and 122.45 MHz. It also transmits on 114.6 MHz. In addition it has two-way high-frequency communications capability on 5680.

The flight route runs across Canyon VOR on 113.9 MHz with the identifier CNY. Note that it does not have DME because there is no small D before the frequency. Also note that River Radio remotes through it, transmitting on the VOR frequency and receiving on 122.1 MHz. The letter G following the frequency 122.1 indicates that it guards (listens to) that frequency but cannot transmit over it. The letter RIV following the G lets you know that you should use River Radio as the calling facility.

Sometimes you will find a *remote communications outlet* (RCO), here shown as diamond. This is not a VOR; hence, there is no VOR frequency, identifier, or Morse-code symbology, but you can see above the box that River Radio transmits and receives on 122.6 MHz, and the location of the antenna is shown by the dot enclosed in the circle.

You might run across an L/MF facility such as Phantom (364 MHz PTM) that is used by both River Radio on 122.3 MHz and Phantom Radio on 122.6 MHz.

Finally, selected VORs enable an FSS to transmit on the VOR frequency but do not have any receiving capability. Such a situation is illustrated at LAVA (115.3 MHz LVA).

The telephone symbol tells you that the facility has communications capabilities other than those shown on the charts. These will be found in the communications panel under the name of the facility. Transcribed weather broadcasts are indicated by the letters TWEB in parentheses over the name of the facility (Fig. 13-5). An asterisk (*) indicates that a facility's operation or service is not continuous.

As far as restricted airspace is concerned, it is important to recognize that the words and figures found near the restricted airspace block have a given order that will include the designation, both the upper and lower limits, the hours of operation, and the controlling agency. Many of them will have infrequent hours of operation and will list NOTAMs rather than days and times; check the current NOTAMs to see if these areas will be activated during the time you plan to be near the area.

Airports are depicted similar to the way they are on an airway or aeronautical chart; specific symbols can be seen in Fig. 13-6. An airport that does not have a Jeppesen approach chart is designated by printing the airport name in both uppercase and lowercase letters. The elevation shown below the name is in feet above mean sea level.

If an airport has a Jeppesen approach chart, the name of the location, by which it

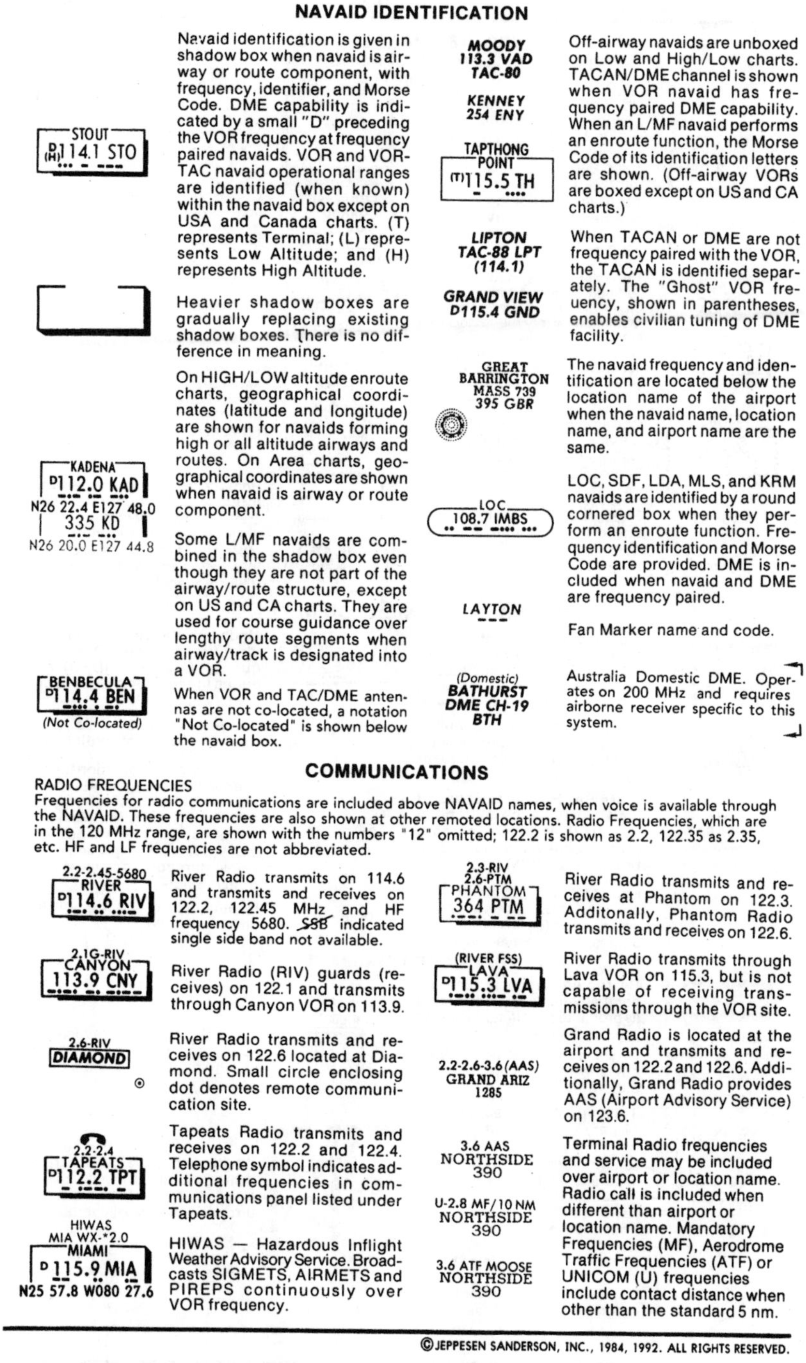

NAVAID IDENTIFICATION

Navaid identification is given in shadow box when navaid is airway or route component, with frequency, identifier, and Morse Code. DME capability is indicated by a small "D" preceding the VOR frequency at frequency paired navaids. VOR and VORTAC navaid operational ranges are identified (when known) within the navaid box except on USA and Canada charts. (T) represents Terminal; (L) represents Low Altitude; and (H) represents High Altitude.

STOUT
(H) 114.1 STO

Heavier shadow boxes are gradually replacing existing shadow boxes. There is no difference in meaning.

On HIGH/LOW altitude enroute charts, geographical coordinates (latitude and longitude) are shown for navaids forming high or all altitude airways and routes. On Area charts, geographical coordinates are shown when navaid is airway or route component.

KADENA
D 112.0 KAD
N26 22.4 E127 48.0
335 KD
N26 20.0 E127 44.8

Some L/MF navaids are combined in the shadow box even though they are not part of the airway/route structure, except on US and CA charts. They are used for course guidance over lengthy route segments when airway/track is designated into a VOR.

BENBECULA
D 114.4 BEN
(Not Co-located)

When VOR and TAC/DME antennas are not co-located, a notation "Not Co-located" is shown below the navaid box.

MOODY
113.3 VAD
TAC-80

KENNEY
254 ENY

TAPTHONG
POINT
(T) 115.5 TH

LIPTON
TAC-88 LPT
(114.1)

GRAND VIEW
D 115.4 GND

GREAT
BARRINGTON
MASS 739
395 GBR

LOC
108.7 IMBS

LAYTON

(Domestic)
BATHURST
DME CH-19
BTH

Off-airway navaids are unboxed on Low and High/Low charts. TACAN/DME channel is shown when VOR navaid has frequency paired DME capability. When an L/MF navaid performs an enroute function, the Morse Code of its identification letters are shown. (Off-airway VORs are boxed except on US and CA charts.)

When TACAN or DME are not frequency paired with the VOR, the TACAN is identified separately. The "Ghost" VOR frequency, shown in parentheses, enables civilian tuning of DME facility.

The navaid frequency and identification are located below the location name of the airport when the navaid name, location name, and airport name are the same.

LOC, SDF, LDA, MLS, and KRM navaids are identified by a round cornered box when they perform an enroute function. Frequency identification and Morse Code are provided. DME is included when navaid and DME are frequency paired.

Fan Marker name and code.

Australia Domestic DME. Operates on 200 MHz and requires airborne receiver specific to this system.

COMMUNICATIONS

RADIO FREQUENCIES
Frequencies for radio communications are included above NAVAID names, when voice is available through the NAVAID. These frequencies are also shown at other remoted locations. Radio Frequencies, which are in the 120 MHz range, are shown with the numbers "12" omitted; 122.2 is shown as 2.2, 122.35 as 2.35, etc. HF and LF frequencies are not abbreviated.

2.2-2.45-5680
RIVER
D 114.6 RIV

River Radio transmits on 114.6 and transmits and receives on 122.2, 122.45 MHz and HF frequency 5680. SSB indicated single side band not available.

2.1G-RIV
CANYON
113.9 CNY

River Radio (RIV) guards (receives) on 122.1 and transmits through Canyon VOR on 113.9.

2.6-RIV
DIAMOND

River Radio transmits and receives on 122.6 located at Diamond. Small circle enclosing dot denotes remote communication site.

2.2-2.4
TAPEATS
D 112.2 TPT

Tapeats Radio transmits and receives on 122.2 and 122.4. Telephone symbol indicates additional frequencies in communications panel listed under Tapeats.

HIWAS
MIA WX-*2.0
MIAMI
D 115.9 MIA
N25 57.8 W080 27.6

HIWAS — Hazardous Inflight Weather Advisory Service. Broadcasts SIGMETS, AIRMETS and PIREPS continuously over VOR frequency.

2.3-RIV
2.6-PTM
PHANTOM
364 PTM

River Radio transmits and receives at Phantom on 122.3. Additonally, Phantom Radio transmits and receives on 122.6.

(RIVER FSS)
LAVA
D 115.3 LVA

River Radio transmits through Lava VOR on 115.3, but is not capable of receiving transmissions through the VOR site.

2.2-2.6-3.6 (AAS)
GRAND ARIZ
1285

Grand Radio is located at the airport and transmits and receives on 122.2 and 122.6. Additionally, Grand Radio provides AAS (Airport Advisory Service) on 123.6.

3.6 AAS
NORTHSIDE
390

U-2.8 MF/10 NM
NORTHSIDE
390

3.6 ATF MOOSE
NORTHSIDE
390

Terminal Radio frequencies and service may be included over airport or location name. Radio call is included when different than airport or location name. Mandatory Frequencies (MF), Aerodrome Traffic Frequencies (ATF) or UNICOM (U) frequencies include contact distance when other than the standard 5 nm.

Fig. 13-4 Reproduced with permission of Jeppesen Sanderson, Inc. Not for use in navigation.

ENROUTE CHARTS

ENROUTE CHART LEGEND
COMMUNICATIONS
(continued)

DEN WX-*2.0
DENVER
ᴰ116.3 DEN
N39 51.6 W104 45.1

US "Enroute Flight Advisory Service". Ident of controlling station to call, using (name of station) FLIGHT WATCH on 122.0 MHz. Charted above VORs associated with controlling station and remoted outlets. Service is provided between 0600 and 2200 hours daily.

ADELAIDE RADIO
124.3

Call and frequencies of control or unit service. For use within geographical defined radio boundaries.

SOUTH EASTERN RADIO
| 2869 | 4678 |
| 5526 | 8876 |

VIRAC RADIO
CRYSTAL
116.1 CRT

The telephone symbol indicates additional communications may be found in the communications tabulation after the associated NAVAID or location name. Telephone symbol does not necessarily mean that voice is available through the NAVAID.

SYDNEY CONTROL
118.5 119.7
123.4 125.6

NASSAU RADIO E-CAR
124.2
| 5566 | 6537 |
| 8871 | 13344 |

Call and frequency of enroute service or control unit. SINGLE SIDE BAND capabilities are available unless specified otherwise.

SECTOR 2
MANILA CONTROL
119.3 126.1
128.2 130.1

Call and frequencies of Control Service for use within graphically portrayed Radio Frequency Sector Boundaries.

TORONTO(R)
(LONDON)
119.4

Remote air/ground antenna for direct communications with control center. Center is named in large type and name of remote site is in parentheses below followed by appropriate VHF frequencies.

BELGRADE
WX
(126.40)

Plain language inflight weather station with name and frequency.

CHICAGO
(CEDAR RAPIDS)
121.4

NAVAID/COMMUNICATION DATA

(May be Shutdown)

(May be Test Only)

(May not be Comsnd)

Operational status at date of publication. Refer to Chart NOTAMS for current status, including substitute routes for VOR and VORTAC shutdowns.

SAARBRUCKEN
343 S̲B̲N̲

Underline shown below navaid identifier, indicates Beat Frequency Oscillator (BFO) required to hear Morse Code identifier.

(TWEB)
MAYBE
326 MBY

(TWEB) indicates continuous automatic weather broadcast is provided on the facility frequency.

*

Asterisk indicates navaid operation or service not continuous.

(WX)
EAST BAY
362 EZB

Class SABH radio beacons of limited navigation suitability indicate their primary purpose of continuous automatic weather broadcast by (WX).

H + 04 & 15(1)

Marine beacon operation times. Transmission begins at 4 minutes past the hour and every 15 minutes thereafter in this illustration; other times will be indicated. Number in parentheses gives duration in minutes of transmission.

(R)

Enroute Radar capability. (All domestic U.S. centers are radar equipped so (R) is omitted from domestic U.S. center boxes.)

FOG:H + 02 & 08

Facility operates in fog only at times indicated.

RESTRICTED AIRSPACE

Restricted airspace. The accompanying label indicates it as prohibited, restricted, danger, etc. See below.

On some charts prohibited areas are shown by a cross-hatch pattern.

Training, Alert, Caution, and Military Operations Areas

R-6001
24000
GND
(JAX ARTCC)

On USA charts K (indicating USA) and parens around the designating letter are omitted.

CY(R)-4207 ◄— Country identifier, designation in parens, and number
FL 450 ◄— Upper Limit
GND ◄— Lower Limit
SR-SS — Hours active
(MSP ARTCC) ◄— Controlling Agency
(Limits may be tabulated)

When restricted airspace areas overlap, a line is shown on the outer edge of each area through the area of overlap.

●ED(R)-7
30000
GND

Dot indicates permanent activation on some chart series.

Fig. 13-5   Reproduced with permission of Jeppesen Sanderson, Inc. Not for use in navigation.

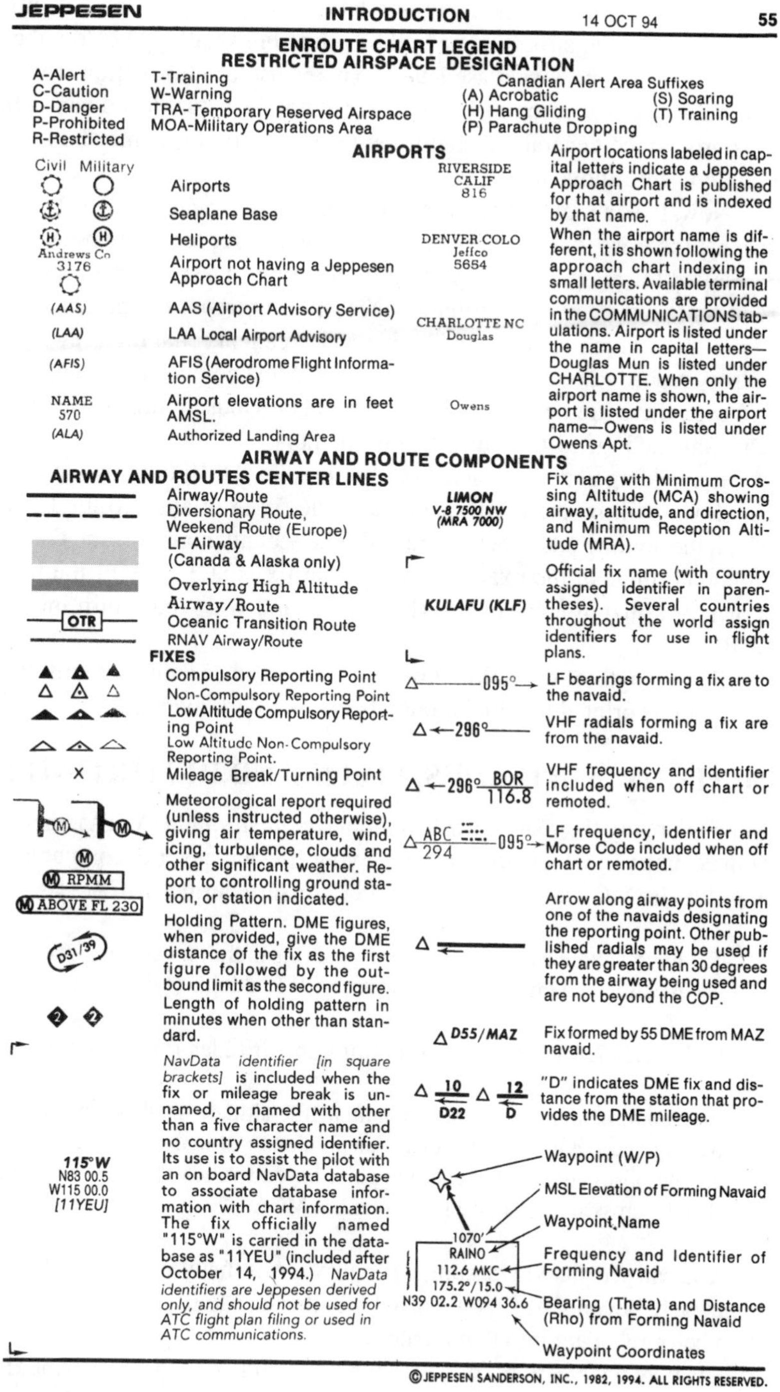

Road maps in the sky

ENROUTE CHART LEGEND
RESTRICTED AIRSPACE DESIGNATION

A-Alert
C-Caution
D-Danger
P-Prohibited
R-Restricted

T-Training
W-Warning
TRA- Temporary Reserved Airspace
MOA-Military Operations Area

Canadian Alert Area Suffixes
(A) Acrobatic   (S) Soaring
(H) Hang Gliding   (T) Training
(P) Parachute Dropping

AIRPORTS

Civil	Military		
○	○	Airports	RIVERSIDE CALIF 816
⚓	⚓	Seaplane Base	
Ⓗ	Ⓗ	Heliports	DENVER COLO Jeffco 5654
Andrews Cn 3176 ○		Airport not having a Jeppesen Approach Chart	
(AAS)		AAS (Airport Advisory Service)	
(LAA)		LAA Local Airport Advisory	CHARLOTTE NC Douglas
(AFIS)		AFIS (Aerodrome Flight Information Service)	
NAME 570		Airport elevations are in feet AMSL.	Owens
(ALA)		Authorized Landing Area	

Airport locations labeled in capital letters indicate a Jeppesen Approach Chart is published for that airport and is indexed by that name.

When the airport name is different, it is shown following the approach chart indexing in small letters. Available terminal communications are provided in the COMMUNICATIONS tabulations. Airport is listed under the name in capital letters—Douglas Mun is listed under CHARLOTTE. When only the airport name is shown, the airport is listed under the airport name—Owens is listed under Owens Apt.

AIRWAY AND ROUTE COMPONENTS

AIRWAY AND ROUTES CENTER LINES

———————	Airway/Route
— — — — —	Diversionary Route, Weekend Route (Europe)
▬▬▬▬▬	LF Airway (Canada & Alaska only)
	Overlying High Altitude Airway/Route
⊣OTR⊢	Oceanic Transition Route
	RNAV Airway/Route

FIXES

▲ ▲ ▲   Compulsory Reporting Point
△ △ △   Non-Compulsory Reporting Point
▲ ▲ ▲   Low Altitude Compulsory Reporting Point
△ △ △   Low Altitude Non-Compulsory Reporting Point.
X   Mileage Break/Turning Point

Ⓜ Ⓜ   Meteorological report required (unless instructed otherwise), giving air temperature, wind, icing, turbulence, clouds and other significant weather. Report to controlling ground station, or station indicated.

Ⓜ
Ⓜ RPMM
Ⓜ ABOVE FL 230

(D31/39)   Holding Pattern. DME figures, when provided, give the DME distance of the fix as the first figure followed by the outbound limit as the second figure. Length of holding pattern in minutes when other than standard.

NavData identifier [in square brackets] is included when the fix or mileage break is unnamed, or named with other than a five character name and no country assigned identifier. Its use is to assist the pilot with an on board NavData database to associate database information with chart information. The fix officially named "115°W" is carried in the database as "11YEU" (included after October 14, 1994.) NavData identifiers are Jeppesen derived only, and should not be used for ATC flight plan filing or used in ATC communications.

115°W
N83 00.5
W115 00.0
[11YEU]

LIMON
V-8 7500 NW
(MRA 7000)

Fix name with Minimum Crossing Altitude (MCA) showing airway, altitude, and direction, and Minimum Reception Altitude (MRA).

KULAFU (KLF)

Official fix name (with country assigned identifier in parentheses). Several countries throughout the world assign identifiers for use in flight plans.

△———— 095°→   LF bearings forming a fix are to the navaid.

△←—296°   VHF radials forming a fix are from the navaid.

△←—296° $\frac{BOR}{116.8}$ VHF frequency and identifier included when off chart or remoted.

△ $\frac{ABC \cdots}{294}$ 095°→   LF frequency, identifier and Morse Code included when off chart or remoted.

△⇐   Arrow along airway points from one of the navaids designating the reporting point. Other published radials may be used if they are greater than 30 degrees from the airway being used and are not beyond the COP.

△ D55/MAZ   Fix formed by 55 DME from MAZ navaid.

△ $\frac{10}{D22}$ △ $\frac{12}{D}$ "D" indicates DME fix and distance from the station that provides the DME mileage.

☆ → Waypoint (W/P)

1070' → MSL Elevation of Forming Navaid
RAINO → Waypoint Name
112.6 MKC → Frequency and Identifier of Forming Navaid
175.2°/15.0 → Bearing (Theta) and Distance (Rho) from Forming Navaid
N39 02.2 W094 36.6 → Waypoint Coordinates

Fig. 13-6   Reproduced with permission of Jeppesen Sanderson, Inc. Not for use in navigation.

is indexed, is printed all in uppercase letters. If the airport name is different from the location name, the airport name will be printed in small type below the location using both uppercase and lowercase letters. This is useful information if you know the airport name and its approximate location but not the actual listed name. In this instance, look around the general area until you locate the airport name and note the chart designation name above it.

Now, look about halfway down the left side of the page (Fig. 13-6). Here you can see that there are four different groups of symbols for reporting points listed as FIXES. These are for compulsory reporting points, on-request reporting points, low-altitude reporting points, and low-altitude noncompulsory reporting points.

With so much radar available that has excellent reliability, fewer and fewer compulsory reporting points are on the airways. Most compulsory points are at the VORs, and even these are becoming fewer in number. Unused information is usually forgotten; examine Fig. 13-6 to refresh your memory.

If a holding pattern depicted on the chart is a DME holding pattern, the first number shown will be the DME distance of the fix in relation to the DME facility upon which the holding pattern is predicated. The second number is the DME distance at the outbound limit. In the example shown, the fix is at 31 DME, the holding pattern is shown as utilizing nonstandard (left) turns, and you would turn inbound again at 39 DME.

If the length of the holding pattern will be other than standard, the time (in minutes) will be printed in white numerals inside a dark diamond.

MINIMUM ALTITUDES, FIXES, AND REPORTING POINTS

Although many fixes show a *minimum reception altitude* (MRA), there are many parts of the country in which you can fly all your life and never encounter a *minimum crossing altitude* (MCA). The pilot/controller glossary defines MCA:

> The lowest altitude at certain fixes at which an aircraft must cross when proceeding in the direction of a higher minimum enroute IFR altitude (MEA).

FAR 91.177, which deals with minimum altitudes for IFR operations states:

> (b) *Climb.* Climb to a higher minimum IFR altitude shall begin immediately after passing the point beyond which that minimum altitude applies, except that when ground obstructions intervene, the point beyond which the higher minimum applies shall be crossed at or above the applicable MCA.

You can see that the reasoning for an MCA is that you will find higher obstructions somewhere beyond the fix (and usually quite close to it), and you will want to be above them before you get into that territory.

LIMON intersection's MCA is explained in Fig. 13-6. The symbol will first show the airway on which the MCA is applicable, the altitude of the MCA, and the direction

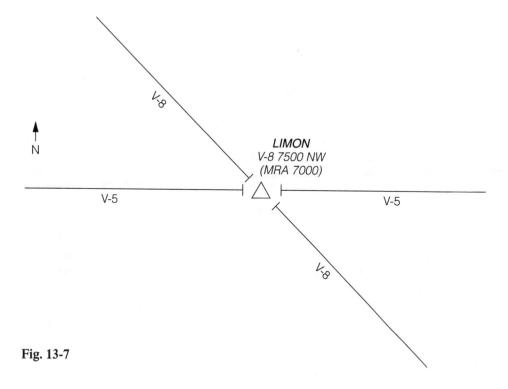

Fig. 13-7

of travel for which it is applicable. Figure 13-7 shows what LIMON might look like on a chart. Let's say that V-8 at LIMON is an NW/SE airway and you are eastbound on V-5, an E/W airway, planning to turn SE on V-8. In this case, the MCA would not apply to you.

If you were either westbound on V-5 and planning to turn to the northwest or you were northwestbound on V-8, the MCA would be in effect and would require crossing the fix (LIMON) at or above the MCA.

Many fixes are formed by a VOR nonairway radial that crosses an airway; take a look at the symbol about midway down the right-hand column of Fig. 13-6. In this case, the airway, which has an on-request reporting point on it, could be oriented in any direction and is not illustrated. The 296-degree radial from the BOR VOR (on VHF frequency 116.8) is not part of any airway, but it helps to identify the on-request reporting point. The VOR itself is off to the right of the on-request reporting point; once again, directions shown in regard to VORs are the radials FROM rather than the bearings TO the facility. Directions with regard to LF facilities, such as NDBs, are printed in green on the chart (as opposed to blue for VHF aids) and are bearings to the station.

If the fix is formed by a VOR radial or an LF bearing that is being remoted or is off the chart, the symbol will include not only the radial or bearing, but also the identifier of the VOR or LF facility above the line and the frequency below the line. You can see both of these illustrated in the case of BOR as explained above and by the LF facility ABC shown just below it.

Two on-request reporting-point symbols are shown a little farther down in the right-hand column of Fig. 13-6. The numbers are shown above the airway running through these points that indicate segment distances. The distance of the segment between the two on-request reporting points is 10 miles. The distance between the on-request reporting point and the next fix to the right (off the chart) is 12 miles. When you look below the course line, you see two more symbols. The one between the fixes is "D22" with a small arrow pointing to the left. This tells you that the left-hand fix (to which the arrow points) is 22 miles from the DME facility. The symbol on the right, a D with an arrow, tells you that the DME distance (from the DME facility) to the right-hand reporting point is the same as the segment distance printed above the course line, in this case, 12 miles.

Note the square star in the last illustration in Fig. 13-6. This is used to illustrate a *waypoint* (W/P) which is used in RNAV systems. These will be used more and more as GPS comes into play. The rest of the illustration indicates a waypoint that is formed in relation to a navigation facility such as a VOR. As we move more and more into GPS waypoints, all we will see are the latitude/longitude coordinates.

At the top of the left-hand column in Fig. 13-8, you can see that the airway and route designations are always shown in reverse (negative) type. About halfway down the left-hand column, take a look at some of the various ways to depict minimum enroute altitudes (MEAs). MEA is defined as follows:

MINIMUM ENROUTE IFR ALTITUDE—The lowest published altitude between radio fixes which assures acceptable navigational signal coverage and meets obstacle clearance requirements between those fixes. The MEA prescribed for a Federal airway or segment thereof, area navigation low or high route, or other direct route applies to the entire width of the airway, segment, or route.

In the United States, an MEA is depicted as either an altitude or flight level, and if a flight level, it will be designated with the letters FL preceding the numerals. At times, the MEA will be higher in one direction than in the other, in which case the altitudes will be shown with appropriate directional arrows.

A *minimum obstruction clearance altitude* (MOCA) is depicted with a T following the altitude, while a route *minimum off-route altitude* (MORA) is designated with a lowercase letter "a" following the altitude. What is the difference between the two? Here is MOCA from the pilot/controller glossary:

MINIMUM OBSTRUCTION CLEARANCE ALTITUDE—The lowest published altitude in effect between radio fixes on VOR airways, off-airway routes, or route segments which meets obstacle clearance requirements for the entire route segment and which assures acceptable navigational signal coverage only within 25 statute (22 nautical) miles of a VOR.

This means that if the route segment is more than 50 statute miles long and you opt for the MOCA, you might not have proper VOR reception for part of the flight. So, in effect, the MOCA is almost a last-resort altitude.

MORA is strictly a Jeppesen altitude. You won't find it in the ATC pilot/controller glossary. Jeppesen's definition is:

MINIMUM OFF-ROUTE ALTITUDE (MORA)—This is an altitude derived by Jeppesen. The [route] MORA provides reference point clearance within 10 nm of the route centerline (regardless of route width) and end fixes. A grid MORA altitude provides reference point clearance within the section outlined by latitude and longitude lines. MORA values clear all reference *points* by 1,000 feet in areas where the highest reference points are 5,000 feet MSL or lower. MORA values clear all reference points by 2,000 feet in areas where the highest reference points are 5,000 feet MSL or higher. When a MORA is shown along a route as "unknown" or within a grid as "unsurveyed," a MORA is not shown due to incomplete or insufficient information.

A broken section in the route indicates there is either a change in the MEA, MOCA, or MORA. It is there primarily to show a change in MEA. This symbol will be omitted at a facility.

OTHER SYMBOLS

The total mileage between facilities is shown inside a six-sided polygon that is positioned along and parallel to the centerline of the airway. When two or more airways share the same course, the polygon has directional pointers indicating the airway to which the mileage applies.

If the *changeover point* (COP) for the navigational radio is other than at the midpoint of the leg or at the turning point on the route, it will be shown by a Z-like symbol crossing the airway. (See Fig. 13-8: sixth item from the top right.) The numeral on each side of this symbol shows the distance from the respective facility, at which point you should change the navigational radio's frequency. By doing so, you will be assured of adequate navigational reception along the entire route segment.

Take a look at the upper portion of the left-hand column in Fig. 13-10. This area shows the airway navaid/reporting point bypass illustrations. These illustrations depict how routes are illustrated when they pass through facilities or intersections that are not required for that specific route. Locate the VOR symbol (third from the top); when a facility is used for a particular route, the route centerline ends at the outer circle of the facility symbol. It usually ends just short of the symbol, leaving enough room to show the outbound radial (as in the case of V-15). If the facility is not required, the airway centerline will be extended through the center of the symbol and no radial will be shown (as in the case of V-76). If a report is not required for one of the routes that pass through a reporting point, that route will be shown passing directly through the reporting point symbol, or the route will be shown as a semicircle so as not to fill in the center of an open symbol.

ENROUTE CHARTS

ENROUTE CHART LEGEND
AIRWAY INFORMATION

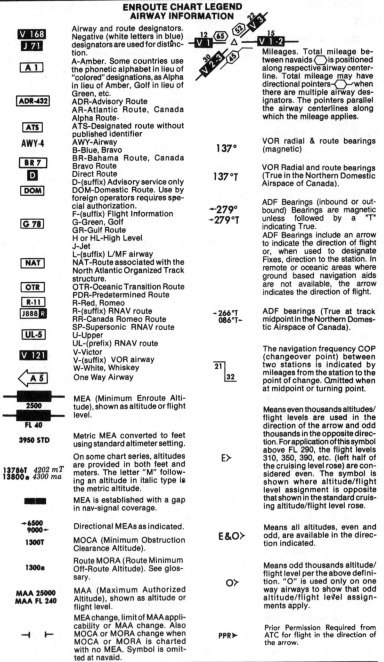

V 168
J 71
Airway and route designators. Negative (white letters in blue) designators are used for distinction.

A 1
A-Amber. Some countries use the phonetic alphabet in lieu of "colored" designations, as Alpha in lieu of Amber, Golf in lieu of Green, etc.

ADR-432
ADR-Advisory Route
AR-Atlantic Route, Canada
Alpha Route·

ATS
ATS-Designated route without published identifier

AWY-4
AWY-Airway
B-Blue, Bravo
BR-Bahama Route, Canada

BR 7
Bravo Route

D
Direct Route
D-(suffix) Advisory service only

DOM
DOM-Domestic Route. Use by foreign operators requires special authorization.
F-(suffix) Flight Information

G 78
G-Green, Golf
GR-Gulf Route
H or HL-High Level
J-Jet
L-(suffix) L/MF airway

NAT
NAT-Route associated with the North Atlantic Organized Track structure.

OTR
OTR-Oceanic Transition Route
PDR-Predetermined Route

R-11
R-Red, Romeo

J888 R
R-(suffix) RNAV route
RR-Canada Romeo Route
SP-Supersonic RNAV route

UL-5
U-Upper
UL-(prefix) RNAV route

V 121
V-Victor
V-(suffix) VOR airway
W-White, Whiskey

◁A 5
One Way Airway

2500
MEA (Minimum Enroute Altitude), shown as altitude or flight level.

FL 40

3950 STD
Metric MEA converted to feet using standard altimeter setting.

13786T   4202 mT
13800ᴀ   4300 ma
On some chart series, altitudes are provided in both feet and meters. The letter "M" following an altitude in italic type is the metric altitude.

MEA is established with a gap in nav-signal coverage.

→6500
9000←
Directional MEAs as indicated.

1300T
MOCA (Minimum Obstruction Clearance Altitude).

1300ᴀ
Route MORA (Route Minimum Off-Route Altitude). See glossary.

MAA 25000
MAA FL 240
MAA (Maximum Authorized Altitude), shown as altitude or flight level.

⊣ ⊢
MEA change, limit of MAA applicability or MAA change. Also MOCA or MORA change when MOCA or MORA is charted with no MEA. Symbol is omitted at navaid.

Mileages. Total mileage between navaids ◯ is positioned along respective airway centerline. Total mileage may have directional pointers—◯— when there are multiple airway designators. The pointers parallel the airway centerlines along which the mileage applies.

137°
VOR radial & route bearings (magnetic)

137°T
VOR Radial and route bearings (True in the Northern Domestic Airspace of Canada).

←279°
←279°T
ADF Bearings (inbound or outbound) Bearings are magnetic unless followed by a "T" indicating True.
ADF Bearings include an arrow to indicate the direction of flight or, when used to designate Fixes, direction to the station. In remote or oceanic areas where ground based navigation aids are not available, the arrow indicates the direction of flight.

←266°T
086°T←
ADF bearings (True at track midpoint in the Northern Domestic Airspace of Canada).

21
32
The navigation frequency COP (changeover point) between two stations is indicated by mileages from the station to the point of change. Omitted when at midpoint or turning point.

E>
Means even thousands altitudes/flight levels are used in the direction of the arrow and odd thousands in the opposite direction. For application of this symbol above FL 290, the flight levels 310, 350, 390, etc. (left half of the cruising level rose) are considered even. The symbol is shown where altitude/flight level assignment is opposite that shown in the standard cruising altitude/flight level rose.

E&O>
Means all altitudes, even and odd, are available in the direction indicated.

O>
Means odd thousands altitude/flight level per the above definition. "O" is used only on one way airways to show that odd altitude/flight level assignments apply.

PPR▶
Prior Permission Required from ATC for flight in the direction of the arrow.

© JEPPESEN SANDERSON, INC., 1982, 1994. ALL RIGHTS RESERVED.

Fig. 13-8 Reproduced with permission of Jeppesen Sanderson, Inc. Not for use in navigation.

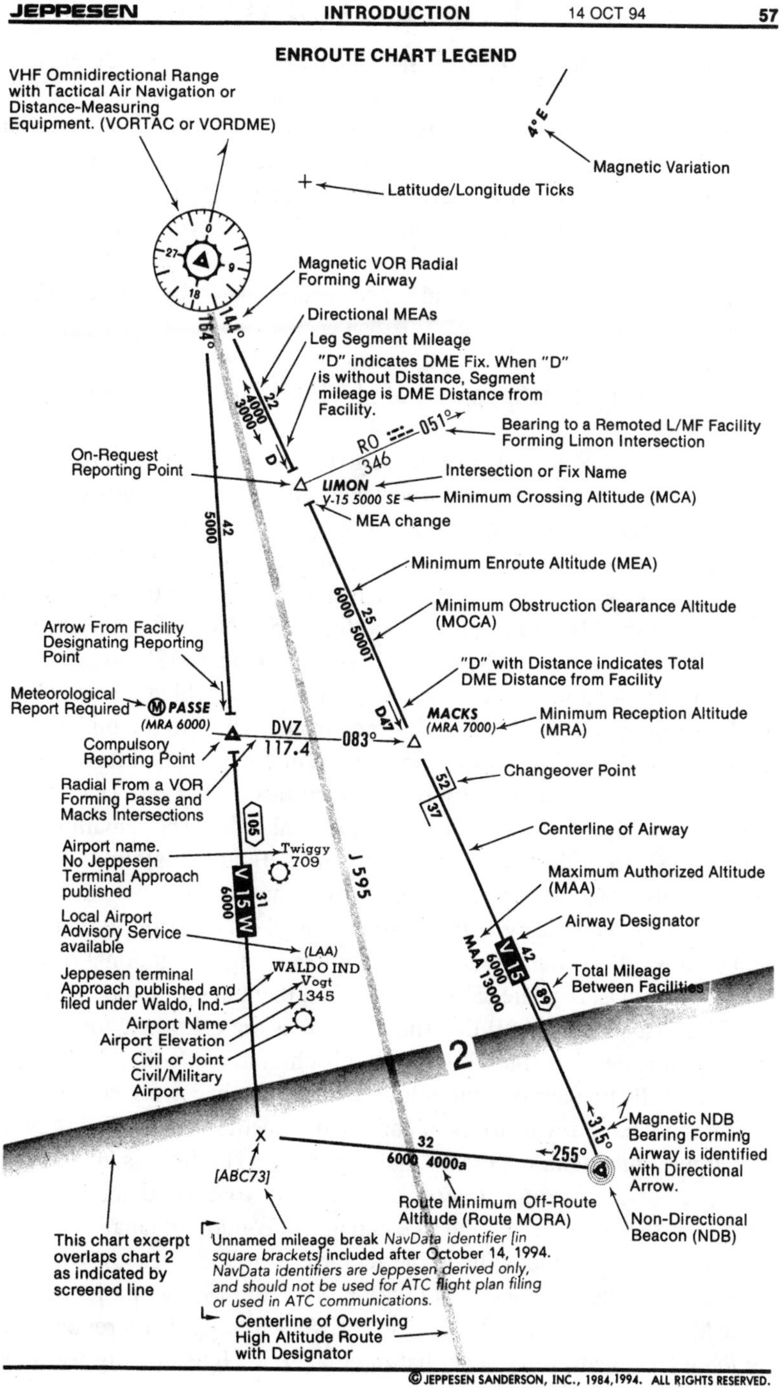

Other symbols

ENROUTE CHART LEGEND

VHF Omnidirectional Range with Tactical Air Navigation or Distance-Measuring Equipment. (VORTAC or VORDME)

Magnetic Variation

Latitude/Longitude Ticks

Magnetic VOR Radial Forming Airway

Directional MEAs

Leg Segment Mileage

"D" indicates DME Fix. When "D" is without Distance, Segment mileage is DME Distance from Facility.

Bearing to a Remoted L/MF Facility Forming Limon Intersection

On-Request Reporting Point

Intersection or Fix Name

LIMON

V-15 5000 SE — Minimum Crossing Altitude (MCA)

MEA change

Minimum Enroute Altitude (MEA)

Minimum Obstruction Clearance Altitude (MOCA)

Arrow From Facility Designating Reporting Point

"D" with Distance indicates Total DME Distance from Facility

Meteorological Report Required — **PASSE** (MRA 6000)

MACKS (MRA 7000) — Minimum Reception Altitude (MRA)

Compulsory Reporting Point

DVZ 117.4 083°

Changeover Point

Radial From a VOR Forming Passe and Macks Intersections

Centerline of Airway

Airport name. No Jeppesen Terminal Approach published

Twiggy 709

Maximum Authorized Altitude (MAA)

Airway Designator

Local Airport Advisory Service available

(LAA)

Total Mileage Between Facilities

Jeppesen terminal Approach published and filed under Waldo, Ind.

WALDO IND Vogt 1345

Airport Name Airport Elevation Civil or Joint Civil/Military Airport

2

Magnetic NDB Bearing Forming Airway is identified with Directional Arrow.

X

[ABC73]

32 6000 4000a

255°

315°

Route Minimum Off-Route Altitude (Route MORA)

Non-Directional Beacon (NDB)

This chart excerpt overlaps chart 2 as indicated by screened line

Unnamed mileage break *NavData identifier [in square brackets]* included after October 14, 1994. *NavData* identifiers are Jeppesen derived only, and should not be used for ATC flight plan filing or used in ATC communications.

Centerline of Overlying High Altitude Route with Designator

Fig. 13-9 Reproduced with permission of Jeppesen Sanderson, Inc. Not for use in navigation.

FITTING ALL THE PIECES TOGETHER

Until now, we've been looking at individual symbols. Let's put them all together to see how they might look as part of a chart; examine Fig. 13-9.

At the top you will see latitude (horizontal) and longitude (vertical) tick marks along the chart edges. To help further, these ticks are shown as small crosses (plus marks) along the face of the charts indicating each half degree of latitude or longitude.

Look down the airway marked V-15W. First off, you can see that it's 42 miles to PASSE, which is a compulsory reporting point when you are not in radar contact. PASSE requires a meteorological report as designated by the M within the circle preceding the name.

PASSE is formed by the intersection of V-15W and the 083-degree radial of the DVZ VOR, which has a frequency of 117.4 MHz and which lies somewhere off the left of the chart.

From the VOR at the top of the page to PASSE, the MEA is 5,000 feet, as you can see by the numerals below the airway centerline. The small arrow just prior to PASSE points from the facility that designates the reporting point.

The perpendicular stubs crossing the airway on either side of the fix at PASSE indicate that the MEA is different on each side. Looking to the southeast of PASSE, you will see that the MEA goes up to 6,000 feet MSL. Notice the absence of those stubs at MACKS (over on V-15) where the MEA is 6,000 feet MSL on both sides of the fix.

Moving along to the southeast side of PASSE (which has an MRA of 6,000 feet MSL, by the way), note that the distance from PASSE to the mileage break (indicated by the X) is 31 nautical miles. The 105 within the six-sided figure tells you that it's a total of 105 nautical miles between the facilities on V-15W. The mileage segments to the break, 42 and 31, only add up to 73 nautical miles. The remaining 32-mile segment extends ESE from the mileage break to an NDB station along the route. The mileage break in this instance also indicates a turn in the airway.

The alphanumerics within the square brackets pointing to that mileage break are Jeppesen NavData identifiers for those pilots using navigational receivers that rely on Jeppesen NavData update cards. More about them in the chapters on loran-C and GPS.

The shaded (screened) line running across the chart just above the mileage break symbol indicates that chart 2 overlaps this chart at that point.

As for the two airport symbols shown on the chart, you can determine that Jeppesen does not have any instrument approach procedure chart of Twiggy Airport because the airport name is in uppercase and lowercase. The field is 709 feet MSL. Jeppesen does provide an instrument approach chart for Vogt Municipal. Vogt is at 1,345 feet MSL, and the chart will be found listed under Waldo, Indiana.

The bearing to the NDB is the reciprocal of 255 degrees, which is 075 degrees. The MEA on this route segment is still 6,000 feet MSL, while Jeppesen has included a route MORA of 4,000 feet MSL. The beacon is a compulsory reporting point. The note by the NDB identifier tells us that the magnetic NDB bearing forming the airway is identified with directional arrows.

The NDB is not only part of V-15W, but also helps to form V-15. The bearing from it on V-15 northbound is 315 degrees. It is 42 nautical miles from the NDB to MACKS intersection, which has an MRA of 7,000 feet MSL. MACKS is formed by V-15 and the 083-degree radial of DVZ VOR. The changeover point from the NDB to the unnamed VOR is 37 nautical miles northwest of the NDB and 52 nautical miles southeast of the VOR. The total distance between these facilities can be found by adding these two changeover point mileages together, adding up the three route segments (22, 25, and 42), or simply by reading the overall distance shown inside the six-sided figure (89).

You can also find a *maximum authorized altitude* (MAA) symbol on this illustration. It's beneath the 6,000-foot MEA below the V-15 airway identifier. The MAA (defined in the glossary of this book) on this airway is 13,000 feet.

Moving up now, past the MACKS on-request reporting-point symbol, you will notice an arrow pointing from the VOR to the fix symbol with D47 below it. This indicates that you can determine the fix by the DME distance from the facility to the fix, which is 47 nautical miles. You can also add the two segment distances of 22 and 25 nautical miles to arrive at the same figure.

Proceeding northwest from MACKS, note that the MEA of 6,000 feet MSL is followed by 5000T, which is the MOCA between MACKS and LIMON. The stubs at LIMON indicate an MEA change similar to that at PASSE. Not only is 5,000 feet MSL the MOCA between LIMON and MACKS, but it is also the MCA at LIMON when heading southeast, as indicated by the wording V-15 5000 SE found under the same LIMON.

Northwest of LIMON, you will see another arrow from the VOR with the letter D below it, indicating that the DME distance from the VOR to LIMON is the same as the segment distance of 22 miles. LIMON is formed by the airway V-15 (the 144-degree radial of the VOR) and the 051-degree bearing to a remote L/MF facility that uses the identifier RO and the frequency 346 MHz. The short line with the small arrow following the bearing indicates that the L/MF facility is either remoted or off the right side of the chart.

Directional MEAs exist northwest of LIMON: 3,000 feet MSL heading toward the VOR and 4,000 feet MSL heading away from the VOR toward LIMON.

Refer to Fig. 13-10 to continue the discussion of enroute charts.

A time zone boundary is indicated by a line of small Ts. This is useful information because the time zones wander around the chart, and you'd hate to arrive somewhere thinking it was 4:30 p.m. only to find that you were in the wrong time zone and everything closed up half an hour ago because it's really 5:30.

The lateral limits of the Class B airspace are shown as a waffled pattern of light blue/gray.

Look at the upper left-hand column in Fig. 13-11; a small grid shows shorelines and latitude/longitude lines. Notice the numbers 62, 75 (with a plus/minus sign), and 28 superimposed on the grids. This is Jeppesen's way of indicating the MORA for each section of the grid. In this case, the left grid section has a MORA of 6,200 feet MSL, the right section has a MORA of 2,800 feet MSL, while the center section has a MORA that is believed not to exceed 7,500 feet MSL, as depicted by the plus/minus sign (±).

ENROUTE CHART LEGEND

AIRWAY NAVAID/REPORTING POINT BY-PASS

When an airway passes over or turns at a navaid or reporting point, but the navaid is not to be utilized for course guidance and/or no report is required, the airway centerline passes around the symbol. In cases where a by-pass symbol cannot be used, an explanatory note is included.

Airway J-26 does not utilize the navaid or reporting point.

Airway J-14 turns at the navaid or reporting point but does not utilize them. A mileage break "X" is included to further indicate a turn point.

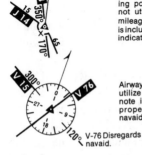

Airway V-76 does not utilize the navaid. A note indicating the proper use of the navaid is included.

V-76 Disregards navaid.

V-76 Disregards Int.

Airway V-76 does not utilize the Int. A note indicating the proper use of the Int is included.

BOUNDARIES

▦▦▦▦▦▦	ADIZ, DEWIZ and CADIZ
•••••••••———	FIR, UIR, ARTCC or OCA boundary.
— · · — · · —	International boundary.
⊢—⊢—⊢—⊢—	Time zone boundary.
QNH / QNE	QNH/QNE-boundaries.

ALTITUDE LIMITS AND TYPES OF CONTROL

$\frac{4000}{\text{CTR, ATZ, TIZ}}$	CTR-Control Zone ATZ-Aerodrome Traffic Zone TIZ-Traffic Information Zone
$\frac{\text{FL 360}}{\text{UTA}}$	UTA-Upper Control Area
$\frac{\text{FL 70}}{4000}$ TMA	TMA-Terminal Control Area OCTA-Oceanic Control Area

CONTROLLED AIRSPACE

Controlled airspace shown in white.
Uncontrolled airspace shown as a tint.

Controlled airway/route.

Uncontrolled airway or advisory route.

Control Area boundary within controlled airspace (CTA, TMA).

U.S. Class B airspace. Waffle screen shows lateral limits.

Radio Frequency Sector Boundary.

Radio boundaries of .control or service unit.

Boundaries within TMAs or CTAs defining different altitude limits and/or sectorizations.

U.S. special VFR weather minimums for fixed wing aircraft are not authorized within the lateral boundaries of the surface areas of Class B, Class C, Class D, or Class E airspace designated for an airport.
Australia Mandatory Traffic Area. Traffic information is exchanged while operating to or from an airport without an operating control tower within the area.

Control Zone or Aerodrome Traffic Zone (controlled).

Aerodrome Traffic Zone (no control). Aircraft broadcast intentions on standard enroute frequency, and listen on same, when within such zones.
Japan Information Zone (no control) within which special VFR may be cleared by an air-ground station.

U.S. Class C airspace.

Canada Class C airspace.

ICAO AIRSPACE CLASSIFICATIONS

Airspace classification is designated by the letters **(A)** thru **(G)**. Classification **(A)** represents the highest level of control and **(G)** represents uncontrolled airspace. The definitions of each classification is found in the Glossary portion of this section and the Enroute and Air Traffic Control section of this manual. The airspace classification letter is displayed in association with the airspace type and vertical limits.

TMA	CTA
FL 145-165 **(A)**	FL 145-165 **(A)**
FL 50-145 **(D)**	TMA
	5000-FL 145 **(D)**
	CTR
FL 45	GND-5000 **(E)**
CTR **(E)**	

CTA**(A)**/UTA**(A)**
(UP TO FL 195**(D)**)

Fig. 13-10

Fitting all the pieces together

ENROUTE CHART LEGEND

ORIENTATION

Grid shown at the intersection of units of latitude and longitude or by complete line.

Magnetic variation isogonic lines are indicated at the edge of the chart or are extended fully across the chart in a continuous dashed line.

Shorelines and large inland lakes are shown.

Grid Minimum Off-Route Altitude (Grid MORA) in hundreds of feet provides reference point clearance within the section outlined by latitude and longitude lines. Grid MORA values followed by a ± denote doubtful accuracy, but are believed to provide sufficient reference point clearance.

BORDER INFORMATION

This area overlapped by chart indicated.

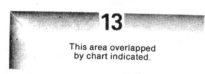

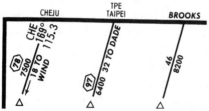

To Notes: Name outside the neatline is the next airway navaid to which the total mileage is given. Navaid identification is shown on all charts except the US(LO) and Canada/Alaska chart series. Reporting point name is shown when it is the airway termination.

To Notes: Name inside the neatline is the first reporting point outside the chart coverage to which the mileage and MEA are shown..

Airway lead information: The frequency and identifier of an off-chart navaid are shown when the navaid designates an on-chart reporting point, changeover point or course change.

MISCELLANEOUS

Outline indicates coverage of separate area chart. Information within this outline for terminal operation, may be skeletonized.

The area chart should be referred to if departure or destination airport is within this boundary to insure pertinent information is available.

On Enroute chart coverage diagrams, shaded symbol denotes Area chart coverage. Area chart name is included with shaded symbol.

Outline indicates an area covered elsewhere on the same or adjoining chart in enlarged scale. Information within this outline may be skeletonized.

Ball Flags: Number or letter symbol used to index information not shown at the point of applicability, but carried in a like-identified note within the same panel.

Reference number for INS Coordinates. These coordinates are tabulated elsewhere on the chart and identified in a like manner.

Fig. 13-11

ENROUTE CHARTS

ENROUTE CHART LEGEND

U.S. SERIES 800 AND 900 DESIGNATED RNAV ROUTES

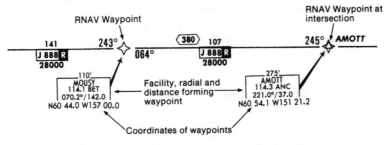

AUSTRALIA AND CANADA T RNAV ROUTES

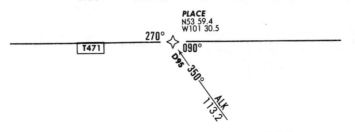

Fig. 13-12 Reproduced with permission of Jeppesen Sanderson, Inc. Not for use in navigation.

This last part is significant: There are times when Jeppesen receives terrain height information where the values are given to them as plus or minus so many feet. In cases like this, Jeppesen will take the highest value and include it in the MORA with the plus/minus figure (±) to indicate that it is not an exact altitude. Because Jeppesen has used the highest elevation provided, they are confident that the terrain does not enter the 1,000- or 2,000-foot clearance space that the MORA is trying to achieve.

Look at the border information given at the bottom of the left-hand column. A name in the margin is the "next airway facility to which the total mileage is given."

Among the examples illustrated, you will see both "18 to WIND" and "32 to DADE," with respective MEAs. Outside the margin, you will see CHEJU and TAIPEI to indicate the next airway facility. The identifier and frequency of CHEJU indicate that the VOR designates an "on-chart reporting point, changeover point, or course change."

Note the next-to-last item on the right. Many times there is too much information to put on the chart; at least it's not possible to put it directly alongside the symbol to which it is referring. Other times the same information might apply to more than one area on the same chart. In these cases, it will be indicated by a number or letter in reverse print, called *ball flags*. When you see one or more of these symbols, you will find the information in a nearby box.

134

Notice the small blue box with DENVER inside it on the right side of Fig. 13-11. This symbol indicates that an area chart is available for that area.

Finalizing this chapter, the square-shaped stars in Fig. 13-12 once again illustrate how Jeppesen presents RNAV waypoints, specifically GPS waypoints (see chapter 27).

CHAPTER QUIZ

1. Jeppesen enroute charts are not all drawn to the same scale.

   True _____False _____

2. What does two numerals separated by a period (such as 2.2) over a communication block indicate?

3. Why are some airport names printed in all uppercase letters, while others are printed in both uppercase and lowercase letters?

4. A compulsory reporting point is indicated by a _____.

5. What would the following number and letter combinations mean when printed below an intersection name?

   V-5 8500 SE

   (MRA 6000)

6. The following numerals are inside a holding pattern symbol. What do they designate?

   25/38

7. The MEA assures two things. What are they?

8. How does an MEA differ from a MOCA?

Answers are in the appendix.

14
Area charts, SIDs, STARs, Class B, profile descents, and charted visual approaches

ALTHOUGH IT SOUNDS LIKE THIS CHAPTER IS GOING TO BE COVERING A LOT of ground, it is actually going to just hit the highlights of a lot of subject matter because most of the symbology has been discussed.

AREA CHARTS EASE CLUTTER

Recall that area charts are large-scale charts for high-density areas. By using them, pilots arriving or departing from airports within these areas will have all the information they need without cluttering up the enroute chart.

The lower section of Fig. 14-1 shows extra symbols that are found on the area charts. There is a communications section for the major airports shown on each chart. Also, major airports are illustrated by airport symbols that show runways. If the departure and arrival routes are different, the departure route is indicated by a solid line with an arrow, while the approach route uses a dashed line with an arrow. If the arrival and departure routings are the same, a heavy solid line is used without the arrow.

The area chart acts as a form of transition chart between the enroute and the approach charts. If the terrain rises above 4,000 feet above the main airport on the chart, this information may be shown by depicting the terrain. When shown, it will be in one of two forms.

Prior to June 24, 1994, *area minimum altitudes* (AMAs) are something like MORAs, except they are not depicted in latitude/longitude grids. Instead, a general layout of the terrain is depicted (Fig. 14-2). The different heights of the terrain are shown by gradient tints *of green*. The AMA is shown within the different tinted sections, or envelopes, the same way that the grid MORA is shown on the enroute charts, with the larger of the numerals depicting thousands of feet and the smaller numerals depicting hundreds of feet.

As in the MORA altitudes, values of 5,000 feet or less allow for a 1,000-foot obstruction clearance, while values above 5,000 feet will clear obstructions within that area by 2,000 feet. Sometimes the AMA value will be higher than the MEA for a specific area because the MEA is only for the terrain beneath the airway itself.

On charts printed after June 24, 1994, the terrain will be shown in brown tints, and the heights (in mean sea level) will be printed along the terrain contour lines. The highest terrain in the specific contour area may be indicated by a dot and black print, but, and this is very important, these contour areas are for general information only. Manmade obstacles are not indicated, nor are all of the terrain heights. Read what Jeppesen says about it in the note alongside the symbols for the generalized terrain contours. These figures are for general information only.

As a rule, these terrain features will only be found on charts where some of the terrain might be higher than 4,000 feet above the area surface.

DME circles are drawn around certain major airports, with specific radials drawn on them. These are for reference points in relation to the AMA envelopes. Figure 14-3, the San Francisco Area Chart 10-1, shows this information.

Three major airports are depicted on this chart: Oakland, San Francisco, and San Jose. More than a dozen other fields are shown. Some of those within the SFO Class B airspace include Navy Moffett, Palo Alto, San Carlos, and Hayward.

That circle of green dots around SFO can be explained by referring to Fig. 13-10 and looking halfway down the right-hand column: This symbol is used to designate United States Class B, C, D, or E airspace within which special VFR weather minimums for fixed-wing aircraft are not authorized.

Runways at the major airports are depicted on the *area* chart, as are the ILS approaches at those airports on the chart that have an ILS available. Study the chart during preflight or during enroute cruise because by the time you get there, it will be too late.

ENROUTE CHART LEGEND
HIGH ALTITUDE CHARTS

The following legend, applicable to High Altitude Charts only, is in addition to the preceding legend. Many items in the preceding legend are also applicable to the High Altitude Charts.

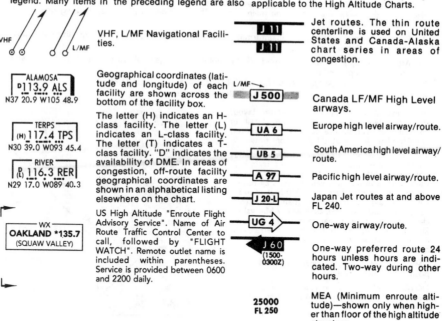

VHF, L/MF Navigational Facilities.

Geographical coordinates (latitude and longitude) of each facility are shown across the bottom of the facility box.

The letter (H) indicates an H-class facility. The letter (L) indicates an L-class facility. The letter (T) indicates a T-class facility. "D" indicates the availability of DME. In areas of congestion, off-route facility geographical coordinates are shown in an alphabetical listing elsewhere on the chart.

US High Altitude "Enroute Flight Advisory Service". Name of Air Route Traffic Control Center to call, followed by "FLIGHT WATCH". Remote outlet name is included within parentheses. Service is provided between 0600 and 2200 daily.

Jet routes. The thin route centerline is used on United States and Canada-Alaska chart series in areas of congestion.

Canada LF/MF High Level airways.

Europe high level airway/route.

South America high level airway/route.

Pacific high level airway/route.

Japan Jet routes at and above FL 240.

One-way airway/route.

One-way preferred route 24 hours unless hours are indicated. Two-way during other hours.

MEA (Minimum enroute altitude)—shown only when higher than floor of the high altitude structure.

AREA CHARTS

The following legend, applicable to Area Charts only, is in addition to the preceding legends. Many items in the preceding legends are also applicable to the Area Charts.

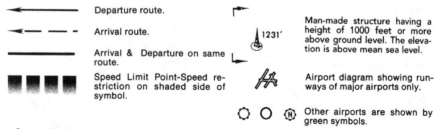

Departure route.

Arrival route.

Arrival & Departure on same route.

Speed Limit Point-Speed restriction on shaded side of symbol.

Man-made structure having a height of 1000 feet or more above ground level. The elevation is above mean sea level.

Airport diagram showing runways of major airports only.

Other airports are shown by green symbols.

Communications frequencies for the major airports shown on an area chart are given in a block as illustrated below.

	App(R)	Dep(R)	Twr	Gnd	ATIS
Chicago-Midway	Chicago 119.35	Chicago 119.35	118.7	121.7 121.85 C	120.05
Chicago O'Hare Int'l	Chicago 119.0	Chicago (340°-159°) 125.0 (160°-219°) 127.4 (220°-339°) 125.4	(N) 118.1 (S) 120.75	121.9 121.6 Cpt	135.15

Fig. 14-1

TERRAIN INFORMATION

Terrain information may be depicted on area charts when terrain within the area chart coverage rises more than 4000 feet above the main airport. This information is portrayed using one of the two following methods:

1) Prior to June 24, 1994, terrain information was depicted as Area Minimum Altitude (AMA) envelopes printed in green.

2) After June 24, 1994 AMAs will gradually be replaced with generalized contour lines, values and gradient tints printed in brown.

AREA MINIMUM ALTITUDE (AMA) ENVELOPES
(Prior to June 24, 1994)

AMA envelopes portray an exaggerated layout of terrain when compared to the detail of contour lines. Terrain rise between two charted envelope lines is indicated by gradient tints.

The area between each envelope line includes an AMA figure which represents the terrain high point/man-made structure clearance altitude for the envelope area. AMA values clears all terrain and man-made structures by 1000 feet in areas where the highest terrain and man-made structures are 5000 feet MSL or lower. AMA values clear all terrain and man-made structures by 2000 feet in areas where the highest terrain and man-made structures are 5001 feet MSL or higher.

DME arcs and radials are included for relating position to AMA envelope.

NOTE: An MEA may be lower than an AMA because of locally lower terrain beneath an airway.

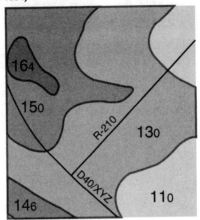

GENERALIZED TERRAIN CONTOURS
(After June 24, 1994)

Generalized terrain contour lines and contour values are depicted. Gradient tints indicate the elevation change between contour intervals. Contour lines, values and tints are printed in brown. Within the highest contour interval some, but not all, terrain high points may be included along with their elevation above mean sea level.

THE TERRAIN CONTOUR INFORMATION DEPICTED DOES NOT ASSURE CLEARANCE ABOVE OR AROUND TERRAIN OR MAN-MADE STRUCTURES. THERE MAY BE HIGHER UNCHARTED TERRAIN OR MAN-MADE STRUCTURES WITHIN THE SAME VICINITY. TERRAIN CONTOUR INFORMATION IS USEFUL FOR ORIENTATION AND GENERAL VISUALIZATION OF TERRAIN. IT DOES NOT REPLACE THE MINIMUM ALTITUDES DICTATED BY THE AIRWAY AND AIR ROUTE STRUCTURE. Furthermore, the absence of terrain contour information does not ensure the absence of terrain or structures.

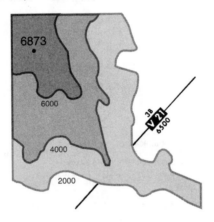

Fig. 14-2 Reproduced with permission of Jeppesen Sanderson, Inc. Not for use in navigation.

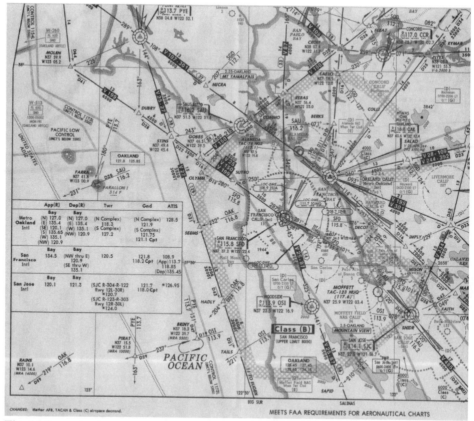

Fig. 14-3 Reproduced with permission of Jeppesen Sanderson, Inc. Not for use in navigation. Reduced image for reproduction.
© JEPPESEN SANDERSON, INC. 1984, 1995. ALL RIGHTS RESERVED.

THE CLASS B TRAP

There is a trap in the Class B procedures for unwary IFR pilots. Refer to Fig. 14-4, the San Francisco (B) Chart 10-1A.

If you're like me, you probably don't like Class B terminal areas. They're too confusing the way they're designed, and if you're operating VFR, you're spending more time looking at the chart to be sure that you're within the proper airspace than you are looking outside for traffic. For that reason alone I'd rather file IFR. Here's where the trap comes in.

Each area of Class B has two figures in it, one above and one below a line. The figure above the line is the top of the Class B airspace for that sector. In other words, if you're flying above 8,000 feet, you're legally above the San Francisco Class B area and have nothing to worry about.

It's the lower number that's the most confusing. This is the floor of Class B for that sector. If you're below that floor, you're also legally clear; however, if you're operat-

(B) TCA

JEPPESEN   23 JUL 93 (10-1A)   **SAN FRANCISCO, CALIF**

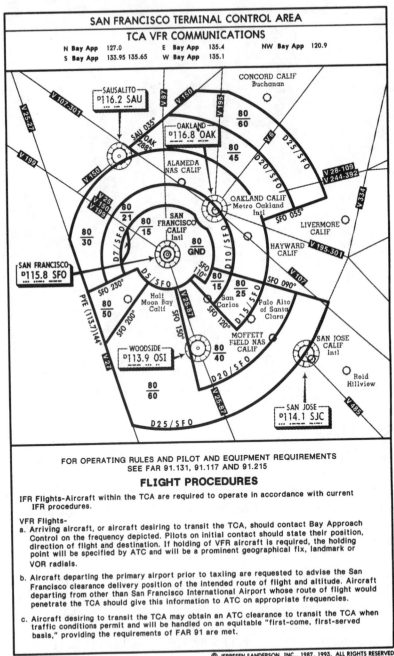

SAN FRANCISCO TERMINAL CONTROL AREA

TCA VFR COMMUNICATIONS

N Bay App 127.0   E Bay App 135.4   NW Bay App 120.9
S Bay App 133.95 135.65   W Bay App 135.1

FOR OPERATING RULES AND PILOT AND EQUIPMENT REQUIREMENTS
SEE FAR 91.131, 91.117 AND 91.215

FLIGHT PROCEDURES

IFR Flights-Aircraft within the TCA are required to operate in accordance with current IFR procedures.

VFR Flights-
a. Arriving aircraft, or aircraft desiring to transit the TCA, should contact Bay Approach Control on the frequency depicted. Pilots on initial contact should state their position, direction of flight and destination. If holding of VFR aircraft is required, the holding point will be specified by ATC and will be a prominent geographical fix, landmark or VOR radials.

b. Aircraft departing the primary airport prior to taxiing are requested to advise the San Francisco clearance delivery position of the intended route of flight and altitude. Aircraft departing from other than San Francisco International Airport whose route of flight would penetrate the TCA should give this information to ATC on appropriate frequencies.

c. Aircraft desiring to transit the TCA may obtain an ATC clearance to transit the TCA when traffic conditions permit and will be handled on an equitable "first-come, first-served basis," providing the requirements of FAR 91 are met.

CHANGES: Airspace reclassification.

Fig. 14-4 Reproduced with permission of Jeppesen Sanderson, Inc. Not for use in navigation.

ing IFR, and have been cleared for a visual approach, watch out. You're not allowed to descend below the floor of the Class B airspace on a visual approach. That rule is there to protect the VFR aircraft that might be flying around just under the floor. There is no floor once you're inside the traffic area or thereabouts. As you can see in the illustration, the floor is the ground all around SFO, for a distance of from 5 to 7 DME.

Then beware that if you accept a visual approach, and there are scattered clouds in the area, you won't be able to duck below them to remain visual if that move will take you below the floor of the Class B sector that you're in. That loophole gives you more reason to be careful before accepting a visual approach. Other than that warning, the Class B chart is fairly straightforward.

SIDs, STARs, AND PROFILE DESCENTS

Before talking about approach charts, let's take a look at some of the specific symbols on the SID and STAR charts. Figure 14-5 illustrates the heading information that will be found on these charts. As a rule, you will find the departure frequency for a SID in a box at the upper left of the heading. If there is more than one frequency sector involved in the area that the chart covers, the different frequencies will be shown on the plan view of the chart, separated by sector boundary symbols.

There is a note telling us that a full explanation of transition altitudes and transition levels can be found on the Jeppesen introductory page 103 (chapter 15, Fig. 15-3).

The charts are identified both by index numbers: 10-2 with suffixes for STARs and profile descents; 10-3 with suffixes for SIDs; and by the actual type of chart denoted in reverse print (white print on black space).

The bottom half of Fig. 14-5 shows various route identifications along with computer codes that are used. It also shows two different types of SIDs. These are the pilot nav SIDs, which means the pilot shall fly the entire SID, including the transition, from the information provided on the SID itself. There is also the vector SID, which indicates that the pilot shall be provided with radar vectors to an assigned route or fix depicted on the SID itself.

This does not mean that you won't receive radar vectors when performing a pilot nav SID because you can receive radar vectors at anytime throughout your flight.

Certain SIDs, STARs, and profile descents do not incorporate computer codes, examples of which are on the bottom of Fig. 14-5.

Notice in Fig. 14-6 that many of the symbols are the same as those found on enroute charts. The routes are shown as solid lines with arrows, while transition tracks use a dashed line. For the transition portion, the name and computer identification of the route are found above the track while the MEA and segment mileage are below it.

If a SID includes a heading, it will be shown with the letters "hdg" following the heading to be flown. Visual flight tracks are depicted by a series of small arrows, while radar vectoring tracks will be illustrated by a series of short arrowheads.

Figure 14-7 shows various crossing restrictions and course guidance information. *Profile descent* tracks are shown using heavy solid lines with arrows. (A profile de-

AREA CHARTS, SIDS, STARS, CLASS B

SID, STAR, AND PROFILE DESCENT LEGEND

The following legend is applicable to Standard Instrument Departure (SID), Departure, Standard Terminal Arrival (STAR), Profile Descents, and Arrival Charts. Refer to the Chart Glossary for more complete definition of terms.

These charts are graphic illustrations of the procedures prescribed by the governing authority. A text description is provided, in addition to the graphic, when it is furnished by the governing authority. In some areas text information is required to perform a SID or STAR procedure. *Not all items apply in all areas.*

All charts meet FAA requirements for aeronautical charts. All altitudes shown on SIDs, STARs, and Profile Descent charts are MSL, unless otherwise specified.

COMMUNICATIONS AND ALTIMETER SETTING DATA

Departure Control frequencies are included with SIDs. The frequencies are listed in the heading of the chart or when frequency sectors are specified they may be displayed in the planview of the chart.

HEADING | TERPS Departure (R) 126.9 |

PLANVIEW

sector boundary → symbol

EAST SECTOR

| TERPS DEPARTURE CONTROL 126.9 |

The ATIS frequency is provided on STARs in the heading of the chart.

| ATIS 120.3 |

The Transition Level and Transition Altitude are listed below the Communications. For a complete explanation of Transition Level and Transition Altitude see Introduction page 103.

| TRANS LEVEL: FL 140 |
| TRANS ALT: 13000' |

CHART IDENTIFICATION

STARS/PROFILE DESCENTS   SIDS

(10-2) (10-2A) , etc.   Index number   (10-3) (10-3A) , etc.   Index number

[10-2] [10-3]   Special chart issued to special coverages only. Contains modified information for your company.

STAR   Standard Terminal Arrival   **SID**   Standard Instrument Departure

ARRIVAL   Arrival Procedure   **DEPARTURE**   Departure Procedure

PROFILE DESCENT   Profile Descent

ROUTE IDENTIFICATION
TYPICAL EXAMPLES USING COMPUTER LANGUAGE

STARS   SIDS

MOORPARK FOUR ARRIVAL (FIM.MOOR4)   MILIS (ROCKI1.MILIS)

└ Arrival Name   Arrival Code ┘ Transition Name ┘   Transition Code ┘

PILOT NAV SIDS

FRESNO (FAT.MOOR4)

Transition Name ↑   Transition Code ↑

Departure Name ┐

ROCKI ONE DEPARTURE (ROCKI1.ROCKI) (PILOT NAV)

Departure Code ┘
Primary Navigation is by pilot, not radar

PROFILE DESCENTS

Transition origination FACILITY/FIX Code

─FILLMORE─
| (D)(L) 112.5 FIM |
N34 21.4 W118 52.8

| CIVET |
D52/ILAX
D52/LAX
N34 02.1 W117 23.3

VECTOR SIDS

DENVER FIVE DEPARTURE (DEN5.DEN) (VECTOR)

SID where ATC provides radar navigational guidance to an assigned route or to a fix depicted on the SID. Vector SIDs indicate the fix or route to which the pilot will be vectored.

TYPICAL EXAMPLES NOT USING COMPUTER LANGUAGE

STARS   SIDS

ALPHA ARRIVAL (RWY 10)

Arrival Name ┘   Specified runway to be used

INDIA DEPARTURE

┌ Departure Name ┘

RUNWAY 13 ARRIVAL

RUNWAY 13 DEPARTURE

PROFILE DESCENTS

RWYS 8L, 9R, 27L ← Identification shown in chart heading.

Fig. 14-5 Reproduced with permission of Jeppesen Sanderson, Inc. Not for use in navigation.

SIDs, STARs , and profile descents

SID, STAR, AND PROFILE DESCENT LEGEND
GRAPHIC
(Charts are not drawn at a specific scale)

RADIO SYMBOLS

VORTAC/VORDME

VOR (VHF Omnidirectional Range)

TACAN (Tactical Air Navigation) or DME (Distance Measuring Equipment)

NDB (Nondirectional Radio Beacon)

LOC, LDA, or SDF Front Course

LOC Back Course

Locator with Outer Marker (LOM)

Outer or Middle Marker (OM) (MM)

RADIO IDENTIFICATION

Navaid identification is given in shadow box with frequency, identifier, Morse Code and latitude & longitude coordinates. DME capability is indicated by a small "D" preceding the VOR frequency at frequency paired navaids. VOR and VORTAC facility operational ranges are identified (when known) within the navaid box. (T) represents Terminal; (L) represents Low Altitude; and (H) represents High Altitude.

— DENVER —
D
(H) 116.3 DEN
N39 51.6 W104 45.1

— PRACHINBURI —
201 PB
N14 06.0 E101 22.0

Localizer navaids are identified by a round cornered box. Frequency identification and Morse Code are provided. DME is included when navaid and DME are frequency paired. Localizer back course facility boxes include front course bearing for HSI setting.

— LOC —
108.7 IMBS

LOC (BACK CRS)
089° 109.7 IMEX
(FRONT CRS 269°)

VERTICAL NOISE ABATEMENT PROCEDURES

RWY	VNAP
07, 15	A
25, 33	A or B

Vertical Noise Abatement Procedures (VNAP). For explanation of procedures, see Air Traffic Control section.

RESTRICTED AIRSPACE

PROHIBITED, RESTRICTED, DANGER AREAS
Prohibited, Restricted & Danger Areas are charted when referenced in SID or STAR source, plus any Prohibited Area within five (5) nautical miles of route centerline or primary airport.

R-2713 ← Designation (Type of area can be determined by P-Prohibited, R-Restricted, D-Danger.)
UNL ← Upper Limit
GND ← Lower Limit
(0800-2200 LT MON-SAT) ← Hours active
(IND ARTCC) ← Controlling Agency

ROUTE PORTRAYAL

SID/STAR Track

BOLES ← Transition name
← Transition track
12000 ← Minimum enroute altitude (MEA)
25 ← Segment mileage

BOLES
(REX.BOLES3)
12000
25
On charts dated on or after Jul 26, 1985 the Transition name will include the route identification code, when assigned.

DF 11 ─▶ SID or STAR label of a particular route in some coverage areas

Radar vectoring

Johns
25

Visual flight track

150° hdg

Flight Track segment flown with heading only.

3.0

Cross at **TL+10** and descend to **3000'**

Crossing altitude instructions, Transition Level plus 1000'

Fig. 14-6 Reproduced with permission of Jeppesen Sanderson, Inc. Not for use in navigation.

SID, STAR AND PROFILE DESCENT LEGEND
GRAPHIC (Continued)
ROUTE PORTRAYAL (Continued)

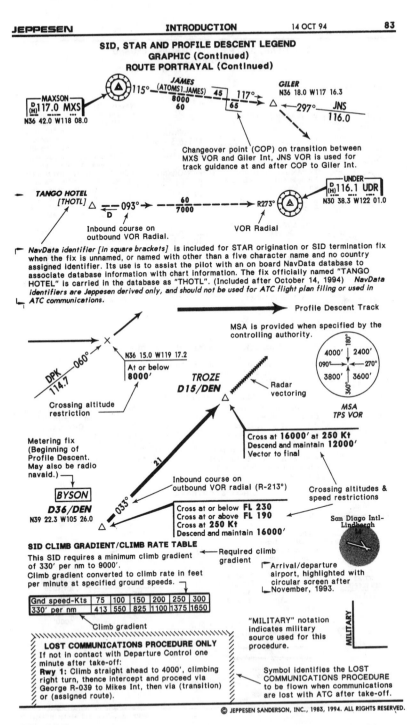

Changeover point (COP) on transition between MXS VOR and Giler Int, JNS VOR is used for track guidance at and after COP to Giler Int.

Inbound course on outbound VOR Radial.

VOR Radial

NavData identifier [in square brackets] is included for STAR origination or SID termination fix when the fix is unnamed, or named with other than a five character name and no country assigned identifier. Its use is to assist the pilot with an on board NavData database to associate database information with chart information. The fix officially named "TANGO HOTEL" is carried in the database as "THOTL". (Included after October 14, 1994) NavData identifiers are Jeppesen derived only, and should not be used for ATC flight plan filing or used in ATC communications.

Profile Descent Track

MSA is provided when specified by the controlling authority.

Radar vectoring

Crossing altitude restriction

MSA
TPS VOR

Metering fix (Beginning of Profile Descent. May also be radio navaid.)

Cross at **16000'** at **250 Kt**
Descend and maintain **12000'**
Vector to final

Inbound course on outbound VOR radial (R-213°)

Crossing altitudes & speed restrictions

Cross at or below **FL 230**
Cross at or above **FL 190**
Cross at **250 Kt**
Descend and maintain **16000'**

San Diago Intl-Lindbergh

SID CLIMB GRADIENT/CLIMB RATE TABLE

This SID requires a minimum climb gradient of 330' per nm to 9000'.
Climb gradient converted to climb rate in feet per minute at specified ground speeds.

Required climb gradient

Arrival/departure airport, highlighted with circular screen after November, 1993.

Gnd speed-Kts	75	100	150	200	250	300
330' per nm	413	550	825	1100	1375	1650

Climb gradient

"MILITARY" notation indicates military source used for this procedure.

LOST COMMUNICATIONS PROCEDURE ONLY
If not in contact with Departure Control one minute after take-off:
Rwy 1: Climb straight ahead to 4000', climbing right turn, thence intercept and proceed via George R-039 to Mikes Int, then via (transition) or (assigned route).

MILITARY

Symbol identifies the LOST COMMUNICATIONS PROCEDURE to be flown when communications are lost with ATC after take-off.

Fig. 14-7 Reproduced with permission of Jeppesen Sanderson, Inc. Not for use in navigation.

scent is an uninterrupted descent from cruising altitude to initial approach.) Some of the fixes require airspeed and/or altitude crossing restrictions that might include minimum and/or maximum crossing altitudes.

Near the bottom of Fig. 14-7 is a SID climb gradient/climb rate table. If a SID does not have a published minimum climb gradient, you can assume that there are no terrain or obstacle problems. In this event, a minimum climb gradient of 200 feet per nautical mile should be flown to the MEA or assigned altitude, unless any climb reductions are necessary to comply with published restrictions. During this climb, the aircraft is expected to cross the departure end of the runway at 35 feet AGL. You must also climb to 400 feet above the airport elevation before initiating any turn, unless one is specified in the procedures.

The standard FAA obstacle clearance slope is based on 152 feet per nautical mile. Climbing at a rate of 200 feet per nautical mile will assure a minimum of 48 feet of obstacle clearance per nautical mile of flight. "That ain't much," so be sure to keep climbing at a good, steady rate.

If, however, there are obstacles or terrain that will penetrate the 40-to-1 slope ratio that results from a climb of 152 feet per nautical mile, you will have a steeper climb gradient shown on the chart.

Many times Jeppesen will publish a climb gradient/climb rate table to help calculate the necessary rate of climb for an aircraft. This is similar to the descent/time-conversion tables published at the bottom of the approach plates that are explained in a subsequent chapter.

All you need to know is the actual *ground speed* in knots. Once you have that, just read the required rate of climb from the chart, interpolating as necessary. Using the chart in Fig. 14-7, for example, with a ground speed of 120 knots, you would need a rate of climb of approximately 660 feet per minute to result in a climb gradient of 330 feet per nautical mile. At 240 knots ground speed, the rate of climb would have to be 1,320 feet per minute.

This is an important item to check because as mentioned before there will be times when the aircraft won't be able to meet the requirement. And there will be times (wind shear or other factors) when you won't know until you are airborne that you can't make the necessary climb gradient. In such a case, you will have to let ATC know immediately so it can vector you to a safe area.

Finally, at the very bottom of Fig. 14-7 you will find an example (self-explanatory) of a lost communications block.

LOOKING AT A PROFILE DESCENT

Figure 14-8 is the RUNWAY 24/25 PROFILE DESCENT for Los Angeles International Airport, and as you can see from the index number it is only one of a series for this airport.

The profile descent is a transitional routing that will take the aircraft from the enroute phase of flight and join it to a visual or instrument approach by allowing the air-

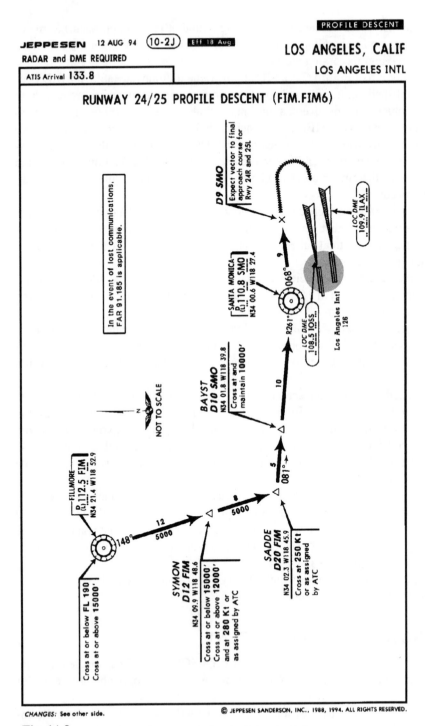

Fig. 14-8 Reproduced with permission of Jeppesen Sanderson, Inc. Not for use in navigation.

craft to descend and position itself at a steady rate of descent with the least amount of communications.

This procedure starts at the FILLMORE VOR, and there is one inherent trap in the profile depiction that has caught a number of high-time airline pilots. You are to cross FIM at an altitude between FL 190 and 15,000 feet. From the VOR, you will fly the 148-degree radial to SADDE intersection where you will turn left to join the Santa Monica SMO VOR 261-degree radial inbound.

Enroute to SADDE, you will be expected to cross the SYMON fix, which is 12 DME from FIL, at between 15,000 and 12,000 feet and at an airspeed of 280 knots (or as assigned by ATC). You will then be expected to slow down further to 250 knots (or as assigned by ATC) by SADDE.

From SADDE, you will only have 5 miles to descend to 10,000 feet at BAYST, which is 10 DME from SMO. At SMO, turn left to track on the SMO 068-degree radial and at 9 DME you should expect vectors to a final approach.

After beginning the profile descent, if ATC revises any part of the route or altitude, ATC will cancel the rest of the profile descent, and all routes, altitudes, and speeds will be provided by ATC. If ATC revises the speed, however, such a revision will void only the charted speed restrictions, and you will still be obliged to comply with the charted routes and altitudes. If you are unable to comply with the required routes and altitudes because of a speed change by ATC, you must notify the controller that you can no longer comply.

The trap is the minimum enroute altitude figures shown between FIL and SADDE. These are for your information and emergency use only. You must comply with the altitudes shown at the fixes. If you go below the lower limit, or bust the upper limit, you will be subject to a violation.

It is important to note that a clearance for a profile descent is not a clearance for an instrument approach procedure. The last altitude shown on the profile descent is the final altitude unless cleared lower by ATC or cleared for a specific instrument approach procedure. In Fig. 14-8, descent below 10,000 feet is prohibited until cleared for a lower altitude.

CHARTED VISUAL APPROACHES

Many high traffic airports are beginning to use charted visual approaches, which are designed to provide an orderly flow of traffic, like SIDs, STARs, profile descents, and instrument approach procedures.

The charted visual approach headings are similar to IAP headings discussed in the next chapter. Two are included here to show what they look like and also to show you that you can get into trouble if you don't pay attention.

Take a look at Figs. 14-9 and 14-10. You will see that there are a number of similarities. Both require radar. Both begin at a point over the SMO VOR and track on the 068-degree radial. Both require crossing the 3.5 DME fix at or above 5,000 feet because the floor of the Class B airspace in that area is 5,000 feet. From there, descent is

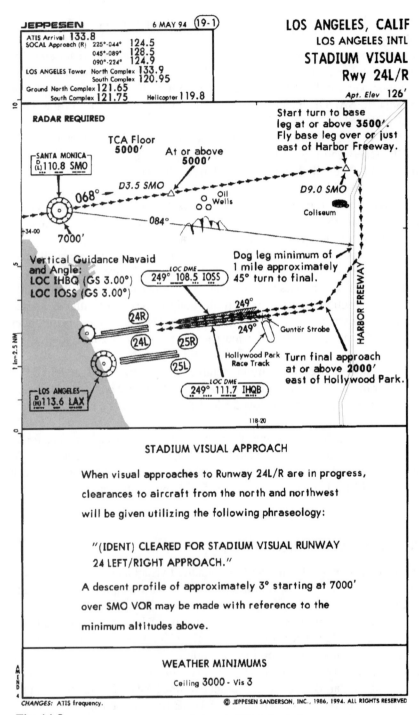

Fig. 14-9 Reproduced with permission of Jeppesen Sanderson, Inc. Not for use in navigation.

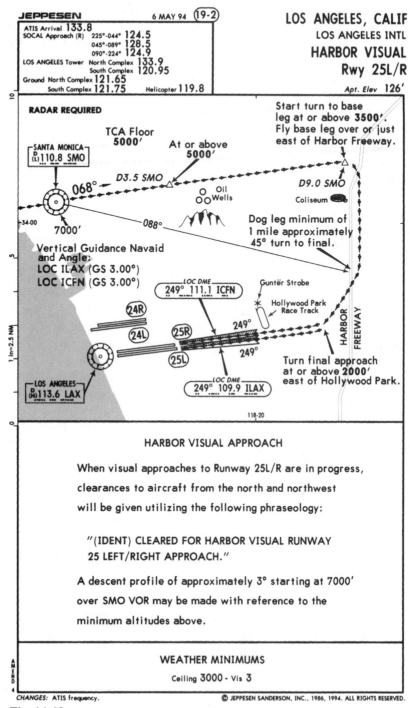

JEPPESEN   6 MAY 94 (19-2)

ATIS Arrival 133.8
SOCAL Approach (R)   225°-044° 124.5
045°-089° 128.5
090°-224° 124.9
LOS ANGELES Tower North Complex 133.9
South Complex 120.95
Ground North Complex 121.65
South Complex 121.75   Helicopter 119.8

LOS ANGELES, CALIF
LOS ANGELES INTL
HARBOR VISUAL
Rwy 25L/R
Apt. Elev 126'

RADAR REQUIRED

Start turn to base
leg at or above **3500'**.
Fly base leg over or just
east of Harbor Freeway.

TCA Floor **5000'**   At or above **5000'**

SANTA MONICA
(L) 110.8 SMO

068°   D3.5 SMO

O Oil
OO Wells

D9.0 SMO
Coliseum

-34-00   7000'   088°

Dog leg minimum of
1 mile approximately
45° turn to final.

Vertical Guidance Navaid
and Angle:
LOC ILAX (GS 3.00°)
LOC ICFN (GS 3.00°)

LOC DME
249° 111.1 ICFN

Guntёr Strobe

Hollywood Park
Race Track

24R

24L

25R   249°

25L   249°

LOC DME
249° 109.9 ILAX

HARBOR FREEWAY

Turn final approach
at or above **2000'**
east of Hollywood Park.

LOS ANGELES
(H) 113.6 LAX

118-20

HARBOR VISUAL APPROACH

When visual approaches to Runway 25L/R are in progress,
clearances to aircraft from the north and northwest
will be given utilizing the following phraseology:

"(IDENT) CLEARED FOR HARBOR VISUAL RUNWAY
25 LEFT/RIGHT APPROACH."

A descent profile of approximately 3° starting at 7000'
over SMO VOR may be made with reference to the
minimum altitudes above.

WEATHER MINIMUMS
Ceiling 3000 - Vis 3

CHANGES: ATIS frequency.   © JEPPESEN SANDERSON, INC., 1986, 1994. ALL RIGHTS RESERVED.

Fig. 14-10 Reproduced with permission of Jeppesen Sanderson, Inc. Not for use in navigation.

allowed to 3,500 feet by the 9.0 DME, then execute a turn to the right to pass east of the Coliseum and the Harbor Freeway. Both procedures require a dogleg with a minimum of a 1-mile, 45-degree turn to final, and that turn has to be at or above 2,000 feet east of Hollywood Park.

Look at the bottom of each chart page to see that both require the same ceiling and visibility of 3,000 feet and 3 miles. Just above the weather requirements you will see the note telling you that both can be performed using a 3-degree descent profile if started at 7,000 feet over the SMO VOR.

Here's where the similarities end and where you have to be careful. The STADIUM VISUAL approach is to Runway 24L or 24R, while the HARBOR VISUAL approach is to Runway 25L or 25R.

On the Stadium Visual, you shall use the 084-degree radial of SMO as a lead-in radial, pass to the *north* of the Hollywood Park Race Track, and use one of the Runway 24 ILSs for vertical guidance and alignment angle. The LOC for 24R is 108.5 MHz, using an identifier of IOSS, while the LOC for 24L is 111.7 MHz with an identifier of IHQB. Both have a descent path of 3 degrees.

The Harbor Visual uses the SMO 088-degree radial as a lead-in radial, passes *south* of the Hollywood Park Race Track, and uses *one of* the Runway 25 ILSs. Runway 25R is on a frequency of 111.1 and has an identifier of ICFN, while Runway 25R uses a frequency of 109.9 with an identifier of ILAX. Like the Stadium Visual, both use a descent path of 3 degrees, and all four runways have the same inbound course of 249 degrees.

It is easy to make a mistake and use the improper chart, especially after a long day of flying on instruments, then landing during heavy haze into the setting sun, *and* with a lot of traffic around you.

Pay attention to the clearance you're given. Make sure you identify the chart itself, set the proper LOC frequency in the radio, and *make sure you positively identify the localizer*.

CHAPTER QUIZ

1. AMAs are shown on area charts. They act like MORAs to provide terrain clearance information, but they depict _____ rather than _____.

2. Once cleared for a visual approach, you are not allowed to descend below the floor of the TCA.

   True ____ False ____

3. What is the difference between a pilot nav SID and a vector SID?

4. What is a profile descent?

5. On an instrument departure, you are expected to be at least _____ feet above the runway at the departure end, to climb to at least _____ feet AGL before turning unless instructed otherwise, and to maintain a rate of climb of at least

_____ feet per nautical mile to remain above the standard obstruction clearance slope of _____ feet per nautical mile unless a greater rate of climb is indicated on the procedure.

6. While executing a profile descent, you can descend to the MEA, but no lower, without ATC permission.

    True _____ False _____

7. If ATC gives you a speed change during a profile descent, the change cancels the rest of the profile descent restrictions and ATC will then provide you with headings, speeds, and altitudes.

    True _____ False _____

8. After crossing the last fix depicted on the profile descent, you can continue to the airport provided that you are in VFR conditions.

    True _____ False _____

Answers are in the appendix.

15
Approach chart plan view

AIRPORTS WITH A PUBLISHED INSTRUMENT APPROACH MIGHT HAVE ONE approach or perhaps 10 or more. Each approach is depicted individually, with very few exceptions, such as an NDB or LOC approach that might be combined with an ILS when both use the same routing.

The first approach to the airport is printed on the first page of the series; the plan view of the airport, as well as airport data and the takeoff and alternate minimums, are usually printed on the reverse side of that first page. The remainder of the approach chart pages for that airport will normally be printed on both sides of the page.

Figure 15-1 shows the general format for the approach chart and the airport chart. At many major airports the airport charts, taxiway charts, gate positions, and INS coordinates are printed on charts that precede the 11-1 chart. In this case, charts are numbered 10-9, 10-9A, 10-9B, and the like. This has been done because some of these airport layouts have become so very complex that even veteran pilots get lost without detailed information that won't fit on one page.

Each approach chart is a storehouse of information. Take the time to familiarize yourself with the chart legend so you can derive the necessary information. Review this information periodically. Remember, these approach charts are designed to lead you down the rosy approach path to the airport runways. Oftentimes they will allow

APPROACH CHART PLAN VIEW

Approach charts are graphic illustrations of instrument approach procedures prescribed by the governing authority. All charts meet FAA requirements for aeronautical charts. The following legend pages briefly explain symbology used on approach charts throughout the world. *Not all items apply to all locations.* The approach chart is divided into specific areas of information as illustrated below.

FORMATS

The first approach procedure published for an airport has the procedure chart published on the front side with the airport chart on the back side. On major airports, the airport chart may preceed the first approach procedure. These locations will have expanded airport information that may occupy more than one side. When an airport has more than one published approach procedure, they are shown front and back on additional sheets. Blank pages will indicate "INTENTIONALLY LEFT BLANK".

APPROACH PROCEDURE CHART FORMAT	AIRPORT CHART FORMAT
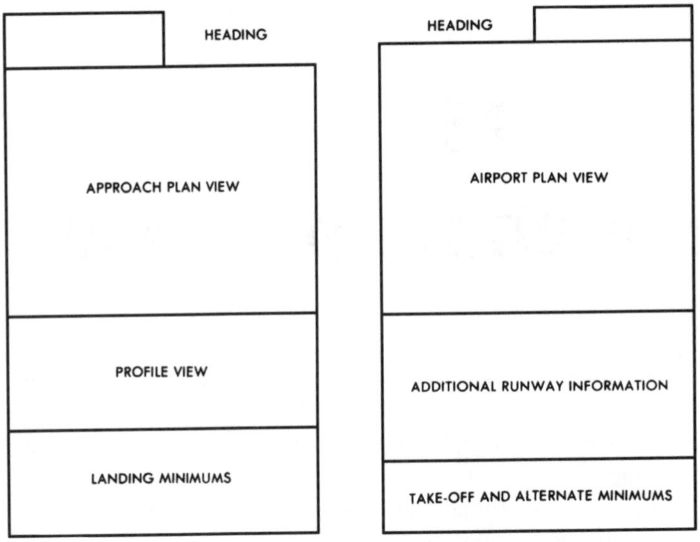 HEADING	HEADING
APPROACH PLAN VIEW	AIRPORT PLAN VIEW
PROFILE VIEW	ADDITIONAL RUNWAY INFORMATION
LANDING MINIMUMS	TAKE-OFF AND ALTERNATE MINIMUMS

Fig. 15-1 Reproduced with permission of Jeppesen Sanderson, Inc. Not for use in navigation.

you to thread the needle between mountains, antenna farms, or high-rise buildings when forward visibility is down to bare minimums.

Then, if you get to the missed approach point and still can't see the runway, the charts will lead you safely through the missed approach, but only if you understand and follow the approach and missed approach exactly. Figure 15-2 shows what you can learn from the chart's heading.

First of all, check the calendar date against the chart *effective* date. You don't want to use a chart before it becomes effective. Why would you have a new chart before an effective date? If a very important change is scheduled in a procedure, the cartographers will issue the charts early enough to assure that all subscribers receive their copies in time to note the change. Additionally, all revisions are Friday dated, and changes effective after the printing date will be shown with an effective date noted. If the chart does not have an effective date shown, it is current and effective when received.

CREATING THE CHARTS

Instrument procedures are developed under the United States Standard Terminal Procedures (TERPs). There are no regulations regarding the appearance of approach charts, so it is up to the cartographers to determine appearance. This is why the NOS and Jeppesen formats are so different.

Information that must be provided to the users comes through three sources: letters of transmittal from the *Federal Register*, the daily *National Data Flight Digest*, and NOTAMs. It is up to the cartographers to study these publications to assure that all charts are up-to-date.

The letters of transmittal include either a form 8260-3 for precision approaches or 8260-5 for nonprecision approaches. These forms print out all the necessary information for each specific approach. The cartographers then use this printed information to create a chart.

HOWIE KEEFE'S UPDATE CONCEPT

Many hours are spent by pilots to keep their manual revisions up-to-date. Not only that, because the changes to the Jeppesen charts come out weekly, a pilot on an extended flight might end up having old approach plates for her return flight. Most of the information is available about seven weeks before the changes take place.

Howie Keefe has done a lot of flying: long-time pilot, ex-Navy pilot, national air racer (modified P-51 *Miss America*), and holder of the transcontinental piston speed record (6 hours and 21 minutes from Los Angeles to Washington, D.C., set in *Miss America* in 1972). Tired of having out-of-date charts, tired of spending many hours revising manuals, and realizing that over 97 percent of the changes can be accomplished by pen and ink changes to the existing charts, Howie started the Air Chart Company in Venice, California.

He sends his revision notices, called the *Universal-Enroute Chart Update* and the *Universal-Approach Chart Update*, to his subscribers six weeks before they become

APPROACH CHART PLAN VIEW

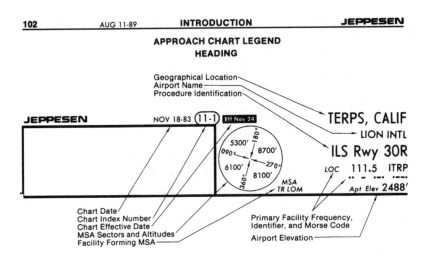

**APPROACH CHART LEGEND
HEADING**

Geographical Location
Airport Name
Procedure Identification

JEPPESEN   NOV 18-83 (11-1) Eff Nov 24

TERPS, CALIF
LION INTL
ILS Rwy 30R
LOC 111.5 ITRP
Apt Elev 2488'

5300' / 180° / 8700'
090° / 270°
6100' / 8100'
360°
MSA
TR LOM

Chart Date
Chart Index Number
Chart Effective Date
MSA Sectors and Altitudes
Facility Forming MSA

Primary Facility Frequency,
Identifier, and Morse Code

Airport Elevation

The geographical name used is generally the major city served by the civil airport or installation name if a military airport. A hyphen before the airport name is used when the location name is part of the airport name. The charts are arranged alphabetically by the geographical location served.

NOTE: U.S. Airway Manual: The civil approach charts covering the United States are arranged alphabetically *by state*. Within each state, the charts are arranged alphabetically by the name of the city served.

For each location, the charts are sequenced by the chart index number. This index number will appear as shown below:

First Digit: represents the airport number and is an arbitrary assignment.

Second Digit: represents the chart type as shown below:

0-area, SID, etc.	5-RESERVED
1-ILS, MLS, LOC, LDA, SDF, KRM	6-NDB
	7-DF
2-PAR	8-ASR
3-VOR	9-RNAV, vicinity chart,
4-TACAN	Visual Arrival or Visual Departure chart.

Third Digit: represents the filing order of charts of the same type.

Oval outlines of chart index numbers represent:

⬭ Standard chart issued to Airway Manual subscribers.

◖ Special chart issued to special coverages only.

⬭M Standard chart that uses metric system units of measure.

In this numerical system—both procedure and airport—there will be gaps in the filing sequence because of deletions, expected expansion, selected distribution and tailoring for specific subscribers. Two procedures may be combined. Numbering, in this case, will be for the lowest number of the pair. ILS and NDB is a typical combination indexed as 11-1, 21-1, etc.

All chart dates are Friday dates. This chart date is not to be confused with the effective date. The effective date is charted when a chart is issued prior to the changes being effective. Charts under USA jurisdiction with an effective date are effective at 0901Z of that date.

Procedure identification is given below the airport name. This identification is per the applicable authoritative source (e.g. VOR-1, NDB (ADF) Rwy 16, NDB Rwy 16, etc.). The use of an alphabetical suffix indicates a procedure does not meet criteria for straight-in landing minimums (e.g. VOR-A, VOR-B, LOC (BACK CRS)-A, etc.).

MSA provides 1000 feet of obstruction clearance within the circle (or sector) within 25 nautical miles of the facility identified just to the lower right of the circle. If the protected distance is other than 25 nautical miles, the effective radius is stated beside the identifier of the central facility. The MSA value is supplied by the controlling authority.

Fig. 15-2   Reproduced with permission of Jeppesen Sanderson, Inc. Not for use in navigation.

current. No other changes can be made for an additional six weeks, so the user can now take an extended trip and know that the charts will be up-to-date. NOS and Jeppesen users can avail themselves of this service, which is really handy for professional people who don't have the time to make numerous manual revisions.

The approach chart updates are all in written, cryptic form on both sides of one sheet of paper. The subscriber checks her route to see what areas she will be flying through, then looks on the list to see if any of the changes will affect her. If they do, she merely makes a pen-and-ink correction to that specific chart.

Figure 15-3 shows the changes made to the Orlando Executive chart for the LOC BC RWY 25. The amended number was changed from 18 to 19, and the new date was inked in; a new fix was added called VITTU, which can be identified as the 9 DME or by radar; the minimum altitude for VITTU is 1,600 feet; the minimum altitude for the MARYB fix was changed to 1,500 feet; and the final approach fix was moved from MARYB to the old ORL 4 DME/radar fix that was named BRICE, and its minimum altitude was changed to 1,100 feet. In addition, the ceiling requirements were lowered to 480 feet for the straight-in approaches.

This encompassed many more changes than the average revision, which is usually no more than a radio frequency, yet, as you can see, these changes were handled neatly with a pen.

Examples from the approach chart updates are seen in Figs. 15-4 and 15-5. These revisions cover all changes made from March 1, 1989, through January 25, 1990. The important changes are listed more than once.

For example, under the SUMMARY OF MAJOR CHANGES in Fig. 15-4, look under GA (for Georgia) and see where it says that the VIDALIA (VDI) NDB was renamed ONYUN (UON) and moved.

This is expanded in Fig. 15-5 to tell you that the NDB has been moved 5 miles east to 32°13.4' north, and 082°17.9' west. The symbol following that information indicates the end of that item.

The next item explains that VIDALIA approach control frequency has been changed from 132.5 to 132.3 MHz. The next item notes the effective dates of the NDB change.

Keefe includes other useful information in block form such as the NOTAM CAUTION in the upper right of Fig. 15-5. This information doesn't necessarily concern itself with chart changes.

The enroute chart update is also handled on one large piece of paper. In addition to the cryptic symbols, a map of the United States is included. Stylized symbols appear on the map to speed changes.

Figure 15-6 is the northwestern United States. Simple changes are printed on the map, such as the Fresno Air Terminal Tower frequency being changed to 118.1 MHz; this is amplified in the other listings.

Sometimes there will be a major change in a routing. Note the boxed numeral 3 at Denver. This number refers to another section of the chart, which is labeled VIS-AIDS.

VIS-AIDS have been prepared to IFR specifications to be used with a low altitude

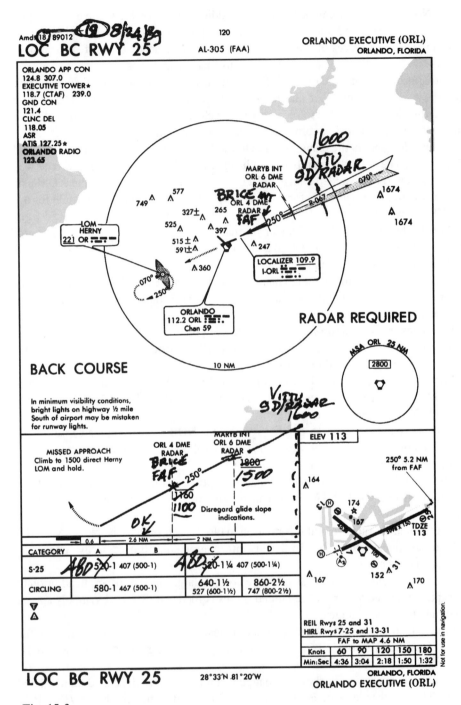

Fig. 15-3

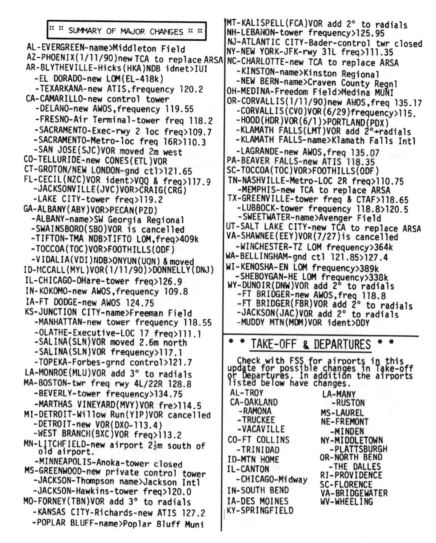

```
:: :: SUMMARY OF MAJOR CHANGES :: ::

AL-EVERGREEN-name>Middleton Field
AZ-PHOENIX(1/11/90)new TCA to replace ARSA
AR-BLYTHEVILLE-Hicks(HKA)NDB idnet>IUI
  -EL DORADO-new LOM(EL-418k)
  -TEXARKANA-new ATIS,frequency 120.2
CA-CAMARILLO-new control tower
  -DELANO-new AWOS,frequency 119.55
  -FRESNO-Air Terminal-tower freq 118.2
  -SACRAMENTO-Exec-rwy 2 loc freq>109.7
  -SACRAMENTO-Metro-loc freq 16R>110.3
  -SAN JOSE(SJC)VOR moved 2m west
CO-TELLURIDE-new CONES(ETL)VOR
CT-GROTON/NEW LONDON-gnd ctl>121.65
FL-CECIL(NZC)VOR ident>VQQ & freq>117.9
  -JACKSONVILLE(JVC)VOR>CRAIG(CRG)
  -LAKE CITY-tower freq>119.2
GA-ALBANY(ABY)VOR>PECAN(PZD)
  -ALBANY-name>SW Georgia Regional
  -SWAINSBORO(SBO)VOR is cancelled
  -TIFTON-TMA NDB>TIFTO LOM,freq>409k
  -TOCCOA(TOC)VOR>FOOTHILLS(ODF)
  -VIDALIA(VDI)NDB>ONYUN(UQN) & moved
ID-MCCALL(MYL)VOR(1/11/90)>DONNELLY(DNJ)
IL-CHICAGO-OHare-tower freq>126.9
IN-KOKOMO-new AWOS,frequency 109.8
IA-FT DODGE-new AWOS 124.75
KS-JUNCTION CITY-name>Freeman Field
  -MANHATTAN-new tower frequency 118.55
  -OLATHE-Executive-LOC 17 freq>111.1
  -SALINA(SLN)VOR moved 2.6m north
  -SALINA(SLN)VOR frequency>117.1
  -TOPEKA-Forbes-grnd control>121.7
LA-MONROE(MLU)VOR add 3° to radials
MA-BOSTON-twr freq rwy 4L/22R 128.8
  -BEVERLY-tower frequency>134.75
  -MARTHAS VINEYARD(MVY)VOR fre>114.5
MI-DETROIT-Willow Run(YIP)VOR cancelled
  -DETROIT-new VOR(DXO-113.4)
  -WEST BRANCH(BXC)VOR freq>113.2
MN-LITCHFIELD-new airport 2½m south of
   old airport.
  -MINNEAPOLIS-Anoka-tower closed
MS-GREENWOOD-new private control tower
  -JACKSON-Thompson name>Jackson Intl
  -JACKSON-Hawkins-tower freq>120.0
MO-FORNEY(TBN)VOR add 3° to radials
  -KANSAS CITY-Richards-new ATIS 127.2
  -POPLAR BLUFF-name>Poplar Bluff Muni
```

```
MT-KALISPELL(FCA)VOR add 2° to radials
NH-LEBANON-tower frequency>125.95
NJ-ATLANTIC CITY-Bader-control twr closed
NY-NEW YORK-JFK-rwy 31L freq>111.35
NC-CHARLOTTE-new TCA to replace ARSA
  -KINSTON-name>Kinston Regional
  -NEW BERN-name>Craven County Regnl
OH-MEDINA-Freedom Field>Medina MUNI
OR-CORVALLIS(1/11/90)new AWOS,freq 135.17
  -CORVALLIS(CVO)VOR(6/29)frequency>115.
  -HOOD(HDR)VOR(6/1)>PORTLAND(PDX)
  -KLAMATH FALLS(LMT)VOR add 2°→radials
  -KLAMATH FALLS-name>Klamath Falls Intl
  -LAGRANDE-new AWOS,freq 135.07
PA-BEAVER FALLS-new ATIS 118.35
SC-TOCCOA(TOC)VOR>FOOTHILLS(ODF)
TN-NASHVILLE-Metro-LOC 2R freq>110.75
  -MEMPHIS-new TCA to replace ARSA
TX-GREENVILLE-tower freq & CTAF>118.65
  -LUBBOCK-tower frequency 118.8>120.5
  -SWEETWATER-name>Avenger Field
UT-SALT LAKE CITY-new TCA to replace ARSA
VA-SHAWNEE(EEY)VOR(7/27)is cancelled
  -WINCHESTER-TZ LOM frequency>364k
WA-BELLINGHAM-gnd ctl 121.85>127.4
WI-KENOSHA-EN LOM frequency>389k
  -SHEBOYGAN-HE LOM frequency>338k
WY-DUNOIR(DNW)VOR add 2° to radials
  -FT BRIDGER-new AWOS,freq 118.8
  -FT BRIDGER(FBR)VOR add 2° to radials
  -JACKSON(JAC)VOR add 2° to radials
  -MUDDY MTN(MDM)VOR ident>DDY
```

```
* * TAKE-OFF & DEPARTURES * *

Check with FSS for airports in this
update for possible changes in Take-off
or Departures. In addition the airports
listed below have changes.
AL-TROY              LA-MANY
CA-OAKLAND            -RUSTON
  -RAMONA            MS-LAUREL
  -TRUCKEE           NE-FREMONT
  -VACAVILLE           -MINDEN
CO-FT COLLINS        NY-MIDDLETOWN
  -TRINIDAD            -PLATTSBURGH
ID-MTN HOME          OR-NORTH BEND
IL-CANTON              -THE DALLES
  -CHICAGO-Midway    RI-PROVIDENCE
IN-SOUTH BEND        SC-FLORENCE
IA-DES MOINES        VA-BRIDGEWATER
KY-SPRINGFIELD       WV-WHEELING
```

Fig. 15-4 Air Chart Systems. Not for use in navigation.

enroute chart. You can see this change at Denver in Fig. 15-7. In addition to the change itself, Keefe includes a synopsis of why the change was made.

Keefe also provides similar services for VFR pilots. With the increasing use of loran and GPS routings, Keefe has a very helpful bound volume called the *LORAN/GPS Navigator Atlas*, which among other things includes the lat/long of all fixes in the United States. It is also an excellent aid for the right-seat passenger, and is highly recommended for RNAV pilots as well as for long cross-country pilots who want the utmost in reference material.

SANDERSVILLE-if no lcl AS on CTAF,use Macon AS & MDAs +200'Ⅱ this in these 3/9 amdts:···NDB 12(A2)MSA 2400Ⅱ Sl & Ci 980-1Ⅱ···VOR/DME-A(A3)23DΔ 1340MⅡ Ci 1000-1Ⅱ
SAVANNAH-NDB 9(11/16-A2O)MAYAR÷SA 2500MⅡ CiA 480Ⅱ···ILS 9(11/16-A25),MAYAR÷SA 132/12.7/2500Ⅱ Ci 460Ⅱ if no control tower, GS unusableⅡ···ILS 36(11/16-A4) 14D÷DANNA 1600MⅡ GS incpt 1600MⅡ S-LOC & Ci 560Ⅱ···VOR 27(11/16-Am15)MAP also 4.4DⅡ DME mins:Sl & CiA 460,CiB 520Ⅱ
SWAINSBORO(SBO)VOR(9/21)is cancelledⅡ
SWAINSBORO-new NDB 13 eff 11/16***Ⅱ ···VOR/DME-A(11/16-Am1)minor word changesⅡ
THOMSON-VOR/DME-A(11/16-Am1)Ci 1120Ⅱ if no Augusta AS,use Athens AS & MDAs +100'
TIFTON(8/24)TMA NDB>TIFTO LOM(ident TM) frequency>409kⅡ
TIFTON-cancel NDB 33(TMA NDB)eff 8/24Ⅱ ···new NDB 33 effective 8/24*** ···new ILS 33 effective 8/24***
TOCCOA(TOC)VOR(9/21)>FOOTHILLS(ODF) >TOCCOA(1/3/90) AC 118.9>134.8Ⅱ
VIDALIA(6/29)Vidalia(VDI)NDB>ONYUN(UON) and moved 5m east to 32-13.4/082-17.9Ⅱ
VIDALIA-AC 132.5>132.3Ⅱ
VIDALIA-cncl NDB 24(VDT NDB)eff 6/29Ⅱ ···new NDB 24(UON NDB)eff 6/29*** ···new LOC 24 effective 6/29***
WAYCROSS-NDB 10(3/9-A5)FAC,PT & MA hold subtract 1°Ⅱ if no lcl AS on CTAF,use Valdosta AS & MDAs +240'Ⅱ
WAYNESBORO-NDB 7>NDB 8(2/9/89-A2) rwy 7/25>8/26Ⅱ

IDAHO

• GENERAL •
>MCCALL(MYL)VOR(1/11/90)>DONNELLY(DNJ)

BOISE-LOC/DME(BC)28L(6/1-A5)1.6DΔ 3600MⅡ Sl & sidestep 3300Ⅱ···VOR/DME 28L(6/1-Am1)Sl & Ci 3320Ⅱ
COEUR D ALENE-AC 125.8>132.1Ⅱ
COEUR D'ALENE-new VOR 1 effective 7/27*** ▨▨▨VOR 1(9/21-Am1)minor word changesⅡ
GOODING-new NDB 25 effective 6/1***
IDAHO FALLS-rwy 16/34>17/35Ⅱ
IDAHO FALLS-NDB 20(2/1/89-A9)minor word changesⅡ···ILS 20(2/1/89-A8)S-ILS 4931Ⅱ ···LOC(BC)2(2/1/89-A4)minor word change
>MCCALL(MYL)VOR(1/11/90)>DONNELLY(DNJ)

ILLINOIS
BELVIDERE-AC 126.0>121.0Ⅱ
BLOOMINGTON(6/1)gnd ctl 121.8>121.65Ⅱ
BLOOMINGTON-VOR 11(10/19-Am12)BMI 2DΔ 1520M(1680 if Peoria AS)Ⅱ DME mins NA if Peoria ASⅡ

NOTAM CAUTION: Be certain to ask FSS for NOTAMS printed in the "Notices to Airmen," formerly called Class II.(FSS will normally give you NOTAMS that are "on the circuit". You must ask for those in "NOTICES TO AIRMEN" **2**

MACOMB-cncl NDB 26(A9)eff 2/9/89(MQB NDB)···new NDB 26(JZY NDB) & LOC 26 eff 2/9/89***Ⅱ···VOR/DME-A(2/9/89-A5) RevAMⅡ Burlington AS: CiB 1340-1Ⅱ ▨▨▨runway 8/26>9/27Ⅱ this in these 6/21 amdts:▨▨▨NDB 27(Am1)▨▨▨LOC 27 (Am1)Ⅱ
MONTICELLO-new VOR-A eff 2/9/89*** ▨▨▨VOR-A(6/29-Am1)MAP 4.1m after FAF or at 13.1DⅡ
MT VERNON-new AWOS 113.8Ⅱ
MT VERNON-ILS 23(2/8/99-A8)Scott AFB AS MDAs +220'···visibilities +¼Ⅱ···VOR5(2/9/ 89-Am13)Si 920-1,Ci 960-1Ⅱ Scott AFB AS,MDAs +220'Ⅱ···VOR 23(2/9/89-Am13) C*±Ⅱ
MT VERNON-lcl AS on AWOS freq 113.8Ⅱ this in these 10/19 amdts:···ILS 23(A9) ···VOR 5(Am14)···VOR 23(Am14)
OLNEY/NOBLE-NDB 3(6/29-Am11)Evansville AS SiA & CiA 1220-1,B 1220-¾Ⅱ ···LOC 10(6/29-A3)new OLY÷LYMON 288/ 4.6/2000Ⅱ MA:crt÷2000 via I-LZW÷LYMON & hold Lt 106°IBⅡ cncl teardropⅡ new PT at LYMON,right side course 286° out- bound 2000MⅡ Evansville AS mins:Si 1140 Ⅱ···VOR/DME-A(6/29-A7)MA:clt÷2000 via SAM-341÷AXTEL & hold Rt,341°IBⅡ
PEKIN-VOR-A(11/16-A5)MAP 2.6m after FAF or at 12.6DⅡ
PEORIA-gnd ctl 121.9>121.6Ⅱ CD 121.7> 121.85Ⅱ
PEORIA-Mt Hawley-end Lites:Key CTAFⅡ >PERU-new LOC 36 effective 1/11/90***
QUINCY-NDB 4(6/1-Am16)MAP 3.6m after FAF Ⅱ CiA 1200Ⅱ···ILS 4(6/1-Am16)new UIN÷ UI 021/2.6/2400Ⅱ MA:now at UI LOM,hold Rt,038°IBⅡ PT at UI LOM,218° outboundⅡ CiA 1200Ⅱ···LOC/DME(BC)22(6/1-A6)Sl 1140Ⅱ CiA 1200Ⅱ···VOR 4(6/1-Am1)Sl 1160Ⅱ CiA 1200Ⅱ···VOR/DME 22(6/1-A7) Si 1140Ⅱ CiA 1200Ⅱ
ROCHELLE-VOR-A(6/29-A7)cncl 9D arcsⅡ
ROCKFORD-AC 126.0>121.0Ⅱ
ST JACOB-VOR-A(4/6-A3)minor word changeⅡ
SALEM-NDB 18(11/16-A8)cancel CRATS÷SLO & HOOKE÷SLOⅡ BIB÷SLO & ENL÷SLO 2600MⅡ MA:2100>2200Ⅱ add 2° to SLO bearingsⅡ PT>2200MⅡ
STERLING ROCKFALLS-new AWOS 254kⅡ
STERLING ROCKFALLS-if no lcl AS on AWOS (freq 254k),use Rockford AS & MDAs/DHs +180'Ⅱ this in these 10/19 amdts: ···NDB 7(A4)···ILS 25(A9)···LOC(BC)7(A4)

Fig. 15-5 Air Chart Systems. Not for use in navigation.

Contact Air Chart for more information. The address and phone number are in the resources section at the back of this book.

FILING THE CHARTS

Returning to the Jepp charts, the number circled to the right of the chart issue date (Fig. 15-2) is the chart index number. The first digit represents the airport. If there are two

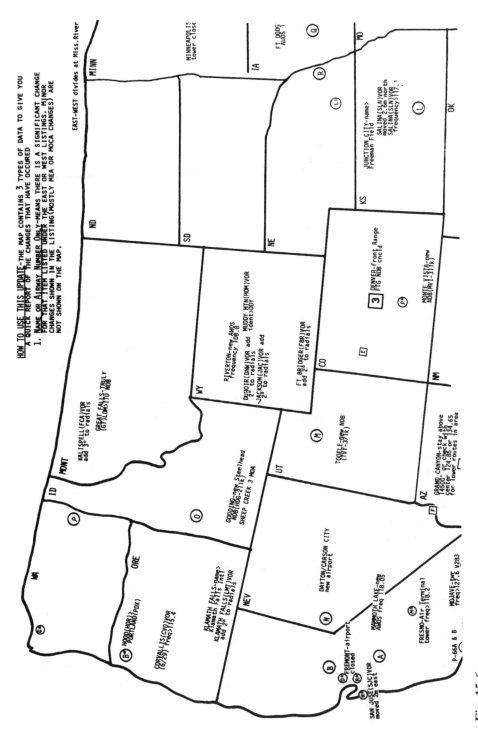

Fig. 15-6 Air Chart Systems. Not for use in navigation.

APPROACH CHART PLAN VIEW

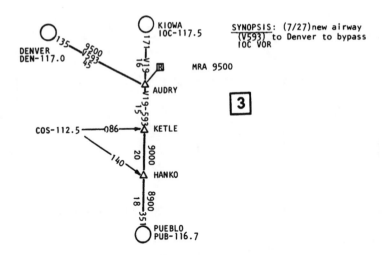

Fig. 15-7

or more airports in the same vicinity, the chartmakers will make one number 1, another number 2, and so on. These numbers are purely discretionary.

The second digit will indicate the type of approach or the type of chart. The third digit establishes a filing order for charts of the same type at the same airport. For example, many airports will have more than one ILS or one VOR approach. In the case of the VOR approaches, they will be numbered 13-1, 13-2, 13-3, 13-4, and the like.

In the case of ILS approaches, the indexing is further broken down; 11-1 would be a CAT I approach to a specific runway, and 11-1A would be the CAT II and CAT IIIA approaches to the same runway.

The charts that have a zero (0) for the second digit are for SIDs, STARs, area charts, and the like. In these cases, the third digit is used to designate the type of chart and the suffix will be the filing index. For example, the area chart is a 10- 1, the Class B terminal chart is a 10-1A, STARs are 10-2 (suffixed by A, B, C), SIDs are 10-3 (also suffixed by letters), noise abatement charts are 10-4, taxi charts are 10-5, and the newest charts of all, the airport charts and their attendant pages, are 10-9 (again with letter suffixes).

Let's say that you are looking at the approaches to John Q Airport and note an approach numbered 13-2 but can't find a 13-1. Well, don't panic because there might not be a 13-1. Perhaps the procedure was abandoned, or perhaps ATC is planning on developing a 13-1 in the future. Jeppesen issues a check sheet every six months to verify that the manuals are up-to-date.

The best way to double check that the charts are up-to-date is to save the last check sheet and the revision notes from that last check sheet to the present time. The check sheet is a listing of all of the pages in the manuals. Check off any page you might be missing. When you get a new check sheet, keep it, and throw away all the old check sheets and revision notices. That way you always have a reference. If the check sheet doesn't list a 13-1 for that airport, chances are there isn't one. If you are still in doubt, go through the revision notices to see if one was issued in the meantime. Most of the time Jeppesen will leave a blank page in that spot anyway and insert a note that the page was intentionally left blank.

What if the check sheet does list a 13-1? Review the revision notices to see if you were to have destroyed it in the meantime. If the search indicates that you should have a 13-1 and you still can't find it, drop a note to Jeppesen and get a replacement by return mail.

Notice the big circle under the chart's effective date. This is the *minimum safe altitude* (MSA) circle.

The MSA is set up to provide a 1,000-foot obstacle clearance within 25 nautical miles from a specific navigational facility. This facility is not necessarily within the ATA. The facility being used is identified outside the circle on the lower right side. If, for any reason, the radius of the MSA circle is other than 25 nautical miles, it shall be so noted.

If the circle is broken up into different sectors—defined in this case with inbound magnetic bearings so you can identify the proper sector directly from the compass—the altitudes then become known as *minimum sector altitudes*. They are designed for obstruction clearance only and will not always provide navigational reception. In fact, Jeppesen's glossary states that ". . . this altitude is for EMERGENCY USE ONLY and does not necessarily guarantee NAVAID reception." (Emphasis is Jeppesen's.) To reemphasize, another important thing to remember is that because the center of the circle is located at a navigational facility that the approach procedure is predicated upon, the MSA is not necessarily a 25-nautical-mile radius around the *airport*.

The last column to the right in the heading lists the geographical location of the airport and under that, the airport name. The charts are filed alphabetically by geographical location.

The procedure identification is listed below the airport name, and here is another area where caution must prevail. Certain airports have many approaches and it becomes necessary to identify each of them individually. But if you are bouncing around in moderate to severe turbulence or if you are tired and in a hurry to get down on the ground, you might hear "cleared for a VOR DME . . . approach." The airport might have several VOR DME approaches, and you might in haste turn to the VOR DME 20 chart when you were cleared to the VOR DME-A approach. So it behooves you to be sure of the approach you have been cleared for; one way to help is to always read back the approach clearance for confirmation.

If the approach has a letter suffix, such as VOR-A, or VOR DME-A, or DME-B, it means that the approach will not meet the criteria for straight-in minimums and is therefore a circling approach.

The primary facility frequency, the identifier, and the Morse-code dots and dashes fall in below the procedure identification followed by other pertinent information such as "Ops not continuous." The airport elevation is shown in feet above sea level (MSL).

The upper left corner of the approach charts (Fig. 15-8) shows the arrival

APPROACH CHART LEGEND
HEADING (continued)

COMMUNICATION AND ALTIMETER SETTING DATA

Communications for "arrivals" are given in normal sequence of use as shown below. See Airport Chart Legend, Introduction page 116, for other communications.

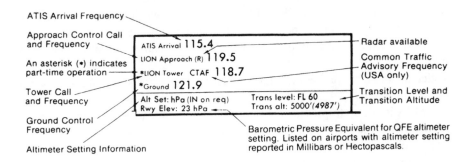

ATIS Arrival Frequency

Approach Control Call and Frequency

An asterisk (∗) indicates part-time operation

Tower Call and Frequency

Ground Control Frequency

Altimeter Setting Information

ATIS Arrival 115.4
LION Approach (R) 119.5
∗LION Tower CTAF 118.7
∗Ground 121.9
Alt Set: hPa (IN on req)   Trans level: FL 60
Rwy Elev: 23 hPa   Trans alt: 5000'(4987')

Radar available

Common Traffic Advisory Frequency (USA only)

Transition Level and Transition Altitude

Barometric Pressure Equivalent for QFE altimeter setting. Listed on airports with altimeter setting reported in Millibars or Hectopascals.

Transition level and transition altitude are listed on the bottom line of the communications and altimeter setting data box. Transition level and transition altitude are provided for all areas outside the 48 conterminous United States, Alaska and Canada.

Trans level: FL 60   The transition level (QNE) is the lowest level of flight using standard altimeter setting (29.92 inches of mercury or 760 millimeters of mercury or 1013.2 millibars or 1013.2 hectopascals.)

Trans alt: 5000'(4987')   The transition altitude (QNH) is the altitude at and below which local pressure setting must be used.

Altimeter setting units are listed on the bottom line of communications data box.

Barometric Pressure Equivalent in millibars or hectopascals enables aircraft operators who use QFE altimeter setting for landing to establish the QFE altimeter setting by subtracting the hectopascal or millibar equivalent from the reported QNH altimeter setting. The value shown is the barometric pressure equivalent for the height reference datum for straight in landing. The height reference datum will be the runway threshold elevation (Rwy), airport elevation (Apt), or the runway touchdown elevation (TDZ), as applicable.

Letter designations behind a frequency indicate operation as follows:

G-guards only
T-transmits only
X-on request

Bearings defining frequency sectors are clockwise outbound
(e.g., 270° to 090° would be north of the airport.)

air/ground communications data, listed systematically in the proper sequence as used on approach: ATIS, approach, tower, and ground control frequencies.

For awhile, prior to October 1984, Jeppesen was only putting the approach control frequency on the first chart at a location. On all other charts for that location, a note would indicate the first chart for that frequency. This saved time when making revisions because many times every chart at a location had to be reissued when only a frequency was changed, but the hassle of having to leaf back and forth in the approach charts prompted the change back to the original method of putting the frequencies on each chart.

Transition altitudes, where aircraft operating at flight levels change back to altitudes, and other pertinent altimeter setting information are shown in the lower part of the communications box.

Jeppesen uses a three-letter code that is found in the communications section. G means that the frequency is guarded (listened to) only, T means that the ATC only uses that frequency to transmit, and X means that the frequency is available upon request.

THE BIRD'S-EYE VIEW

Jeppesen defines the plan view at the top of Fig. 15-9. In effect, the plan view is a bird's-eye view of the approach with the flight path drawn in (appearing to be what you would *like* to see on a tracing paper after you get out of a simulator).

The note at the top of the page tells you that most approach plan views are drawn at a scale of 1 inch = 5 nautical miles. If they are drawn at a different scale, that is noted.

The plan view offers a tremendous amount of information, and you must understand each and every symbol to fly in a safe, professional manner. Many of the symbols require little or no thought, but some of them could use a little more explanation. For example, notice the symbol for an offset localizer, you will have to make some sort of turn to the landing runway when you get down to minimums, and because of this, the minimums will be higher than they would be for a straight-in ILS.

Notes on the page will provide such information as how many degrees the localizer is offset from the runway heading, as well as how far from the threshold the approach course crosses the runway centerline. These offset localizers are usually LDAs:

LOCALIZER TYPE DIRECTIONAL AID—A navaid, used for nonprecision instrument approaches with utility and accuracy comparable to a localizer but which is not a part of a complete ILS and is not aligned with the runway.

An example of the notes mentioned above can be seen on the Honolulu, Hawaii, LDA DME Runway 26L approach (Fig. 15-10):

"Use IEPC LDA DME when on LOC course. Localizer course offset from landing runway by 45°. Final approach course crosses runway centerline 8100' from threshold."

APPROACH CHART PLAN VIEW

APPROACH CHART LEGEND
APPROACH PLAN VIEW

The plan view is a graphic picture of the approach, usually presented at a scale of 1 in = 5 NM. Plan views at scales other than 1 in = 5 NM are noted. Latitude and longitude are shown in 10 minute increments on the plan view neatline. Symbols used in the plan view are shown below.

NAVAIDS

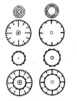

NDB (Non-Directional Radio Beacon)

VOR (VHF Omni-Directional Range)

TACAN (Tactical Air Navigation facility) or DME (Distance Measuring Equipment)

VORTAC or VOR/DME

ILS, LOC, LDA, SDF, MLS or KRM Front Course

LOC Back Course

OFFSET LOC — Offset Localizer

Markers with or without locator, NDB, or Intersection. The triangle or circle in a marker or NDB symbol represents co-located intersection.

┌─ TERPS ─┐
│ ᴰ 115.4 TRP │
└─────────┘

┌─ THORNTON ─┐
│ 281 TOT │
└────────────┘

Navaid facility boxes include facility name, identifier, Morse code, and frequency. The shadow indicates the primary facility upon which the approach is predicated. In VORTAC and VORDME facility boxes the letter "D" indicates DME capability.

┌─ TERPS ─┐
│ ᴰ(H)115.4 TRP │
└─────────┘

VOR, VORTAC and VORDME class is indicated by a letter "T" (Terminal), "L" (Low Altitude), or "H" (High Altitude) when available.

┌─ SAARBRUCKEN ─┐
│ 343 S̲B̲N̲ │
└───────────────┘

Underline shown below navaid identifier, indicates Beat Frequency Oscillator (BFO) required to hear Morse Code identifier.

(OP NOT CONT) or ✱   Indicates part-time operation.

┌─ TAC-112 ─┐
│ CUSTARD │
│ ᴰ(116.5) CUS │
└───────────┘

TACAN facility box with "Ghost" VOR frequency for civil tuning of TACAN - only facilities to receive DME information.

┌─ Domestic DME ─┐
│ BIBOOHRA │
│ CH-4 BIB │
└────────────────┘

Australia Domestic DME Operates on 200 MHz and requires airborne receiver specific to this system.

NAVAIDS (continued)

┌── ILS DME ──┐
│ 257° 110.3 IDE̲N̲ │
└─────────────┘

ILS, LOC, LDA, or SDF facility box. It includes inbound magnetic course, frequency, identifier, and Morse code.

┌── LOC (BACK CRS) ──┐
│ 077° 110.3 IDEN │
│ (FRONT CRS 257°) │
└────────────────────┘

Localizer Back Course facility box. Front course included for HSI setting.

┌── MLS DME ──┐
│ 035°Ch 516 MTRP │
│ ᴰ(109.7) │
└─────────────┘

MLS facility box including inbound magnetic final approach course, MLS channel, identifier with Morse code and VHF "Ghost" frequency for manually tuning DME.

BEARINGS

106°←   Magnetic course

106°T←   True course

DEN
116.3 — 135°
←315° EWD iss
379

VOR cross radials and NDB bearings forming a position fix are "from" a VOR and "to" an NDB.

Morse code ident is charted on VOR radial/NDB bearing when forming facility is outside of planview.

Fig. 15-9 Reproduced with permission of Jeppesen Sanderson, Inc. Not for use in navigation.

The bird's-eye view

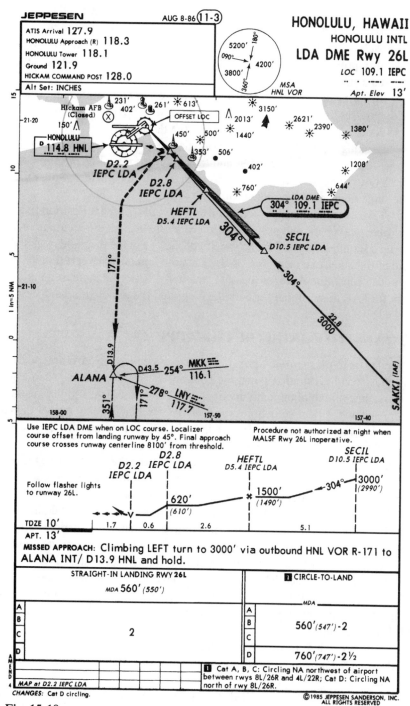

Fig. 15-10   Reproduced with permission of Jeppesen Sanderson, Inc. Not for use in navigation.

Even though you have to make a 45-degree turn to get lined up with the runway, you have more than a mile and a half to accomplish it. The minimum visibility for this approach is 2 miles, so even though the course change is over 30 degrees, the 2-mile visibility provides enough time to line up with the centerline so the approach is considered a straight-in.

Referring back to Fig. 15-9, under bearing symbols, notice that bearings are magnetic courses unless the letter T is after the course direction, in which case it will be a true course. You will find true courses in the Far North.

Looking a little farther down, note that the symbol for EWD in the example also shows the Morse-code identifier and the explanation for this information: "charted on the VOR radial/NDB radial when forming facility is outside of plan view." You saw the same thing on the enroute charts.

Take a look at the upper left-hand column of Fig. 15-11. Position fixes are depicted by filled and open triangles, like enroute charts. If there are alternate means of identifying a fix, these means will be specified, such as in the example, where the fix can be either the outer marker or 6.2 DME. The note here also reveals that if you so request, you can substitute ASR for the outer marker. Due to the increased precision, you can ask for PAR to substitute for both the outer and the middle markers.

TRANSITIONING FOR THE APPROACH

Moving on to the *approach transition* (formerly called the terminal route) information. In the second illustration down the column, the nautical mileage is shown above the course line, the minimum altitude is shown below the line, and the magnetic course is depicted on the line. Sometimes the route is merely a heading (rather than a bearing to or from a facility), in which case "hdg" will follow the magnetic course symbol.

The upper illustration on the right-hand column shows a NoPT (no procedure turn) sector. The NoPT sector is indicated by radials from the VOR. These radials are shaded on the NoPT side. If arriving on an airway within this sector, you are not allowed to make any type of course reversal without permission from ATC.

The NoPT is one of the most misunderstood symbols on the charts. Some pilots will say this means that you are not required to make a procedure turn, while others will say that procedure turns are not authorized. I have heard pilots argue both points, yet they are both half-right. The procedure turn is not required, nor is it authorized without ATC clearance. These procedures have been set up to increase the flow of traffic. Airspace is getting too congested to have aircraft wandering around procedure turns that take 2 minutes (minimum) to complete or as much as 5 minutes for the published procedure.

The procedure turn is merely designed to allow you to reverse direction so you will be on the inbound course. It also provides time to get down to the initial approach altitude.

The NoPT is found on DME arc approaches, straight-in approaches, and various approach transitions depicted on the charts, which also show procedure turns from

Transitioning for the approach

APPROACH CHART LEGEND
APPROACH PLAN VIEW (continued)

POSITION FIXES

Position fixes are portrayed by a triangle. △ ▲

DME value will be portrayed as D10.0. When fix and co-located navaid name are the same, only the navaid name is displayed.

Allowable substitutions for identifying a fix are noted in the planview. At the pilot's request, where ATC can provide the service, ASR may be substituted for the OM. In addition, PAR may be substituted for OM and MM.

APPROACH TRANSITIONS

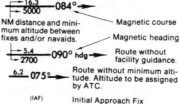

NM distance and minimum altitude between fixes and/or navaids.

Magnetic course

Magnetic heading

Route without facility guidance.

Route without minimum altitude. Altitude to be assigned by ATC.

(IAF)   Initial Approach Fix

(IF)   Intermediate Approach Fix

NoPT   No procedure turn, Race track pattern or any other type of course reversal procedure required or authorized without ATC clearance.

❶   Flag notes –see applicable reference notes elsewhere on the plan view.

Cross at FL 110 and descend to 3000'

WAKER   Crossing altitude and descent instructions.

TERPS VOR

Approach transition inset. (Dog leg route, with off-chart turn). Also provided when route originates at an off-chart intersection designated only for approach use—such fixes are not charted on enroute and area charts.

JOHNS

APPROACH TRANSITIONS (continued)

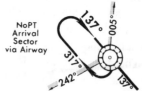

NoPT Arrival Sector via Airway

NoPT arrival sectors depict an area of approach transition routing to an approach fix. No procedure turn, Race Track Pattern or any type course reversal is required nor authorized without ATC clearance when an arrival course is within the charted sector and on an established airway radial to the fix.

Approach transition track, distance, and altitude from a defined fix is illustrated below.

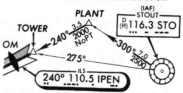

Note that the routes from STO to Plant to Tower are approach transitions, whereas the STO R-275° is not an approach transition. The STO R-275° has a small arrowhead and is a cross radial forming Tower. The STO R-300° has a large and small arrowhead indicating both an approach transition and a cross radial forming Plant. Plant and Tower are also formed by the IPEN localizer course.

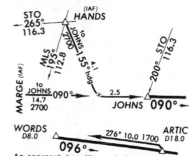

An approach transition coincidental with the approach procedure flight track is charted offset from the flight track for clarity.

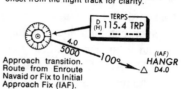

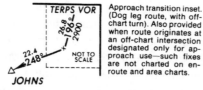

Approach transition. Route from Enroute Navaid or Fix to Initial Approach Fix (IAF).

Fig. 15-11   Reproduced with permission of Jeppesen Sanderson, Inc. Not for use in navigation.

overhead approaches. This is to help differentiate the various initial approaches and let you use the same charts if the terminal radar fails.

With more and more aircraft being compressed into the airspace, more and more routes seem to crop up on enroute and approach charts. At times, these routings result in a mess of lines crisscrossing the charts, intermixed with numbers and symbols. It is important to understand such subtle things as the differences in the widths of the lines, for example, or in the position of the numbers in relation to the lines so that you will have a full understanding of what the charts are trying to explain.

The approach transitions are tracks that are defined by courses, minimum altitudes, and fixes that are designed to bring you from the *initial approach fix* (IAF) to the *final approach fix* (FAF). The mileage figures shown on these transitions are only between the fixes shown on the transition. They are not the mileage to the airport.

Again, this is obvious while sitting in an easy chair under a no-stress condition, but it is possible to misread or misunderstand it while you're bouncing around in a rainstorm with flickering panel lights at night, especially if it is at the end of a 14- or 16-hour day.

On the bottom of the left-hand column, you can see how Jepp insets a dogleg route with an off-chart turn. It is important to note that these insets are not to scale; also, the dogleg turn fixes are not charted on enroute and area charts.

Look at the triangular-shaped transition halfway down the right-hand column and notice a route from Stout (STO) to TOWER. The route goes via PLANT intersection. Transition routes are depicted in heavy lines; they are the routes you must fly. You are not authorized to fly the 275-degree course from STO to TOWER because this light line with a small arrow only shows a cross-radial that helps to form the fix. You are only assured obstacle clearance when you are on the published route. The heavy line from STO to PLANT ends in a light line that indicates both an approach transition and a cross-radial.

In the next diagram below, you see two IAFs leading to an approach. HANDS is located by two cross-radials, one from STO and the other from MLS. Both facilities are off the chart as indicated by the complete identification of them. There is a dogleg 4.1 miles southeast of HANDS. From the dogleg, it is another 2.5 miles to JOHNS, which is identified by the 090-degree course and the 200-degree cross-radial from STO.

The second IAF is off the chart to the left. The IAF in this case is known as MARGE, and it is 14.7 miles to JOHNS as noted below the transition course line. There is also a minimum altitude of 2,700 feet shown on this section of the transition.

Because the approach procedure flight track is portrayed by a bold line, it would be difficult to show the approach transition segment when the segment coincides with the approach procedure track. The answer is to draw the approach transition alongside the approach-path line. The line signifying the approach transition will jut out from a fix and terminate in a heavy arrow pointing parallel to the approach path, as in the WORDS-ARTIC example in Fig. 15-11.

The upper left-hand column of Fig. 15-12 indicates how the approach transitions are depicted using DME arcs. The DME distance is shown alongside the arc itself, in this case the 18 DME. The minimum altitude is shown just inside the arc.

Transitioning for the approach

APPROACH CHART LEGEND
APPROACH PLAN VIEW (continued)

APPROACH TRANSITIONS (continued)

Approach transitions via DME arcs are illustrated below with distance from facility, direction of flight, start and termination points of the arc. DME arc approach transitions may be started from any airway or authorized direct route which intercepts the arc. DME arc altitude is maintained until established on approach course.

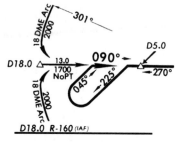

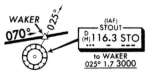

Lead radials may be provided as an advisory point for turning to the approach course.

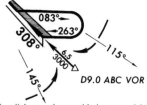

Approach transitions may be described under the originating navaid with course, distance, altitude, and terminating point.

APPROACH PROCEDURE FLIGHT TRACK

The approach procedure flight track is portrayed by a bold line. This track begins in the plan view at the same location where the profile begins.

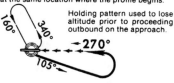

Holding pattern used to lose altitude prior to proceeding outbound on the approach.

················ High level approach track
◄ ◄ ◄ ◄ ◄ ◄ ◄ Visual flight track

PROCEDURE TURNS - COURSE REVERSALS

Schematic portrayal of procedure turn

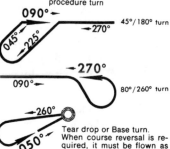

45°/180° turn

80°/260° turn

Tear drop or Base turn. When course reversal is required, it must be flown as charted.

Holding pattern or Racetrack pattern. When course reversal is required, it must be flown as charted.

When a procedure turn, Racetrack pattern, Teardrop or Base turn is not portrayed, they are not authorized.

ALTITUDES

2300′ — All altitudes in the plan view are "MINIMUM" altitudes unless specifically labeled otherwise. Altitudes are above mean sea level in feet. May be abbreviated "MIM."

MANDATORY 2400′ — Mandatory altitudes are labeled "MANDATORY" and mean at the fix or glide slope intercept.

MAXIMUM 1900′ — Maximum altitudes are labeled "MAXIMUM." May be abbreviated "MAX."

RECOMMENDED 2000′ — Recommended altitudes are labeled "RECOMMENDED."

MISSED APPROACH

▬ ▬ ▬ ▬ ▶ Initial maneuvering course for missed approach. Details of the missed approach are specified below the profile diagram.

Missed approach fix inset.

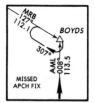

Fig. 15-12

The next illustration down shows how lead radials are depicted as advisory points of when to begin the turn inbound.

THE REST OF THE WAY IN

An interesting example of an approach procedure flight track is shown near the bottom of the left-hand column. It shows a holding pattern designed to lose altitude over an NDB, after which the outbound leg of the approach procedure is a 105-degree magnetic course followed by a left turn to a 270-degree magnetic course inbound. As the holding pattern is not really part of the approach procedure flight track, it is depicted with a fine line rather than a bold one. Once inbound, the series of small arrows indicate that the remainder of the approach is a *visual* flight path.

The right-hand column shows procedure turns and course reversals. Four are illustrated here. The upper one is a schematic of a procedure that might be called the "generic" procedure turn. Remember that this is just a schematic and need not be followed exactly. The same is true of the 80/260 turn that is shown. All you are required to do in these two cases is to make the reversal on the same side of the approach course as depicted and to stay within the protected airspace at or above the minimum altitude.

The next two course reversals, the teardrop and the holding pattern, however, must be followed as published. This is an important point to remember.

ODDS AND ENDS

Moving on to Fig. 15-13, as far as the missed approach is concerned, about all that is pictured on the chart is a heavy dashed line with a heavy arrowhead that shows the initial maneuvering course. The remainder of the procedure is written out in text form and can be found below the approach profile diagram.

Remember that if forced to execute a missed approach out of a circling approach, the initial climbing turn must be made toward the landing runway, then continue the turn until established on the missed approach course. The missed approach fix inset, shown near the top of the left-hand column, is depicted on charts when the missed approach fix is at a location outside the chart boundaries.

As a VFR pilot, you are conditioned to the color-coded sectional charts on which you can visualize what the enroute terrain will look like just by looking at the topographical color on the chart. As you transition from VFR to IFR flying, you have to reevaluate the information available on the charts. As an IFR pilot, you will require even more information from charts, but color coding it would make the other information too hard to find and hard to read. Although the airport chart shows more ground detail, about all you will get from the approach plate plan view is the type of airport, large masses of water, restricted areas, specific obstructions that might encroach upon your airspace, and a 5-statute-mile-radius circle around the airport. This circle has been omitted on charts published after October 1, 1993.

Carefully study orientation details and reference points. In the first place, not all of the obstructions will be charted.

APPROACH CHART LEGEND
APPROACH PLAN VIEW (continued)

HOLDING PATTERN

Holding pattern not part of the approach procedure. DME figures, when provided, give the DME distance of the fix as the first figure followed by the outbound limit as the second figure. 3000 indicates the minimum holding altitude, (MHA).

Length of holding pattern in minutes when other than standard.

Holding patterns are generally not charted to scale.

← Indicates procedure for leaving the holding pattern.

AIRPORTS

IFR airports in the area and VFR airports underlying the final approach are depicted.

	Airport to which the approach is designed
O	Nearby Military airport
⊙	Nearby Civil or joint use Military airport
	Heliport
	Civil Seaplane Base
⊕	Military Seaplane Base
☼	Airport with light beacon
⊗	Abandoned or closed airport
	An airport reference circle, 5 statute miles in radius, centered on the airport. Omitted after 1 OCT 93.

AIRSPACE

 Restricted airspace (Refer to the enroute chart for limitations.)

 ——PROHIBITED AREA SC(P)-23

ORIENTATION DETAILS

Lake or large water area

River

★ Aeronautical Light/Beacon

TERRAIN HIGH POINTS AND MAN-MADE STRUCTURES

1. Some, but not all, terrain high points and man-made structures are depicted, along with their elevation above mean sea level. THIS INFORMATION DOES NOT ASSURE CLEARANCE ABOVE OR AROUND THE TERRAIN OR MAN-MADE STRUCTURES

TERRAIN HIGH POINTS AND MAN-MADE STRUCTURES (continued)

AND MUST NOT BE RELIED ON FOR DESCENT BELOW THE MINIMUM ALTITUDES DICTATED BY THE APPROACH PROCEDURE. Generally, terrain high points and man-made structures less than 400 feet above the airport elevation are not depicted.

2. Symbols for terrain high points and man-made structures:

✳	Natural terrain (peak, knoll, hill, etc.) Used prior to August 12, 1988.
•	Unidentified natural terrain or man-made. Used prior to August 12, 1988.
●	Natural terrain (peak, knoll, hill, etc.) Used after August 12, 1988.
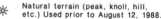	Man-made (tower, stack, tank, building, church)
⋀	Unidentified man-made structure
4460'	Mean Sea Level elevation at top of TERRAIN HIGH POINT/ MAN-MADE STRUCTURE.
±	Denotes unsurveyed accuracy
▼	Arrow indicates only the highest of portrayed TERRAIN HIGH POINTS AND MAN-MADE STRUCTURES in the charted planview. Higher terrain or man-made structures may exist which have not been portrayed.

⌐GENERALIZED TERRAIN CONTOURS

1. Generalized terrain contour information may be depicted when terrain within the approach chart planview exceeds 4000 feet above the airport elevation, or when terrain within 6 nautical miles of the Airport Reference Point (ARP) rises to a least 2000 feet above the airport elevation. THIS INFORMATION DOES NOT ASSURE CLEARANCE ABOVE OR AROUND THE TERRAIN AND MUST NOT BE RELIED ON FOR DESCENT BELOW THE MINIMUM ALTITUDES DICTATED BY THE APPROACH PROCEDURE. Furthermore, the absence of terrain contour information does not endure the absence of terrain or structures.

2. Terrain features are depicted using one of the two following methods:

   a) Prior to June 24, 1994, terrain information was depicted as screened contour lines with contour values.

   b) After June 24, 1994, screened contour lines will gradually be replaced with generalized contour lines, values and gradient tints printed in brown. Gradient tints indicate the elevation change between contour intervals.

Fig. 15-13

Prior to August 1988, many of the obstructions were indicated. Now, reference points lower than 400 feet above the airport elevation are not depicted, and none of the reference points shown can be relied upon to provide terrain or obstruction clearance because other higher obstacles might be in the same area.

"Why is that?" you ask. Well, it's to avoid clutter on the chart for one thing, and for another you aren't supposed to descend that low anyway, so the obstacles shouldn't really concern you. Remember, as long as you are on the prescribed approach course at or above the minimum allowable altitude, you won't have any problems with obstructions.

CHAPTER QUIZ

1. Jeppesen approach charts are effective when you receive them.

   True _____ False _____

2. The three sources that provide the information for chart updates are:

   1. _____ from the Federal Register,

   2. the daily _____, and

   3. _____.

3. In the Jeppesen method of indexing charts, what is the difference between an 11-1 chart and a 21-1 chart? Which is more important?

4. What does the second numeral in the index (such as the 3 in 13-1) denote?

5. The MSA is designed to provide the pilot with _____.

6. You might not always receive navigational signals when flying within the sectors of the MSA.

   True _____ False _____

7. What does the letter suffix on approach charts indicate?

8. The symbol NoPT on a chart indicates that if you are low enough, you can make a straight-in approach without using a course reversal.

   True _____ False _____

9. All holding patterns must be flown as indicated on the approach chart.

   True _____ False _____

Answers are in the appendix.

16
Approach
chart profile view

OFFICIALLY, THE PROFILE VIEW OF THE APPROACH CHART IS DESCRIBED AS the "vertical cross-section of the plan view." It is like watching the aircraft descend while standing off to the side of the approach path. The plan view depicts the flight path over the ground; the profile view shows the aircraft's altitude above the surface and is, therefore, a very crucial tool for the instrument pilot.

Three types of nonprecision approach profiles are shown in Fig. 16-1. Above them is a table of recommended altitudes/heights at various DME fixes. This table is designed to allow for a constant rate of descent; however, the altitudes/heights are only *recommended* figures, and the minimums depicted in the profile view still apply.

Regarding the tables, they do not always read from left to right as most other tables do. They are orientated to read in the same direction as the profile is depicted.

NONPRECISION APPROACHES

Examine the uppermost approach depicted on Fig. 16-1, which is the standard nonprecision approach that includes an overhead approach, an outbound leg, a procedure

APPROACH CHART PROFILE VIEW

APPROACH CHART LEGEND
PROFILE VIEW

The top of the profile view on certain *non-precision* approaches contains a table of *recommended* altitudes/heights at various DME fixes to allow a constant rate of descent. The altitudes/heights are *recommended* only; minimum altitudes in the profile view apply. The table is sequenced in the same direction as the profile is portrayed.

LOC (GS out)	BMN DME	7.0	6.0	5.0	4.0	3.0	2.0
	ALTITUDE *(HAT)*	2240'(2227')	1920'(1907')	1600'(1587')	1330'(1317')	960'(947')	650'(637')

↱ DME fixes ↰

↳ Approach type when combined with precision approach

Recommended altitudes/heights ↰

Notes pertaining to conditional use of the procedure are shown at the top of the profile. The note "Pilot controlled lighting" indicates that pilot activation is required as specified on the airport chart under Additional Runway Information.

The profile view schematically (not to scale) portrays the approach procedure flight track as a vertical cross section of the plan view.

NON-PRECISION APPROACH PROFILE (LOC, VOR, VORTAC, NDB, etc.)
M symbol representing the non-precision missed approach point (MAP), as shown below, is used on charts dated on or after 5 FEB 93. This symbol is omitted when more than one non-precision approach track is depicted.

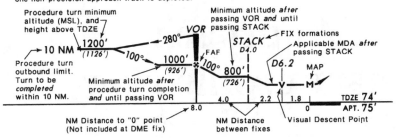

NON-PRECISION APPROACH PROFILE (LOC, VOR, VORTAC, NDB, etc.)
with constant rate of descent

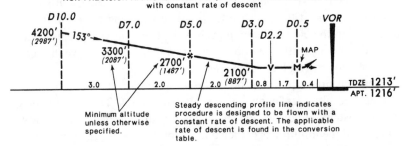

Minimum altitude unless otherwise specified.

Steady descending profile line indicates procedure is designed to be flown with a constant rate of descent. The applicable rate of descent is found in the conversion table.

NON-PRECISION APPROACH PROFILE (VISUAL APPROACH)

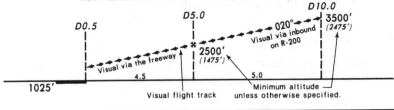

Visual flight track

Minimum altitude unless otherwise specified.

Fig. 16-1 Reproduced with permission of Jeppesen Sanderson, Inc. Not for use in navigation.

turn, and inbound leg. You begin by passing over the VOR and proceeding outbound on the 280-degree radial. Notice a group of numbers to the left of the profile. These numbers represent the procedure turn and define the turn's limits. In this case, the procedure turn must be completed within 10 nautical miles of the VOR, the fix that the turn is predicated upon. Remember this: The protected airspace begins at the fix where the outbound track begins, not necessarily from the final approach fix, unless they are collocated. Also, the turn *must be completed* within the distance specified.

The large number above the line (1200') is the minimum altitude for the procedure turn, and the smaller number in parentheses below the line (1126') is the height in feet above the TDZE (touchdown zone elevation), the runway end, or the airport.

The most complete definition of the TDZE is in the pilot/controller glossary:

> TOUCHDOWN ZONE ELEVATION—The highest elevation in the first 3,000 feet of the landing surface. TDZE is indicated on the instrument approach procedure chart when straight-in landing minimums are authorized.

For more on the TDZE, look ahead and refer to Fig. 16-4, about midway down from the top left of the figure and notice that the number shown in parentheses (1200') is the:

> Height in feet above airport, runway end, or TDZ elevation. Height is measured from airport elevation unless TDZE or runway end elevation is noted at the airport symbol.

The airport symbol referred to is the heavy horizontal bar on the ground reference line (which is the next symbol down from the top left of Fig. 16-4, as well as that shown in the right side of the two top illustrations in Fig. 16-1). Going back to the non-precision approach mentioned above, you will see that after completing the procedure turn and inbound on the 280-degree radial (equivalent to a magnetic course of 100 degrees, or 100 degrees TO on the VOR), you are allowed to descend a little lower, in this case down to 1,000 feet MSL (926 feet above the TDZE), until reaching the FAF.

INBOUND FROM THE FAF

The nonprecision FAF is identified by a Maltese cross symbol on the profile view. The FAF is described in the chart glossary:

> FINAL APPROACH FIX (FAF)—The fix from which the final approach (IFR) to an airport is executed and which identifies the beginning of the final approach segment. It is designated in the profile view of Jeppesen Terminal charts by the Maltese Cross symbol for nonprecision approaches and by the glide slope/path intercept point on precision approaches. The glide slope/path symbol starts at the FAF. When ATC directs a lower-than-published Glide slope/path Intercept Altitude, it is the resultant actual point of the glide slope/path intercept.

APPROACH CHART PROFILE VIEW

APPROACH CHART LEGEND
PROFILE VIEW (continued)

PRECISION APPROACH PROFILE [ILS with LOC (GS out), or with NDB Approach]

M symbol representing the non-precision missed approach point (MAP), as shown below, is used on charts dated on or after 5 FEB 93. This symbol is omitted when more than one non-precision approach track is depicted.

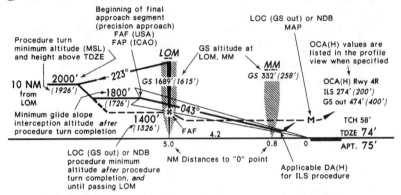

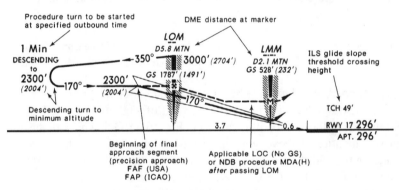

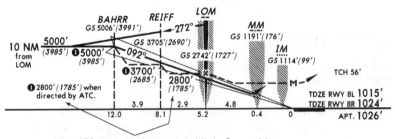

When ATC directs the lower noted altitude: For precision approaches, the altitude becomes the minimum glide slope intercept altitude and the resultant actual point of glide slope intercept becomes the FAF (USA).

Fig. 16-2 Reproduced with permission of Jeppesen Sanderson, Inc. Not for use in navigation.

Inbound past the FAF (in this case the VOR), the course to the runway will be the 100-degree radial of the VOR (100 degrees FROM on the OBI). The numeral 8.0 under the VOR symbol and below the ground reference line indicates the distance, in nautical miles, between that point and the 0 point (in this case, the runway threshold). The zero point can be shown under middle markers, inner markers, or other points as well. It is not shown when a DME fix is at the same location. As an example, there is no mileage shown under the ground reference line at STACK. Indicated by D4.0, STACK is 4.0 miles from the VOR. The VOR in this case is also the FAF.

On the other hand, look at the center illustration on Fig. 16-2, and you will see underneath the letters LOM (outer compass locator) a DME distance of 5.8 from MTN, while the 4.7 is below the ground reference line.

Similar data is printed for the LMM (inner compass locator). The reason for this is that the DME to the markers is measured from a geographical point other than the 0 point, whereas the numerals beneath the ground reference line show the distance to the 0 point at the runway threshold.

Continuing with Fig. 16-1, after you pass the FAF inbound, use a step-down descent, descending first to 800 feet MSL until past STACK, which is a fix 4.0 DME along the 100-degree radial on the final approach course. Once past STACK, you can descend to the MDA.

VISUALIZING THE VDP

Above the ground-reference line, notice 4.0 between the FAF and STACK, 2.2 between STACK and the V symbol, and 1.8 between the V symbol and the runway threshold. These are the segment distances between these points, all of which add up to the 8.0 miles from the FAF to the 0 point.

The V symbol is the visual descent point (VDP) that is described in the chart glossary:

> VISUAL DESCENT POINT/VDP—A defined point on the final approach course of a nonprecision straight-in approach procedure from which normal descent from the MDA to the runway touchdown point may be commenced, provided the approach threshold of that runway, or approach lights, or other markings identifiable with the approach end of that runway are clearly visible to the pilot.

In other words, you are not to go below the MDA until you are past the VDP. When flying VFR, it's also a good idea to stay at or above the MDA until the VPD; this will give you a mental picture of what the runway environment will look like under real-life instrument conditions.

To save the trouble of having to add up all of the segment distances, the distance from the applicable facility, in this case D6.2, is included above the descent profile line.

In the center illustration of Fig. 16-1, notice a nonprecision profile using a steady rate of descent. You can find the rate of descent in the conversion table (which is discussed later), but the minimum altitudes shown at the various points of the approach still apply. In this example, the VOR is on the airport surface, and the missed approach point is 0.4 mile from the runway threshold. The small arrow pointing toward the runway indicates that the rest of the approach (from the MAP in this case) must be flown visually.

At times, you will find a nonprecision profile utilizing a visual approach as illustrated at the bottom of Fig.16-1, but this is self-explanatory.

A new symbol "M" has been appearing on the nonprecision approach profiles since February 1993. This indicates the missed approach point. It will be omitted if there is more than one nonprecision approach depicted on the chart.

PRECISION APPROACHES CUT A FINE LINE

Precision approaches feature additional symbols. Take a look at the top illustration in Fig. 6-2. The first difference is between the procedure turn information and the FAF. The descent profile has been split into two different lines, one solid and one dashed.

Many airports will use locater beacons in conjunction with the outer marker. Sometimes this beacon will be incorporated into an NDB approach and the dashed line will signify the descent profile for the NDB approach. At other times, the glide slope might malfunction—either the airborne equipment or the ground equipment—in which case the ILS will revert to a LOC approach (minimums will be affected) and again the dashed line will signify the profile flight path.

Why do you see two different approach altitudes (1800' and 1400') inbound after the procedure turn? Because the entry to each type of approach is based on different thinking. Without glide path or DME information, you are never really sure where you are along the ground track, unless of course you are crossing one of the fixes. So, you want to get down as low as possible as soon as possible to reach the MDA before arriving at the MAP. On the other hand, when you do have the glide path information, you'll usually want to have the aircraft stabilized on the glide slope as soon as possible, certainly prior to crossing the LOM inbound.

The nonprecision FAF, as indicated by the Maltese cross, is the LOM in this illustration; however, the FAF for precision approaches is always the published glide slope intercept point, which in this case is reached prior to the LOM (unless ATC has authorized a lower-than-normal glide slope intercept altitude). The inbound ILS course of 043 degrees is illustrated inside the localizer symbol, and the glide slope altitude of 1,689 feet (1,615 feet above TDZE) at the LOM is under the two-dash Morse code identifier of the LOM.

To illustrate these points further, realize that from the glide path intercept point, which is slightly before crossing the FAF, to the DH, an aircraft on an ILS approach will continue down a steady descent path; however, an aircraft flying the localizer or NDB approach will descend to 1,400 feet MSL before crossing the FAF. Then it will descend to the MDA, level off, and maintain the MDA until it reaches the MAP.

Again, note the distances from fixes to the 0 point listed below the ground-reference line. The 4.2 above the line is the distance between the LOM and the MM.

Recall the last sentence in the earlier definition of the final approach fix. A lower glide slope/path intercept point can be used when directed by ATC. The lower diagram on Fig. 16-2 illustrates this very well. The step-down altitudes are shown for the nonprecision approach on the chart, but the note states that the lower 2,800-foot altitude can be used as the glide slope/path intercept point when directed by ATC. In this case, the final approach point for the precision approach will still begin at the glide slope/path intercept point, not at the nonprecision FAF point at the LOM as indicated by the Maltese Cross symbol. You must always have a definite point at which to begin the final approach segment; without the glide slope/path indication in the cockpit, you will have to wait until the LOM can be identified.

DH, MAP, AND OTHER ACRONYMS

Look at the differences in altitudes and geographical positions between the DH and the MAP. In the first place, understand that the DH is the altitude you will be at when you arrive at the MAP on an ILS approach, *if* you are properly on the glide slope.

On the other hand, on a nonprecision approach, when you reach the MDA, you are allowed to fly out the *time* to the MAP before initiating the missed approach procedure. In this case, descent as low as an ILS is not allowed due to a lack of precision either in altitude or azimuth or both. After all, if you are timing the approach, the actual ground position can vary slightly from the charted MAP, and if you don't get down to the MDA before reaching the MAP, you will still have to break off the approach if you don't have the runway environment in sight. The higher minimum altitude provides adequate obstruction clearance, compensating for the lack of precision.

Other notes might be placed in the profile view. One found in this illustration is the *threshold crossing height* (TCH), which in this case is 58 feet. You will only find this on precision approaches as it signifies the height at which the glide slope crosses the threshold. On some charts, its placement might lead you to believe that it refers to the nonprecision approach path that it appears to be attached to, but remember that it is the threshold crossing height *for the glide slope*.

If the *obstruction clearance altitude* (OCA) is lower than the charted DH or MDA, it will be listed as shown in the illustration. In this case, it is depicted (even though it is the same as the DH) because it is definitely lower than the MDA.

The center profile of Fig. 16-2 shows a descending turn in combination with the procedure turn. The procedure turn is to be started after flying outbound for a specific time (in this case, 1 minute). It also shows an LMM rather than just the MM shown in the upper illustration.

CAT II AND CAT IIIA

Moving on to the top of Fig. 16-3, we find the granddaddies of all instrument approaches. You might fly your entire career and never get into equipment that will allow you to fly down to these minimums—as low as zero/zero on a CAT IIIC. Still, you should be aware of how they are portrayed.

APPROACH CHART PROFILE VIEW

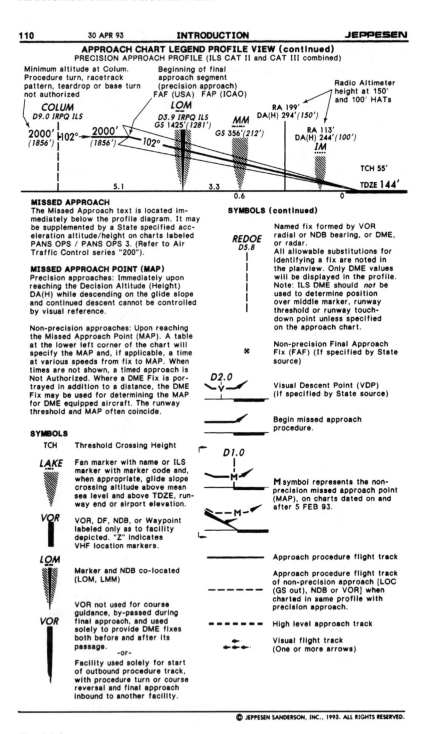

APPROACH CHART LEGEND PROFILE VIEW (continued)
PRECISION APPROACH PROFILE (ILS CAT II and CAT III combined)

Minimum altitude at Colum. Procedure turn, racetrack pattern, teardrop or base turn not authorized

Beginning of final approach segment (precision approach) FAF (USA) FAP (ICAO)

Radio Altimeter height at 150' and 100' HATs

COLUM
D9.0 IRPQ ILS

LOM
D3.9 IRPQ ILS
GS 1425'(1281')

MM
GS 356'(212')

RA 199'
DA(H) 294'(150')

2000'
(1856')
⊢102°

2000'
(1856')
102°

RA 113'
DA(H) 244'(100')
IM

TCH 55'

TDZE **144'**

5.1   3.3   0
         0.6

MISSED APPROACH

The Missed Approach text is located immediately below the profile diagram. It may be supplemented by a State specified acceleration altitude/height on charts labeled PANS OPS / PANS OPS 3. (Refer to Air Traffic Control series "200").

MISSED APPROACH POINT (MAP)

Precision approaches: Immediately upon reaching the Decision Altitude (Height) DA(H) while descending on the glide slope and continued descent cannot be controlled by visual reference.

Non-precision approaches: Upon reaching the Missed Approach Point (MAP). A table at the lower left corner of the chart will specify the MAP and, if applicable, a time at various speeds from fix to MAP. When times are not shown, a timed approach is Not Authorized. Where a DME Fix is portrayed in addition to a distance, the DME Fix may be used for determining the MAP for DME equipped aircraft. The runway threshold and MAP often coincide.

SYMBOLS

TCH   Threshold Crossing Height

LAKE   Fan marker with name or ILS marker with marker code and, when appropriate, glide slope crossing altitude above mean sea level and above TDZE, runway end or airport elevation.

VOR   VOR, DF, NDB, or Waypoint labeled only as to facility depicted. "Z" indicates VHF location markers.

LOM   Marker and NDB co-located (LOM, LMM)

VOR   VOR not used for course guidance, by-passed during final approach, and used solely to provide DME fixes both before and after its passage.
      -or-
Facility used solely for start of outbound procedure track, with procedure turn or course reversal and final approach inbound to another facility.

SYMBOLS (continued)

REDOE
D5.8   Named fix formed by VOR radial or NDB bearing, or DME, or radar.
All allowable substitutions for identifying a fix are noted in the planview. Only DME values will be displayed in the profile. Note: ILS DME should *not* be used to determine position over middle marker, runway threshold or runway touchdown point unless specified on the approach chart.

＊   Non-precision Final Approach Fix (FAF) (If specified by State source)

D2.0   Visual Descent Point (VDP) (if specified by State source)

Begin missed approach procedure.

D1.0   M symbol represents the non-precision missed approach point (MAP), on charts dated on and after 5 FEB 93.

Approach procedure flight track

Approach procedure flight track of non-precision approach [LOC (GS out), NDB or VOR] when charted in same profile with precision approach.

High level approach track

Visual flight track (One or more arrows)

Fig. 16-3   Reproduced with permission of Jeppesen Sanderson, Inc. Not for use in navigation.

In the first place, these are straight-in approaches in which neither procedure turns, base turns, nor any other turn is authorized. The aircraft has to be specially equipped and certified, and you have to be certified as well. The beginning of the approach is just like any other ILS, but notice where the descent ends. That's right, the runway. It flies you right to the ground.

The letters RA appear twice, once at the inner marker (IM) not used in normal ILS approaches, and again at a point between the MM and the IM. The numbers shown after the RA are for the radio altimeter height above the ground at those points. Those points are at 150 and 100 feet above touchdown or height above touchdown (HAT).

If that's the case, why don't the radio altimeters read 150 and 100 at these points? That's because radio altimeters read directly off the ground, and the ground at any given distance from the runway is very seldom the same elevation as the runway itself. In the first instance, the radio altimeter would read 199 feet, so the ground is 49 feet below the touchdown elevation. In the second instance the radio altimeter would read 113 feet, so the ground there is 13 feet lower than the touchdown zone.

Get an uncluttered look at some of the profile symbols by looking at the rest of the symbols on Fig. 16-3. Here is the VDP, the FAF, the visual flight track path, and others.

A recent new symbol is DA(H). Although this is really an ICAO symbol, Jeppesen is using it on its charts so it might as well be discussed. The DA is the decision altitude referenced to MSL (the DH is the decision height referenced to the touchdown elevation). Another new symbol is MDA(H), with the same mean-sea-level explanation.

MISSED APPROACH

Recall the approach chart format; the heading information was at the top of the page, followed by the approach plan view, under that is the profile view, and finally, at the bottom of the page are the landing minimums.

The missed approach procedures are written out below the profile view just before the landing minimums. The missed approach is a very crucial area of the approach. Here you are at a minimum altitude, tooling along in the dark (so to speak), with the aircraft all dirtied up and ready to land. If you can't see the airport when you get to the MAP, it's time to get back up in the ozone where you will be safe. But in order to clean up, climb, and miss all of the buildings, trees, poles, mountains, and the like, the missed approach must be executed in an orderly fashion.

When reviewing the approach plates prior to filing the flight plan, you also reviewed the missed approach procedure. When there are two pilots aboard, it's a good idea for the one not flying to read the missed approach procedure aloud after passing the FAF inbound.

When there is only one pilot on board, I find it useful to copy the missed approach procedure in advance on a small file card or on one of those pages from the telephone answering pad and tape it to the glare shield where I can see it without having to take my hands off the controls. (Naturally, when taping the card up it has to be placed where

APPROACH CHART PROFILE VIEW

APPROACH CHART LEGEND
PROFILE VIEW (continued)

SYMBOLS (continued)

2300'
All altitudes in the profile view are "MINIMUM" altitudes unless specifically labeled otherwise. Altitudes are above mean sea level in feet. May be abbreviated "MIM".

MANDATORY 2400'
Mandatory altitudes are labeled "MANDATORY" and mean at the fix or glide slope intercept.

MAXIMUM 1900'
Maximum altitudes are labeled "MAXIMUM". May be abbreviated "MAX".

OCL Rwy 04R 274' (200')
Obstruction Clearance Limit

OCA(H) Rwy 26 720' (263')
Obstruction Clearance Altitude (Height)

RECOMMENDED 2000'
Recommend altitudes are labeled "RECOMMENDED".

(1200')
Height in feet above airport, runway end, or TDZ elevation. Height is measured from airport elevation unless TDZE or runway end elevation is noted at the airport symbol.

TDZE 74'
Touchdown Zone Elevation. (Runway End or Threshold Elevation when labeled RWY).

APT. 75'
Official Airport Elevation

10 NM 1200' (1126')
Procedure turn minimum altitude (MSL)

Height above TDZE, runway end, runway threshold, or airport.

Procedure turn outbound limit. When the outbound procedure track is depicted in the profile view, the turn limit is from the fix where the outbound track begins. The turn must be carried out within the specified distance.

Combined procedure turn (course reversals) and NoPT procedure flight tracks

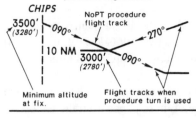

Minimum altitude at fix.

NoPT procedure flight track

Flight tracks when procedure turn is used

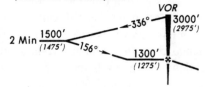

1 Min 080° → ← 260° 2000' (1900')
Racetrack used in lieu of procedure turn with holding limit, outbound and inbound bearings, and minimum altitude.

For a racetrack and holding in lieu of procedure turn, the outbound track corresponds to the plan view depiction beginning at a point abeam the facility/fix.

Procedure based on 120 KT TAS.
When airspeeds are indicated in profile note, higher airspeeds require shortened times to assure remaining in the protected area.

Radar required.
Radar vectoring is required when it is the only approved method for providing a procedure entry and/or for identifying a terminal fix.

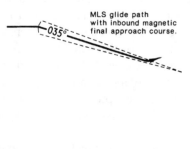

Glide Slope with inbound magnetic course of Localizer.

Glide Slope, Glide path intercept is the Final Approach Fix (FAF USA), Final Approach Point (FAP ICAO) for precision approaches. The glide slope symbol starts at the FAF/FAP.

MLS glide path with inbound magnetic final approach course.

Fig. 16-4 Reproduced with permission of Jeppesen Sanderson, Inc. Not for use in navigation.

it won't block the instruments from view.) I put the initial turn and altitude information in large capital letters so they'll catch my eye.

Remember, when the time comes to execute the missed approach, you will be pretty busy applying power, retracting the gear and flaps, transitioning from a descent to a climb regime, turning, resetting navigational radios, and reporting to the proper control facility, so you won't have time to scan a page in the manual for the procedure *and you definitely don't want to rely on your memory.*

Figure 16-4 presents a few more symbols that might be of interest. The bottom illustration in the left-hand column shows how a procedure turn and a NoPT flight path would be symbolized at the same facility.

You have already reviewed the procedure turn symbol. The upper right-hand symbol shows a holding pattern used in lieu of a procedure turn. Here notice the inbound and outbound bearings as well as the time of the inbound leg and the minimum altitude. Below this symbol is another one that shows a holding pattern and racetrack in lieu of a procedure turn that is depicted somewhat differently. Here you have the outbound track shown in the descending line that would begin abeam the VOR, and the inbound track showing how you would descend from the holding pattern when cleared for an approach.

Note the words "Procedure based on 120 KT TAS" in the next example. This indicates that if you have a faster aircraft, you will have to reduce all times to remain within the protected airspace.

LANDING MINIMUMS

Landing minimums are presented in a standard-format table depending on the type of approach. To simplify the understanding of these minimums, the only information shown in each table will be those items that specifically affect that particular approach.

Examine the USA FORMAT found at the top of Fig. 16-5. The letters A, B, C, and D running down the left-hand border of the format signify the aircraft categories.

The table is broken up into various blocks. The DA(H) or MDA(H) will be shown in the upper part of the table, while the visibility requirements necessary to initiate the approach will be shown in the blocks below.

The format shown in Fig. 16-5 is just an illustration. The headings used on the actual charts might be somewhat different, depending upon which lights and auxiliary systems are available on a particular approach. Furthermore, the delineations of the various blocks will depend on many factors, like the airport itself, the surrounding terrain or aircraft performance, for instance.

The lowest minimums listed in any format will be found on the left side of the chart. Less-desirable minimums are shown in descending order to the right. In this case, note that all minimums to the left of the vertical line running from top to bottom are predicated upon straight-in approaches. The minimums to the right side of the line are for circling approaches.

Notice that the top two formats are for United States charts. The upper example is

APPROACH CHART LEGEND LANDING MINIMUMS (continued)

USA FORMAT - Prior to 15 October 1992 Effective date.

STRAIGHT-IN LANDING RWY 36L — CIRCLE-TO-LAND

	ILS DA(H) 212′ (200′) FULL	ILS DA(H) 212′ (200′) TDZ or CL out	ILS DA(H) 212′ (200′) ALS out	DA(H) 262′ (250′) MM out	LOC (GS out) MDA(H) 400′ (388′)	LOC (GS out) ALS out	Max Kts	MDA(H)
A	RVR 18 or ½	RVR 24 or ½	RVR 40 or ¾	RVR 24 or ½	RVR 24 or ½	RVR 50 or 1	90	560′ (533′)-1
B							120	
C							140	560′ (533′)-1½
D				RVR 40 or ¾	RVR 40 or ¾	RVR 60 or 1¼	165	580′ (553′)-2

USA FORMAT - Effective 15 October 1992 and all succeeding revisions.

STRAIGHT-IN LANDING RWY 36L — CIRCLE-TO-LAND

	ILS DA(H) 212′ (200′) FULL	ILS DA(H) 212′ (200′) TDZ or CL out	ILS DA(H) 212′ (200′) ALS out	LOC (GS out) MDA(H) 400′ (388′)	LOC (GS out) ALS out	Max Kts	MDA(H)
A	RVR 18 or ½	RVR 24 or ½	RVR 40 or ¾	RVR 24 or ½	RVR 50 or 1	90	560′ (533′)-1
B						120	
C						140	560′ (533′)-1½
D				RVR 40 or ¾	RVR 60 or 1¼	165	580′ (553′)-2

WORLD-WIDE FORMAT

STRAIGHT-IN LANDING RWY 36L — CIRCLE-TO-LAND

	ILS DA(H) 212′ (200′) FULL	ILS DA(H) 212′ (200′) TDZ or CL out	ILS DA(H) 212′ (200′) ALS out	LOC (GS out) MDA(H) 400′ (388′)	LOC (GS out) ALS out	Max Kts	MDA(H)
A	RVR 550m VIS 800m	RVR 720m VIS 800m	1200m	RVR 720m VIS 800m	RVR 1500m VIS 1600m	100	560′ (533′) -1600m
B						135	
C						180	630′ (603′) -2800m
D				1200m	RVR 1800m VIS 2000m	205	730′ (703′) -3600m

SIDESTEP INOPERATIVE COMPONENTS

For a runway identified as sidestep, such as SIDESTEP RWY 24L:
Inoperative light components shown in Rwy 24L column are those for the lights installed on *Rwy 24L, not* the lights for Rwy 24R.

CIRCLE-TO-LAND

Starting with charts dated July 28, 1989, *maximum aircraft speeds* for circling are shown in lieu of Aircraft Approach Categories. The maximum indicated airspeeds are shown in knots (kilometers per hour on Metric Edition charts).

U.S. STANDARD FOR TERMINAL INSTRUMENT APPROACH PROCEDURES (TERPS)

CIRCLE-TO-LAND

Max Kts	MDA(H)
90	560′ (533′)-1
120	
140	560′ (533′)-1½
165	580′ (553′)-2

NEW INTERNATIONAL CIVIL AVIATION ORGANIZATION (ICAO) FLIGHT PROCEDURES

CIRCLE-TO-LAND

Max Kts	MDA(H)
100	560′ (533′) -1600m
135	
180	630′ (603′) -2800m
205	730′ (703′) -3600m

Known deviations to the above speeds are charted. For the few countries that have not published maximum circling speeds, aircraft approach categories A,B,C and D will continue to be shown.

Aircraft Approach Categories in the straight-in minimum column can be read across the chart from left to right for referencing the circle-to-land information.

The fact that straight-in-minimums are not published does not preclude the pilot from landing straight-in, using published circling minimums, if he has the straight-in runway in sight in sufficient time to make a normal approach for landing. Under such conditions, and when Air Traffic Control has cleared him for landing on that runway, he is not expected to circle even though straight-in minimums are not published. If he desires to circle, he should advise ATC.

Fig. 16-5 Reproduced with permission of Jeppesen Sanderson, Inc. Not for use in navigation.

for charts published prior to October 15, 1992, while the next illustration down is for charts published after October 15, 1992.

Since October 15, 1992, none of the approaches in the United States require higher minimums for the loss of the MM.

Whenever you see a horizontal line, it will tell you that visibility minimums are different above and below the line. These differences are not always the same for each category in each situation, so very carefully check the landing minimums for the approach charts. This statement cannot be repeated too often.

CIRCLING MINIMUMS

To the right of the vertical line are the landing minimums for circling approaches. A recent change (July 28, 1989) has made the circling minimums easier to understand. Now, instead of category letters being shown on the left side of the columns, you will find speeds listed. These are the same V_{SO} speeds as you will find for the categories, but they simplify planning for you.

Recall that if an aircraft had to circle at a speed higher than what was listed for its category, the aircraft would occupy the next higher category for a circling approach. These speeds simplify that process.

That will not happen in most general aviation aircraft, but as you progress in flying you will probably move up to a high performance business aircraft or an airliner. Many of these will maneuver at a flap setting lower than the landing flaps, termed *maneuvering* or *approach flaps*. The V_{S1} will increase with these different flap settings, and may very well throw you into the higher approach category. It's a lot easier to read the numbers than it is to have to convert to letters.

The worldwide formats are also shown in Fig. 16-5. The biggest differences are that the worldwide charts show the distances in meters or kilometers, rather than in feet or miles. If meters are used, the full value is shown as well as the letter m; if only a number is shown, it is feet or miles. Also, the circling speeds are slightly higher.

Conversion tables are useful for a couple of reasons, but to give them more meaning, let's look at the examples shown in Fig. 16-6.

The obvious time to use this table is when you are flying an approach that uses time/speed to determine the MAP. It's also a good backup for any approach in which it can be utilized, especially nonprecision approaches. On precision approaches it gives a fairly good estimate of the rate of descent you'll need to stay on the glide slope. If you maintain this rate of descent, yet find yourself deviating from the glide slope, sometimes this will be the first indication that a wind shear exists.

The conversion table at the top left of Fig. 16-6 is for a precision approach. The upper line is ground speed in knots. This means that you will have to convert from statute miles per hour, unless the airspeed indicator is calibrated in knots, and then add or subtract the known or estimated headwind or tailwind components. Naturally, you will have to interpolate, but that should be no major problem. The second line shows the glide slope angle, in this case it is 2.50 degrees, as well as what the rate of descent should be, based upon the estimated ground speed, to stay on the glide slope.

APPROACH CHART PROFILE VIEW

APPROACH CHART LEGEND
LANDING MINIMUMS (continued)

CONVERSION TABLE

At the bottom of the approach chart page, there is a conversion table as shown below.

Gnd speed-Kts		70	90	100	120	140	160
GS	2.50°	315	405	450	541	631	721
LOM to MAP	5.0	4:17	3:20	3:00	2:30	2:09	1:53

Gnd speed-Kts	70	90	100	120	140	160
VOR to MAP 3.9	3:21	2:36	2:20	1:57	1:40	1:28

The speed table relates aircraft approach speeds to the rate of descent for the ILS glide slope (descent in feet per minute). For non-precision approaches it relates speed to the distance shown from the final approach fix (FAF) or other specified fix to the missed approach point (MAP).

Some missed approach points are calculated on a time/speed basis after completion of the procedure turn inbound on final approach. The absence to time/speed table means the MAP cannot be determined by time and a timed approach is Not Authorized.

Gnd speed-Kts	70	90	100	120	140	160
Descent rate D7.0 to D3.0	466	600	667	800	934	1067
MAP at D1.5						

Non-precision approaches designed to be flown at a constant rate of descent have a rate of descent provided in the conversion table. The conversion table specifies a rate of descent that allows arrival at minimum altitudes shown in the profile view. The descent rate is a recommended rate only. Minimum altitudes shown in the profile view apply.

Gnd speed-Kts		70	90	100	120	140	160
Rwy 5, 23, PAR GS	2.50°	315	405	450	541	631	721
Rwy 30 PAR GS	2.55°	322	413	459	551	643	735

On PAR charts:
Speed table with rates of descent on PAR glide slope is provided.

Gnd speed-Kts	70	90	100	120	140	160
Descent Gradient 5.9%	418	538	597	717	836	956
MAP at VOR						

When provided by the State, a non-precision descent gradient is provided with a descent table in feet per minute.

Gnd speed-Kts	70	90	100	120	140	160
ILS GS 3.00° or LOC Descent Gradient 5.2%	377	484	538	644	753	861
MAP at MM						

For combined ILS and non-precision approaches, only one descent table is provided when the ILS glide slope angle and the descent gradient are coincidental.

Gnd speed-Kts		70	90	100	120	140	160
Glide path Angle 3.00°		377	485	539	647	755	863
FAF to MAP	5.1	4:22	3:24	3:04	2:33	2:11	1:55

On MLS charts the Glide path angle authorized for the procedure and rate of descent table is provided.

Amendment number of a procedure. An amendment number increase generally indicates a procedure change.

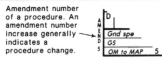

"MILITARY" notation, shown here on charts dated on and after JUN 8-90 indicates military source used for the procedure.

ON CHARTS DATED ON OR AFTER DEC 16-88 (NOT APPLICABLE TO USA AND CANADA)

⌐ "PANS-OPS" margin notation indicates that the State has specified that the instrument approach procedure complies with the ICAO Procedures for Air Navigation Services-Aircraft Operations (PANS-OPS) Document 8168, Volume II, 1st or 2nd Edition. Aircraft handling speeds for these procedures are shown on Introduction Page 2 under "AIRCRAFT APPROACH CATEGORY (ICAO)". Known deviations to these handling speeds are charted.

"PANS-OPS 3" further indicates that holding speeds to be used are those specified in Document 8168, Volume II, Third Edition.

"PANS-OPS 4" further indicates that the acceleration segment criteria have been deleted, as formerly published in Document 8168, Volume II, Third Edition.

Jeppesen International Air Traffic Control ("200" Series) pages provide an extract of the latest PANS-OPS Document 8168, Volume I. They highlight the major differences of Document 8168, Volume I and the earlier version, concerning holding speeds. Holding speed tables for both the earlier revision, and the later Edition 3 and 4, of PANS-OPS are included in ⌊ these pages.

Fig. 16-6 Reproduced with permission of Jeppesen Sanderson, Inc. Not for use in navigation.

The bottom line gives the amount of time (in minutes and seconds) from the non-precision FAF to the MAP, useful for timed localizer approaches when the glide slope is out of service. In the example, it shows that the distance from the LOM to the MAP is 2.6 nautical miles, and time ranges from 2 minutes and 14 seconds to just 59 seconds, depending on the ground speed.

In the nonprecision approach table on the right, the glide slope line is omitted. The distance from the VOR to the MAP is 3.9 miles. The rest is self-explanatory.

If the time/speed table is missing, it means that you are unable to determine the MAP by time. In such a case, a timed approach is not authorized.

CHAPTER QUIZ

1. The profile view is officially the _____ and depicts _____.

2. The table of recommended altitudes for nonprecision approaches on Jeppesen charts don't always read from left to right. True _____ False _____

3. The numbers near the procedure turn symbols _____, and _____ the _____, the procedure turns.

4. On the profile views, large numbers indicate _____, while small numbers in parentheses depict the _____ in feet above the _____, the _____, or the _____.

5. The nonprecision FAF is depicted on the profile view by a _____, while the precision approach FAF is _____.

6. After reaching the DH, you should level off and fly out the time to the airport. True _____ False _____

7. The letters TCH on a precision approach stand for _____ and indicate the _____.

8. You will find the missed approach instructions on the (plan/profile) view, located just _____ and _____.

9. The time/speed table is useful in a precision approach to determine the approximate_____. Many times this will be a first indication of _____.

Answers are in the appendix.

17
Airport charts

AIRPORT LAYOUT CHARTS ARE NORMALLY FOUND ON THE REVERSE SIDE OF the first approach chart for the airport. As mentioned in chapter 15 though, some of the airports are becoming so large and complex that it is necessary to produce even larger charts of the airport, the taxiways, and the gate locations at the terminals in some instances.

Refer back to Fig. 15-1; the airport format is made up of four sections just like the approach chart. The upper portion is the heading, the next one down is the airport plan view, below that you will see the runway data, and finally, at the bottom of the page, you find the takeoff and alternate airport minimums.

Examine a sample heading in Fig. 17-1. The location and airport name in this example are on the left side of the heading. The latitude and longitude are listed directly under the airport name; these coordinates are shown for the *airport reference point* (ARP), when one is charted at the airport; otherwise, the source of the coordinates will be shown. In the example you will also see that the airport is 7.7 miles from the TRP VOR.

The ICAO or United States airport identifier is printed in bold type just to the left of the chart index number.

The communications block is divided into two sections; the left side pertains primarily to frequencies used on the ground; the right side is for frequencies used in flight.

APPROACH CHART LEGEND
AIRPORT CHART FORMAT

The airport chart appears on the back side of the first approach chart. It contains information pertaining to the airport, air/ground communications, take-off minimums, alternate minimums, and departure procedures. At major terminals, the airport chart may be expanded and indexed separately to provide detailed information pertaining to taxiways, ramp or terminal parking areas, aircraft parking spot coordinates, start-up procedures, and low visibility procedures.

HEADING

Geographic name, airport name, latitude and longitude, elevation, magnetic variation, location identifier, index number, revision date and communications are given at the top of the page as illustrated below. All communications for departing the airport are listed in order of use. The designated Common Traffic Advisory Frequency (CTAF) is shown for U.S. public airports without control tower or where the tower is part-time. UNICOM, when available, is charted when other local communication capabilities are not available.

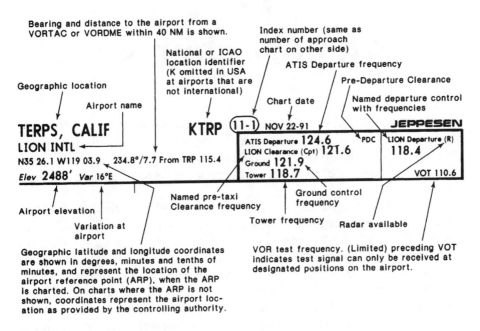

Fig. 17-1   Reproduced with permission of Jeppesen Sanderson, Inc. Not for use in navigation.

The frequencies are listed top to bottom in the order used during departure: ATIS, clearance delivery, ground, and tower. The departure control frequencies and the VOR test frequency, if applicable, are found on the right side of the block.

NEW SYMBOLS

Some airport plan symbols will be new to you. To help understand them, examine Fig. 17-2 and Fig. 17-3. As on the approach chart, the symbols on the airport plan are all in

APPROACH CHART LEGEND
AIRPORT PLAN VIEW

SYMBOLS

Physical feature symbols used on the airport chart are illustrated below.

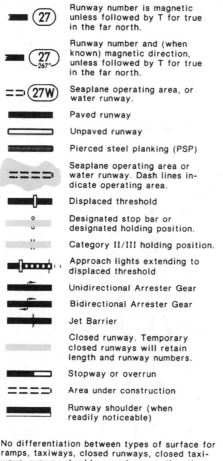

Runway number is magnetic unless followed by T for true in the far north.

Runway number and (when known) magnetic direction, unless followed by T for true in the far north.

Seaplane operating area, or water runway.

Paved runway

Unpaved runway

Pierced steel planking (PSP)

Seaplane operating area or water runway. Dash lines indicate operating area.

Displaced threshold

Designated stop bar or designated holding position.

Category II/III holding position.

Approach lights extending to displaced threshold

Unidirectional Arrester Gear

Bidirectional Arrester Gear

Jet Barrier

Closed runway. Temporary closed runways will retain length and runway numbers.

Stopway or overrun

Area under construction

Runway shoulder (when readily noticeable)

No differentiation between types of surface for ramps, taxiways, closed runways, closed taxiways, runway shoulders, and areas other than runways. Stopways and overruns are shown regardless of surface, with the length, when known. Stopway and overrun lengths are not included in runway lengths.

ADDITIONAL INFORMATION

Runway end elevations are shown on the airport diagram if source is available.

Approach lights and beacons are the only lighting symbolized on the airport diagram. Approach lights are normally shown to scale in a recognizable form. For approach light symbols see page 121.

A representative selection of reference points known to Jeppesen is depicted. The elevation of reference points depicted is above mean sea level (MSL).

Latitude and longitude ticks at tenths of a minute interval are charted around most planview neatlines.

Taxiway and apron

Permanently closed taxiway

Authorized Landing Area

Helicopter landing pad

Airport Reference Point. Off-runway. Center of cross positioned at exact location.

Airport Reference Point. Located on runway centerline. Arrow points to exact location.

RVR measuring site, may have identifying letter or number.

Airport/Aerodrome/ Identification beacon.

On-airport navaid - VOR, NDB or LCTR (locators, other than locators associated with ILS). Depicted on charts dated on and after 5 FEB 93.

Railroad

⊤―⊤― Pole line

Lighted Pole

Road

Bluff

Trees

Cone

Tee

Tetrahedron

Buildings

Large building

Feet 0 1000 2000 3000 4000 5000
Meters 0   500   1000   1500
Bar Scale

Fig. 17-2 Reproduced with permission of Jeppesen Sanderson, Inc. Not for use in navigation.

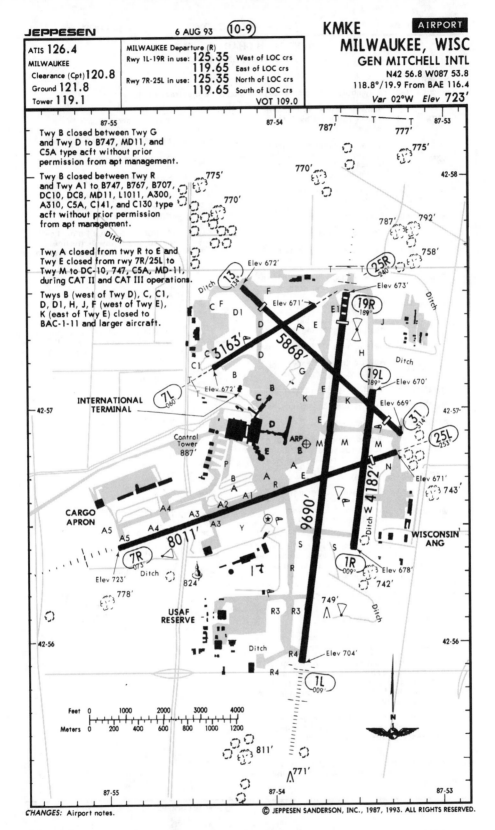

ATIS **126.4**
MILWAUKEE
Clearance (Cpt)**120.8**
Ground **121.8**
Tower **119.1**

MILWAUKEE Departure (R)
Rwy 1L-19R in use: **125.35** West of LOC crs
119.65 East of LOC crs
Rwy 7R-25L in use: **125.35** North of LOC crs
119.65 South of LOC crs
VOT 109.0

N42 56.8 W087 53.8
118.8°/19.9 From BAE 116.4
Var 02°W Elev 723'

Twy B closed between Twy G and Twy D to B747, MD11, and C5A type acft without prior permission from apt management.

Twy B closed between Twy R and Twy A1 to B747, B767, B707, DC10, DC8, MD11, L1011, A300, A310, C5A, C141, and C130 type acft without prior permission from apt management.

Twy A closed from twy R to E and Twy E closed from rwy 7R/25L to Twy M to DC-10, 747, C5A, MD-11, during CAT II and CAT III operations.

Twys B (west of Twy D), C, C1, D, D1, H, J, F (west of Twy E), K (east of Twy E) closed to BAC-1-11 and larger aircraft.

INTERNATIONAL TERMINAL

CARGO APRON

USAF RESERVE

WISCONSIN ANG

Control Tower 887'

Feet 0 1000 2000 3000 4000
Meters 0 200 400 600 800 1000 1200

Fig. 17-3 Reproduced with permission of Jeppesen Sanderson, Inc. Not for use in navigation.

white, black, and shades of gray. This reduces the amount of detail that can be shown; therefore, many symbols are used. Basically, paved runways are black, unpaved runways are white, and taxiways and ramps are gray. Permanently closed taxiways are shown by gray Xs.

The runway numbers are all magnetic unless they are followed by a "T" to indicate that they are true headings. True headings are only found in the Far North. Most runways have the magnetic heading shown in smaller numbers below the runway number as seen in the second example down in the left-hand column of Fig. 17-2. A "W" will follow the runway number if it is a seaplane-operating area or a water runway.

Let's begin examining the Milwaukee airport chart by glancing at the communications block in Fig. 17-3 to see how KMKE delegates its departure control frequencies, depending on which runway is in use, and the departure route after takeoff.

THE AIRPORT AS SEEN FROM THE AIR

On the airport plan view, notice that Runways 25L, 31, 19R, and 13 all have displaced landing thresholds as indicated by the white crossbar placed across the runway. The *airport reference point* (ARP), where the latitude and longitude coordinates are measured, can be seen just to the west of the midpoint of Runway 1L/19R.

The legend in the right-hand column of Fig. 17-2 explains that if the ARP is located off the runway, a circle with a cross inside it will be placed so that the center of the cross is on the ARP. The letters ARP will be below the circle. If the ARP is on a runway, the position will be indicated by an arrow from the letters ARP, and the circle and cross symbol will be omitted.

Every runway at Milwaukee has the elevation of both ends marked on the chart. If this information is omitted, the information is not available. Taxiways are identified alphabetically: G, M, DD.

ADDITIONAL RUNWAY INFORMATION

The only lights shown on the airport plan view are approach lights and beacons, and according to Jeppesen, while the approach lights are "normally shown to scale in a recognizable form," the easiest way to determine what type of system(s) is (are) installed is to read the information in the additional runway information table that is often located below the airport plan view.

In Milwaukee's case, however, this table appears on the reverse side of the plan view (Fig. 17-4). Some airports show this table on the reverse side of the plan view, Milwaukee uses the 10-9A series (Fig. 17-4). For a complete listing of the abbreviations and an example of an additional runway information table, see Figs. 17-5 and 17-6.

This example shows the wealth of information that can be derived from this one small block. The definitions of the abbreviations are quite straightforward, but there are a few that might benefit from discussion. CL, for example, means centerline lights. If shown by itself, it means that these lights are arranged in what is considered to be a

GENERAL
Birds in vicinity of airport.
Low-level wind shear alert system.

ADDITIONAL RUNWAY INFORMATION

RWY		LANDING BEYOND Threshold	LANDING BEYOND Glide Slope	USABLE LENGTHS Threshold to Intersecting Runway	TAKE-OFF	WIDTH
1R ❶ 19L	MIRL			13/31 3450'	Turbojet NA	150'

❶ Closed 2200-0600 LT except to lightweight single engine aircraft.

RWY		LANDING BEYOND Threshold	LANDING BEYOND Glide Slope	USABLE LENGTHS	TAKE-OFF	WIDTH
1L ❷	HIRL CL ALSF-I TDZ ❸PAPI-R RVR		8439'	7R/25L 4500' 13/31 7200'		200'
19R	HIRL CL MALSR ❸PAPI-R RVR	8915'	7861'	7R/25L 3700'		

❷ Runway grooved.
❸ (angle 3.00°)

RWY		LANDING BEYOND Threshold	LANDING BEYOND Glide Slope	USABLE LENGTHS	WIDTH
7R ❹	HIRL SSALR ❺PAPI-L RVR		6837'	1L/19R 5450' 1R/19L 6500'	150'
25L	HIRL REIL VASI-L	7339'			

❹ Runway grooved.
❺ (angle 3.00°)

RWY		WIDTH
7L ❻	MIRL VASI-L (angle 3.1°)	100'
25R	MIRL VASI-L (angle 3.5°)	

❻ Closed to all jet aircraft and aircraft over 12,500 lbs.
     Closed 2200-0600 LT except to lightweight single engine aircraft.

RWY		LANDING BEYOND Threshold	USABLE LENGTHS	WIDTH
13 ❼	MIRL VASI-L	5137'	1L/19R 2150' 1R/19L 3550'	150'
31	MIRL VASI-R	5344'	7L/25R 3650'	

❼ Closed to turbojet aircraft without prior permission from airport manager.
     Closed 2200-0600 LT except to lightweight single engine aircraft.

TAKE-OFF

	Rwy 1L			Rwys 13,19R 19L,25R,25L,31		Rwy 7R			Rwys 1R, 7L
	CL & RCLM any RVR out, other two req.	Adequate Vis Ref	STD	Adequate Vis Ref	STD	With Mim climb of 299'/NM to 1100' Adequate Vis Ref	STD	Other	
1 & 2 Eng	TDZ RVR 6 Mid RVR 6	RVR 16 or ¼	🔲 RVR 50 or 1	RVR 16 or ¼	🔲 RVR 50 or 1	RVR 16 or ¼	🔲 RVR 50 or 1	300-1	300-1
3 & 4 Eng	Rollout RVR 6		🔲 RVR 24 or ½		RVR 24 or ½		RVR 24 or ½		

🔲 FAR 135: Rwy 1L, RVR 18.
🔲 FAR 135: Rwy 19R, RVR 24.
🔲 FAR 135: RVR 24.

FOR FILING AS ALTERNATE

	Precision	Non-Precision	NDB Rwy 7R
A B C D	600-2	800-2	NA

CHANGES: Usable lengths, take-off minimums.

AMEND 4

Fig. 17-4   Reproduced with permission of Jeppesen Sanderson, Inc. Not for use in navigation.

APPROACH CHART LEGEND
ADDITIONAL RUNWAY INFORMATION (continued)

RWY	ADDITIONAL RUNWAY INFORMATION		USABLE LENGTHS — LANDING BEYOND —			
			Threshold	Glide Slope	TAKE-OFF	WIDTH
4R	HIRL CL ALSF-I TDZ grooved RVR					150'
22L	HIRL CL grooved RVR			6641'		
4L	HIRL CL HIALS SFL				NA	150'
22R						
7	RL VASI (angle 2.4°, TCH 10')					200'
25						
13	HIRL CL VASI LDIN		11, 972'			150'
31	HIRL CL SSALR VASI (non-std) HST-H		11, 252'			

RUNWAY LIGHTS-ABBREVIATIONS

RL.........Low Intensity Runway Lights or intensity not specified.

HIRL......High Intensity Runway Edge Lights

Runway edge lights are white, except on instrument runways amber replaces white on the last 2000' or half of the runway length, whichever is less.

MIRL......Medium Intensity Runway Edge Lights

REIL......Runway End Identifier Lights (threshold strobe)

TDZ.......Touchdown Zone Lights

HST-H... High Speed Taxiway turn-off with green centerline lights. H indicates taxiway identification.

CL.........Standard Centerline Light configuration white lights then alternating red & white lights between 3000' and 1000' from runway end and red lights for the last 1000'.
-or-
Exact configuration is not known. Known non-standard configurations are stated as listed below

CL (white).......all lights are white full length of runway.

CL (non-std)....non-standard, configuration unknown

CL(50W, 20R & W, 20R)...non-standard, configuration known...first 5000' white lights; next 2000' alternating red & white lights; last 2000' red lights.

APPROACH LIGHTS-ABBREVIATIONS

ALS.......Approach Light System. Color of lights, if known to be other than white, is included.

HIALS....High Intensity Approach Light System

MIALS....Medium Intensity Approach Light System

SFL........Sequenced Flashing Lights

F...........Condenser-Discharge Sequential Flashing Lights/Sequenced Flashing Lights

ALSF-I....Approach Light System with Sequenced Flashing Lights

ALSF-II..Approach Light System with Sequenced Flashing Lights and Red Side Row Lights the last 1000'. May be operated as SSALR during favorable weather conditions.

SSALF....Simplified Short Approach Light System with Sequenced Flashing Lights

SALSF....Short Approach Light System with Sequenced Flashing Lights

MALSF...Medium Intensity Approach Light System with Sequenced Flashing Lights

RAI...... Runway Alignment Indicator

RAIL......Runway Alignment Indicator Lights (Sequenced Flashing Lights which are installed only in combination with other light systems)

RLLS......Runway Lead-in Lighting System

SSALR...Simplified Short Approach Light System with Runway Alignment Indicator Lights

MALSR...Medium Intensity Approach Light System with Runway Alignment Indicator Lights

SALS.....Short Approach Light System

SSALS...Simplified Short Approach Light System

MALS.....Medium Intensity Approach Light System

LDIN......Sequenced Flashing Lead-in Lights

ODALS...Omni-Directional Approach Light System

VASI......Visual Approach Slope Indicator (L or R indicates left or right side of runway only)

AVASI... Abbreviated Visual Approach Slope Indicator (L or R indicates left or right side of runway only)

VASI (3 bar)....Visual Approach Slope Indicator for high cockpit aircraft (L or R indicates left or right side of runway only)

T-VASI.. Tee Visual Approach Slope Indicator

AT-VASI.Abbreviated Tee Visual Approach Slope Indicator (L or R indicates left or right side of runway only)

VASI (non-std)..Visual Approach Slope Indicator when known to be non-standard

Fig. 17-5

APPROACH CHART LEGEND
ADDITIONAL RUNWAY INFORMATION (continued)

APPROACH LIGHTS-ABBREVIATIONS (continued)

VASI......VASI/AVASI/NON-STD angles are shown when known to be less than 2.5° or more than 3.0°. T-VASI/ AT-VASI angles are shown at all times. VASI (3 bar) descent angles are shown when other than upwind angle 3.25°, downwind angle 3.00°.

PAPI......Precision Approach Path Indicator (L or R indicates left or right side of runway only)

PLASI....Pulsating Visual Approach Slope Indicator, normally a single light unit projecting two colors. (L or R indicates left or right side of runway only)

TRCV.....Tri-Color Visual Approach Slope Indicator, normally a single light unit projecting three colors. (L or R indicates left or right side of runway only)

TCH.......Threshold Crossing Height. Height of the effective visual glide path over the threshold.

MEHT....Minimum Eye Height over Threshold. Lowest height over the threshold of the visual on glide path indication.

MEHT or TCH is shown (when known) when less than 60' for the upwind bar of a VASI (3 bar) system or less than 25' for all other systems including PAPI.

Fig. 17-6 Reproduced with permission of Jeppesen Sanderson, Inc. Not for use in navigation.

standard configuration. Centerline lights are white from the approach end of the runway until 3,000 feet from the departure end; from that point until 1,000 feet from the departure end, you will see alternating red and white lights; all of the centerline lights in the final 1,000 feet are red. These are a tremendous help during low-visibility conditions. Some airports use all-white centerline lights, and in that case, the symbol will be CL (white). If the centerline lights are in a nonstandard configuration, and the configuration is not known, the symbol is CL (non-std).

If the nonstandard configuration is known, it will be specified in the symbol. Look at the example shown in Fig. 17-5 to see CL (50W, 20R & W, 20R), which means that the first 5,000 feet from the approach end are white, the next 2,000 feet are red and white, and the last 2,000 feet are red.

Remember that this refers only to centerline lights, directly in the center of the runway, not the runway edge lights. Some people get the two confused. It is also important to fix the configuration of the lights in your mind. It would be very embarrassing to be rolling out at a high rate of speed, expecting red and white alternating lights and then red lights at the end of the runway, only to be on a runway that has all white lights.

A recent change in the abbreviations is the meaning of RL in the upper left. In the past it simply meant runway edge lights. Now it means that they are of low intensity or that the intensity has not been specified by the airport. High- and medium-intensity lights have always been identified by the addition of the letters MI or HI in front of the RL.

WHAT YOU SEE AIN'T ALWAYS WHAT YOU GET

Look again at the additional runway information table on Fig. 17-5, and find the columns listing the usable lengths for the runways. These are set up for three conditions: landing beyond the threshold, landing beyond the glide slope, and takeoff.

You will not see anything in the landing-beyond-threshold column unless the runway has a displaced threshold. Then, the figure shown is the effective length of the runway from the displaced threshold to the departure (rollout) end of the runway.

Just because there is a displaced runway for landing, that does not mean that the displaced part cannot be used for takeoff. There are times when there will be a takeoff displacement as well. This usually has to do with noise abatement or jet blast considerations. If no signs have been posted on the runway itself, or no notes are listed in the additional runway information columns, then all of the runway is available for takeoff.

For the usable length, landing beyond the glide slope, the figure is taken from a point abeam the glide slope transmitter to the departure (rollout) end of the runway. For a runway using PAR, it is from the point of the theoretical glide path/runway intersection to the departure end of the runway.

Glance at Fig. 17-4 and examine the data for Runway 1L/19R in the additional runway information table. Although the runway is shown on the plan view as being 9,690 feet long, the displaced threshold on 19R reduces its effective length to 8,915 feet when landing beyond the threshold. Wouldn't it be embarrassing if you figured the weight and balance for landing on a 9,690-foot runway by just taking a cursory glance at the plan view without looking at the additional information?

There is no reduction in usable length for landing beyond the threshold in the other direction (Runway 1L); therefore, that box is left blank. Because glide slope angles are set up to effect touchdown somewhere between 750 and 1,500 feet from the threshold, notice that for landing beyond the glide slope, Runway 1L has a usable length of 8,439 feet, and Runway 19R has a usable length of 7,861 feet. Runway 25L is restricted to 7,339 feet when landing beyond the threshold, and Runways 13 and 31 are restricted to 5,137 and 5,344 feet, respectively, when landing beyond the threshold.

Although takeoff usable lengths are not listed for any of the runways at Milwaukee, had they been, they would have been measured from the point the takeoff roll commences, to the end of the pavement that is usable for takeoff.

The note "Turbojet NA" in that column indicates that Runway 1R is not available for jet departures. At times, there are also other restrictions for a runway. These are indicated by small numbers in reverse print in black circles (1, 2, 3, and the like, appearing in white). Milwaukee is a good example of this. The reasoning behind some of the restrictions, besides sounding confusing at first, is hard to understand at times.

Tax your brains a bit and look at the restrictions concerning Runway 13/31; see if you can figure out why some of them came about.

TAKEOFF MINIMUMS

The last section of the airport chart is the takeoff and alternate minimums table. This block is explained quite well in Fig. 17-7. The block might be broken down into two main sections: takeoff minimums and alternate minimums. Or the takeoff minimum block might appear above the alternate minimum block, as in Milwaukee's case (Fig. 17-4), depending on the amount of information printed.

Notice that the takeoff minimums apply only to Part 121, 123, 125, 129, and 135 operators, but Part 91 operators would be wise to heed them.

Study Fig. 17-7 very carefully. There is a lot of good information included. Runway 4 information is presented in three columns. The first two columns are headed by the words "With Mim climb of 290'/NM to 1000'." The first column under that specifies the visibility required under the definition of "adequate Vis Ref," which is defined in the upper left-hand side of the page. The next column is for "STD" visibility requirements, and although the standard takeoff visibilities are just that, standard, they are printed out in case someone were to forget. It would appear that there are no transmissometers installed on Runway 11L, 22, and 29R because the standard visibilities are only printed in terms of miles, not RVR feet.

Getting back to the breakdown for Runway 4, the other column is the visibility requirements for aircraft that cannot meet the climb criteria specified of 290'/NM to 1000'. The minimum climb criteria would certainly be indicative of obstructions above the normal obstruction clearance plane.

Reexamine Milwaukee and note how many options are available, depending on the runway and the equipment in use.

Here is another very important point. Some day you will run across instances where the takeoff minimums are higher than many of the landing minimums, due to obstructions; therefore, read the notes on the applicable airport charts very carefully.

As mentioned, these takeoff minimums are not for Part 91 operators, but it would certainly be wise to abide by them.

ALTERNATE MINIMUMS

The alternate minimums block is very straightforward; for one example, see Fig. 17-8. This column is divided into two sections. The section on the left is further divided into three sections. The furthest to the left lists the minimums for the precision approach. The next column indicates the minimums required for using localizer or NDB approaches to Runway 2 or the localizer DME back course to Runway 20. The next column indicates the minimums required to use the NDB approach to Runway 20. All of these columns require that the control zone be effective.

You can use the minimums for the VOR 20 or VOR DME 20 approaches provided you have approved weather service. What is approved weather service? The weather bureau will suffice when it is operating, but when it is closed, you will be out of luck unless you happen to fly for a commuter or an air carrier that has its own certificated weather people.

APPROACH CHART LEGEND
TAKE-OFF AND ALTERNATE MINIMUMS (continued)
USA FORMAT

The title TAKE-OFF & IFR DEPARTURE PROCEDURE is used to indicate that both take-off minimums and IFR departure procedures are specified. In such cases, refer to the note IFR DEPARTURE PROCEDURE to the left and immediately below the minimum columns for the procedure.

"Adequate Vis Ref" is shown as a reminder that at least one of the following visual aids must be available. The Touchdown Zone RVR report, if available, is controlling. The Mid RVR report may be substituted for the Touchdown Zone RVR report if the Touchdown Zone RVR is not available.
(1) Operative high intensity runway lights (HIRL).
(2) Operative runway centerline lights (CL).
(3) Runway centerline marking (RCLM).
(4) In circumstances when none of the above visual aids are available, visibility or RVV ¼ statute mile may still be used, provided other runway markings or runway lighting provide pilots *with adequate visual reference* to continuously identify the take-off surface and maintain directional control throughout the take-off run.
("Forward Vis Ref", in lieu of "Adequate Vis Ref", is used on charts dated prior to July 28, 1989.)

STD denotes standard take-off minimums for FAR 121, 123, 125, 129 and 135 operators. Standard is RVR 50 or 1 for 1 & 2 Eng. RVR 24 or ½ for 3 & 4 Eng.

The IFR Departure for runways 29L/R require (when the weather is below 1000' ceiling-7 miles) a climb to 1800' MSL on runway heading before initiating a turn.

Applicable to FAR 121 and 129 operators. Applicable to FAR 135 operators of large aircraft and small transport category aircraft.

Operative Touchdown Zone and Rollout RVR reporting systems serving the runway to be used, both of which are controlling, or three RVR reporting systems serving the runway to be used, all of which are controlling. However, if one of the three RVR reporting systems has failed, a take-off is authorized provided the remaining two RVR values are at or above the appropriate take-off minimums.

To be eligible for the minimum shown in the columns below, a climb gradient of at least 290'/NM is required until reaching 1000' MSL.

If unable to meet climb requirement, 300' ceiling-1 mile apply.

Restrictions in this column, if any, apply to all operators.

Approaches with electronic glide slope.

LOC, VOR, etc. approaches.

TAKE-OFF & IFR DEPARTURE PROCEDURE								FOR FILING AS ALTERNATE	
Rwys 11R, 29L			Rwys 11L, 29R		Rwys 4, 22				
CL & RCLM any RVR out, other two req.	Adequate Vis Ref	STD	Adequate Vis Ref	STD	With Min climb of 290'/NM to 1000' Adequate Vis Ref / STD		Other	Precision	Non-Precision
1 & 2 Eng	TDZ RVR 6	RVR 16 or ¼	RVR 50 or 1	RVR 16 or ¼	RVR 50 or 1		300-1	A	600-2	800-2
	Mid RVR 6		RVR 24 or ½					B		
3 & 4 Eng	Rollout RVR 6			½	RVR 24 or ½			C / D	700-2	

IFR DEPARTURE PROCEDURE: Rwys 29L & 29R, when weather is below 1000-7 northbound departures (296° clockwise 116°) climb rwy heading to 1800' before turning.

Figures shown with RVR (runway visual range) represent readings in hundreds of feet. The figures without the RVR prefix represent visibility in statute miles or fractions thereof. For example: RVR 50 or 1 means 5000 feet RVR or one statute mile visibility; RVR 24 or ½ means 2400 feet RVR or one-half statute mile visibility.

Individual runway columns are shown whenever minimums are not the same for all runways The best opportunity runway is shown at the far left. Within each runway column, all conditions are specified, and minimums are positioned in ascending order, left to right. Columns are not established solely to identify runways with and without RVR when all other conditions are the same.

Altitudes listed in climb gradient requirements or for IFR departure procedures are above Mean Sea Level (MSL). Ceiling specified for Take-off minimums or Alternate minimums are heights Above Airport Level (AAL).

Fig. 17-7 Reproduced with permission of Jeppesen Sanderson, Inc. Not for use in navigation.

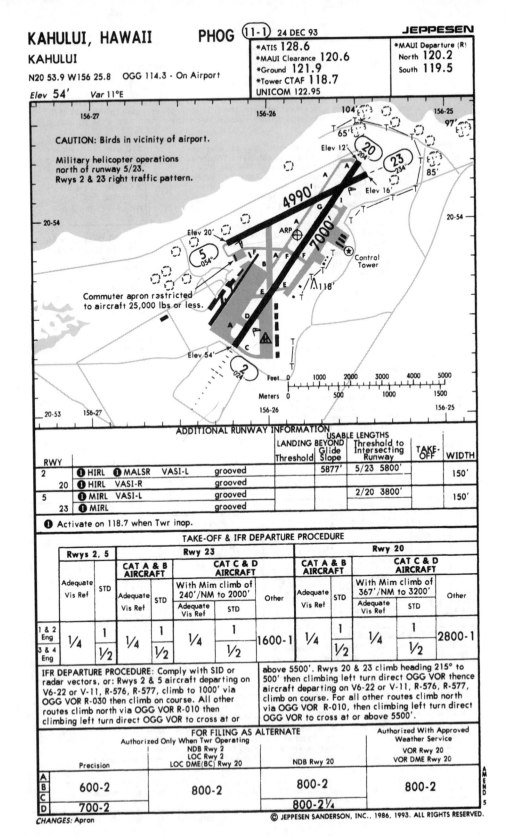

KAHULUI, HAWAII
KAHULUI

PHOG (11-1) 24 DEC 93

N20 53.9 W156 25.8   OGG 114.3 - On Airport

Elev 54'   Var 11°E

JEPPESEN

*ATIS **128.6**	*MAUI Departure (R)
*MAUI Clearance **120.6**	North **120.2**
*Ground **121.9**	South **119.5**
*Tower CTAF **118.7**	
UNICOM **122.95**	

CAUTION: Birds in vicinity of airport.

Military helicopter operations
north of runway 5/23.
Rwys 2 & 23 right traffic pattern.

Commuter apron restricted
to aircraft 25,000 lbs or less.

Feet	0	1000	2000	3000	4000	5000'
Meters	0	500	1000	1500		

ADDITIONAL RUNWAY INFORMATION

RWY					USABLE LENGTHS		TAKE-OFF	WIDTH
				LANDING BEYOND Glide Slope	Threshold to Intersecting Runway		
				Threshold			
2	❶HIRL ❶MALSR VASI-L	grooved		5877'			150'
20	❶HIRL VASI-R	grooved			5/23 5800'		
5	❶MIRL VASI-L	grooved			2/20 3800'		150'
23	❶MIRL	grooved					

❶ Activate on 118.7 when Twr inop.

TAKE-OFF & IFR DEPARTURE PROCEDURE

	Rwys 2, 5		Rwy 23				Rwy 20			
			CAT A & B AIRCRAFT		CAT C & D AIRCRAFT		CAT A & B AIRCRAFT		CAT C & D AIRCRAFT	
	Adequate Vis Ref	STD	Adequate Vis Ref	STD	With Mim climb of 240'/NM to 2000'	Other	Adequate Vis Ref	STD	With Mim climb of 367'/NM to 3200'	Other
					Adequate Vis Ref	STD			Adequate Vis Ref	STD	
1 & 2 Eng	1/4	1	1/4	1	1/4	1	1600-1	1/4	1	1/4	1	2800-1
3 & 4 Eng		1/2		1/2		1/2			1/2		1/2	

IFR DEPARTURE PROCEDURE: Comply with SID or radar vectors, or: Rwys 2 & 5 aircraft departing on V6-22 or V-11, R-576, R-577, climb to 1000' via OGG VOR R-030 then climb on course. All other routes climb north via OGG VOR R-010 then climbing left turn direct OGG VOR to cross at or above 5500'. Rwys 20 & 23 climb heading 215° to 500' then climbing left turn direct OGG VOR thence aircraft departing on V6-22 or V-11, R-576, R-577, climb on course. For all other routes climb north via OGG VOR R-010, then climbing left turn direct OGG VOR to cross at or above 5500'.

FOR FILING AS ALTERNATE

	Authorized Only When Twr Operating			Authorized With Approved Weather Service
	Precision	NDB Rwy 2 LOC Rwy 2 LOC DME(BC) Rwy 20	NDB Rwy 20	VOR Rwy 20 VOR DME Rwy 20
A B C	600-2	800-2	800-2	800-2
D	700-2		800-2¼	

AMEND 5

CHANGES: Apron

© JEPPESEN SANDERSON, INC., 1986, 1993. ALL RIGHTS RESERVED.

EXPANDED AIRPORT CHARTS

I talked earlier about the new expanded airport charts that are coming out for some of the major airports. Take a look at those that have been produced for Los Angeles International (Figs. 17-9 through 17-11).

Figure 17-9, in its original form, is a fold-out chart to show the complexity of LAX. There are cargo buildings, terminals, and outbuildings scattered all over the field, and the taxiways are quite complex. Another interesting thing about LAX is that there are three different tower frequencies shown in the communications block.

As at Milwaukee, the additional runway information section as well as the takeoff and landing minimum blocks are shown on the new series 10-9A chart, which need not be illustrated again.

The terminal area (gates and taxiways), Imperial Cargo Complex, and the West Pads with their attendant taxiways are complex enough that two additional charts (Figs. 17-10 and 17-11) have been created exclusively to illustrate those specific areas of the airport.

These two pages also list the latitude and longitude coordinates of every gate for the benefit of those pilots who are flying aircraft equipped with any form of area navigation equipment.

You can see that as terminals and airspace become more and more congested, the charts change to keep pace. Keep up with these rapid changes by periodic reviews.

Hopefully, by now you have learned the importance of studying all of the information available to you on Jeppesen charts, as well as in the explanatory pages. In the next chapter we'll take a look at the NOS charts to see how they compare.

CHAPTER QUIZ

1. The initials ARP stand for_____, and is the spot at which the _____ of the airport are determined.

2. A white bar across a runway on an airport plan view indicates a _____.

3. While runways are identified_____, taxiways are designated _____.

4. What does CL (30W, 20R & W, 20R) in the additional runway information mean?

5. Why is a runway takeoff length usually longer than the usable length when landing beyond the threshold?

6. There are no takeoff minimums for general aviation aircraft.

   True _____ False _____

7. Takeoff minimums are always lower than landing minimums.

   True _____ False _____

Answers are in the appendix.

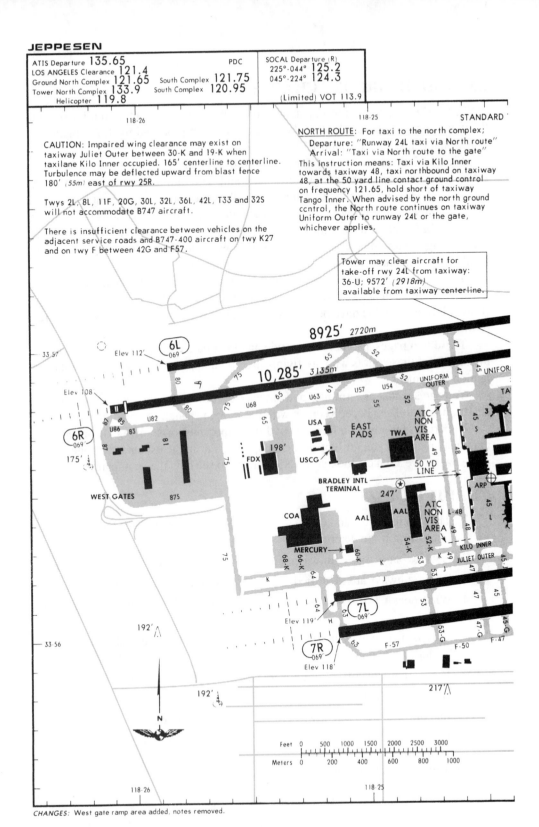

JEPPESEN

ATIS Departure 135.65		PDC	SOCAL Departure (R)
LOS ANGELES Clearance 121.4			225°-044° 125.2
Ground North Complex 121.65	South Complex 121.75		045°-224° 124.3
Tower North Complex 133.9	South Complex 120.95		
Helicopter 119.8			(Limited) VOT 113.9

118-26   118-25   STANDARD

CAUTION: Impaired wing clearance may exist on
taxiway Juliet Outer between 30-K and 19-K when
taxilane Kilo Inner occupied. 165' centerline to centerline.
Turbulence may be deflected upward from blast fence
180' (55m) east of rwy 25R.

Twys 2L, 8L, 11F, 20G, 30L, 32L, 36L, 42L, T33 and 32S
will not accommodate B747 aircraft.

There is insufficient clearance between vehicles on the
adjacent service roads and B747-400 aircraft on twy K27
and on twy F between 42G and F57.

NORTH ROUTE: For taxi to the north complex;
   Departure: "Runway 24L taxi via North route"
   Arrival: "Taxi via North route to the gate"
This instruction means: Taxi via Kilo Inner
towards taxiway 48, taxi northbound on taxiway
48, at the 50 yard line contact ground control
on frequency 121.65, hold short of taxiway
Tango Inner. When advised by the north ground
control, the North route continues on taxiway
Uniform Outer to runway 24L or the gate,
whichever applies.

Tower may clear aircraft for
take-off rwy 24L from taxiway:
36-U; 9572' (2918m)
available from taxiway centerline.

8925' 2720m

10,285' 3135m

6L -069-
6R -069-
Elev 112'
Elev 108'
175'

WEST GATES

U82 U86 83 81 875

FDX 198' USCG USA

EAST PADS TWA

ATC NON VIS AREA

50 YD LINE

BRADLEY INTL TERMINAL 247'

COA AAL AAL

ATC NON VIS AREA

MERCURY 60-K

KILO INNER JULIET OUTER

7L -069-
7R -069-
Elev 119'
Elev 118'

192'

192'

217'

Feet 0 500 1000 1500 2000 2500 3000
Meters 0 200 400 600 800 1000

N

118-26   118-25

CHANGES: West gate ramp area added, notes removed.

Fig. 17-9 Reproduced with permission of Jeppesen Sanderson, Inc. Not for use in navigation.

TAXI ROUTES

SOUTH ROUTE: For taxi to the south complex;
   Departure: "Runway 25R taxi via South route"
   Arrival: "Taxi via South route to the gate"
This instruction means: If the aircraft is west of taxiway 49, taxi eastbound on taxiway Uniform Outer and turn right on taxiway 49, if the aircraft is east of taxiway 49, taxi westbound on taxiway Tango Inner and turn left on taxiway 49, at the 50 yard line contact ground control on frequency 121.75, hold short of taxiway Kilo Inner. When advised by south ground control, the South route continues on taxiway Juliet Outer to runway 25R or the gate, whichever applies.

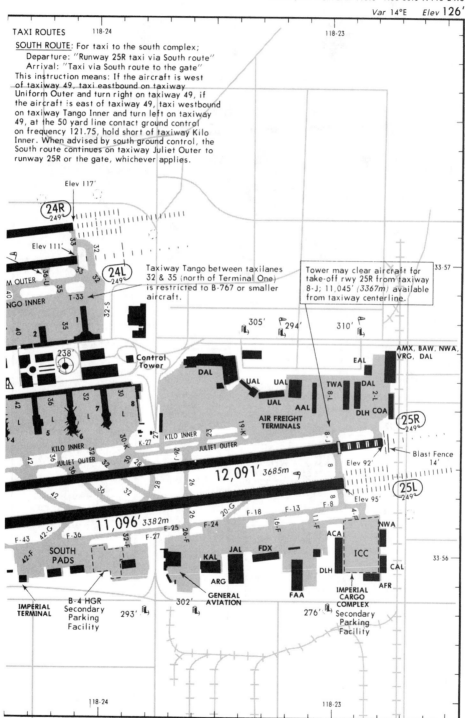

Taxiway Tango between taxilanes 32 & 35 (north of Terminal One) is restricted to B-767 or smaller aircraft.

Tower may clear aircraft for take-off rwy 25R from taxiway 8-J; 11,045' (3367m) available from taxiway centerline.

12,091' 3685m

11,096' 3382m

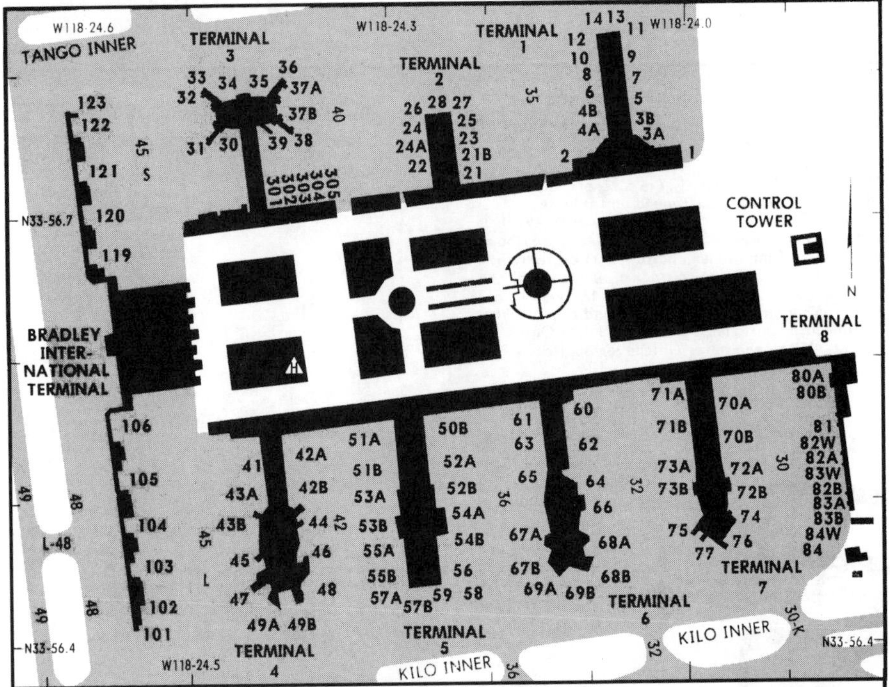

PARKING BAY COORDINATES

BAY No.	COORDINATES	BAY No.	COORDINATES
Bradley International Terminal			**Terminal 4 (con't)**
101	N33 56.4 W118 24.6	46	N33 56.4 W118 24.3
102 thru 104	N33 56.4 W118 24.5	47	N33 56.4 W118 24.4
105, 106	N33 56.5 W118 24.5	48	N33 56.4 W118 24.3
119 thru 120	N33 56.7 W118 24.5	49A	N33 56.4 W118 24.3
121	N33 56.6 W118 24.6	49B	N33 56.4 W118 24.3
			Terminal 5
122, 123	N33 56.8 W118 24.5	50B	N33 56.5 W118 24.2
Passenger Terminal		51A, 51B	N33 56.5 W118 24.3
Terminal 1		52A thru 53A	N33 56.5 W118 24.2
1	N33 56.8 W118 23.9	53B	N33 56.5 W118 24.3
2	N33 56.7 W118 24.1	54A	N33 56.5 W118 24.2
3A thru 10	N33 56.8 W118 24.0		
11	N33 56.9 W118 24.0	54B thru 59	N33 56.4 W118 24.2
12	N33 56.8 W118 24.0	**Terminal 6**	
		60 thru 63	N33 56.5 W118 24.1
13, 14	N33 56.9 W118 24.0	64	N33 56.5 W118 24.0
		65	N33 56.5 W118 24.0
Terminal 2		66	N33 56.5 W118 24.0
21 thru 22	N33 56.7 W118 24.2	67A, 67B	N33 56.4 W118 24.1
23 thru 28	N33 56.8 W118 24.2		
		68A, 68B	N33 56.4 W118 24.0
		69A, 69B	N33 56.4 W118 24.1
Terminal 3			
30 thru 35	N33 56.8 W118 24.4		
36 thru 38	N33 56.8 W118 24.3		
39	N33 56.8 W118 24.4	**Terminal 7**	
301	N33 56.7 W118 24.4	70A, 70B	N33 56.5 W118 23.9
302 thru 305	N33 56.7 W118 24.3	71A	N33 56.6 W118 24.0
		71B	N33 56.5 W118 24.0
		72A, 72B	N33 56.5 W118 23.9
Terminal 4		73A, 73B	N33 56.5 W118 24.0
41	N33 56.5 W118 24.4		
42A, 42B	N33 56.5 W118 24.3	74	N33 56.5 W118 23.9
43A, 43B	N33 56.5 W118 24.4	75 thru 77	N33 56.4 W118 23.9
44	N33 56.4 W118 24.3	**Terminal 8**	
45	N33 56.4 W118 24.4	80A, 80B	N33 56.6 W118 23.8
		81 thru 83B	N33 56.5 W118 23.8
		84, 84W	N33 56.4 W118 23.8

CHANGES: Terminal 8 gates.

Fig. 17-10 Reproduced with permission of Jeppesen Sanderson, Inc. Not for use in navigation.

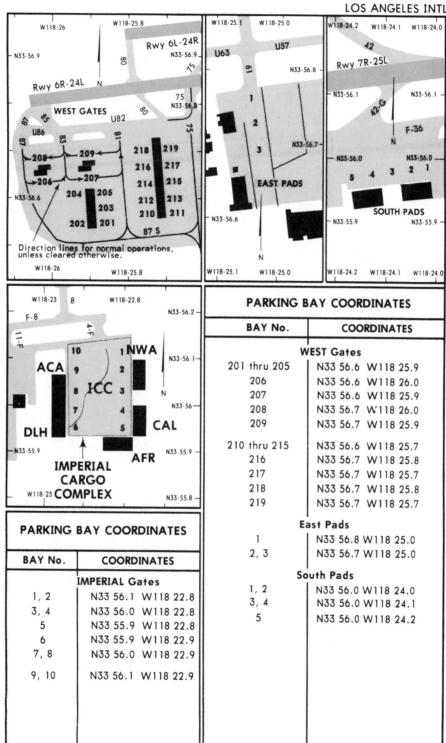

Fig. 17-11 Reproduced with permission of Jeppesen Sanderson, Inc. Not for use in navigation.

18
NOS approach charts

RECALL FROM CHAPTER 15 THAT THERE ARE NO HARD AND FAST RULES FOR cartographers to follow when producing approach plates, as long as all necessary information is presented. Many pilots think that the National Ocean Service (NOS) charts are confusing because they cram a lot of information on one sheet of paper. Others say the NOS charts are much better than the Jeppesen products because NOS charts give you all the information you need on one piece of paper without making you turn pages to discover items such as the airport diagram. This all boils down to personal choice, which will depend, to an extent, on what you used during instrument training.

The NOS charts come in volumes that are updated every 56 days with a change notice volume issued on the 28th day. This change notice is being replaced by NOTAMs. It is possible, though, to get them in either a spiral ring-type or loose-leaf style held together by metal clips or nonmagnetic plastic rings. These versions are available through the Air Chart Company in Venice, Calif. (chapter 15), whose unique update service works equally well for Jeppesen charts.

General information and abbreviations for NOS charts appear near the front of the volume: Distances are in nautical miles (NM), except for the visibility, which will be in statute miles (SM); RVR will be in hundreds of feet; ceilings shown will be in feet above the airport elevation; and radials, bearings, headings, and courses are magnetic.

The approaches are arranged by airport name, and, if the airport has more than one, the approaches are listed with the NDB approach first, followed by ILS, LOC, LOC/DME, VOR, VOR/DME, and RNAV.

ILS BY NOS

Figure 18-1 shows the ILS approach for Runway 9L at Opa Locka, Florida. The upper and lower left margins of the chart identify the specific approach (ILS RWY 9L) in bold letters. The upper and lower right margins identify the airport's name in upper-case letters and by its geographical location in smaller uppercase letters. The three-letter identifier follows the airport name. In the center of the lower margin (called the *trailer*), you will find the latitudinal and longitudinal coordinates.

The plan view comprises the upper two-thirds of the plate. The profile view is below the plan view on the left. The minimums information is below the profile view, followed by any notes. The airport diagram is located below the plan view on the right side of the plate (large airports will have a separate airport chart), including any appropriate notes, and the distance and time from the FAF to the MAP is under the airport diagram, when applicable.

Obviously, there is a great deal of information on one side of an approach plate, but some of it is difficult for an old or tired pair of eyes to read, and the pulp paper it's printed on doesn't make it any easier. If I were using these plates, I would make a magnifying glass part of my flight kit.

You should be aware of the large circle on the plan view. In Fig. 18-1, this circle depicts a 10-nautical-mile radius. It is not necessarily drawn around the airport, but rather around the final approach fix. This is just a reference circle, and although it is usually of 10-nm radius, it can vary. So check the radius when you look at the chart. The radius can be found along the edge of the circle. The airport might not even be within the circle, as in the case of Fig. 18-1, where this 10-mile ring just barely chops across some of the runways.

The MSA circle will be found somewhere within the plan view. Look at the bottom left portion of the plan view and see the MSA circle for Opa Locka. The data above the circle explains which facility the MSA is predicated on, in this case, the Miami (MIA) VOR, and the radius is 25 nautical miles. Note that in the northwest sector from a bearing to the VOR of 040 degrees (220-degree radial) clockwise through a bearing of 180 degrees (360-degree radial), the MSA is 1,500 feet MSL. The MSA for the rest of the circle is 2,900 feet MSL.

The radio frequencies you will use on approach are listed in the upper-left corner of the plan view. With the exception of the ATIS frequency, these are listed in the order that you will use them, beginning with approach control and continuing down through ground control. Any note concerning the airport, in this case the note about the highway lights, is printed near the bottom of the plan view.

Missed approach instructions are printed in the profile view, as are any procedure turn instructions. In the case of an ILS, both the glide slope angle and the threshold crossing height of the glide slope are indicated in the profile view section.

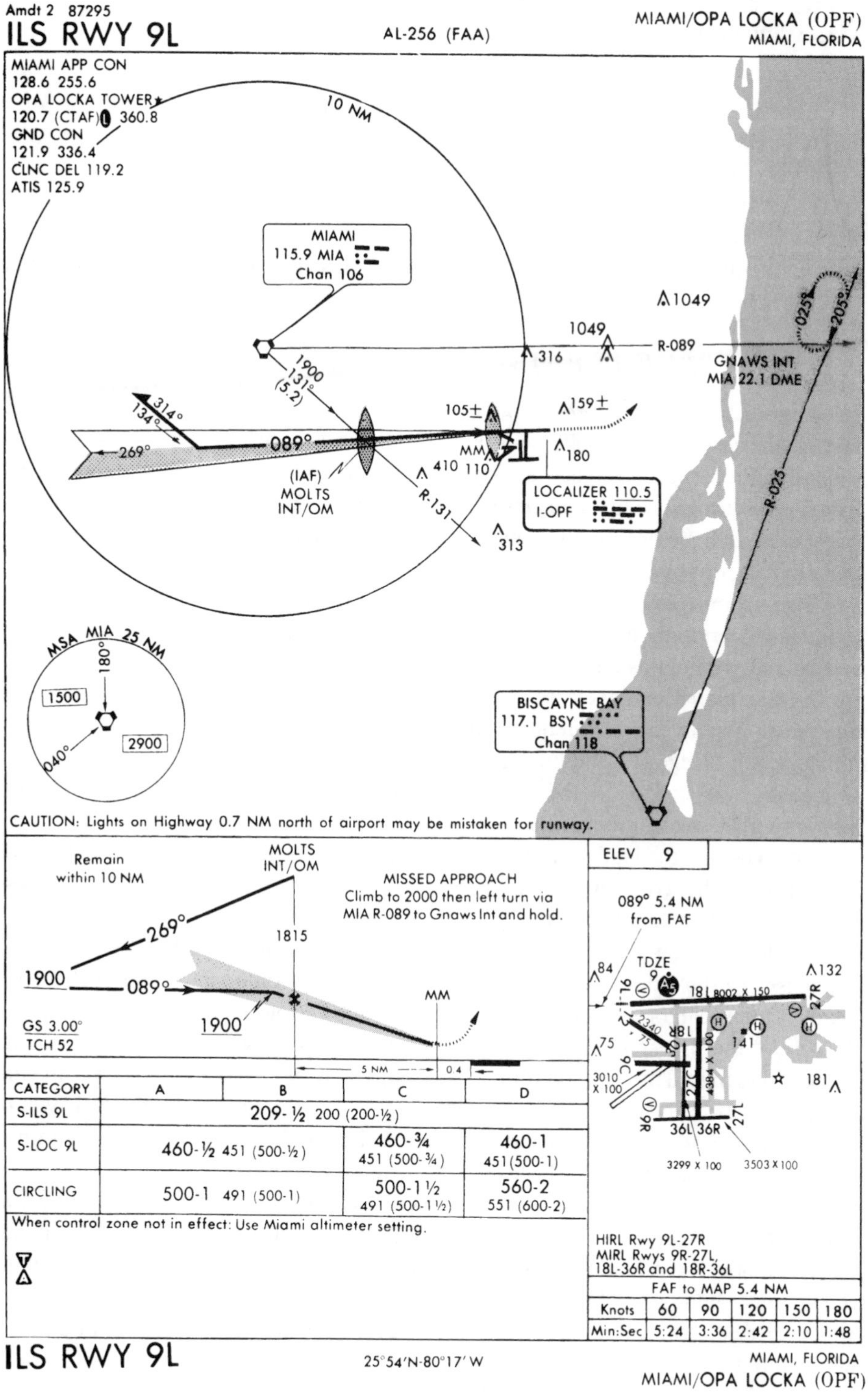

ILS RWY 9L

AL-256 (FAA)

MIAMI/OPA LOCKA (OPF)
MIAMI, FLORIDA

MIAMI APP CON
128.6 255.6
OPA LOCKA TOWER
120.7 (CTAF) 360.8
GND CON
121.9 336.4
CLNC DEL 119.2
ATIS 125.9

10 NM

MIAMI
115.9 MIA
Chan 106

△1049

1049
△ 316   R-089

GNAWS INT
MIA 22.1 DME

1900
(131°)
(5.2)

314°
134°
269°
089°

105±

△159±

△ 180

MM

314°

(IAF)
MOLTS
INT/OM

410 110

R-131

△ 313

LOCALIZER 110.5
I-OPF

MSA MIA 25 NM
180°
1500
040°
2900

BISCAYNE BAY
117.1 BSY
Chan 118

CAUTION: Lights on Highway 0.7 NM north of airport may be mistaken for runway.

	MOLTS INT/OM	MISSED APPROACH
Remain within 10 NM		Climb to 2000 then left turn via MIA R-089 to Gnaws Int and hold.

269°
1815
1900   089°
MM
GS 3.00°
TCH 52   1900

5 NM   0.4

ELEV   9

089° 5.4 NM
from FAF

△84   TDZE
△76   9
A5   18L 8002 X 150   27R
△75   18R   141
3010 X 100   27C   4384 X 100   181 △
36L 36R   27L
3299 X 100   3503 X 100

CATEGORY	A	B	C	D
S-ILS 9L		209-½ 200 (200-½)		
S-LOC 9L	460-½ 451 (500-½)		460-¾ 451 (500-¾)	460-1 451 (500-1)
CIRCLING	500-1 491 (500-1)		500-1½ 491 (500-1½)	560-2 551 (600-2)

When control zone not in effect: Use Miami altimeter setting.

HIRL Rwy 9L-27R
MIRL Rwys 9R-27L,
18L-36R and 18R-36L

FAF to MAP 5.4 NM					
Knots	60	90	120	150	180
Min:Sec	5:24	3:36	2:42	2:10	1:48

ILS RWY 9L

25°54'N-80°17'W

MIAMI, FLORIDA
MIAMI/OPA LOCKA (OPF)

Fig. 18-1 Not for use in navigation.

Notes concerning displaced thresholds and lighting are included with the airport diagram. On approaches other than ILS and LOC, a helpful arrow indicates the direction from which you will be approaching the airport.

Look at the minimums table of the approach plate. Notice the categories listed along the top and various approaches listed down the left side. In this case, the approach minimums are for straight-in approaches (ILS and LOC) to Runway 9L and for circling approaches to the airport.

A LOT OF PAGE TURNING

The next section of the approach plate contains information that doesn't fit anywhere else. In the case of Opa Locka, you find a T and an A in reverse type set within black triangles. The T indicates that the takeoff minimums are not standard, or there are published departure procedures, or both. The A indicates that the alternate minimums are not standard. In either or both cases, you must turn to the list of tabulated data for airports in the front of the booklet.

There is only so much room on one 5 x 8 piece of paper; it's virtually impossible to include everything on one plate. As a result, NOS charts show nonstandard takeoff and landing minimums on pages other than the approach chart.

NOS explanatory pages are in the front of the book. Although the pages are laid out quite logically, they still require you to do a lot of page turning. The explanation of the approach categories is quite straightforward, especially regarding how you must change the category to a higher one if you are using a circling approach in which the aircraft will be maneuvering in a configuration that increases the stall speed.

You will find the landing minima format at the bottom of Fig. 18-2 (as a tribute to NOS, I'll use the word minima for awhile!). It is different enough from the Jeppesen format to justify an explanation.

While Jeppesen puts the categories in a vertical column and breaks up the horizontal row to show the various minima for inoperative-components approaches, NOS charts list the categories horizontally, then show the various approaches in columns. In the case of the ILS approach, if the glide slope is inoperative, you only look down to the next line to find the minima for the LOC approach. Notice that in Fig. 18-2 the minima for the ILS and LOC are for straight-in approaches, signified by the S. If you use the ILS or LOC to reach the airport, but plan to circle to land, you will find the minima on the bottom line, labeled CIRCLING.

Unlike the Jeppesen charts, with the NOS versions, if you have inoperative components for the approach, you are obliged to turn to another page to see what changes must be made to the minima (Fig. 18-3). Although this format is fairly easy to understand, you would be hard pressed to find the correct page if you were already on the approach when something decided to quit. In fact, unless you had a copilot on board who could do the research, you would probably have to execute a missed approach until everything was straightened out. With the Jeppesen chart, you could glance at the bottom of the page and make the necessary adjustments to the MDA more efficiently.

IFR LANDING MINIMA

Landing minima are established for six aircraft approach categories (ABCDE and COPTER). In the absence of COPTER MINIMA, helicopters may use the CAT A minimums of other procedures. The standard format for portrayal of landing minima is as follows:

AIRCRAFT APPROACH CATEGORIES

Speeds are based on 1.3 times the stall speed in the landing configuration of maximum gross landing weight. An aircraft shall fit in only one category. If it is necessary to maneuver at speeds in excess of the upper limit of a speed range for a category, the minimums for the next higher category should be used. For example, an aircraft which falls in Category A, but is circling to land at a speed in excess of 91 knots, should use the approach Category B minimums when circling to land. See following category limits:

MANEUVERING TABLE

Approach Category	A	B	C	D	E
Speed (Knots)	0-90	91-120	121-140	141-165	Abv 165

RVR/Meteorological Visibility Comparable Values

The following table shall be used for converting RVR to meteorological visibility when RVR is not reported for the runway of intended operation. Adjustment of landing minima may be required – see Inoperative Components Table.

RVR (feet)	Visibility (statute miles)	RVR (feet)	Visibility (statute miles)
1600	¼	4000	¾
2000	⅜	4500	⅞
2400	½	5000	1
3200	⅝	6000	1¼

LANDING MINIMA FORMAT

In this example airport elevation is 1179, and runway touchdown zone elevation is 1152.

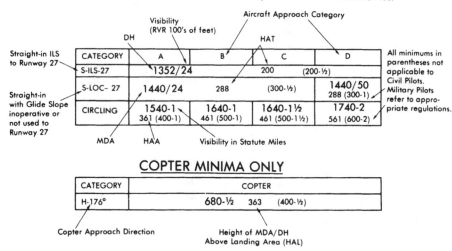

COPTER MINIMA ONLY

CATEGORY	COPTER		
H-176°	680-½	363	(400-½)

Copter Approach Direction   Height of MDA/DH Above Landing Area (HAL)

No circling minimums are provided

Fig. 18-2 Not for use in navigation.

Landing minimums published on instrument approach procedure charts are based upon full operation of all components and visual aids associated with the particular instrument approach chart being used. Higher minimums are required with inoperative components or visual aids as indicated below. If more than one component is inoperative, each minimum is raised to the highest minimum required by any single component that is inoperative. ILS glide slope inoperative minimums are published on instrument approach charts as localizer minimums. This table may be amended by notes on the approach chart. Such notes apply only to the particular approach category(ies) as stated. See legend page for description of components indicated below.

(1) ILS, MLS, and PAR

Inoperative Component or Aid	Approach Category	Increase DH	Increase Visibility
MM*	ABC	50 feet	None
MM*	D	50 feet	¼ mile
ALSF 1 & 2, MALSR, & SSALR	ABCD	None	¼ mile

*Not applicable to PAR, MLS, and Operators Authorized in their Operations Specifications.

(2) ILS with visibility minimum of 1,800 RVR.

MM*	ABC	50 feet	To 2400 RVR
MM*	D	50 feet	To 4000 RVR
ALSF 1 & 2, MALSR, & SSALR	ABCD	None	To 4000 RVR
TDZL, RCLS	ABCD	None	To 2400 RVR
RVR	ABCD	None	To ½ mile

*Not applicable to Operators Authorized in their Operations Specifications.

(3) VOR, VOR/DME, VORTAC, VOR (TAC), VOR/DME (TAC), LOC, LOC/DME, LDA, LDA/DME, SDF, SDF/DME, RNAV, and ASR

Inoperative Visual Aid	Approach Category	Increase MDA	Increase Visibility
ALSF 1 & 2, MALSR, & SSALR	ABCD	None	½ mile
SSALS, MALS & ODALS	ABC	None	¼ mile

(4) NDB

ALSF 1 & 2, MALSR, & SSALR	C	None	½ mile
	ABD	None	¼ mile
MALS, SSALS, ODALS	ABC	None	¼ mile

Fig. 18-3 Not for use in navigation.

This is an important point, particularly when making an approach to an alternate, when low on fuel, or if landing at a busy field and a miss would put you way back in a long daisy chain.

Also noteworthy in Fig. 18-3 is the caution that reads:

This table may be amended by notes on the approach chart. Such notes apply only to the particular approach category(ies) as stated.

Certain amendments are indicated in the block below the minima block (Fig. 18-4). The note's text increases the required visibility to RVR 5,000 for Category D aircraft conducting straight-in localizer approaches to Miami International's Runway 9L when the middle marker is inoperative. Once again, you have to carefully read everything on every chart.

BASIC TAKEOFF AND ALTERNATE MINIMA

The basic regulations that apply to minima are FAR 91.175(f) and 91.169(c). In effect, these regulations set up standard takeoff and alternate minimums. For takeoff, these require 1 statute mile visibility for airplanes with one or two engines, and one-half statute mile visibility for those with more than two engines, except for Part 91 operators, as explained earlier.

Standard alternate minima require a 600-foot ceiling and 2-statute-mile visibility for precision (ILS and PAR) approaches and an 800-foot ceiling with 2-statute-mile visibility for nonprecision approaches. In the Jeppesen format, all of this information, including any nonstandard requirements, is listed under the takeoff and alternate minimum formats that are found on each airport chart.

The NOS charts present this information in a different manner. NOS lists takeoff and alternate minima in the front of the booklet. These pages (Figs. 18-5 through 18-8) spell out the standard minima as mentioned above and list each airport that has minima different from standard. To find out if the airport you are operating at has nonstandard minimums, you need only look at the note section of the individual approach chart.

There you will find a white T in an inverted black triangle if the takeoff minima are nonstandard and a white A in a black triangle if the alternate minima are nonstandard. Then turn to the appropriate page in the front of the book and check out the differences, or you can just look up the airports in these pages to begin with. In either case, it amounts to a lot of page turning or trying to memorize the standard minima, which leads to errors. The less you commit to memory, the better off you are.

As with all minima, the takeoff and alternate minima are based on obstacle clearance and aircraft performances. You will see, for example, that although there are no ceiling requirements in the standard takeoff minima, you might have them in nonstandard situations, such as seen in Figs. 18-5 through 18-8.

In the note section for Albert Whitted Airport at St. Petersburg, Florida (Fig.18-9):

When control zone not effective the following applies:
1. Use Tampa, FL altimeter setting.
2. Increase all MDAs 40 feet.
3. Alternate minimums not authorized.

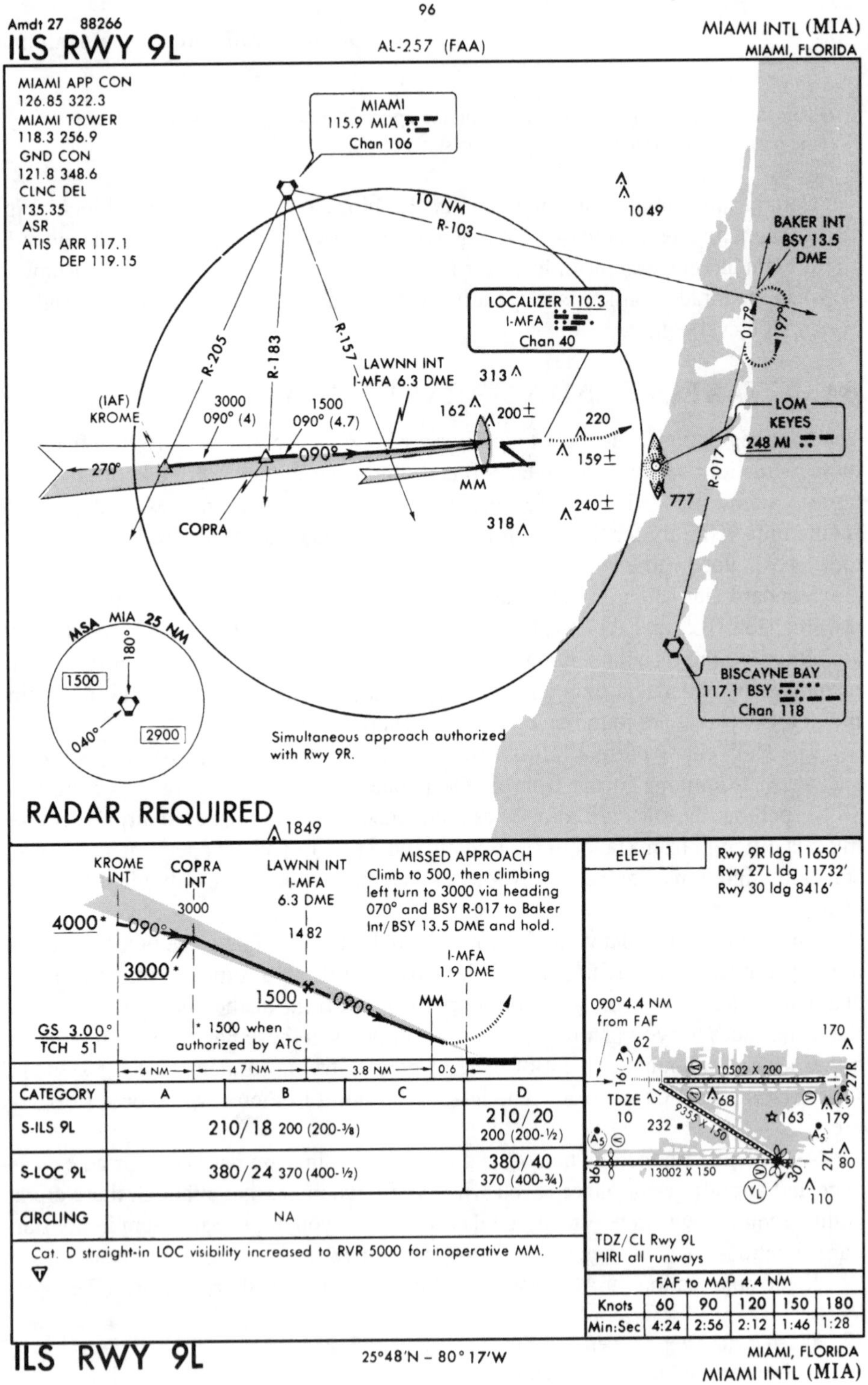

CATEGORY	A	B	C	D
S-ILS 9L	210/18 200 (200-3/8)			210/20 200 (200-1/2)
S-LOC 9L	380/24 370 (400-1/2)			380/40 370 (400-3/4)
CIRCLING	NA			

Cat. D straight-in LOC visibility increased to RVR 5000 for inoperative MM.

FAF to MAP 4.4 NM					
Knots	60	90	120	150	180
Min:Sec	4:24	2:56	2:12	1:46	1:28

Fig. 18-4 Not for use in navigation.

INSTRUMENT APPROACH PROCEDURES (CHARTS)

⚠️ IFR ALTERNATE MINIMUMS
(NOT APPLICABLE TO USA/USN/USAF)

Standard alternate minimums for nonprecision approaches are 800-2 (NDB, VOR, LOC, TACAN, LDA, VORTAC, VOR/DME or ASR); for precision approaches 600-2 (ILS or PAR). Airports within this geographical area that require alternate minimums other than standard or alternate minimums with restrictions are listed below. NA - means alternate minimums are not authorized due to unmonitored facility or absence of weather reporting service. Civil pilots see FAR 91. USA/USN/USAF pilots refer to appropriate regulations.

NAME	ALTERNATE MINIMUMS	NAME	ALTERNATE MINIMUMS

ALBERT WHITTED — SEE ST. PETERSBURG, FL

ALEXANDER HAMILTON — SEE CHRISTIANSTED, ST. CROIX, VI

CHARLOTTE AMALIE, ST. THOMAS, VI
CYRIL E KING . . . . VOR-A
ILS Rwy 10
   1200-3

CHRISTIANSTED, ST. CROIX, VI
ALEXANDER HAMILTON . . . . NDB Rwy 9, 1200-3†
ILS Rwy 9†
VOR Rwy 27*
   *Non-DME equipped aircraft 900-3.
   †NA when control tower closed.

CRAIG MUNI — SEE JACKSONVILLE, FL

CYRIL E KING — SEE CHARLOTTE AMALIE, ST. THOMAS, VI

DAYTONA BEACH REGIONAL, FL
VOR Rwy 16
   Category D, 800-2¼

EUGENIO MARIA DE HOSTOS — SEE MAYAGUEZ, PR

FORT LAUDERDALE, FL
FORT LAUDERDALE EXECUTIVE . . . . . RNAV Rwy 8
NDB Rwy 8*
ILS Rwy 8†
   NA when control zone not in effect.
   *Category D, 800-2¼
   †ILS, Category D, 700-2

FORT LAUDERDALE-HOLLYWOOD INTL
ILS Rwy 9L
ILS Rwy 27R
   ILS, 700-2

FORT MYERS, FL
SOUTHWEST FLORIDA REGIONAL . . . NDB Rwy 6
ILS Rwy 6*
VOR Rwy 24
RADAR-1
   *ILS, Category E, 700-2¼; LOC, Category E, 800-2¼
   NA when control tower closed.

GAINESVILLE REGIONAL, FL
VOR-A
   Category C, 800-2¼; Category D, 800-2½.

JACKSONVILLE, FL
CRAIG MUNI . . . . VOR Rwy 13
   Category D, 800-2¼.

KEY WEST INTL, FL
NDB-A
   NA when control tower closed.

LAKELAND MUNI, FL
NDB Rwy 5
ILS Rwy 5
VOR Rwy 13
VOR Rwy 27†
   †Categories C, D, 800-2½
   NA when control zone not in effect.

LUIS MUNOZ MARIN INTL — SEE SAN JUAN, PR

MAYAGUEZ, PR
EUGENIO MARIA DE HOSTOS . . . . . VOR Rwy 9
   Categories A, B, C, 900-2½

SE-3

Fig. 18-5 Not for use in navigation.

89348

INSTRUMENT APPROACH PROCEDURES (CHARTS)

IFR ALTERNATE MINIMUMS
(NOT APPLICABLE TO USA/USN/USAF)

Standard alternate minimums for nonprecision approaches are 800-2 (NDB, VOR, LOC, TACAN, LDA, VORTAC, VOR/DME or ASR); for precision approaches 600-2 (ILS or PAR). Airports within this geographical area that require alternate minimums other than standard or alternate minimums with restrictions are listed below. NA - means alternate minimums are not authorized due to unmonitored facility or absence of weather reporting service. Civil pilots see FAR 91. USA/USN/USAF pilots refer to appropriate regulations.

NAME	ALTERNATE MINIMUMS

ALBERT WHITTED — SEE ST. PETERSBURG, FL

ALEXANDER HAMILTON — SEE CHRISTIANSTED, ST. CROIX, VI

CENTRAL FLORIDA REGIONAL – SEE SANFORD, FL

CHARLOTTE AMALIE, ST. THOMAS, VI
CYRIL E KING ....VOR-A
ILS Rwy 10, 1200-3

CHRISTIANSTED, ST. CROIX, VI
ALEXANDER HAMILTON .... NDB Rwy 9, 1200-3†
ILS Rwy 9†
VOR Rwy 27*
*Non-DME equipped aircraft 900-3.
†NA when control tower closed.

CRAIG MUNI — SEE JACKSONVILLE, FL

CYRIL E KING — SEE CHARLOTTE AMALIE, ST. THOMAS, VI

DAYTONA BEACH REGIONAL, FL
VOR Rwy 16
Category D, 800-2¼

EUGENIO MARIA DE HOSTOS — SEE MAYAGUEZ, PR

FORT LAUDERDALE, FL
FORT LAUDERDALE EXECUTIVE .....RNAV Rwy 8
NDB Rwy 8*
ILS Rwy 8†
NA when control zone not in effect.
*Category D, 800-2¼
†ILS, Category D, 700-2

FORT LAUDERDALE-HOLLYWOOD INTL
ILS Rwy 9L
ILS Rwy 27R
ILS, 700-2

FORT MYERS, FL
SOUTHWEST FLORIDA REGIONAL ... NDB Rwy 6
ILS Rwy 6*
VOR Rwy 24
RADAR-1
*ILS, Category E, 700-2¼; LOC, Category E, 800-2¼
NA when control tower closed.

GAINESVILLE REGIONAL, FL
VOR-A
Category C, 800-2¼; Category D, 800-2½.

JACKSONVILLE, FL
CRAIG MUNI .... VOR Rwy 14*
ILS Rwy 32†
*Category D, 800-2¼.
†NA when control tower closed.

KEY WEST INTL, FL
NDB-A
NA when control tower closed.

LAKELAND REGIONAL, FL
NDB Rwy 5
ILS Rwy 5
VOR Rwy 9
VOR Rwy 13
VOR Rwy 27†
†Categories C, D, 800-2½
NA when control zone not in effect.

LUIS MUNOZ MARIN INTL — SEE SAN JUAN, PR

MAYAGUEZ, PR
EUGENIO MARIA DE HOSTOS ..... VOR Rwy 9
Categories A, B, C, 900-2½

SE-3

Fig. 18-6 Not for use in navigation.

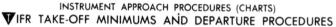

▼IFR TAKE-OFF MINIMUMS AND DEPARTURE PROCEDURES

INSTRUMENT APPROACH PROCEDURES (CHARTS)

Civil Airports and Selected Military Airports

CIVIL USERS: FAR 91 prescribes take-off rules and establishes take-off minimums as follows:
(1) Aircraft having two engines or less – one statute mile. (2) Aircraft having more than two engines – one-half statute mile.

MILITARY USERS: Special IFR departure procedures, not published as Standard Instrument Departure (SIDs), and civil take-off minima are included below and are established to assist pilots in obstruction avoidance. Refer to appropriate service directives for take-off minimums.

Airports with IFR take-off minimums other than standard are listed below. Departure procedures and/or ceiling visibility minimums are established to assist pilots conducting IFR flight in avoiding obstructions during climb to the minimum enroute altitude. Take-off minimums and departures apply to all runways unless otherwise specified. Altitudes, unless otherwise indicated, are minimum altitudes in feet MSL.

NAME	TAKE-OFF MINIMUMS	NAME	TAKE-OFF MINIMUMS

ALBERT WHITTED — SEE ST. PETERSBURG, FL

ALEXANDER HAMILTON — SEE
CHRISTIANSTED, ST. CROIX, VI

BONIFAY, FL
TRI COUNTY
IFR DEPARTURE PROCEDURES: Rwys 1, 19, climb runway heading to 2000' before turning west.

BUNNELL, FL
FLAGLER COUNTY
IFR DEPARTURE PROCEDURE: Rwy 29, aircraft departing on a course between 270° clockwise to 360° climb on heading 270° to 1300' before proceeding on course.

CENTRAL FLORIDA REGIONAL – SEE
SANFORD, FL

CHARLOTTE AMALIE, ST. THOMAS, VI
CYRIL E KING . . . . Rwy 10, 400-1
IFR DEPARTURE PROCEDURES: Rwy 10, immediate climbing right turn to heading 120°. Continue climb to 2000 before turning north. Rwy 28, climb runway heading to 2000 before turning north.

CHRISTIANSTED, ST. CROIX, VI
ALEXANDER HAMILTON
Rwy 9, 1000-3 or standard with minimum climb of 300' per NM to 500.
IFR DEPARTURE PROCEDURE: Rwy 27, climb runway heading to 1100 before turning north. Rwy 9, for departures 250° clockwise thru 095°, climbing left turn to 1400 via heading 045° before proceeding on course.

CRAIG MUNI — SEE JACKSONVILLE, FL

CYRIL E KING — SEE CHARLOTTE AMALIE, ST. THOMAS, VI

DAYTONA BEACH REGIONAL, FL
Rwys 7R, 16, 25L/34, 300-1

DELAND MUNI-SIDNEY H. TAYLOR FIELD, FL
IFR DEPARTURE PROCEDURE: Rwys 5, 12, 30, 36, aircraft proceeding on a course between 120° CW to 260°, fly runway heading to 1800. Rwy 18, aircraft proceeding on a course between 120° CW to 260°, fly heading 120° to 1800. Rwy 23, aircraft proceeding on a course between 120° CW to 260°, fly heading 260° to 1800.

DESTIN-FORT WALTON BEACH, FL
IFR DEPARTURE PROCEDURE: Rwy 14, climb runway heading to 400 before making turn.

EUGENIO MARIA DE HOSTOS —
SEE MAYAGUEZ, PR

FLAGLER COUNTY — SEE BUNNELL, FL

FORT LAUDERDALE, FL
FORT LAUDERDALE-EXECUTIVE
IFR DEPARTURE PROCEDURE: Rwy 8, fly runway heading to 300 feet before turning north. Rwy 26, fly runway heading to 500 feet before turning south.

FORT LAUDERDALE-HOLLYWOOD INTL
Rwys 13, 27L, 300-1
IFR DEPARTURE PROCEDURE: Rwys 9L/R, climb runway heading to 500 before turning.

FORT MYERS, FL
PAGE FIELD . . . . Rwy 31, 300-1
or standard with minimum climb of 280 feet per NM to 300'.

SE-3

Fig. 18-7 Not for use in navigation.

NAME	TAKE-OFF MINIMUMS	NAME	TAKE-OFF MINIMUMS

FORT PIERCE, FL
ST. LUCIE COUNTY INTL . . . . Rwy 18, 600-1*
Rwy 36, 600-1†
*or standard with minimum climb of 300' per
NM to 600 or turn right heading 270° to 600
before proceeding on course.
†or standard with minimum climb of 250' per
NM to 600.
IFR DEPARTURE PROCEDURE: Rwy 14 climb
runway heading to 600 before turning right.

JACKSONVILLE, FL
CRAIG MUNI
Rwy 23, 1100-3 or standard with minimum climb
of 320' per NM to 1100'
IFR DEPARTURE PROCEDURE: Rwy 14, climb
runway heading to 1000' before turning right.

KEY WEST INTL, FL
IFR DEPARTURE PROCEDURE: Rwy 9, climb
runway heading to 200 before turning north.
Rwy 27, climb runway heading to 200 before
turning south.

KISSIMMEE MUNI, FL
Rwy 6, 300-1

LUIS MUNOZ MARIN INTL — SEE
SAN JUAN, PR

MARCO ISLAND, FL
IFR DEPARTURE PROCEDURE: Rwy 35,
aircraft proceeding on a course between
270° clockwise to 030° fly heading 030° to
1000' before proceeding on course.

MAYAGUEZ, PR
EUGENIO MARIA DE HOSTOS
Rwy 9, 700-1 or standard with minimum climb of
350' per NM to 2300.
IFR DEPARTURE PROCEDURE: Rwy 9, climbing
left turn to 2500 direct MAZ VOR/DME, climb in
holding pattern to 2700 for Route-1, 3300 for
G-3. Rwy 27, climbing ritht turn to 2500 direct
MAZ VOR/DME, climb in holding pattern to 2700
for Route-1, 3300 for G-3.

MERCEDITA — SEE PONCE, PR

MIAMI, FL
MIAMI INTL . . . . Rwy 9L, 800-1*
Rwy 9R, 800-1†
Rwy 12, 800-1↓
*or standard with minimum climb of 220'
per NM to 1100 or climb runway heading to
1100 before turning right.
†or standard with minimum climb of 220'
per NM to 1100 or comply with RADAR
vectors.
↓or standard with minimum climb of 220'
per NM to 1100 or climb runway heading
to 1100 before turning left.

OPA LOCKA
Rwys 9R, 9C, 12, 18R, 27L, 27C, 30, 36L, NA.
IFR DEPARTURE PROCEDURE: Rwys 9L and
36R, climb runway heading to 1100 before
proceeding on course.

TAMIAMI
IFR DEPARTURE PROCEDURE: All Rwys climb
runway heading to 1400' before turning south.

NEW PORT RICHEY, FL
TAMPA BAY EXECUTIVE
IFR DEPARTURE PROCEDURE: Rwy 8 climb rwy
heading to 1000 feet before turning. Rwy 26,
departures between 270° clockwise to 360°
climbing right turn heading 320° to 2100 feet
before proceeding on course. Departures between
269° counter clockwise to 180° climbing left turn
heading 200° to 2100 feet before proceeding on
course.

NEW SMYRNA BEACH MUNI, FL
Rwys 2, 6, 300-1

OPA LOCKA — SEE MIAMI, FL

ORLANDO EXECUTIVE, FL
Rwy 25: 500-2 or standard with minimum climb
of 300'/NM to 700'. Rwy 31: 300-2 or standard
with minimum climb of 250'/NM to 700'.

PAGE FIELD — SEE FORT MYERS, FL

PAHOKEE, FL
PALM BEACH COUNTY GLADES
Rwys 7, 35, 400-1
Rwy 17, 300-1

PALM BEACH COUNTY GLADES — SEE
PAHOKEE, FL

PERRY-FOLEY, FL
IFR DEPARTURE PROCEDURE: Rwys 6, 12, 30, 36,
climb on runway heading to 800 before turning.

SE-3

Fig. 18-8 Not for use in navigation.

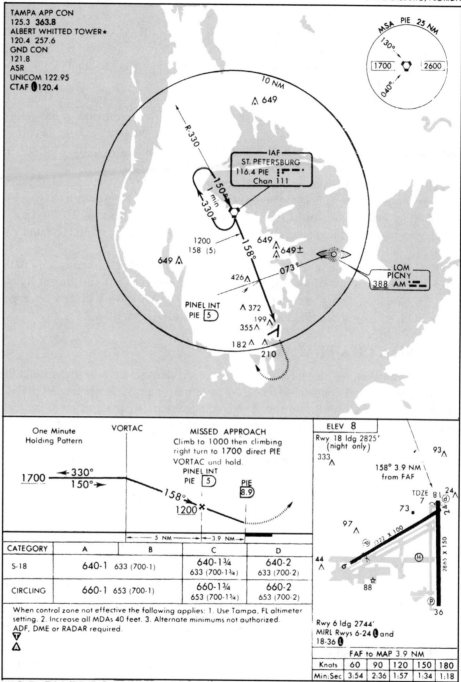

TAMPA APP CON
125.3 **363.8**
ALBERT WHITTED TOWER★
120.4 257.6
GND CON
121.8
ASR
UNICOM 122.95
CTAF 120.4

MSA PIE 25 NM
130°
1700   2600
040°

IAF
ST. PETERSBURG
116.4 PIE
Chan 111

R-330

150°
1 min
330°

158°

1200
158 (5)

649

649±

073°

LOM
PICNY
388 AM

426

PINEL INT
PIE 5

372

199
355

182   210

649

649

649

One Minute Holding Pattern

VORTAC

MISSED APPROACH
Climb to 1000 then climbing right turn to **1700** direct PIE VORTAC and hold.

ELEV 8

Rwy 18 ldg 2825'
(night only)

158° 3.9 NM
from FAF

1700   330°
150°

158°

PINEL INT
PIE 5

1200 ✕

PIE
8.9

5 NM   3.9 NM

93

333

TDZE 8

73

97

44

88

36

CATEGORY	A	B	C	D
S-18	640-1	633 (700-1)	640-1¾ 633 (700-1¾)	640-2 633 (700-2)
CIRCLING	660-1	653 (700-1)	660-1¾ 653 (700-1¾)	660-2 653 (700-2)

When control zone not effective the following applies: 1. Use Tampa, FL altimeter setting. 2. Increase all MDAs 40 feet. 3. Alternate minimums not authorized.
ADF, DME or RADAR required.

Rwy 6 ldg 2744'
MIRL Rwys 6-24 and
18-36

FAF to MAP 3.9 NM					
Knots	60	90	120	150	180
Min:Sec	3:54	2:36	1:57	1:34	1:18

Fig. 18-9 Not for use in navigation.

The note goes on to say that you need ADF, DME, or RADAR for this approach. Looking below the table, you find the symbols that tell you that nonstandard takeoff and alternate minimums are specified for this airport, so look at the tabulations in the front of the book.

Figure 18-5 lists the standard alternate minimums at the top of the page. Then look down at ALBERT WHITTED only to find an answer like you'd find in the yellow pages: SEE ST. PETERSBURG, FL. So, turn to St. Petersburg on the next page (Fig. 18-6), where you see that Whitted is not authorized for use as an alternate airport via the VOR Rwy 18 approach when the control zone is not effective.

Then look up the nonstandard takeoff minimums (Fig. 18-7). Once again, the standard minimums are spelled out at the top of the page, and you have to turn the page (to Fig. 18-8) to find the note for ALBERT WHITTED airport: Runway 6, 18, 24, and 36 (in other words, all of the runways) takeoffs require both a ceiling of 200 feet and visibility of 1 mile.

Review some of the other nonstandard takeoff and landing minimums on these pages to anticipate some of the differences you will experience in instrument flying. Next time you look through a complete set of approach charts, whether they be Jeppesen or NOS, see if you can find the possible reasons for the variations.

PICKING A CHART APART

Further examination of the Albert Whitted approach chart (Fig. 18-9) reveals that the procedure turn for this approach is a holding pattern over the St. Petersburg VORTAC, which is also the IAF for the airport. The holding pattern, when depicted in lieu of a procedure turn, is mandatory except when radar vectors are being provided.

Note that the holding pattern procedure turn is shown in both the plan and profile views. The inbound leg of the holding pattern should be 1 minute in duration.

The distance from the IAF to the FAF is 5 nautical miles. The FAF is PINEL intersection, which can be identified three ways:

- 5 DME from St. Petersburg VOR (PIE)
- The 073-degree bearing to PICNY (an outer compass locator for another approach)
- A radar fix (Now you can see why ADF, DME, or radar is required for this approach.)

From PINEL to the MAP is another 3.9 nautical miles or 8.9 DME from the VOR. Under the airport diagram you can see a table to estimate time from the FAF to the MAP. Remember, the speed you want to use is ground speed in knots. Another thing to note here is the manner in which the NOS charts depict DME distances. They put the numeral inside a stylized letter D that is attached to the vertical line leading upward from the ground plane that identifies the fix.

An arrow runs from the upper part of the airport diagram down toward Runway 18. The note on it reads "158 degrees 3.9 NM from FAF." This helps you visualize the path the aircraft will fly on the approach.

AIRPORT LIGHTING

The airport diagram in Fig. 18-10 includes a V within a circle alongside the numerals for Runways 18R, 9/27, and 18L, and a VL in a circle next to Runway 36R. The right-hand side of Fig. 18-11 has an explanation that these letters indicate that the runways are equipped with visual approach slope indicators (VASI). The V is for the two-bar VASI that most of us are familiar with, which provides approach slope guidance for most aircraft. The VL indicates a three-bar VASI that uses an upper bar to provide a higher threshold crossing height to accommodate long-bodied or jumbo aircraft.

In the two-bar system, if both upper and lower bars are white you are too high; if both are red, too low; red on top and white on the bottom, on the glide slope. A good way to remember this is by the saying, "Red over white, you're all right. Red over red, you're dead."

Three-bar systems give large aircraft adequate gear clearance when crossing the threshold. Pilots flying light aircraft and even carriers flying other than wide- or long-bodies can use the lower pair of light bars. Pilots of larger aircraft use the upper pair. If you've ever seen a wide-bodied jet on approach and have noticed how high the pilot sits above the landing gear, you can see why the third bar is there. His main gear is 50 feet lower than his eyes, so when following the standard VASI, there would be too great a chance of landing short.

Figure 18-10 shows A1, A3, and A5 inside circles on the airport diagram. These are symbols representing various approach light systems, which are illustrated on Fig. 18-11. The dot at the top of those circles means the runway also has sequence flashing lights. Additionally, at the top of Fig. 18-11 notice that if these circles and numerals are in reverse print, they indicate pilot-controlled lighting.

You can find the instructions for activating the pilot radio-controlled airport lighting systems at the front of the approach plate book. If you are flying to a field with such a system, all of the pilot-activated lights are indicated by the symbols in reverse print as noted above or by the specific lights noted in the airport diagram. The VOR/DME-A chart for Lake City, Florida (Fig. 18-12), has the note "MIRL Rwy 10-28" followed by an L in reverse print. You will also see that the VASI symbols for those runways are printed in reverse type. The frequency to be used to activate the lights can be found in the communications grouping in the upper left hand corner, identified by an L in reverse print. In this case, it's the unicom frequency 122.7. To operate the system, tune the transmitter to 122.7, and key the mike five times within 5 seconds. This will turn on the medium intensity lights.

At some airports, if you were to key the mike seven times within 5 seconds, that would activate the highest intensity lights available, while three keys in 5 seconds

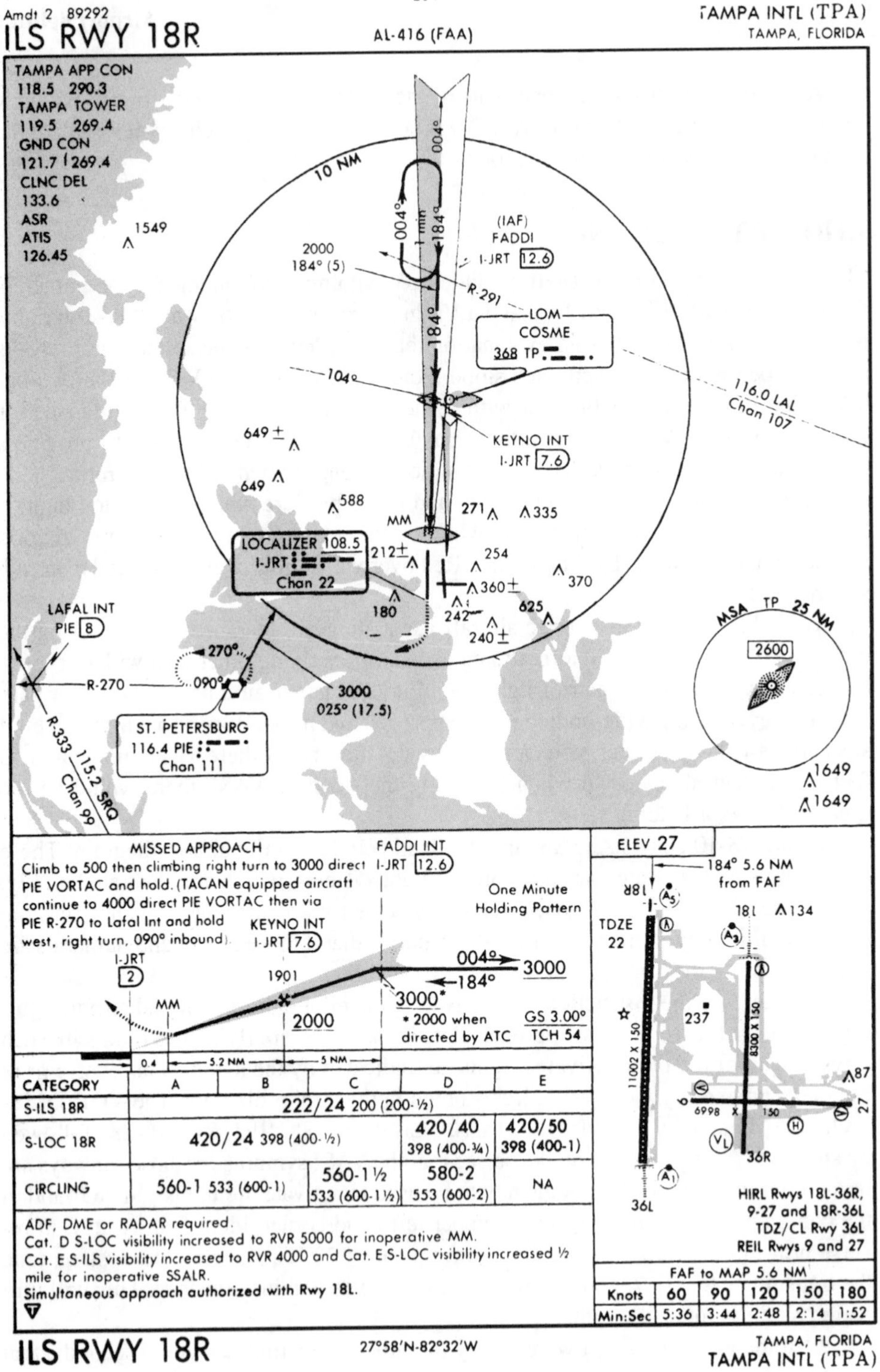
Amdt 2 89292
ILS RWY 18R
AL-416 (FAA)
TAMPA INTL (TPA)
TAMPA, FLORIDA
TAMPA APP CON
118.5 290.3
TAMPA TOWER
119.5 269.4
GND CON
121.7 269.4
CLNC DEL
133.6
ASR
ATIS
126.45
1549
10 NM
004°
004°
1 min
184°
2000
184° (5)
(IAF)
FADDI
I-JRT 12.6
R-291
LOM
COSME
368 TP
184°
104°
116.0 LAL
Chan 107
KEYNO INT
I-JRT 7.6
649 ±
649
588
271
335
MM
LOCALIZER 108.5
I-JRT
Chan 22
212 ±
254
360 ±
370
180
242
625
240 ±
LAFAL INT
PIE 8
270°
R-270
090°
3000
025° (17.5)
ST. PETERSBURG
116.4 PIE
Chan 111
R-333
115.2 SRQ
Chan 99
MSA TP 25 NM
2600
1649
1649
MISSED APPROACH
Climb to 500 then climbing right turn to 3000 direct PIE VORTAC and hold. (TACAN equipped aircraft continue to 4000 direct PIE VORTAC then via PIE R-270 to Lafal Int and hold west, right turn, 090° inbound).
FADDI INT
I-JRT 12.6
One Minute
Holding Pattern
KEYNO INT
I-JRT 7.6
I-JRT
2
1901
MM
004°
3000
184°
3000*
2000
* 2000 when directed by ATC
GS 3.00°
TCH 54
0.4
5.2 NM
5 NM
ELEV 27
184° 5.6 NM from FAF
18R
18L
134
TDZE 22
237
11002 X 150
8300 X 150
6998 X 150
9
27
87
36R
36L
HIRL Rwys 18L-36R, 9-27 and 18R-36L
TDZ/CL Rwy 36L
REIL Rwys 9 and 27
ILS RWY 18R
27°58′N-82°32′W
TAMPA, FLORIDA
TAMPA INTL (TPA)

CATEGORY	A	B	C	D	E
S-ILS 18R	222/24 200 (200-½)				
S-LOC 18R	420/24 398 (400-½)			420/40 398 (400-¾)	420/50 398 (400-1)
CIRCLING	560-1 533 (600-1)		560-1½ 533 (600-1½)	580-2 553 (600-2)	NA

ADF, DME or RADAR required.
Cat. D S-LOC visibility increased to RVR 5000 for inoperative MM.
Cat. E S-ILS visibility increased to RVR 4000 and Cat. E S-LOC visibility increased ½ mile for inoperative SSALR.
Simultaneous approach authorized with Rwy 18L.

FAF to MAP 5.6 NM

Knots	60	90	120	150	180
Min:Sec	5:36	3:44	2:48	2:14	1:52

Fig. 18-10 Not for use in navigation.

Each approach lighting system indicated on Airport Diagrams will bear a system identification indicated in legend.

A dot " • " portrayed with approach lighting letter identifier indicates sequenced flashing lights (F) installed with the approach lighting system e.g., (A₁). Negative symbology, e.g.,(A₁), Ⓥ indicates Pilot Controlled Lighting (PCL).

RUNWAY TOUCHDOWN ZONE AND CENTERLINE LIGHTING SYSTEMS

TDZ/CL

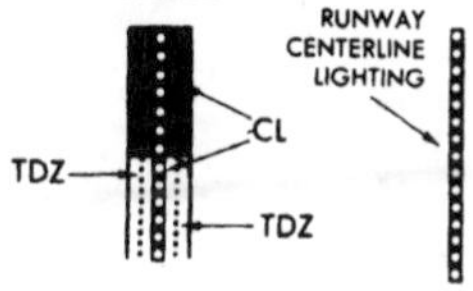

RUNWAY CENTERLINE LIGHTING
CL
TDZ
TDZ

AVAILABILITY of TDZ/CL will be shown by NOTE in SKETCH e.g. "TDZ/CL Rwy 15"

APPROACH LIGHTING SYSTEM
(A)
ALSF-2

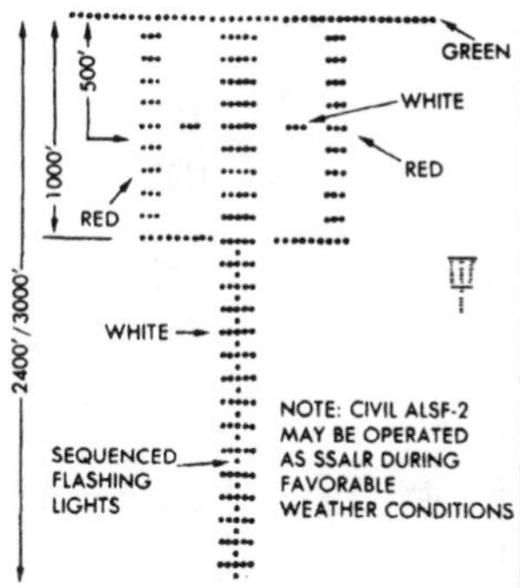

GREEN
WHITE
RED
RED
WHITE
SEQUENCED FLASHING LIGHTS

NOTE: CIVIL ALSF-2 MAY BE OPERATED AS SSALR DURING FAVORABLE WEATHER CONDITIONS

(High Intensity)
LENGTH 2400/3000 FEET

APPROACH LIGHTING SYSTEM
(A₁)
ALSF-1

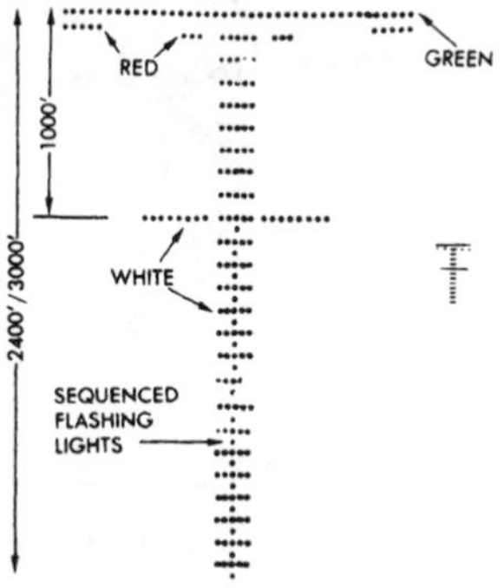

RED
GREEN
WHITE
SEQUENCED FLASHING LIGHTS

(High Intensity)
LENGTH 2400/3000 FEET

SHORT APPROACH LIGHTING SYSTEM
(A₂)
SALS/SALSF
(High Intensity)

SAME AS INNER 1500' OF ALSF-1

SIMPLIFIED SHORT APPROACH LIGHTING SYSTEM
with Runway Alignment Indicator Lights
(A₃)
SSALR

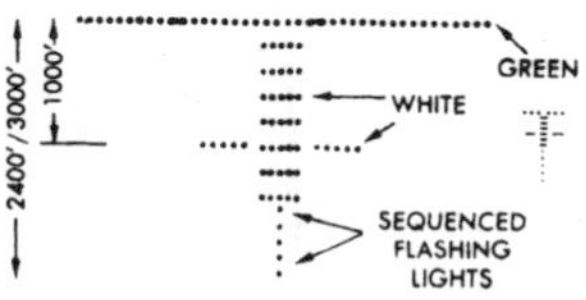

GREEN
WHITE
SEQUENCED FLASHING LIGHTS

(High Intensity)
LENGTH 2400/3000 FEET

MEDIUM INTENSITY (MALS and MALSF) OR SIMPLIFIED SHORT (SSALS and SSALF) APPROACH LIGHTING SYSTEMS
(A₄)

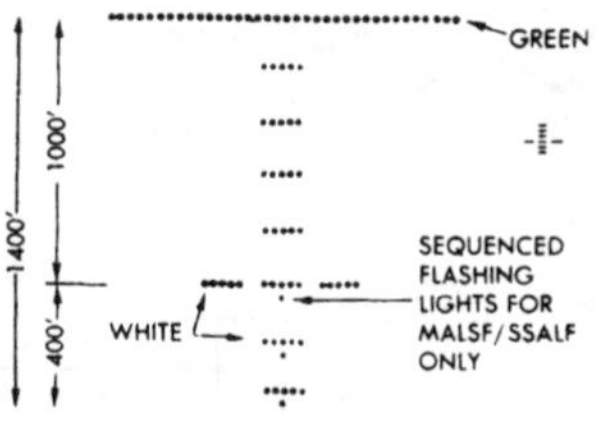

GREEN
SEQUENCED FLASHING LIGHTS FOR MALSF/SSALF ONLY
WHITE

LENGTH 1400 FEET

MEDIUM INTENSITY APPROACH LIGHTING SYSTEM
with Runway Alignment Indicator Lights
(A₅)
MALSR

SAME LIGHT CONFIGURATION AS SSALR.
-I-

OMNIDIRECTIONAL APPROACH LIGHTING SYSTEM
ODALS

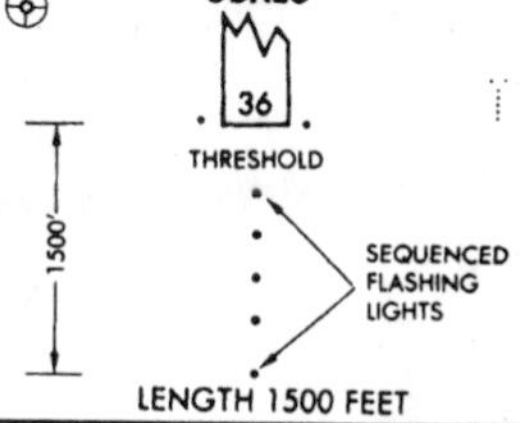

36
THRESHOLD
SEQUENCED FLASHING LIGHTS

LENGTH 1500 FEET

Ⓥ VISUAL APPROACH SLOPE INDICATOR
VASI

VISUAL APPROACH SLOPE INDICATOR WITH STANDARD THRESHOLD CLEARANCE PROVIDED.

ALL LIGHTS WHITE — TOO HIGH
FAR LIGHTS RED } ON GLIDE SLOPE
NEAR LIGHTS WHITE }
ALL LIGHTS RED — TOO LOW

VASI 2   VASI 4

36   36
THRESHOLD   THRESHOLD

VASI 12

36
THRESHOLD

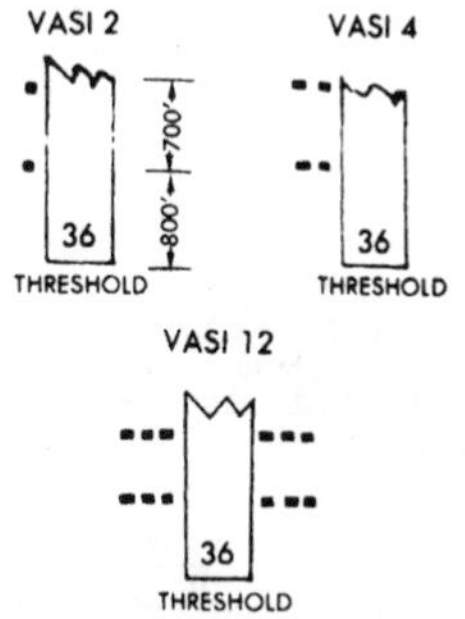

Ⓥₗ VISUAL APPROACH SLOPE INDICATOR
VASI

VISUAL APPROACH SLOPE INDICATOR WITH A THRESHOLD CROSSING HEIGHT TO ACCOMODATE LONG BODIED OR JUMBO AIRCRAFT.

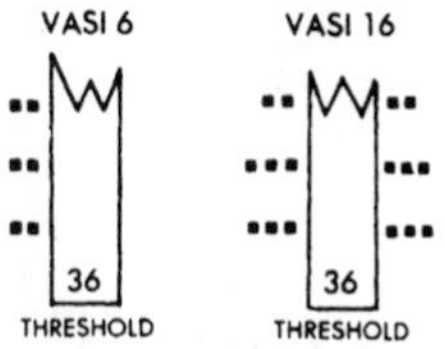

VASI 6   VASI 16

36   36
THRESHOLD   THRESHOLD

Fig. 18-11 Not for use in navigation.

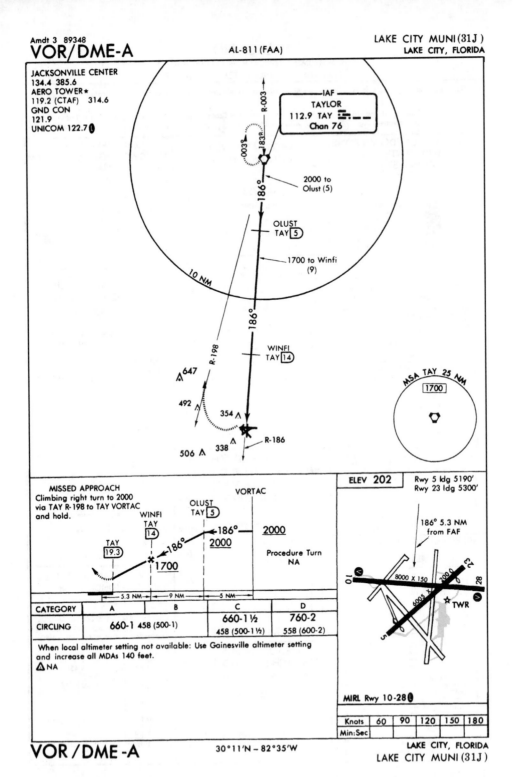

JACKSONVILLE CENTER
134.4 385.6
AERO TOWER★
119.2 (CTAF) 314.6
GND CON
121.9
UNICOM 122.7

IAF
TAYLOR
112.9 TAY
Chan 76

R-003

003°

183°

186°

2000 to
Olust (5)

OLUST
TAY 5

1700 to Winfi
(9)

10 NM

186°

R-198

WINFI
TAY 14

647

492

354

338

R-186

506

MSA TAY 25 NM
1700

MISSED APPROACH
Climbing right turn to 2000
via TAY R-198 to TAY VORTAC
and hold.

VORTAC

OLUST
TAY 5

WINFI
TAY 14

186°

186°

2000

2000

TAY
19.3

186°

1700

Procedure Turn
NA

5.3 NM   9 NM   5 NM

CATEGORY	A	B	C	D
CIRCLING	660-1 458 (500-1)		660-1½ 458 (500-1½)	760-2 558 (600-2)

When local altimeter setting not available: Use Gainesville altimeter setting
and increase all MDAs 140 feet.
⚠ NA

ELEV 202

Rwy 5 ldg 5190'
Rwy 23 ldg 5300'

186° 5.3 NM
from FAF

8000 X 150

6005 X 150

TWR

MIRL Rwy 10-28

Knots	60	90	120	150	180
Min:Sec					

Fig. 18-12 Not for use in navigation.

would operate the lowest intensity lights available. Check the approach plates to determine the highest intensity lights available and key the mike to bring them up initially to that intensity. This will allow you to see the lights at the greatest distance, which is especially useful in low visibility conditions or around strange airports. Then, as you get closer, when the lights might be too bright, use the keying technique to reduce the intensity.

Another symbol to be aware of is the holding pattern symbol in which the race track is made up of a series of hash marks such as is found over the TAYLOR VOR. This is not a procedure-turn holding pattern. The note in the profile view explains that a procedure turn is not available. The holding pattern depicted by hash marks is a missed approach holding pattern only.

NOS PROCEDURE TURNS

An actual approach procedure begins at the IAF. From this point on, the procedure track will be indicated by a heavy line with arrowheads indicating the proper direction to be flown. These, and other symbols used on the plan view, are in Fig. 18-13. Follow this track on an ILS approach to Orlando Executive Airport (Fig. 18-14).

The procedure turn is indicated in the upper left-hand column of Fig. 18-13 as half an arrowhead with the inbound and outbound magnetic courses (also illustrated on Fig. 18-14).

About midway down the left-hand column in Fig. 18-13, note four different holding patterns. The dark, heavy line indicates a holding pattern that is being used in lieu of a procedure turn. The second type, with a finer line, indicates a normal arrival holding pattern. The third type, shorter and finer still, is the old type that depicts a holding pattern used in conjunction with a missed approach, and above that is the new missed approach holding pattern, mentioned earlier, that uses the hash marks to differentiate it. The new missed approach is in Fig. 18-14 at OVIDO.

For some reason, the NOS charts don't have any plan view symbol for the teardrop procedure turn, but they do indicate it on the profile view. The upper left-hand symbol on Fig. 18-15 signifies a teardrop procedure turn, and you can see how it differs from the profile of a normal procedure turn. The teardrop has a continuous line, while the normal procedure turn shows a break at the outbound end.

Review the normal procedure turn illustration at the top center of Fig. 18-15; the procedure turn altitude is 2,400 feet as depicted by the numeral above the line, near the break in the procedure turn track. Note the lightning bolt figure pointing to the inbound leg just prior to the LOM; it has a number (in this case 2400) above another line. Look down at the PROFILE SYMBOLS in the lower right-hand column of the page and see that this symbol indicates the glide slope intercept point and altitude. Recall from chapter 16 that the glide slope intercept point is always the FAF on precision approaches.

Note the small 2156 above the Maltese cross symbol. This indicates the glide slope altitude at the outer marker. This is a good checkpoint when flying an ILS ap-

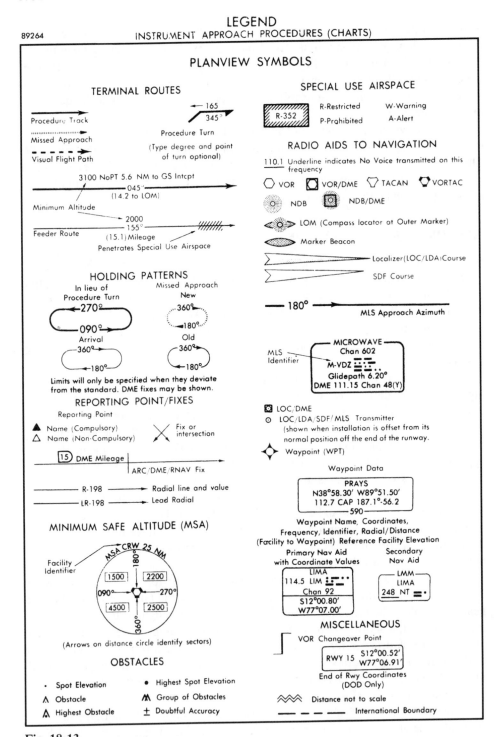

LEGEND
INSTRUMENT APPROACH PROCEDURES (CHARTS)

Fig. 18-13 Not for use in navigation.

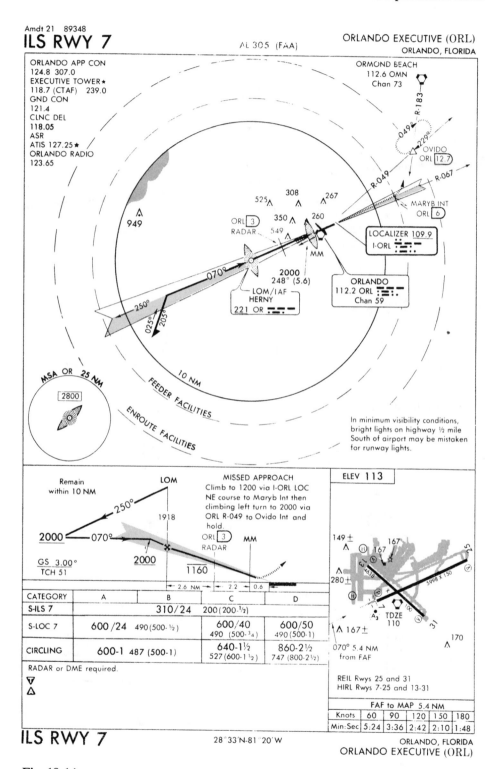

Fig. 18-14 Not for use in navigation.

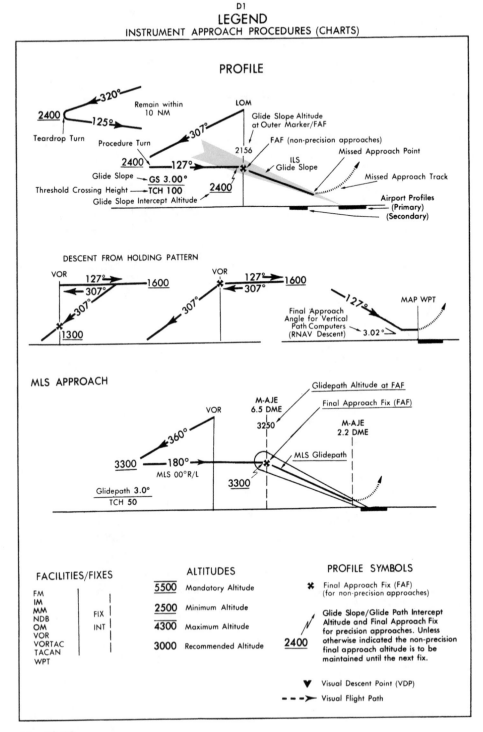

D1
LEGEND
INSTRUMENT APPROACH PROCEDURES (CHARTS)

PROFILE

DESCENT FROM HOLDING PATTERN

MLS APPROACH

FACILITIES/FIXES

FM
IM
MM
NDB   FIX
OM   INT
VOR
VORTAC
TACAN
WPT

ALTITUDES

5500 Mandatory Altitude

2500 Minimum Altitude

4300 Maximum Altitude

3000 Recommended Altitude

PROFILE SYMBOLS

✱ Final Approach Fix (FAF)
(for non-precision approaches)

Glide Slope/Glide Path Intercept
Altitude and Final Approach Fix
for precision approaches. Unless
otherwise indicated the non-precision
final approach altitude is to be
maintained until the next fix.

▼ Visual Descent Point (VDP)

- - - ► Visual Flight Path

Fig. 18-15 Not for use in navigation.

proach to let you know that you are not on a false glide slope.

So you can see that, in this case, you should intercept the glide slope at 2,400 feet, prior to reaching the LOM, then descend on the glide slope, arriving at the LOM when the altimeter reads about 2,156 feet.

Look at the altitudes depicted in the bottom center of Fig. 18-15. These are self-explanatory, but make sure that you understand them. Basically, the line drawn over, under, or both over and under a numeral, indicates a barrier that should not be penetrated; therefore, if the altitude has lines at both top and bottom, it is a mandatory altitude. A line above the numeral means that you must stay at or below that altitude; it is a maximum altitude. A line beneath the numeral indicates a minimum altitude, and no lines mean the altitude is merely recommended.

CLIMB AND DESCENT GRADIENTS

Remember that the glide slope intercept altitude will give you a clue about whether or not the aircraft is on the true glide slope. Another check would be to determine what the rate of descent should be. You know the indicated approach speed, and when you get the ATIS or the numbers from approach control, you can apply the correction to the airspeed to determine approximate ground speed on approach. Then you look at the symbol at the bottom of the profile view to determine the glide slope angle for the airport. In both the example shown in Fig. 18-15 and the actual approach in Fig. 18-14, the glide slope angle is 3.0 degrees. Taking this angle and the ground speed in knots, you can look at the rate-of-descent table in Fig. 18-16 and determine that the rate of descent for a ground speed of, say, 120 knots, should be 635 feet per minute. Use this recommended rate to also check for wind shear during the approach. If you need to descend at a very high sink rate, you are probably experiencing a tailwind; a very low sink rate would indicate a headwind.

The introductory pages also contain tables to help determine the rate of climb necessary to meet certain airport or runway climb-gradient restrictions (Fig. 18-17).

This chapter was included to give you some insight into the layout of the NOS charts. Comparing NOS to the Jeppesen charts should help you decide which type you prefer. Whichever type you decide upon, remember that the legends and explanatory pages should be reviewed periodically. Each time you review them, you will run across forgotten symbols or explanations or new symbols and explanations.

Remember, pilots never know enough. One mark of a professional pilot is that he or she is willing to open the manuals to review procedures, even when there isn't a check flight coming up or a cloud in the sky.

INSTRUMENT APPROACH PROCEDURE CHARTS
RATE OF DESCENT TABLE
(ft. per min.)

A rate of descent table is provided for use in planning and executing precision descents under known or approximate ground speed conditions. It will be especially useful for approaches when the localizer only is used for course guidance. A best speed, power, attitude combination can be programmed which will result in a stable glide rate and attitude favorable for executing a landing if minimums exist upon breakout. Care should always be exercised so that the minimum descent altitude and missed approach point are not exceeded.

ANGLE OF DESCENT (degrees and tenths)	GROUND SPEED (knots)										
	30	45	60	75	90	105	120	135	150	165	180
2.0	105	160	210	265	320	370	425	475	530	585	635
2.5	130	200	265	330	395	465	530	595	665	730	795
3.0	160	240	320	395	480	555	635	715	795	875	955
3.5	185	280	370	465	555	650	740	835	925	1020	1110
4.0	210	315	425	530	635	740	845	955	1060	1165	1270
4.5	240	355	475	595	715	835	955	1075	1190	1310	1430
5.0	265	395	530	660	795	925	1060	1190	1325	1455	1590
5.5	290	435	580	730	875	1020	1165	1310	1455	1600	1745
6.0	315	475	635	795	955	1110	1270	1430	1590	1745	1905
6.5	345	515	690	860	1030	1205	1375	1550	1720	1890	2065
7.0	370	555	740	925	1110	1295	1480	1665	1850	2035	2220
7.5	395	595	795	990	1190	1390	1585	1785	1985	2180	2380
8.0	425	635	845	1055	1270	1480	1690	1905	2115	2325	2540
8.5	450	675	900	1120	1345	1570	1795	2020	2245	2470	2695
9.0	475	715	950	1190	1425	1665	1900	2140	2375	2615	2855
9.5	500	750	1005	1255	1505	1755	2005	2255	2510	2760	3010
10.0	530	790	1055	1320	1585	1845	2110	2375	2640	2900	3165
10.5	555	830	1105	1385	1660	1940	2215	2490	2770	3045	3320
11.0	580	870	1160	1450	1740	2030	2320	2610	2900	3190	3480
11.5	605	910	1210	1515	1820	2120	2425	2725	3030	3335	3635
12.0	630	945	1260	1575	1890	2205	2520	2835	3150	3465	3780

Fig. 18-16 Not for use in navigation.

INSTRUMENT TAKEOFF PROCEDURE CHARTS
RATE OF CLIMB TABLE
(ft. per min.)

A rate of climb table is provided for use in planning and executing
takeoff procedures under known or approximate ground speed conditions.

REQUIRED CLIMB RATE (ft. per NM)	GROUND SPEED (KNOTS)						
	30	60	80	90	100	120	140
200	100	200	267	300	333	400	467
250	125	250	333	375	417	500	583
300	150	300	400	450	500	600	700
350	175	350	467	525	583	700	816
400	200	400	533	600	667	800	933
450	225	450	600	675	750	900	1050
500	250	500	667	750	833	1000	1167
550	275	550	733	825	917	1100	1283
600	300	600	800	900	1000	1200	1400
650	325	650	867	975	1083	1300	1516
700	350	700	933	1050	1167	1400	1633

REQUIRED CLIMB RATE (ft. per NM)	GROUND SPEED (KNOTS)					
	150	180	210	240	270	300
200	500	600	700	800	900	1000
250	625	750	875	1000	1125	1250
300	750	900	1050	1200	1350	1500
350	875	1050	1225	1400	1575	1750
400	1000	1200	1400	1600	1700	2000
450	1125	1350	1575	1800	2025	2250
500	1250	1500	1750	2000	2250	2500
550	1375	1650	1925	2200	2475	2750
600	1500	1800	2100	2400	2700	3000
650	1625	1950	2275	2600	2925	3250
700	1750	2100	2450	2800	3150	3500

Fig. 18-17 Not for use in navigation.

CHAPTER QUIZ

1. NOS charts are updated every _____ days with a change notice issued every _____ days.

2. The NOS chart reference circle is usually _____ nm in radius.

3. On NOS charts, straight-in approaches are indicated by an " _____ " in the _____.

4. Takeoff and alternate minima tables are found on the back of the NOS approach plates. True _____ False _____

5. NOS inoperative components are found in the minima columns on the airport page. True _____ False _____

6. Pilot controlled lighting is indicated by _____.

7. A lightning bolt symbol on a profile view of a NOS chart indicates the _____.

Answers are in the appendix.

19
VOR approaches

RETURNING TO THE JEPPESEN CHARTS, YOU WILL NOW BE LOOKING OVER some actual approach plates, rather than explanatory pages, and I'll talk you through the approaches. I'll try to make my explanations general enough to work in any aircraft. When I speak of flying at an approach airspeed, you will have to realize that this is good for learning and practice, but if you are at a busy airport in actual IFR conditions and flying an aircraft with an approach speed of less than 120 knots, you might have to fly up to the V_A speed so as not to force that 747 or L-1011 behind you into a holding pattern.

Before we go too far, here are a few helpful hints for IFR flight:

- Always keep the volume of the navigational radio high enough to hear the identifier. Although this is a very distracting sound in some situations, it will let you know at once if the facility goes off the air. It will also give ATC a way of communicating with you if you lose communications capabilities and are not aware of it.

- Use every navigational aid you have on board. Have them all tuned and identified. This way, if one fails, you will have an immediate backup.

- Once cleared for an approach, get a final check on the weather. It might have gone down below your particular minimums, and the controller might be too busy to notice. Remember that you will be the one left holding the bag if you land when conditions are below the authorized minimums. This last check on the weather will also give you some idea of what you can expect to see when you break out.

- In order to establish a consistent pattern for setting up VOR radios in a single-pilot cockpit, *try* to use the number 1 VOR for the course you are actually flying. Set the number 2 VOR to indicate intersections, turning points, lead-in radials, missed approaches, or for the next course you will be flying. Once reaching the new course point, fly using the number 2 VOR as a reference until you are able to reset the number 1 VOR to the new course. This procedure might not always be practical, especially on a series of short approach segments, as you'll be able to see in some of the sample approaches throughout the remainder of this book.

EXECUTING A VOR APPROACH

Let's plan a simple IFR flight to Kaunakakai Airport on the island of Molokai in Hawaii. By looking at the upper-right corner of the approach plate (Fig. 19-1), notice that Kaunakakai has a VOR approach based on the Molokai VOR (116.1) with the identifier MKK. In the upper left, you also note that it is controlled by Molokai Tower on 125.7, but that the tower operation is not continuous, as indicated by the asterisk and the letters CTAF, which means common traffic advisory frequency. The tower frequency is used as the CTAF when the tower is closed.

The airport elevation is 454 feet MSL and a glance at both the plan view and the airport diagram reveals that the airport is in a bowl, surrounded by hills ranging from 552 feet (about one-half mile northeast on the airport diagram), to 1,485 feet (the highest elevation on the plan view), which is the hilltop on which the VOR is located, to the west of the field.

Without even looking in the minimums block, you know that this is not a straight-in approach because of the suffix A after the approach type (VOR-A). Still, by looking at the inbound course, you see that the final approach course is well within the 30 degrees to Runway 5, which should qualify for straight-in minimums. "Aha," you say, remembering our earlier discussions. "Here's one of those approaches requiring a steeper-than-normal descent angle." That, plus the surrounding high terrain, necessitates the high circling minimums.

Turn the chart over to the back and examine the airport diagram (Fig. 19-2). There are two runways. The main one, 5/23, is 4,494 feet long, and the shorter one, 17/35, is 3,118 feet long. Hills and power lines (not shown on the chart) on the approach ends of Runways 17 and 23 necessitate the displaced thresholds shown by the white blocks across the runways. The additional runway information table shows that when landing on Runway 17, the effective runway length is reduced to 2,692 feet. Usable landing

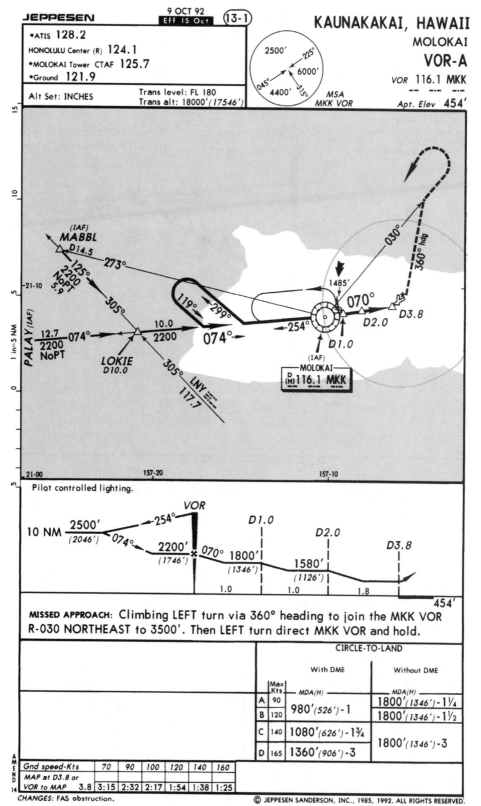

JEPPESEN   9 OCT 92 Eff 15 Oct   (13-1)

*ATIS 128.2
HONOLULU Center (R) 124.1
*MOLOKAI Tower CTAF 125.7
*Ground 121.9

Alt Set: INCHES   Trans level: FL 180
Trans alt: 18000'(17546')

KAUNAKAKAI, HAWAII
MOLOKAI
VOR-A
VOR 116.1 MKK
Apt. Elev 454'

MSA
MKK VOR
2500' — 225°
045° — 6000° — 315°
4400'

Pilot controlled lighting.

10 NM — 2500' (2046') — 254° — VOR
074° — 2200' (1746') — 070° 1800' (1346')
D1.0 — 1.0 — D2.0 — 1580' (1126') — 1.8 — D3.8 — 454'

MISSED APPROACH: Climbing LEFT turn via 360° heading to join the MKK VOR R-030 NORTHEAST to 3500'. Then LEFT turn direct MKK VOR and hold.

		Max Kts	CIRCLE-TO-LAND	
			With DME MDA(H)	Without DME MDA(H)
A		90	980'(526')-1	1800'(1346')-1¼
B		120		1800'(1346')-1½
C		140	1080'(626')-1¾	1800'(1346')-3
D		165	1360'(906')-3	

Gnd speed-Kts	70	90	100	120	140	160
MAP at D3.8 or VOR to MAP 3.8	3:15	2:32	2:17	1:54	1:38	1:25

AMEND 14

CHANGES: FAS obstruction.

© JEPPESEN SANDERSON, INC., 1985, 1992. ALL RIGHTS RESERVED.

Fig. 19-1 Reproduced with permission of Jeppesen Sanderson, Inc. Not for use in navigation.

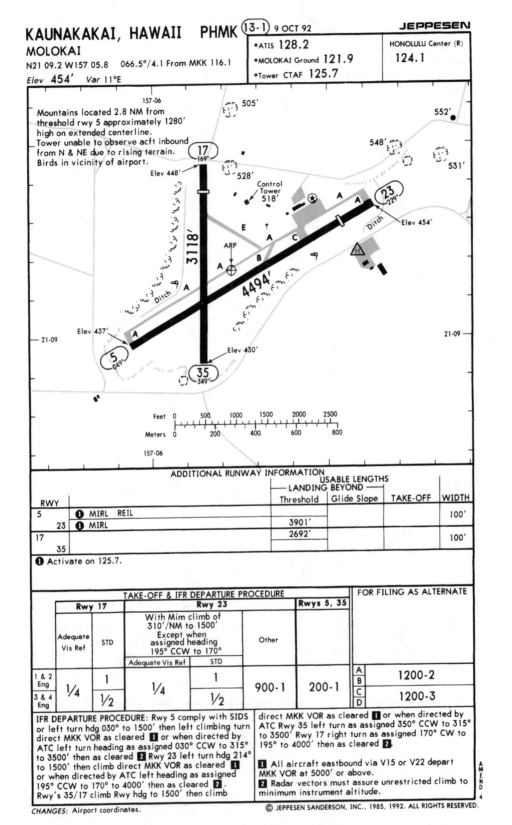

KAUNAKAKAI, HAWAII PHMK (13-1) 9 OCT 92   JEPPESEN

MOLOKAI

N21 09.2 W157 05.8   066.5°/4.1 From MKK 116.1

Elev 454'   Var 11°E

*ATIS 128.2

*MOLOKAI Ground 121.9

*Tower CTAF 125.7

HONOLULU Center (R)
124.1

Mountains located 2.8 NM from threshold rwy 5 approximately 1280' high on extended centerline. Tower unable to observe acft inbound from N & NE due to rising terrain. Birds in vicinity of airport.

| Feet | 0 | 500 | 1000 | 1500 | 2000 | 2500 |
| Meters | 0 | 200 | 400 | 600 | 800 | |

ADDITIONAL RUNWAY INFORMATION

RWY		USABLE LENGTHS — LANDING BEYOND — Threshold	Glide Slope	TAKE-OFF	WIDTH
5	❶ MIRL REIL				100'
23	❶ MIRL	3901'			
17		2692'			100'
35					

❶ Activate on 125.7.

TAKE-OFF & IFR DEPARTURE PROCEDURE

	Rwy 17		Rwy 23		Rwys 5, 35		FOR FILING AS ALTERNATE	
	Adequate Vis Ref	STD	With Mim climb of 310'/NM to 1500' Except when assigned heading 195° CCW to 170°		Other			
			Adequate Vis Ref	STD			A / B	1200-2
1 & 2 Eng	1/4	1	1/4	1	900-1	200-1		
3 & 4 Eng		1/2		1/2			C / D	1200-3

IFR DEPARTURE PROCEDURE: Rwy 5 comply with SIDS or left turn hdg 030° to 1500' then left climbing turn direct MKK VOR as cleared ❶ or when directed by ATC left turn heading as assigned 030° CCW to 315° to 3500' then as cleared ❷ Rwy 23 left turn hdg 214° to 1500' then climb direct MKK VOR as cleared ❶ or when directed by ATC left heading as assigned 195° CCW to 170° to 4000' then as cleared ❷. Rwy's 35/17 climb Rwy hdg to 1500' then climb

direct MKK VOR as cleared ❶ or when directed by ATC Rwy 35 left turn as assigned 350° CCW to 315° to 3500' Rwy 17 right turn as assigned 170° CW to 195° to 4000' then as cleared ❷.

❶ All aircraft eastbound via V15 or V22 depart MKK VOR at 5000' or above.
❷ Radar vectors must assure unrestricted climb to minimum instrument altitude.

A M E N D 4

CHANGES: Airport coordinates.

© JEPPESEN SANDERSON, INC., 1985, 1992. ALL RIGHTS RESERVED.

Fig. 19-2 Reproduced with permission of Jeppesen Sanderson, Inc. Not for use in navigation.

length of Runway 23 is 3,901 feet. Both runways are 100 feet wide, Runway 5/23 has medium intensity runway lights, and the approach end to Runway 5 has REIL. These lights are pilot-actuated after 1830 local time as can be seen in the note at the bottom of the table. (This was mentioned in chapter 18 and will be discussed further in chapter 21.)

Some interesting notes are found along the upper-left side of the airport plan view, specifically, the one about the 1,280-foot mountain located 2.8 nautical miles (northeast) from the threshold of Runway 5 on the extended centerline. That explains the IFR departure procedure (at the bottom of the chart) requiring all eastbound aircraft off Runway 5 to fly a heading of 030 degrees after takeoff and climb to 1,500 feet before making a climbing left turn to the MKK VOR. The additional note (1) says that all eastbound aircraft via V15 or V22 depart MKK VOR at 5,000 feet or above.

There are also some interesting climb gradient restrictions in the takeoff minimums block. Aircraft departing Runway 23 can go with visibility less than 1 mile if they have adequate visibility reference as specified and can climb at 310 feet per nautical mile to 1,500 feet. The climb performance will not be necessary if the aircraft is assigned a heading of 195 degrees counterclockwise to 170 degrees. This is because the land drops away to sea level to the south, although nothing on the charts will indicate that, which is another good reason to consult sectional charts.

A good idea of the abrupt mountains in the area can be gleaned from the MSA altitudes where aircraft to the east must be above 6,000 feet. This is true in all volcanic areas. The mountains seem to rise straight up out of nowhere.

The profile view on the approach chart (Fig. 19-1) shows a *double* step-down approach. From the VOR inbound, the initial descent is down to 1,800 feet. At 1.0 DME, you can descend farther to 1,580 feet to the 2.0 DME, and then down to the final minimums. Notice that if you *are not* DME equipped, you cannot descend any lower than the initial step-down altitude of 1,800 feet MSL.

I mentioned earlier that the airport is in a bowl surrounded by higher terrain. A good indication of just how close the terrain is to the field can be seen by the 280-foot increase in the MDA between Category C (1,080 feet) and Category D aircraft (1,360 feet), and the high circling minimums without DME (1,800 feet).

APPROACHING FROM THE EAST

From Maui, you will be westbound approaching the VOR. You should double-check that both VOR receivers are tuned to the MKK VOR (check the Morse code identifier). Then set the number 2 OBS to the outbound course of 254 degrees, check the DME, and request current weather. After making sure that the DME is operating, take a quick look at the chart to confirm minimums. If you are in most light aircraft, look under Category A. Because you have an operating DME, you can use the lowest minimums. You must have 1 mile visibility, and you will be able to descend to 1,800 feet after crossing the VOR, down to 1,580 feet when you pass the 1.0 DME, and down to the MDA of 980 feet after crossing the 2.0 DME inbound to the airport.

The field is reporting a zero-wind condition (for a change) so the ground speed will be the same as the approach speed, which is around 100 knots. Glance at the conversion chart under the minimums table and find that at a ground speed of 100 knots, it will take 2 minutes and 17 seconds to fly from the FAF at the VOR to the MAP.

As you approach the VOR, slow to approach speed and complete the descent and in-range checklists. Crossing the VOR, track outbound on the 254-degree radial (already tuned on number 2) and begin the descent. The profile view shows that you must complete the procedure turn within 10 nautical miles, that the initial turn will be made to the northwest, and that the minimum procedure turn altitude is 2,500 feet MSL (2,046 feet above the airport elevation).

Even though you know you can make any type of course reversal you choose on this particular approach (as long as you remain on the north side of the course, at or above the procedure turn minimum altitude), you decide to use the standard procedure turn as depicted because it will give you a little more time to get all squared away for the approach.

After you turn right to a heading of 299 degrees, fly outbound for 1 minute. During this time, descend to and maintain 2,500 feet. After the 1-minute outbound leg, make a standard-rate, 180-degree turn to the left, rolling out on a heading of 119 degrees. While waiting to intercept the inbound course, you can set the number 1 OBS to 074 degrees. At the same time, set the number 2 OBS to 070 degrees, which will be the final approach track after crossing the MKK VOR, which is the FAF. As the number 1 needle centers, indicating approach course interception, turn inbound. Once established on the inbound course (and not before), continue the descent to 2,200 feet MSL.

As you fly inbound to the VOR, you want to get the airway bracketed to within 10 degrees because once past the FAF, you don't want to have to turn more than 5 degrees to stay on course.

How do you tie down a course this close? Well, it becomes a matter of concentration and setting up tighter and tighter brackets. The ultimate goal is to find the correct heading to properly compensate for the wind drift. You first turn to the published inbound heading. One of three things will happen. You will either stay on course, drift to the right, or drift to the left. If you drift right or left, you will have to correct for the drift. If you are to the right of the course, make an immediate turn of 10 degrees to the left of the published inbound course and *hold* that heading. Again, one of three things will happen:

- The needle (OBI) will stay where it is, indicating that you have turned just enough to correct for the wind.

- The needle can continue drifting to the left, indicating that you have not turned far enough to compensate for the wind.

- It will start back toward the center, indicating that you have overcorrected for the wind.

If you have not corrected enough, you will turn another 10 degrees to the left and watch what happens. Again, you will have one of the three results described. When the correction is enough to stop the drift of the needle, you will turn an additional 10 degrees to start it back toward the center.

When the needle centers, remove 5 degrees of the last correction and *hold* this new heading. From then on, a 10-degree correction (really a 5-degree, if you are sharp) to either side of this new heading should be enough to bring you back on course. You would have a good idea of the initial correction necessary if you had properly tied down the *outbound* course between the VOR and the procedure turn. But if you had other problems and never got around to working out a wind correction angle, the procedure mentioned earlier will get you on course in a short time. Remember, though, that this has to be accomplished before you get into the cone of confusion above the VOR.

APPROACHING FROM THE WEST

Let's suspend this approach from Maui and join up with it later. In the meantime, let's see how it would go up to this point if you had departed from Honolulu.

After leaving Honolulu International Airport, you would have been routed to either of two IAFs. One is MABBL intersection, which is the intersection of the MKK 273-degree radial and the Lanai (LNY) 305-degree radial. The other is PALAY intersection, which is 12.7 miles southwest of LOKIE on the MKK 254-degree radial.

At either point, reset both of the navigational radios. I would set the number 1 VOR to MKK, tune and identify it, and set the OBS to 074 degrees TO. This will provide a double-check on LOKIE intersection, which is 10 DME west of the MKK VOR on the 254-degree radial, and/or the intersection of the two radials. Naturally, if you are approaching from MABBL, you would fly the number 2 VOR (tuned to LNY) until reaching LOKIE, while if you are coming in from PALAY, you would track in on number 1.

As in the approach from Maui, now would be a good time to get the current weather and check the minimums. When cleared for the approach, you would begin the descent to 2,200 feet MSL. The note on both transition courses says you can descend to 2,200 feet. It also says that you will not make a procedure turn (NoPT). By the time you reach LOKIE, you should have completed the descent and in-range checklists, airspeed should be down to approach speed, and you should have the wind correction angle pretty well worked out.

I might be confusing some of you when I speak of approach speed. A complex aircraft would normally still be in the clean configuration at this point, so the approach speed would be higher (faster) than when we lower the landing gear and flaps. If you are used to differentiating between this segment and the final approach segment by calling the speed "maneuvering speed" in this part of the approach and "approach speed" in the final approach, be my guest, just so long as you recognize that for our purposes here, we are referring to the same thing.

At LOKIE intersection, reset the number 2 radio to MKK, identify it, and set the OBS to 070 degrees, which again will be your final approach course after crossing the FAF at MKK VOR. Review the approach and missed approach procedures, and tie down the inbound heading to determine the approximate wind correction angle.

INBOUND FROM THE FAF

Now we're back to the point where we left the approach from Maui, and from this point on, both approaches will be the same. When you cross the FAF, simultaneously check the time, lower the gear if the aircraft has retractable gear, extend approach flaps, initiate a descent of about 1,000 feet per minute, set the number 1 VOR's OBS to 070 degrees FROM, turn to intercept the 070-degree radial, call the controlling facility to report passing the FAF inbound and leaving the altitude, and complete the prelanding checklist. This sounds like a lot, so let's take the items one at a time.

In this approach, the time check is important. If you have a DME failure, you can still fly-out the time to the MAP, even though you will have to use a higher MDA. It will also give you a fairly good cross-check about how well the descent is progressing. A stopwatch mounted on the instrument panel or the yoke would be best, but if none is available, you can always use a wristwatch with a sweep-second hand. If the watch has a stopwatch function, so much the better.

Depending on the type of aircraft, lower the gear and select approach flaps. This is a simple matter of moving two handles or switches, depending upon the aircraft. If you control the attitude properly, most airplanes will end up descending at close to 1,000 fpm at approach airspeed just by adding the drag. Power changes should be very slight. A 450-fpm rate of descent is sufficient on this approach, but most pilots —and I'm one of them—would rather descend a little faster, get to the MDA sooner, and fly out the time, than take a chance on hitting an unexpected updraft, or be distracted for a moment, and not get down in time.

Because you have so many things to do at practically the same time, it wouldn't be too much of a problem if you took a little longer to get the number 1 radio set up because you could track on the number 2 VOR for awhile. In this case, there's a heading difference of only 4 degrees, and it will take the omnis 10 seconds or more to settle down after passing the VOR.

Turning to intercept the 070-degree radial is no big thing. Again, it's only a change of 4 degrees and a little rudder pressure alone will yaw the aircraft that far, without hardly dipping a wing.

Under radar, your radio report of crossing the FAF inbound is *not required*, unless requested by the controller, but it is a good idea nevertheless. And like any radio report, it is only made after you have the aircraft well under control and have started the descent. I have seen student pilots so anxious to get the radio report out of the way that they give it immediately upon crossing the FAF. Some have even flown to the MAP without ever starting a descent because other aircraft were on the frequency and they couldn't get their report in. Remember, the aircraft doesn't stop in space while you're waiting to talk. FLY THE PLANE FIRST. *Talk later.*

Finally, complete the prelanding checklist. If the controller is busy talking to someone else, you can even finish this before talking to her.

All of this time, you have been subconsciously flying the aircraft. You are past the FAF, so you shouldn't have to turn any more than 5 degrees in either direction to stay on course. Remember that you are flying a VOR circling approach, the object of which is to position the aircraft so that, when it breaks out of the cloud, you will see the airport environment. If you are scanning properly, you should be able to hold the heading pretty well. With most aircraft, it's easier to just use rudder pressure to yaw it left or right a few degrees. It won't be a coordinated turn, but it can be, and should be, smooth.

Once you get to 1,800 feet, level off until you get to 1.0 DME, and then reestablish the descent to 1,580 feet until 2.0 DME, and then down to the MDA of 980 feet. (If the aircraft does not have DME, you must not descend below 1,800 feet.)

If you break out early, you might be able to make a straight-in landing, but if you don't make visual contact until you fly out the time, you will be more than 500 feet above the field and will have to circle to land. Remember to maintain the MDA until you are in a position to make a normal descent to the runway.

FIELD NOT IN SIGHT

If you don't see the field before the time runs out (at the MAP), or if you lose sight of it while circling, you will have to execute the missed approach. The procedure at MKK is to make a climbing left turn, heading 360 degrees, until intercepting the MKK 030-degree radial, then track outbound on that radial until reaching 3,500 MSL (which means that once you are established on a heading of 360 degrees and are in a positive climb, you will reset the number 1 OBS to the 030 degrees FROM) while climbing to 3,500 feet MSL.

Then, make a left turn directly back to the MKK VOR. As you turn, reset the number 1 OBS in order to center the needle TO the MKK VOR, and as you fly toward the VOR, reset the number 2 OBS to 074 degrees because this will be the inbound track to the VOR after you are established in the holding pattern.

Recall the holding pattern entry procedures. Make a teardrop entry in this case. The initial outbound heading to fly after crossing the VOR will be 284 degrees.

In order to accomplish the missed approach, apply takeoff power, retract the gear, and retract the flaps to the normal takeoff position. As soon as the aircraft attains normal climb speed, initiate the climb. When you reach sufficient airspeed, retract the flaps fully and set climb power. If you are flying an aircraft with sufficient power to climb with the gear extended, it is a good procedure to establish a positive rate of climb before retracting the gear.

While doing all of this, you will be reporting to the controller that you are executing a missed approach. It saves time if you can also relay your intentions to her because that will be her first question if you don't tell her on the initial contact.

While on the approach itself and throughout the enroute portion of the flight, you should have been evaluating the weather, flight conditions, and options. If the weather is reported as down, and it is expected to remain that way, you might decide to take a look, and if you can't get in, you'll ask for a clearance to the alternate. If you miss the approach because of a sudden rain or snow squall, or a shower that's passing over the field, you will probably either ask to initiate another approach at once, or perhaps hold for a few minutes to allow conditions to improve. In any case, the decision is yours to make, and you should have some plan of action in mind.

In training, almost all approaches, except the final one of the session, will terminate in a missed approach. Just as you constantly think of an aborted takeoff while on the takeoff roll (until the aircraft is moving faster than the rejection speed or is past the rejection point), on an instrument approach, you should be thinking missed approach until actually flaring out to land.

Perhaps now you are beginning to realize why so much emphasis is put on practicing the basic instrument maneuvers until you can fly the plane without thinking about it. As you can see here, you have too much else on your mind when you actually start the approach.

CHAPTER QUIZ

1. It is important to keep the volume of the navigational radio down because the identifier is too distracting during an actual approach.

   True _____ False _____

2. Have all navigational radios tuned and identified prior to approach.

   True _____ False _____

3. Which of the following applies regarding an instrument approach?

   a. Tune and identify all nav radios.

   b. Get up-to-date weather before beginning approach.

   c. File missed approach route with ATC.

   d. Review the appropriate approach chart including the missed approach procedures.

For answers to the following questions, refer to Fig. 19-1 and Fig. 19-2.

4. Which of the following fixes is not an initial approach fix?

   a. PALAY

   b. MABBL

   c. LOKIE

   d. MKK VOR

5. The asterisks by ATIS and MOLOKAI TOWER in the communications block indicate that

   a. These are new frequency changes.

   b. These are part-time frequencies.

   c. Radar is not available.

   d. a and b are correct.

6. The heavy arrow on the plan view indicates,

   a. The final approach fix.

   b. The Molokai VOR.

   c. The highest obstacle on the chart.

   d. The facility upon which the approach is predicated.

7. In the communications block, the letters CTAF stand for,

   a. Cannot transmit after five.

   b. Common traffic advisory frequency.

   c. Call to Air Force (search and rescue).

   d. Common traffic arrival frequency.

8. The course reversal must be flown,

   a. North of the inbound track.

   b. At or above 2,500 feet.

   c. Within 10 nm of the MKK VOR.

   d. An 80/260-degree reversal can be substituted.

   e. All of the above.

Answers are in the appendix.

20
DME approaches

BEFORE A DISCUSSION OF DME APPROACHES, LET'S TAKE A LOOK AT THE approach to the Waimea-Kohala Airport (Fig. 20-1). There are some interesting aspects to this approach. Start by looking at the airport information at the top of the page. You can see here that the airport elevation is 2,671 feet MSL. You also see that it has a control zone that does not operate continuously. When the zone is effective, you will transmit to Honolulu Radio on 122.1 and receive on the Kamuela VOR (MUE) frequency of 113.3. You will also use 122.9 as the common traffic advisory frequency. There is a note in the communications section telling you that when the control zone is not effective, the procedure is not authorized except for operators with certificated weather reporting service. (This refers to air carriers and commuters, mentioned in chapter 17.) Honolulu Air Route Traffic Control Center works IFR and radar advisory traffic on 126.0.

Notice that the minimum sector altitudes are quite high. If you are approaching from the north, between inbound headings of 045 degrees through 255 degrees, the MSA is 6,600 feet. For headings of 255 degrees through 045 degrees, it goes up to 14,800 feet with the MUE VOR as the center of the sector diagram. It looks like you will be best off staying on the centerline of this approach.

Looking at the airport diagram (Fig. 20-2), you can see that the airport has a single runway, 4/22, and that it is 5,197 feet long and 100 feet wide with no displaced thresholds.

The additional runway information block shows that both runways have medium intensity runway lights and VASIs. The VASI for Runway 4 is to the right side of the runway, while the VASI for Runway 22 is to the left. All of these lights are pilot controlled, as can be determined from the notes. In addition, Runway 4 has runway end identification lights.

LEAD-IN RADIALS

A glance back at the plan view shows that if you are approaching from the UPP VOR, you will have to make a 120-degree turn to the left to get on the final approach course. Because of this, you have a lead-in radial, the MUE 244-degree radial. It crosses the UPP 174-degree radial, forming MURPH intersection. You have a dogleg from MURPH, beginning the approach transition with a minimum altitude of 4,000 feet.

The note says that the dogleg allows no procedure turn. The distance from MURPH to the mileage break is 2.0 miles via the 156-degree heading (although in actual practice you will find that it is really one continuous turn from MURPH to the inbound course), and that the distance from the mileage break to PUAKO intersection, the FAF, is another 6.0 miles.

HOLDING PATTERN IN LIEU OF PROCEDURE TURN

You have two other ways of reaching the FAF. Either straight-in from JASON intersection, or by flying an overhead approach from the MUE VOR, which uses a holding pattern for a course reversal at PUAKO. If you are flying an overhead approach, you can see from the outbound approach transition that the outbound minimum altitude is 6,000 feet on the 234-degree radial, and that it is 5.9 miles to PUAKO. In this case, when you cross the PUAKO intersection outbound, PUAKO is the IAF.

The turns in the holding pattern will be to the right with an inbound course of 054 degrees, and you will be using a teardrop entry with an initial course of 204 degrees when entering the holding pattern. The minimum altitude in the holding pattern is 4,000 feet MSL and the inbound legs should be 1 minute in length. As a backup to the DME, you should tune the number 2 OBS to the 152-degree radial of UPP for a check on PUAKO.

You will note that the ground rises rapidly both to the north *and south*. Two miles north*northeast* is a 3,155-foot obstruction, and at only 6 miles out is a 5,583-foot obstruction. That's why a note in the circle-to-land section says that you are not authorized to circle northwest of the airport. Also note that the terrain rises to 3,265 feet just 3 miles southeast of the field and that the highest point on the chart is above 10,000 feet MSL to the south. A good idea of how fast the terrain rises can be gleaned by a quick glance at the terrain contour lines.

The missed approach procedure calls for a climbing right turn to 4,000 feet via the 234-degree radial of the MUE VOR with holding back at PUAKO.

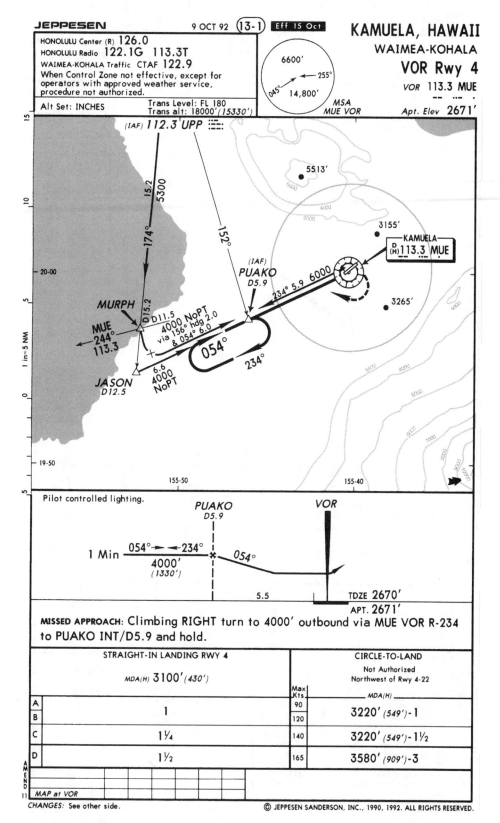

Fig. 20-1 Reproduced with permission of Jeppesen Sanderson, Inc. Not for use in navigation.

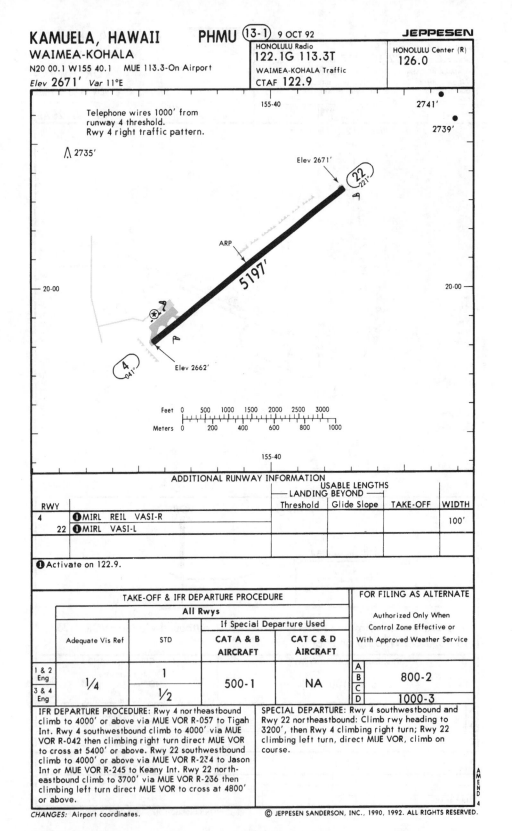

KAMUELA, HAWAII
WAIMEA-KOHALA

N20 00.1 W155 40.1   MUE 113.3-On Airport

Elev 2671'   *Var* 11°E

PHMU (13-1) 9 OCT 92

JEPPESEN

HONOLULU Radio	HONOLULU Center (R)
122.1G 113.3T	**126.0**
WAIMEA-KOHALA Traffic	
CTAF **122.9**	

Telephone wires 1000' from
runway 4 threshold.
Rwy 4 right traffic pattern.

Λ 2735'

2741'

2739'

Elev 2671'

22 221°

ARP

5197'

Elev 2662'

4 041°

Feet	0	500	1000	1500	2000	2500	3000
Meters	0	200	400	600	800	1000	

ADDITIONAL RUNWAY INFORMATION

RWY		USABLE LENGTHS LANDING BEYOND		TAKE-OFF	WIDTH
		Threshold	Glide Slope		
4	❶MIRL REIL VASI-R				100'
22	❶MIRL VASI-L				

❶Activate on 122.9.

TAKE-OFF & IFR DEPARTURE PROCEDURE

All Rwys

			If Special Departure Used	
	Adequate Vis Ref	STD	CAT A & B AIRCRAFT	CAT C & D AIRCRAFT
1 & 2 Eng	1/4	1	500-1	NA
3 & 4 Eng		1/2		

FOR FILING AS ALTERNATE

Authorized Only When
Control Zone Effective or
With Approved Weather Service

A	
B	800-2
C	
D	1000-3

IFR DEPARTURE PROCEDURE: Rwy 4 northeastbound
climb to 4000' or above via MUE VOR R-057 to Tigah
Int. Rwy 4 southwestbound climb to 4000' via MUE
VOR R-042 then climbing right turn direct MUE VOR
to cross at 5400' or above. Rwy 22 southwestbound
climb to 4000' or above via MUE VOR R-234 to Jason
Int or MUE VOR R-245 to Keany Int. Rwy 22 northeastbound climb to 3700' via MUE VOR R-236 then
climbing left turn direct MUE VOR to cross at 4800'
or above.

SPECIAL DEPARTURE: Rwy 4 southwestbound and
Rwy 22 northeastbound: Climb rwy heading to
3200', then Rwy 4 climbing right turn; Rwy 22
climbing left turn, direct MUE VOR, climb on
course.

AMEND 4

CHANGES: Airport coordinates.

Fig. 20-2 Reproduced with permission of Jeppesen Sanderson, Inc. Not for use in navigation.

USING THE LEAD-IN RADIAL

Let's examine the approach to see how you will use the lead-in radial. The UPP VOR is the IAF on this routing, and you will be proceeding southward on the 174-degree radial and descending to the MEA of 5,300 feet. You would naturally have the number 1 VOR receiver tuned to the UPP VOR (and identified) because you will be tracking it outbound. You have 15.2 miles to fly from the VOR to MURPH intersection, so there is plenty of time to take care of the checklists and to get the latest weather. Tune to and identify the MUE VOR on the number 2 VOR receiver. In this case, to identify MURPH, set the OBS at 064 degrees TO because this will put the needle on the proper side of the scale (the right side), giving you a better picture of what's happening.

As you grind out those last few miles to MURPH, recheck the approach plate. Minimums for the straight-in approach are pretty much the same as all aircraft. All aircraft can descend to 430 feet above the TDZE. The visibility for a Category A airplane is one mile, although it increases to as high as 1½ miles for Category D aircraft.

Here, as at Molokai, the high-speed aircraft take a beating in the circle-to-land minimums due to their increased radius of turn. Although the visibility increases one-half mile between Category A/B and Category C aircraft, the MDA remains the same. But moving up to Category D aircraft, the MDA jumps 360 feet to 909 feet, and the visibility increases by another 1½ miles to 3 miles. Perhaps now you can begin to understand the whys and wherefores behind all of these somewhat confusing figures.

There aren't any figures in the conversion box for a timed run from the VOR to the MAP because the VOR is the MAP in this case.

The number 2 OBI (or CDI, if you prefer) is coming off the peg now, so bring the airspeed down to the clean-configuration approach speed, tune the number 1 VOR to MUE, identify it, and set the OBS to 054 degrees TO. The note tells us to fly a heading of 156 degrees for 2.0 miles, and then turn farther to a heading of 054 degrees. The distance to PUAKO should be 6.0 miles. By now, the number 2 needle has centered, and the number 1 is coming off the peg, so start the turn to the left and begin descent to 4,000 feet MSL. Unless you have a strong wind from the south, by the time you are about ready to roll out on the 156-degree heading, the number 1 needle is almost centered, so continue the turn to 054 degrees and begin tracking inbound to PUAKO. While turning, you should have been retuning the number 2 VOR to the UPP VOR, checking the identifier, and setting the OBS to 152 degrees FROM, so that you can identify PUAKO intersection to check against the DME. Inbound to the runway, PUAKO becomes the FAF. (How do you know? The FAF for a nonprecision approach is indicated by the Maltese-cross symbol in the profile view.)

The approach plate shows a total of 8.0 miles (2.0 + 6.0) from MURPH intersection to PUAKO, so you have plenty of time to lose those 1,300 feet from 5,300 feet to 4,000 feet. During this period of time, you should go over the checklist and set the approach flaps. Crossing PUAKO, lower the gear, complete the prelanding checklist, call ATC to report the FAF inbound, and fly down to the MDA of 3,100 feet MSL.

After passing PUAKO, it's a good idea to retune the number 2 VOR receiver to MUE and set the missed approach course (234 degrees) on the OBS. This way, in the event of a missed approach, you won't have to be changing the radios while getting the power up and cleaning up the plane. Another thing to remember is that you will be at 3,000 feet MSL, so more than likely, you won't be getting full performance from the aircraft when you apply the power, unless it's equipped with turbocharged engines.

ON TO HILO

There are many approaches to the HILO Airport in Hilo, Hawaii, but here you will only be concerned about two of them, the VOR DME Rwy 26 (Fig. 20-3) and the VOR DME-A (Fig. 20-4).

Hilo is a controlled field with a part-time tower. The approach plates explain that the tower frequency is 118.1. The field has radar and an approach control that operates on 119.7. When the tower is not operating, use Honolulu Center on 126.6 and give your position reports in the blind on 118.1; ground control is 121.9.

The minimum sector altitudes here are 1,500 feet MSL between a 160-degree inbound heading, east to a 250-degree inbound heading; 2,800 feet MSL from the 250-degree inbound heading, south to a 340-degree inbound heading; and then 14,800 feet MSL from the 340-degree inbound heading, west to a 160-degree inbound heading.

Note here that the circle-to-land MDAs are the same for both approaches even though the VOR DME-A increases the visibility requirements for Category A and B aircraft by one-half mile. The VOR DME Rwy 26 plate shows a straight-in approach. The VOR DME-A, although it is a straight approach to the airport area, requires a circling approach to the runway (due to the angle between the final approach segment and the landing runway). Both approaches, as indicated in the names, require a DME receiver.

IT'S YOUR DECISION

The approach plate for the VOR DME 26 (Fig. 20-3) gives two possible initial approach segments: the 11-mile DME arc and the overhead approach. The FAF is VEWES intersection (as denoted by the Maltese cross), which is 5.0 DME from the ITO VOR on the 079-degree radial. VEWES intersection is also the missed approach holding fix for both approach plates, although the missed approach procedure is different in each case. The VOR DME Rwy 26 approach uses a climbing right turn in the missed approach, while you must make a climbing left turn if you miss on the VOR DME-A approach, proving again that it's necessary to double-check each and every procedure. Also notice that Hilo uses a nonstandard left turn holding pattern.

Let's assume you are approaching from the northwest on the ITO 325-degree radial (145 degrees TO on the number 1 VOR). You have completed the descent checklist and have been cleared for the VOR DME-A approach (Fig. 20-4). You are 20 miles out at 4,000 feet when you get the weather. The tower reports 500 feet scattered, estimated 600 feet broken, 1,000 feet overcast, with 1½ miles visibility in light rain showers. Visibility to the south is poor and a heavier rain shower is approaching from the south. Wind is from the southwest at 5 knots.

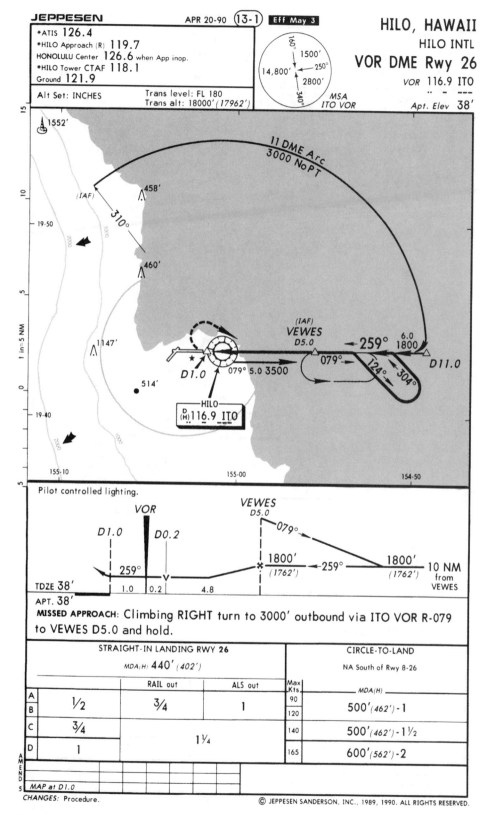

Fig. 20-3 Reproduced with permission of Jeppesen Sanderson, Inc. Not for use in navigation.

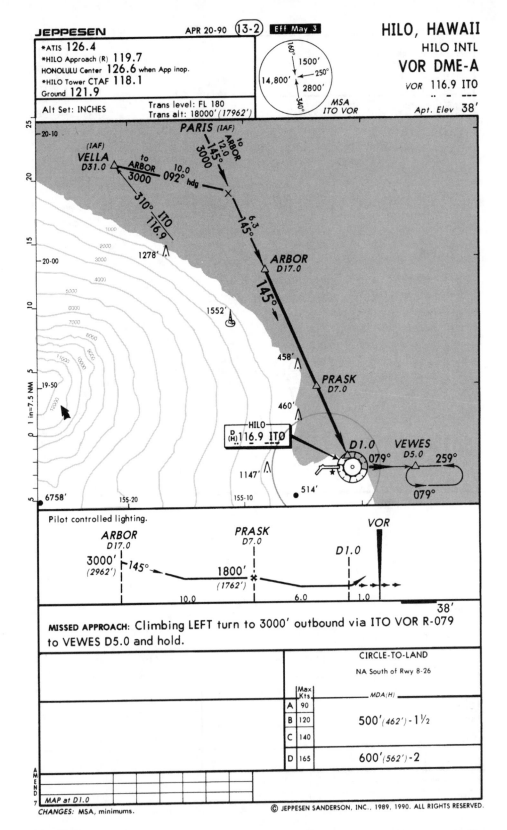

Fig. 20-4 Reproduced with permission of Jeppesen Sanderson, Inc. Not for use in navigation.

Under Part 91, you may *initiate* an instrument approach *regardless* of the reported ceiling and visibility. But you cannot go below the MDA (or DH) and land unless (1) the *flight* visibility meets the applicable minimums shown on the chart, (2) you have the runway environment in sight, and (3) you can make a normal descent to landing.

Take a look at the minimums. You can try either approach, but you have been cleared for the VOR DME-A approach, which will be faster than the VOR DME Rwy 26 (flying the arc is very time-consuming). With the low ceiling and the rain showers, however, you ask to use the VOR DME Rwy 26 arc approach instead.

Why?

Take a look at the plan view on the VOR DME-A approach. If you have to fly it to the minimums, you must initiate a missed approach 1 mile DME before reaching the VOR. The only time you can continue to the VOR (follow the short arrows as shown in the profile view) is when you have *visual reference* with the *runway* environment and can continue to the runway by visual reference. You have to establish this reference prior to reaching the MAP, and the rain showers might be just bad enough to obscure your vision.

Remember, the tower is reporting *ground* visibility, and what you will see outside the aircraft windshield is often much less than that. Also, you have to realize that, even if you do have visual reference prior to the MAP, you will still have to make a 114-degree turn to Runway 26 while close to the ground in rain showers to boot. And don't forget those heavier showers approaching the field from the southwest. Sure, the VOR DME-A might be possible, and it is more expedient, but it's easier and safer to fly the arc approach. (My father always used to tell me that sometimes the long way around is the shortest way home.) In the case of the arc approach, you can get a little closer to the field because the MAP is at the VOR, which is only a mile from the threshold. In addition, should the approaching rain showers lower the ceiling, you will be able to use the straight-in MDA of 440 feet MSL off of the arc, along with the lower ½-mile visibility.

If the weather conditions were better, say 1,500 feet broken with 2 miles visibility and scattered rain showers, I'd be more inclined to take the VOR DME-A, and then only if I'd been there before and was familiar with the terrain and the ground reference points.

FLYING THE DME ARC

Well, you have made your decision, asked approach control, and ATC has cleared you for the 11-mile DME arc approach. As you're on the 315-degree radial, you're east of the standard intercept radial, but you have a long way to go, and ATC clears you to intercept the arc on your present course.

When do you turn on the arc? A good rule of thumb is to allow a 1-mile lead for each 100 knots of airspeed. In a Cessna 172 at 100 knots, you would start your turn at 12 DME, while in a DC-9 at 250 knots, you'd start it at 13.5 DME. In both cases, you would use a standard-rate turn. This would bring you out just about on the arc. From here on in, a series of shallow bank corrections should hold you on the arc.

To get on the arc initially, turn 90 degrees from the inbound track heading. In this case, if you have been approaching the Hilo (ITO) VOR on a heading of about 145 degrees, a left turn to a heading of 055 degrees should put you on the arc. This happens because whenever you cross an arc inbound, you cross it at a 90-degree angle.

To fly an arc, you actually fly a series of tangents to it. After rolling out on the arc, check the DME. If it is exactly 11 miles, you have done everything perfectly. If it's a little less than 11 miles, you turned too slowly, so just maintain the heading of 055 degrees until you get back to 11 miles. If you rolled out a little more than 11 miles, you should turn back toward the VOR (in this case the turn will be to the right) about 10–20 degrees, depending on what you will need to compensate for the wind. After completing the turn, hold the heading until the DME changes slightly. You will have to continue slight turns toward the VOR as you progress around the arc. During this arc, you will descend to the minimum arc altitude of 3,000 feet MSL.

As you turn on the arc, set the number 1 OBS to the inbound course (259 degrees), and set the number 2 OBS to 249 degrees TO, which will give you a 10-degree lead-in radial to use as a guide. With such a long distance left to fly, you can review the chart, paying special attention to the missed approach procedure.

If there happens to be a compass locator (NDB) at or near the VOR site, setting the ADF to that frequency will prove a big help because the relative bearing to the VOR site should remain off the wingtip throughout the arc.

When you have everything set up to your satisfaction, sit back and relax until the needle on the number 2 OBI centers (at which time the number 1 needle should be coming off the peg). By using both needles, you can adjust the rate of turn to intercept the inbound radial without overshooting it. Done properly, you should end up on an 11-*mile* straight-in final, having rolled out on course 6 miles east of VEWES. At this time, you will have to begin your descent to the final approach altitude of 1,800 feet MSL. You will have 6 miles to lose 1,200 feet, so you can't afford to dawdle. When you get time, reset the number 2 OBS to 079 degrees FROM the ITO VOR to prepare for the missed approach. By now you should also be at approach airspeed with the approach flaps set.

As you cross VEWES, lower the gear, and go through the before-landing checklist. And be aware that because this approach has a visual descent point at 0.2 DME (prior to the VOR), you cannot descend below the MDA until you pass that point, even if you do have the runway environment in sight.

You should be at minimums before you reach the VOR. Remember that the closer the VOR facility is to the airport, the more accurate the approach should be. Anytime you hit minimums and can see the runway environment when the safety pilot lifts the hood, you have made a good VOR approach.

If you don't have visual contact with the runway environment by the time you cross the VOR, apply takeoff power, retract flaps to the takeoff flap position, and when you have a positive climb indication, retract the gear and start a climbing right turn to intercept the 079-degree radial outbound. Then clean up the flaps and climb to 3,000 feet. While all of this is going on, set the number 1 OBS to 079 degrees FROM. Until you get around to this, you can use the number 2 OBI for guidance. When you arrive at VEWES, you will turn right to a heading of 109 degrees to establish a tear-drop entry to the left-hand holding pattern.

This example demonstrates that there are times when, as pilot-in-command, you will have to weigh expediency versus safety.

CHAPTER QUIZ

(The following questions are based on Figs. 20-1 and 20-2.)

1. In the plan view, if arriving from UPP VOR, the FAF is shown by the "x" on the turn by JASON. True _____ False _____

2. The solid line with the arrow leading from MUE VOR towards PUAKO shows:
   a. The overhead approach track from the VOR, north of the inbound track for traffic separation.
   b. An approach transition coincidental with the approach flight track.
   c. The missed approach track when cleared back to JASON.
   d. The heading to fly until crossing the UPP VOR 152-degree radial.

3. In the airport view, the two flag symbols to the right of the runway indicate
   a. Right-hand traffic pattern for Runway 4, left-hand pattern for Runway 22.
   b. Wind shears common from the southeast.
   c. Position of wind indicators near runways.
   d. Both a and b.

4. JASON is only an initial approach fix for aircraft conducting straight-in approaches. True ____False ____

The following questions are based on Figs. 22-3 and 22-4.

5. The pilot controlled lighting noted in the profile view, is activated on
   a. 119.7
   b. Unknown—frequency will be shown on airport chart.
   c. 118.1
   d. 121.9

6. VEWES intersection can be identified by Radar when approach control is working. True _____ False _____.

7. For a straight-in approach to Runway 26,
   a. Category D aircraft must increase visibility requirements by ¼ mile if the RAIL is inoperative.
   b. There is no visibility increase for the runway alignment indicator lights (RAIL) being inoperative.

    c. All categories must increase visibility requirements by ¼ if the approach light system is inoperative.

    d. a and c are correct.

8. Aircraft approaching Hilo from the west:

    a. Fly inbound on the ITO VOR 310-degree radial from VELLA to intercept the UPP VOR 097-degree radial to ARBOR.

    b. Fly the UPP VOR 097-degree radial from UPP to ARBOR.

    c. Fly a 092-degree heading from VELLA to intercept the inbound course.

    d. All are correct.

Answers are in the appendix.

21
Localizer-only
and ILS approaches

Descent below the MDA of a VOR approach is not allowed until you have the runway environment in sight, but you usually have a little time to spot the runway before you have to execute a missed approach. An ILS approach allows you to thread the needle, so to speak. The difference in accuracy can best be illustrated by the fact that if you fly the glide slope down to the ground and keep the localizer needle anywhere on the active area of the indicator face, the wheels will hit the runway upon touchdown. This means that at the threshold of the runway, a full deflection of the localizer needle amounts to less than 100 feet of lateral displacement from the centerline. That's cutting it pretty close. It means that if you have the localizer needle centered when you break out, you will be looking right down the runway centerline.

Figure 21-1 is Honolulu's ILS Rwy 8L approach. The airport diagram (Fig. 21-2) is one of the new index 10-9 series for larger, complicated airports. It shows that Runway 8L/26R is 12,357 feet long, with a 648-foot stopway for Runway 8L and a 200-foot stopway for Runway 26R. These stopways used to be called overruns. They are areas beyond the normal takeoff length of the runway that can support the weight of an aircraft after an aborted takeoff. The additional runway information on Fig. 21-3 explains that Runway 8L has high-intensity runway lights and a standard, high-intensity approach light system with sequenced flashing lights in an ILS CAT 1 configuration (ALSF-1). There is a standard VASI on the left side of the approach, the runway is 150 feet wide, and it is grooved. Also, the usable runway length for landing beyond the glide slope is 11,123 feet, which means that the glide slope transmitter is positioned about 1,200 feet from the approach end of the runway.

A new column has been added: "Threshold to Intersecting Runway." It is common practice at many congested airports, Honolulu being one of them, to land or depart aircraft simultaneously on runways that intersect. You might hear, when being cleared to land on Runway 8L, "Cleared to land Runway 8L, hold short of Runway 4 Left for landing and takeoff traffic." That's all well and good, but how much runway do you have left to land and stop on? This column tells you that if you are landing on Runway 8L, 9,800 feet is available from the threshold of Runway 8L to the intersection of Runway 4L. This is very useful information.

THE DUCK-UNDER SYNDROME

Quite a few accidents result from aircraft diving below the glide slope after they break out. These *duck-under* maneuvers are caused by two factors. First, if the aircraft is on the glide slope and breaks out at minimums, it will still be between 50 and 100 feet above the runway at the threshold. This is enough to make some pilots feel that they're too high. The other problem is that they will see a black hole in front of them, and they will be afraid of losing sight of the field. In any case, these reasons will be enough to make some pilots dip below the glide path and either land short, or hit with such a high rate of sink that they severely damage the aircraft. It's such a problem that our big brothers in the FAA have made a regulation prohibiting large and turbine-powered aircraft from flying below the glide slope prior to passing the middle marker. If a runway is equipped with a VASI, aircraft (including small ones) are not allowed to fly below the VASI. (These restrictions apply to controlled airports.)

Anytime you are flying an ILS approach, remember that the glide slope transmitter is located 750 feet or more from the approach end of the runway. With this in mind, you should realize two things.

First, you will, of necessity, cross the threshold higher when flying the ILS glide slope than you usually do when flying VFR. That's why it's a good idea to fly the glide slope from time to time in visual conditions and remain aware of the threshold crossing height. It will look even higher in rain and snow, when visibility is reduced.

Secondly, the designated touchdown point is between 750 and 1,500 feet from the approach end to provide plenty of runway to stop, even if you fly the glide slope to the ground.

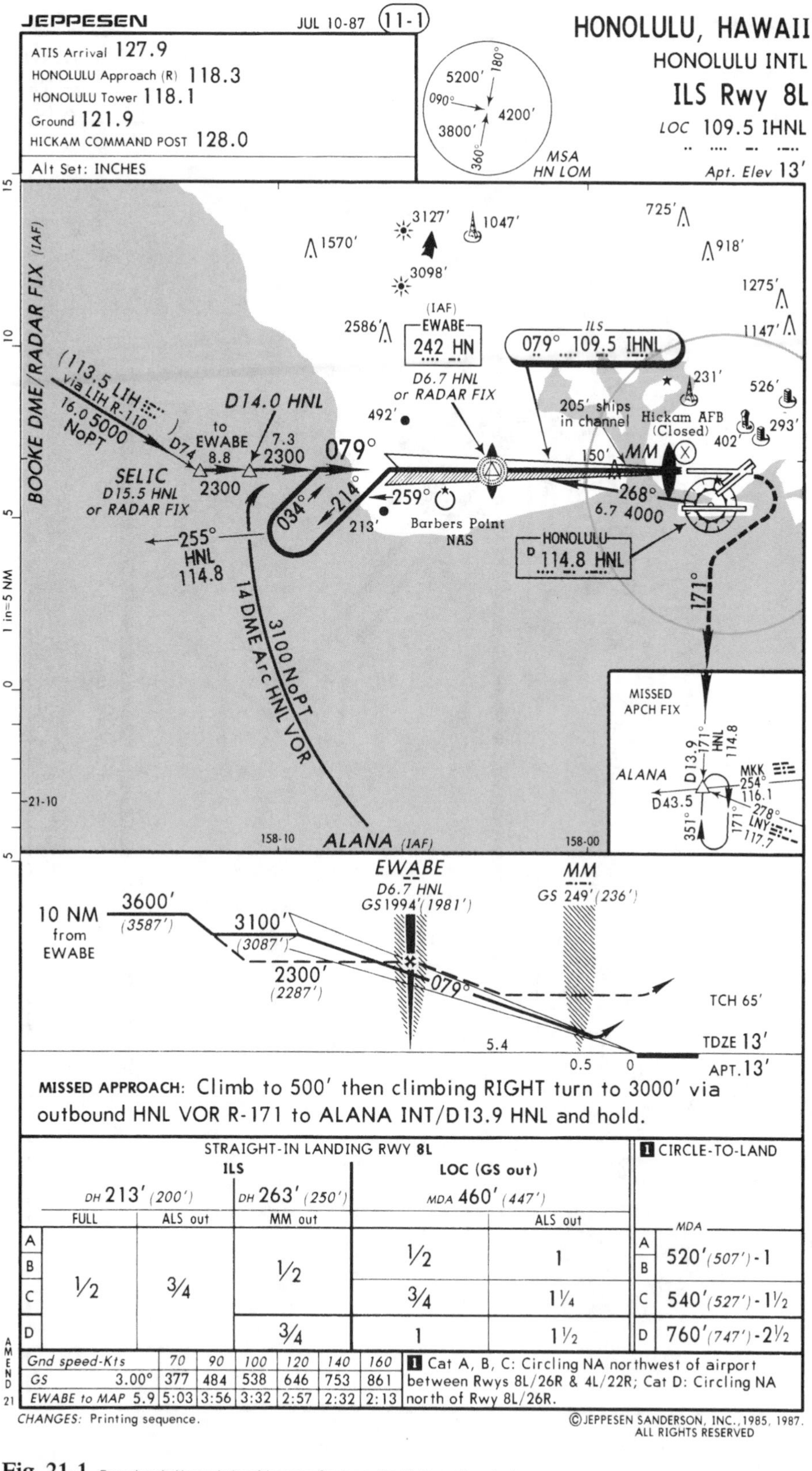
JEPPESEN
JUL 10-87 (11-1)
HONOLULU, HAWAII
HONOLULU INTL
ILS Rwy 8L
LOC 109.5 IHNL
Apt. Elev 13'
ATIS Arrival 127.9
HONOLULU Approach (R) 118.3
HONOLULU Tower 118.1
Ground 121.9
HICKAM COMMAND POST 128.0
Alt Set: INCHES
5200'
180°
090°
4200'
3800'
360°
MSA
HN LOM
BOOKE DME/RADAR FIX (IAF)
(113.5 LIH via LIH R-110
16.0 5000
NoPT
D74
SELIC
D15.5 HNL
or RADAR FIX
2300
D14.0 HNL
to EWABE 8.8
7.3
2300
079°
034°
214°
255°
HNL
114.8
14 DME Arc HNL VOR
3100 NoPT
ALANA (IAF)
(IAF)
EWABE
242 HN
D6.7 HNL
or RADAR FIX
ILS
079° 109.5 IHNL
259°
Barbers Point
NAS
213'
492'
HONOLULU
D 114.8 HNL
205' ships
in channel
Hickam AFB
(Closed)
150'
MM
268°
6.7 4000
171°
MISSED
APCH FIX
ALANA
D13.9
D43.5
MKK
254°
116.1
278°
LNY
117.7
351°
171°
HNL
114.8
3127'
1047'
1570'
3098'
2586'
725'
918'
1275'
1147'
231'
526'
293'
402'
158-10
158-00
21-10
1 in=5 NM
EWABE
D6.7 HNL
GS 1994' (1981')
MM
GS 249' (236')
10 NM
from
EWABE
3600'
(3587')
3100'
(3087')
2300'
(2287')
079°
TCH 65'
TDZE 13'
5.4
0.5
0
APT. 13'
MISSED APPROACH: Climb to 500' then climbing RIGHT turn to 3000' via outbound HNL VOR R-171 to ALANA INT/D13.9 HNL and hold.
STRAIGHT-IN LANDING RWY 8L
ILS
DH 213' (200')
FULL
ALS out
DH 263' (250')
MM out
LOC (GS out)
MDA 460' (447')
ALS out
A
B
C
D
1/2
3/4
1/2
3/4
1/2
1
3/4
1 1/4
1
1 1/2
CIRCLE-TO-LAND
MDA
520' (507')-1
540' (527')-1 1/2
760' (747')-2 1/2
Gnd speed-Kts 70 90 100 120 140 160
GS 3.00° 377 484 538 646 753 861
EWABE to MAP 5.9 5:03 3:56 3:32 2:57 2:32 2:13
Cat A, B, C: Circling NA northwest of airport between Rwys 8L/26R & 4L/22R; Cat D: Circling NA north of Rwy 8L/26R.
AMEND 21
CHANGES: Printing sequence.
© JEPPESEN SANDERSON, INC., 1985, 1987. ALL RIGHTS RESERVED

Fig. 21-1 Reproduced with permission of Jeppesen Sanderson, Inc. Not for use in navigation.

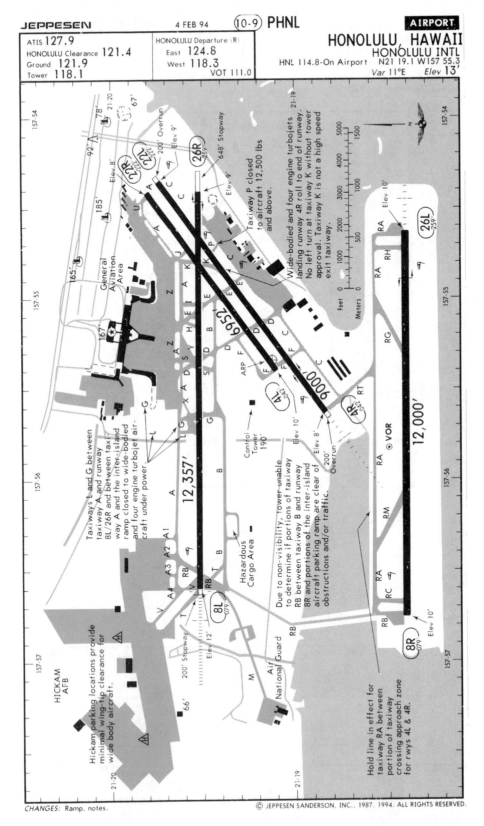

Fig. 21-2

GENERAL CAUTION: Birds in vicinity of airport. Low-level wind shear alert system.
Due to tower location, controllers unable to determine whether acft are on correct final approach to rwys 4L/R and 22L/R.

ADDITIONAL RUNWAY INFORMATION

RWY		USABLE LENGTHS				
			LANDING BEYOND		Threshold to Intersecting Runway	TAKE-OFF	WIDTH
			Threshold	Glide Slope			
4R	HIRL MALSR VASI-L	grooved		7949'	8L/26R 6600'		
22L	HIRL REIL ❶VASI-L	grooved					150'
4L	MIRL REIL VASI-L				8L/26R 3900'		
22R	MIRL REIL						150'
8R	HIRL VASI (3 bar)-L	grooved					
26L	HIRL MALSF ❷ VASI (3 bar)-L	grooved					200'
8L	❸HIRL ALSF-I VASI-L	grooved		11,123'	4L/22R 9800'		
26R	❸HIRL REIL ❹VASI (3 bar)-L	grooved					150'

❶ Unusable beyond 2 NM from threshold due to obstruction.
❷ System canted 5° south of rwy centerline.
❸ Runway lights are outside 200' pavement width; pavement striped 150' wide.
❹ Unusable beyond 3.6 NM from threshold due to obstruction.

TAKE-OFF

	Rwys 22L, 22R, 26R		Rwy 26L			Rwy 8R		
	Adequate Vis Ref	STD	With Mim climb of 285'/NM to 3000'		Other	If Special Departure Used or With Mim climb of 212'/NM to 1000'		Other
			Adequate Vis Ref	STD		Adequate Vis Ref	STD	
1 & 2 Eng	¼	1	¼	1	300-1	¼	1	500-1
3 & 4 Eng		½		½			½	

Rwy 8L

	CAT A & B AIRCRAFT			CAT C & D AIRCRAFT		
	If Special Departure Used or With Mim climb of 210'/NM to 1000'		Other	If Special Departure Used or With Mim climb of 334'/NM to 1700'		Other
	Adequate Vis Ref	STD		Adequate Vis Ref	STD	
1 & 2 Eng	¼	1	600-2	¼	1	1500-2
3 & 4 Eng		½			½	

Rwys 4L, 4R

	CAT A & B AIRCRAFT			CAT C & D AIRCRAFT		
	If Special Departure Used or With Mim climb of 466'/NM to 2000'		Other	If Special Departure Used or With Mim climb of 524'/NM to 3500'		Other
	Adequate Vis Ref	STD		Adequate Vis Ref	STD	
1 & 2 Eng	¼	1	1800-2	¼	1	3200-2
3 & 4 Eng		½			½	

SPECIAL DEPARTURE

Immediate climbing right turn, between headings 150° & 200° to be completed within 2 NM of runway departure end, then as cleared. Turn must be completed prior to HNL VOR D3.6.
Caution: Steeply rising terrain north and east of airport. Tall vessels traverse Pearl Harbor channel.

IFR DEPARTURE PROCEDURE

Comply with SID or RADAR VECTORS, or: Rwys 4L, 4R, 8L, 8R, climbing right turn as soon as practicable, then as cleared. Rwys 22L, 22R, 26L, 26R, climb runway heading to 300' then left climbing as cleared. Left turn must be completed within 2 NM of runway departure end (HNL VOR D3.0).

FOR FILING AS ALTERNATE

	Precision	Non-Precision
A,B	600-2	800-2
C,D		

AMEND 7

CHANGES: See other side.   © JEPPESEN SANDERSON, INC., 1987, 1992. ALL RIGHTS RESERVED.

Fig. 21-3   Reproduced with permission of Jeppesen Sanderson, Inc. Not for use in navigation.

MOUNTAINS AND MOVING OBSTACLES

Examine the face of the chart in Fig. 21-1. On the plan view, you are cautioned by the note to the north of the MM that explains you might encounter 205-foot ships in the channel that leads into Pearl Harbor, which is a busy naval installation. The MM is just past the channel with a glide slope crossing height of 249 feet MSL, so if you are on the glide slope and one of these large ships is in the channel, you will have about 100 feet of clearance, more or less. You certainly don't want to be low on this approach.

The LOM is called EWABE. In addition to its ADF (NDB) signal, this fix can also be determined by radar or by 6.7 DME on the 268-degree radial of the Honolulu (HNL) VOR, which is on a frequency of 114.8.

Both from the plan view and the MSA circle, you can see that like all volcanic areas, Oahu is a high island, and although the runway is at sea level (13 feet MSL), it has high mountains on three sides. You will see more proof of that later on the takeoff minimums page.

No procedure turn is authorized on the straight-in approach from the IAF at BOOKE (which is off the chart to the left) or from the DME arc from ALANA (which is off the bottom of the chart). The procedure turn illustrated is for overhead approaches only, in which case EWABE is the IAF.

While we're at it, SELIC intersection can also be identified by radar as noted in the plan view.

Let's take a look at some of the other information on the chart. On the plan view again, note the thin arrow crossing the DME arc line that is the 255-degree radial of HNL VOR. It is the lead-in radial, marking the location where aircraft should begin to turn from the arc onto the final approach. You can see that the minimum altitude on the arc is 3,100 feet MSL.

Over the runway symbol, on the profile view, is a note that reads "TCH 65'." That is the threshold crossing height for aircraft on the glide slope. The TCH appears on all ILS approach charts because you usually want to know the height at which the glide slope crosses the threshold, especially in wide-bodied aircraft.

The solid line on the profile view shows the approach profile used if flying a full ILS, while the dashed line shows the step-down flight path if flying a localizer-only approach.

The solid transition arrow from the HNL VOR shows that if you are going to fly an overhead ILS approach, you would cross the VOR and fly the 268-degree bearing to EWABE intersection, which is 6.7 miles. The minimum altitude is 4,000 MSL. From EWABE you would track outbound on the ILS, then make the procedure turn and complete the approach.

To set your radios up for this approach, you would have your number 1 VOR receiver tuned on HNL 114.8. The number 2 VOR receiver would be set to the ILS frequency, 109.5, and if you have an ADF, that would be set on EWABE, 242. Crossing the VOR, set the number 1 OBS to the 268-degree radial, and track outbound. The number 2 OBS should be set on the outbound localizer course of 259 degrees for orientation only. The ILS is sense orientated to the inbound course, so tracking outbound will require you to fly opposite the needle indications. (This is explained further in the next chapter describing a BACK-COURSE ILS.)

As you cross EWABE, and turn the required 11 degrees to track outbound on the localizer, you would retune the number 1 VOR receiver to the localizer frequency, and dial in the inbound localizer course of 079 degrees. You would also descend to 3,600 feet MSL and fly the procedure turn. Once on the outbound leg of the procedure turn, you would reset the number 1 OBS to the inbound course. Turning inbound at the end of the procedure turn, you would descend to 3,100 feet MSL. From that point on, you would fly either the ILS or localizer-only approach as described below.

MORE FACTS AND FIGURES

The minimums table shows how inoperative components will change the minimums. Look under the appropriate column to see what minimums you should use.

You can determine an approximate rate of descent from the conversion table at the bottom of the chart, provided that you have the ground speed pretty well figured out. You can also see that the glide slope angle is 3 degrees. Additionally, the conversion table tells you that the distance from the LOM (EWABE) to the MAP is 5.9 miles. Recall the segment mileages shown above and below the ground reference line; in this case, it's 5.4 miles from the LOM to the MM and 0.5 miles from the MM to the runway threshold.

The MAP, indicated where the dashed horizontal line bends upward near the threshold, is the spot where you will begin a missed approach when flying a localizer approach. If flying the full ILS approach, you would be on the solid line and would be flying that down to a lower altitude (the DH), which is just about the vicinity of the MM in this case. This is an absolute go-no-go point. When you reach the DH, you either see the runway environment and land, or you initiate the missed approach.

If you're on the localizer approach, get down to the MDA and fly out the time. When the MM is operational, it will give you an additional check on the missed approach point because you will have another half-mile to go before the MAP, about 15 seconds in the average light aircraft.

Before examining the actual approaches, there are a few more items to consider. Note (1) of the circle-to-land minimums explains that Category A, B, and C aircraft are restricted from circling northwest of the airport between Runways 8L/26R and 4L/22R, while Category D aircraft are restricted from circling anywhere north of Runway 8L/26R.

Look at Fig. 21-3 again, which is one of those new pages Jeppesen has created for major airports. Under many of the takeoff minimums, it reads, "If Special Departure Used Or. . . ." Look down at the next-to-last listing on the page and you'll find the special departure explained:

> Immediate climbing right turn, between headings 150 & 200 to be completed within 2 nm of runway departure end, then as cleared. Turn must be completed prior to HNL VOR D3.6. Caution: Steeply rising terrain north and west of airport. Tall vessels traverse Pearl Harbor channel.

LOCALIZER-ONLY APPROACH

Now that we've covered the information found on the approach charts, let's see how to incorporate it into a successful approach. Begin with a localizer approach (no glide slope) as depicted by the dashed lines on the profile view (Fig. 21-1). The minimums box explains that for your type of aircraft, on a straight-in approach to Runway 8L, you will have an MDA of 460 feet MSL (447 AGL) and a visibility minimum, provided the ALS is operating, of one-half mile. If you lose the ALS, the visibility minimum will increase to 1 mile.

The 3,600-foot MSL altitude shown on the profile view applies only to the procedure turn or overhead approach minimum altitude. Once you complete the procedure turn and are heading inbound, you can descend to 2,300 feet MSL to the FAF, which, in the case of this nonprecision approach, is EWABE.

The same 2,300-foot minimum holds true for the two NoPT approaches. In the case of the 14-mile DME arc approach, you would start the descent from 3,100 feet after you are established on the inbound course. If you were coming in from LIH (Lihue, Kauai), you would cross BOOKE intersection and descend to 5,000 feet MSL until you got to SELIC—as in Tom!—intersection, which is 15.5 DME from the HNL VOR. At SELIC, you would be established on the inbound track and could then descend to 2,300 feet MSL. As you can see on the plan view, SELIC is 8.8 miles from EWABE and you would have 2,700 feet to descend. If the ground speed were 120 knots, it would take about 4 minutes 20 seconds to cover that distance; therefore, you would want a descent rate of 700 fpm, or slightly greater, in order to get down to the minimums prior to the FAF.

Prior to SELIC, tune the number 1 VOR receiver to the HNL ILS (assuming you're on radar vectors and are not using the VOR receiver to navigate from LIH), and identify it. Set the OBS on 079 degrees, check the weather, and complete the descent checklist. If the marker beacon receiver and/or ADF is operable, turn the beacon switch to HI and the speaker on. Check the light bulbs in the marker beacon receiver for proper operation and tune the ADF to EWABE and identify. Tune the number 2 VOR receiver to HNL VOR and identify for DME information, and set the OBS to 171 degrees, to be ready for the missed approach.

If I tend to keep repeating myself regarding proper radio identification, it's only because with extremely reliable avionics as compared to old tube types, many pilots are sloppy about identifying the stations they are tuning to, and it's quite easy to make a mistake. Many times this is caused by too many frequencies being too close together for similar facilities, on the dial and on the ground.

A good example of this is the frequency for the ILS approach to Runway 8L at Honolulu, 109.5, and the frequency for the ILS to Runway 4R at the same airport, 110.5. In the dark, or bouncing around in the clouds, it would be quite easy to miss by just one click of the knob and end up flying the wrong approach. Also, there have been times when the frequency display is out of sync with the actual frequency being received. So, to implant this point in the back of your mind, I'll repeat "and identify" each time I mention tuning radios.

There are two schools of thought regarding setting up the two VOR receivers. One school prefers to have both tuned and identified on the approach frequency in order to detect a failure in one or the other receiver. The second school says to have the primary receiver set on the approach frequency and the secondary receiver set up for the missed approach.

If I am flying in a two-pilot cockpit, I adhere to the first method because I can always tell the other pilot to set up the missed approach on the radios while I am beginning the missed approach procedure. But if I am flying solo, I like to have the missed approach already set up because I'll be busy enough doing everything else by myself.

Once you cross the FAF, you can begin the final descent. You need to positively ascertain the FAF passage, however, and that can be done by the OM indicator light, the aural tone of the marker, the reversal of the ADF needle, the HNL 6.7 DME, or by approach control confirming it on radar.

When you cross the FAF, lower the gear and complete the prelanding checklist, just as you did on the VOR approach. I have made it a habit of always calling for "gear down, landing checklist" whenever I cross the FAF, even if I'm flying solo and even if I know I've lowered the gear earlier. By calling for it, it becomes a habit that will hopefully prevent me from landing with the gear up someday. Remember that Murphy's Law is always waiting to catch us slipping up. In addition to calling for the gear down and the checklist, I also physically touch or point toward the gear lights to ascertain that they are green.

I never fly closer to the airport than the FAF when the aircraft is clean. One reason for this is that I still won't be all that busy that far out, so there is plenty of time to get the gear down and the checklist completed properly. It's also nice to stabilize the approach far enough out so that you're not chasing the aircraft all the way to the runway.

To prevent chasing all around the sky, try to get within 10 degrees of the inbound track before crossing the FAF, and thereafter try to stay within 5 degrees of the track. The heading required to stay on course will usually change somewhat as you descend because the wind shifts around due to surface friction and the Coriolis force, and because the wind is deflected by ground objects, such as trees, small hills, and high buildings.

Keeping heading changes this small requires a lot of practice and a fairly rapid instrument scan. Remember not to chase the needle. As I pointed out earlier, when flying the localizer, a full deflection of the needle will still put you over the runway. If the needle starts drifting off center, make a small 5-degree correction to try and stop that drift. When the drift has stopped, a further correction of 1 or 2 degrees should start it back toward the center.

As mentioned in a previous chapter, although it might not be considered good airmanship by some, I find it easier to apply a little rudder pressure to skid the nose around those few degrees; this keeps the gyro presentation steady and is actually easier on passengers than a lot of wing waving. Once you have stopped the trend of the needle deflection, you have it made. If you can bring the needle slowly back to the centerline and hold it there, you're a real pro.

The reason I emphasize just stopping the trend is that if you work constantly at coming back to centerline as the aircraft gets closer and closer to the runway and the width of the localizer beam narrows to just a few hundred feet, you'll look as though you're doing Dutch rolls on the way in.

THE PRECISION APPROACH

What about the full ILS? What's the difference? Well, it usually means that you'll be descending 200–500 feet lower than on the localizer-only approach, and you'll have one more needle to monitor.

You will go through the same procedure used for the localizer approach, as far as the tuning and identifying of the navigational aids are concerned. You will also be completing the same checklists at the same time, as well as checking on the latest weather. The big thing you will notice is that finally, that little red OFF flag on the side of the OBI is gone, and a "live" horizontal needle has appeared in its place.

As you maneuver to bring the aircraft onto the final approach path, this extra needle will normally be near the top of the indicator or hidden behind the face of the instrument at the top. This is merely a guide indicating that you are below the level of the glide path for this distance from the runway.

Even though you will be flying an electronic glide path down to the runway, you will still tune and identify the LOM on the ADF and still turn on the marker beacon receiver because there are many times when you will be intercepting false glide paths that are sent out as ghost signals from the transmitter. The most dangerous of these would be the ghost signals that indicate a glide slope that is too steep. One indication of such a false signal would be a rate of descent in excess of that shown for the ground speed in the conversion table. If you were to hit wind shear, though, with a resultant tailwind (as happens many times, especially around squalls), you would expect a high rate of descent.

The best indication of wind shear or false glide paths is the aircraft altitude when crossing the outer marker. If it's not close to that shown on the profile view—in the case of the ILS Rwy 8L at Honolulu, it would be 1,994 feet MSL—you're on a false glide path. If your altitude is close to what is shown at the outer marker and you still have a high rate of descent, then you have a strong tailwind. If this is the case and the wind at the field is reported as coming down the runway, then be aware that you will be experiencing wind shear prior to touchdown. If the winds have been strong and gusting in the area, you might even want to abandon the approach and go around once to allow the shear condition to abate.

The solid line at 3,100 feet MSL on the profile view in Fig. 21-1 shows the altitude where you would intercept the glide slope. If you were cleared for an ILS approach, this is the lowest altitude you would descend to until intercepting the glide slope. (By definition, the glide slope intercept point on a precision approach is the FAF.) This is also the time you would extend the gear. That way you would have a stabilized approach all the way down. If you set up a normal descent speed at glide slope interception but left the gear up until the outer marker, you'd have to add power to compensate for the extra drag of the gear. It's a lot smoother to put the gear down when intercepting the glide slope and then just make enough of a power adjustment to establish the required rate of descent.

The next question: How do you fly the glide slope indicator? The answer to that is simple. Just as if it were a horizontal OBI bearing indicator. Am I kidding? Nope, that's all there is to it. As you fly into the glide slope, the needle will move off the upper peg. As it centers itself, lower the gear and begin the descent.

Adjust the rate of descent as necessary to keep the needle near the center. The rate shown in the conversion table will give you a great starting figure. If you suddenly find that the glide slope needle is off center, glance at the vertical speed indicator. Chances are good that you have allowed the rate of descent to get away from you.

Just as with the localizer needle, don't chase the glide slope indicator. Alter the rate of descent by 200 fpm to try and stop any trend the needle makes off center, and when you get the needle stopped, adjust the descent by 100-fpm increments to bring it back to the center again. As with the localizer, as long as you keep the needle from pegging-out, you are in good shape. Big problem here: If the needle were a dot high, you would be too low and might reach the DH before you'd be close enough to the field to see the approach lights. If the needle were a dot low, you'd be too high crossing the approach lights and might not see them.

How low you ask? *Only down to the DH and no lower*, at which time you are required to initiate a missed approach if you don't see the runway or other identifying features. To review what these identifying features are, take a look at FAR 91.175 in chapter 11.

When you make your first full ILS approach, the accuracy will astound you. It will give you the confidence you'll need when the weather goes sour and you end up "on the gauges."

Very little is more satisfying in flying than breaking out of the mist and rain at minimums and seeing those sequence flashers right in front of your nose. It makes all of the hard work, study, and financial expenditure worthwhile.

ANOTHER LOOK AT HONOLULU

Refer to Fig. 21-2, the Honolulu Airport chart, to study more notes. Notice the two different departure control frequencies, depending on which direction you are going after takeoff. Normally, clearance delivery will tell you the frequency to use on departure, but if not told, ATC expects you to know which way you're heading. Listed in the lower-right corner of the communications block, below the departure frequencies, is the VOR test frequency on the field (VOT 111.0).

In the additional runway information in Fig. 21-3, notice that each runway is equipped with a VASI on the left side of the runway, except for 22R, which has no VASI. The VASIs on 8R, 26L, and 26R are three-bar configurations; the rest are two-bar.

So you won't be too surprised when you see feathers flying past the windshield, a CAUTION note at the top of the page mentions birds in the vicinity of the airport. I don't know what could be done in flight because it's impossible to dodge a flock.

Note (2) explains that the VASI on 26L is canted 5 degrees south of the runway centerline. This is because the normal approach to that runway is from offshore to the south, and the canted angle of the VASI allows you to pick it up sooner. Other notes say that you can only expect to see the 22L VASI within 2 nautical miles of the runway and the 26R VASI within 3.6 nautical miles due to obstructions in both cases.

Notice in Fig. 21-3 that takeoff minimums for Runways 4L and 4R are much more restrictive than takeoff minimums on Runway 8L, which are, in turn, more restrictive than those for Runway 8R. This makes sense because in each case you will be farther from the obstructions after takeoff. On Runways 4L and 4R, you will be heading directly at the mountains; on 8L, you will be just about parallel to them; and on 8R, you will be almost completely offshore.

Why do you suppose that the takeoff minimum ceilings for other than special departures are so much higher than straight-in and circling landing minimums? Furthermore, why are they so much higher for Categories C and D than for A and B?

It all boils down to performance, again. The Category A and B aircraft will be getting off the ground sooner, and they will have more room to maneuver. Also, because of their slower speed, they will have a tighter radius of turn than the large aircraft. The heavies will be using up most of the runway before they finally stagger into the air, so they will end up a lot closer to the mountains.

These things should concern you on every departure and every arrival as well. You might be able to get into an airport only to find out that you might not be able to get out for awhile. Yet, if you chose another field nearby, you might have no problem. It's just one more thing you'll have to look at during preflight planning.

CHAPTER QUIZ

1. You are inbound from Lihue, Kauai, at 6,000 feet, pass BOOKE, and are cleared for a Runway 8L localizer approach. You can:

   a. Descend to 5,000 feet because that is the minimum enroute altitude on the chart.

   b. You cannot descend below 3,100 feet until past the 14 DME fix because that altitude is governed by the ARC approach.

   c. You can descend to 2,300 feet anytime past SELIC because that is the MEA to the FAF.

   d. Both a and c.

2. The MDA once past the FAF is

   a. 213 feet

   b. 263 feet

   c. 460 feet

   d. 520 feet if Category A or B; 540 feet if Category C

3. Aircraft category is based on

   a. Indicated airspeed

   b. Calibrated airspeed

   c. True airspeed

   d. 1.3 V_{SO} airspeed

4. The wind is from the east at 10 knots, gusting to 14 knots. The approach speed is normally 110 knots. How long should it take to fly from EWABE to the MAP?

   a. 3 minutes 56 seconds

   b. 3 minutes 32 seconds

   c. 2 minutes 57 seconds

   d. 2 minutes 32 seconds

5. According to the profile view, the distance from the "0" point to the MM is .5 miles, and the distance between the MM and EWABE is 5.4 miles. Yet the DME shown at EWABE is 6.7 miles. Why the discrepancy?

6. Based on information in Fig. 21-3, why is it important that you confirm the landing runway when cleared to land on 4L, 4R, 22L, or 22R?

Answers are in the appendix.

22
NDB and back course approaches

EXAMINE THE NDB APPROACH PLATE TO HONOLULU'S RUNWAY 8 LEFT. AN NDB (nondirectional beacon) approach is the same as an ADF (automatic direction finder) approach (Fig. 22-1). Its relative low degree of accuracy is evidenced by its lowest MDA being 540 feet MSL. Because the MDA is so high, the missed approach procedure is a simple climbing right turn. You don't have to climb to 500 feet before turning as you did on the ILS and localizer approaches to Runway 8L at Honolulu because you are already higher than that.

When you look at the chart, your immediate reaction might be, "Wow, a simple, old, overhead approach." It could be, and it should be, but because of the infrequency of making this type of approach, many students don't really receive enough training in the use of the ADF. It's not only student pilots, though. There have been so many incidents in air carrier operations lately that the FAA is requiring each pilot proficiency check to include at least one NDB approach.

Simply stated, Fig. 22-1 shows you crossing the LOM on what I call "high key," or "high station." Proceeding outbound, track on the 259-degree bearing from the

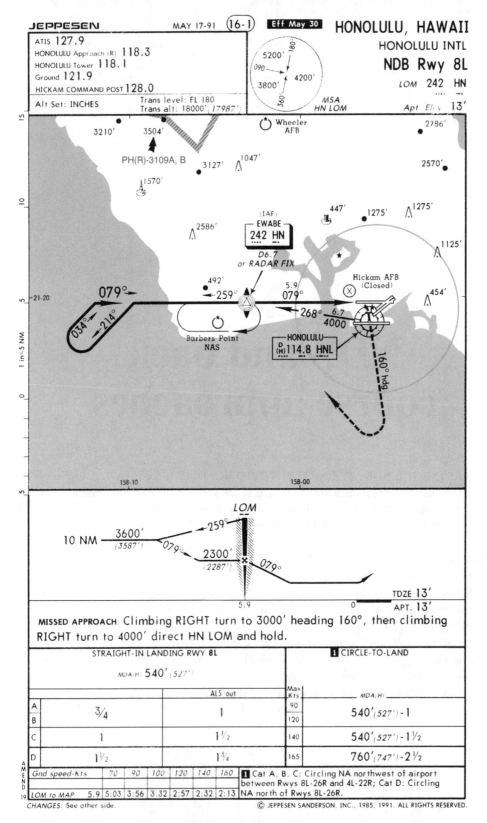

station (EWABE) and descend to 3,600 feet MSL, which is the minimum procedure turn altitude. Notice once again that the procedure turn has to be completed within 10 nautical miles southwest of the facility and that it can be any type of reversal you care to fly.

You should get the latest weather report and take care of the descent and in-range checklists while on descent from the high station. Sometime before or during the procedure turn, take a quick look at the missed approach procedure. After the turn inbound, descend to 2,300 feet MSL and, when you pass the FAF (LOM) inbound, check the time, lower the gear, begin the descent, report the FAF inbound, and take care of the prelanding checklist, all the while tracking on the 079-degree bearing from the station. As in the VOR and localizer approaches, descend to the MDA and fly out the time, which will again bring you to approximately the runway threshold.

TRACKING WITH THE ADF

There are basically three types of ADF presentations. First, the flux gate, or *radio magnetic indicator* (RMI), which is found on most large aircraft, is the best. It has the ADF needle incorporated into the face of the instrument and utilizes a movable face. This works so well that we call it the "no-think" gauge. The instrument does the thinking for us. The face of the instrument, or the azimuth, turns to keep lined up with magnetic north. The RMI is the directional gyro as well, so whatever number shows on the upper indicator is the magnetic heading. Because the ADF needle always points to the station, whatever number it points to on the azimuth is the magnetic bearing to the station. This is what makes it a "no-think" instrument. All you have to remember is that if you want to change the magnetic bearing to the station, you have to turn, and if you can't remember which direction to turn, just remember the old saying, "pull the tail" of the needle.

The second type of ADF presentation has a manually rotatable dial. This requires a three-step procedure. First, check the magnetic compass to set the DG. Second, rotate the dial of the ADF to make it read the same as the DG, and finally, read the magnetic bearing to the station directly off the ADF needle, provided the heading hasn't changed in the meantime.

The least expensive and most common presentation found in general aviation aircraft is the one that uses a fixed-azimuth dial. On this dial, 0 degrees (360 degrees) is always at the top of the face and the needle always reads the relative bearing to the station. That means that you have to mentally compute the magnetic bearing. I've seen a plastic accessory advertised that fits over the face of the fixed azimuth dial. You rotate the accessory to get the same results as in the manually operated dial. It's a good idea, but unfortunately you don't have one during this problem and are faced with flying an NDB approach using a fixed-azimuth ADF.

How do you figure it all out? Like any other type of navigation, one of the first things you have to know is where you are, so you will know which way you need to go. If you're a little confused and are unable to convert all of the numbers at first, you can always turn the aircraft until the needle is reading directly ahead (reading 0 on the dial) and then read the magnetic bearing to the station directly off the DG.

"All right," you say, "but this procedure might not always be possible or practical. Then what?"

"Well," I say, "look here." The sum of the DG plus the azimuth reading (relative bearing to the station), if less than 360 degrees, is the magnetic bearing *to* the station. Its reciprocal (add or subtract 180 degrees) will be the bearing *from* the station.

If the sum of the DG and the azimuth is more than 360 degrees, simply subtract 360 degrees from it, and the remainder will be the magnetic bearing to the station. If you find it difficult to do the math, invest a few dollars in a small electronic calculator.

Throughout this discussion I'll be mentioning bearings *to* and *from* the station, although technically speaking when one refers to bearings in relation to NDBs it should always be in terms of bearings *to*, which is the opposite of working with VORs, where the radials are defined as always *from* the station; however, usage of the terms "radial TO" and "bearing FROM" is becoming more common.

Setting up an example

Let's figure out some magnetic bearings. While we're at it, why not work out a problem showing how to track to the station on a given bearing, compensating for wind drift? It's all a simple matter of addition and subtraction as you can see in Fig. 22-2. In this example, you are directly south of the station in position A, and you want to track inbound to the station on the 330-degree bearing.

At position A, you are heading north, so the DG reads 0 degrees, and because you are due south of the station, the azimuth is also 0 degrees.

Your desired inbound course, 330 degrees, is found (on the ADF dial) to the left of the head of the needle. Now, if the head were on 330 degrees, the tail would be on 150 degrees, right? So, as I said earlier, to know which way to turn, remember to "pull the tail" of the needle. In this case, you want to pull the tail to the right of the bottom of the dial, so you turn to the right. How *much* do you want to turn? That depends on how far you are from the station and what intercept angle you want to use, but to make this simple turn 30 degrees to the right.

At point B, at the moment when you complete the turn to a heading of 030 degrees on the DG (30 degrees to the right of 0), and before the aircraft moved off the 360-degree TO bearing, the azimuth will read 330 degrees. If you add the DG (030 degrees) and azimuth (330 degrees) together, you get 360 degrees, which is the magnetic bearing to the station at that moment.

If you continue on the heading of 030 degrees, how will you know when you are crossing the desired track so that you can turn inbound? Well, you want to track inbound on the 330-degree TO bearing. By subtracting the heading (030 degrees) from 330 degrees, you get 300 degrees. The needle will point to 300 degrees (300 degrees will be the relative bearing on the azimuth) when crossing the 330-degree TO magnetic bearing at position C. When you turn inbound to a 330-degree heading, the relative bearing will be 0 (position D).

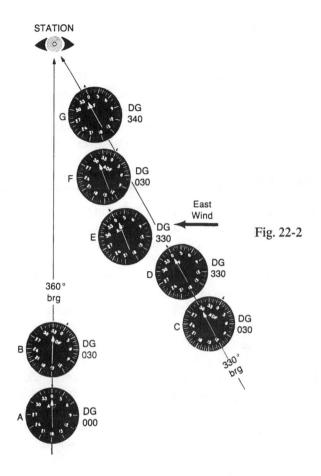

Fig. 22-2

Correcting for the wind

How do you correct for wind drift? It's really just as easy. Let's assume that you have a wind from the east. This will cause you to drift to the west, and before long you'll end up 10 degrees off course, as shown at position E. The heading is still 330 degrees, but the relative bearing is now reading 010 degrees; 330 degrees + 010 degrees = 340 degrees, which is now the new magnetic bearing to the station.

To correct back to course, turn to a heading of 030 degrees (position F). Here you see that the heading is 030 degrees again, but because you were on the 340-degree magnetic bearing to the station when you made the turn, the relative bearing on the azimuth will be reading 310 degrees. Is that correct? Let's confirm it. The DG is 030 degrees, plus the relative bearing of 310 degrees, which produces a magnetic bearing to the station of 340 degrees. Simple enough?

Once again you continue on a heading of 030 degrees until the relative bearing is 300 degrees, and you'll be back at the desired magnetic bearing (330 degrees TO).

This time, however, instead of turning inbound to the station and flying a 330-degree heading, which will only cause you to drift off course again, correct 10 degrees to the right to compensate for wind drift. What will the instruments read now? Well, 010 degrees right of 330 degrees will produce a DG heading of 340 degrees. This will provide a relative bearing of 10 degrees left of center on the ADF azimuth, or 350 degrees. Are you still on the 330-degree magnetic bearing to the station? Check again. Your heading is 340 degrees, plus the relative bearing of 350 degrees, equals 690 degrees. Because this is more than 360 degrees, you have to subtract 360 degrees, which equals 330 degrees. Easy? Well, maybe not, but at least this should take some of the mystery out of it.

The big thing to remember is that when you are flying specific tracks on an NDB facility, decide on a heading to fly and fly it. Any deviation of the azimuth needle will then be an indication of the wind drift involved. The biggest mistake beginning pilots make is to try to keep the azimuth needle centered. With a strong crosswind and starting far enough from the station, you can conceivably end up describing an arc, reaching the station heading directly into the wind.

Tracking away from the station is similar, except you'll be working with reciprocals. Try it out both on paper and in the air.

If you're the type of person who does things easier pictorially rather then mathematically, look at it this way. In Fig. 22-2, to go from A to C, you have to change the relative bearing by 30 degrees (360 degrees magnetic bearing to 330 degrees magnetic bearing). If you stay on the heading of 030 degrees, you will fly until the relative bearing changes the 30 degrees from 330 degrees (at B) to 300 degrees (at C), and you are there.

Either way, it all comes out the same, and although the NDB approach requires more mental labor than the others, once you have mastered the basic rules outlined above and have practiced them a bit, you really will be able to say what you did in the beginning of this chapter: "Wow, a simple, old, overhead approach."

FLYING "AWAY" FROM THE NEEDLE

It is time to discuss one last approach, the localizer back course, with an examination of the Kahului, Hawaii, LOC DME (BACK CRS) Rwy 20 approach (Fig. 22-3).

Two main facts to remember concerning back course approaches are (1) you cannot use the glide slope information and (2) the localizer needle movement is reversed. This means that you have to be extraordinarily cautious and think through the approach because you will have to consciously fight your previous training. On a back course, if the OBI moves to the left, don't turn left to bring it back, turn to the right; if it moves to the right, turn to the left. *Turn away from the needle.* As long as you keep that in mind, you should have no trouble.

The approach chart shows that if you are making arc approaches from the east or west, the lead-in radials are indicated. There are two initial approach fixes from the east, OPANA, where the 069-degree radial of the OGG VOR crosses the 13 DME arc, and an unnamed intersection where the 084-degree radial of the OGG VOR crosses the 13 DME arc.

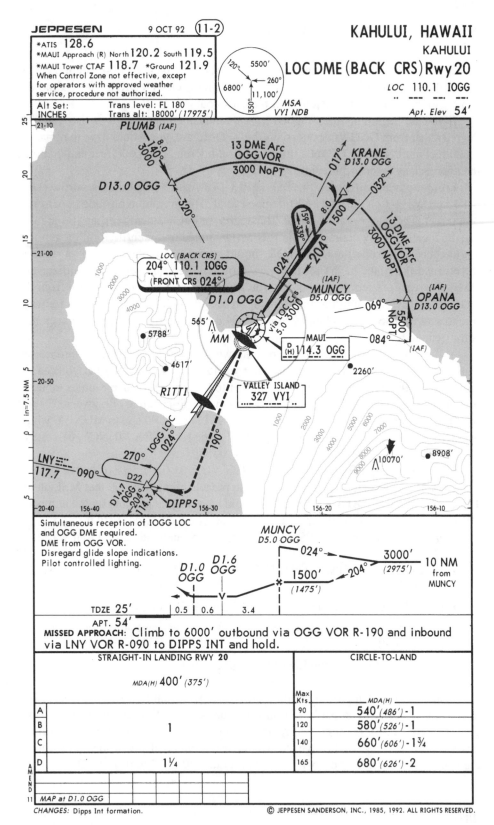

Fig. 22-3 Reproduced with permission of Jeppesen Sanderson, Inc. Not for use in navigation.

If you are beginning the approach from OPANA, remain at 3,000 feet and fly the arc until passing the 032-degree lead-in radial from the OGG VOR, at which time you can begin the turn inbound to intercept the back course.

If you are beginning the approach from the unnamed intersection where the 084-degree radial from OGG VOR intersects the 13 DME arc, you would have to remain at 5,500 feet until crossing OPANA, then you could descend to 3,000 feet and continue the approach as described previously.

From the other direction, the IAF is PLUMB, which is 8.0 miles northwest of the 13.0 DME fix on the OGG 320-degree radial. The minimum altitude here is also 3,000 feet. The lead-in radial is the 017-degree radial. Remember that you are flying the localizer back course, so the ILS will be tuned and identified on the number 1 VOR receiver, while the OGG VOR should be on the number 2 receiver. In fact, if you read the notes in the profile view, you will see that separate localizer and DME receivers are required, and that you are using the DME information from the OGG VOR. Even though the ILS sensing gives you reverse information, I always like to set the OBS to the inbound course (204 degrees in this case) just to keep myself orientated.

You will use the DME to determine letdown points on this specific approach because the approach is made over water. After you turn inbound at KRANE, you can descend to 1,500 feet MSL. You have 1,500 feet to lose, but you have 8 miles (about 4 minutes) to lose them, so if you maintain a reasonable descent rate of between 500 and 600 fpm, you will get down there in plenty of time. Fly at 1,500 feet to MUNCY, which is the 5.0 DME fix from the OGG VOR. It is also the FAF. After MUNCY, descend to minimums, which are 400 feet MSL (377 feet AGL).

The MAP here, 1.0 DME from the OGG VOR, is 0.4 miles from the runway threshold. If you have to execute the missed approach, climb to 3,000 feet MSL on the 190-degree radial of the OGG VOR. You would have set that heading on the number 2 OBS upon turning onto final approach, so now all you have to do is fly it.

You will be holding at DIPPS intersection, which can be identified four ways:

- The intersection of the Lanai (LNY) 090-degree radial and the front course ILS to Kahului
- The LNY 090-degree radial and the OGG VOR 204-degree radial
- The LNY 090-degree radial and the 023-degree bearing to the McGregor Point (MPH) NDB
- The 22.2 DME fix on the LNY 090-degree radial

If, after a missed approach on the back course, you want to try a front course ILS to Kahului, you would probably just turn the number 1 OBS to the inbound (024-degree) ILS course. By the time you're about 10 miles south of the OGG VOR on the missed approach, you should have the heading pretty well tied down, so you can retune the number 2 receiver to the LNY VOR, and set the OBS to 270 degrees TO.

Turn right (toward LNY) as the number 2 needle centers, fly until the number 1 needle (ILS) centers, and make a 30-degree turn to the right for a teardrop entry into the nonstandard (left-hand) holding pattern. While flying the 1-minute outbound leg, you would reset the number 2 (LNY) OBS to 090 degrees FROM, which will be the inbound holding pattern course.

VECTORS TO FINAL—A WARNING

On many approaches, not just the approaches discussed in this chapter, you will be provided radar vectors to the final approach course. In such cases, it is crucial that you be aware of the following from the *Aeronautical Information Manual*:

> After release to approach control, aircraft are vectored to the final approach course (ILS, MLS, VOR, ADF, etc.). Radar vectors and altitude or flight levels will be issued as required for spacing and separating aircraft. *Therefore, pilots must not deviate from the headings issued by approach control.* Aircraft will normally be informed when it is necessary to vector across the final approach course for spacing or other reasons. If approach course crossing is imminent and the pilot has not been informed that he (or she) will be vectored across the final approach course he (or she) should query the controller. . . . The pilot is not expected to turn inbound on the final approach course unless the approach clearance has been issued.

Here we have a possible disaster. A low-time instrument pilot, suffering from fatigue, is vectored through the final approach course for separation purposes. The controller gets busy with another aircraft. The pilot, not familiar with terrain or perhaps misreading the chart, could conceivably fly into a mountain. This points out a good reason to study the entire approach chart, including the heights of all major obstructions, not just the diagram of the approach itself.

CHAPTER QUIZ

1. While heading 020 degrees, the ADF needle is pointing to a station that reads 020 degrees on the face of the dial. What is the bearing of the station from the aircraft?

    a. 10 degrees

    b. 20 degrees

    c. 30 degrees

    d. 40 degrees

2. In question 1, what bearing of the station is the aircraft crossing?

    a. 20 degrees

    b. 40 degrees

    c. 220 degrees

    d. 240 degrees

3. In question 1, in order to track inbound to the station on the 090-degree bearing, you could

    a. Turn left to a heading of 360 degrees and fly until the ADF needle reads 090 degrees and then turn right to the station.

    b. Turn right to a heading of 040 degrees and fly until the ADF needle reads 270 degrees and turn farther right to the station.

    c. Continue flying a heading of 020 degrees until the ADF needle reads 070 degrees and then turn right to the station.

    d. Continue flying a heading of 020 degrees until the ADF needle centers, then fly a heading of 090 degrees to the station.

4. You are tracking away from an NDB on a track of 135 degrees. You notice that with an aircraft heading of 135 degrees your ADF needle is pointing to 170 degrees. To get back on track you should

    a. Turn right 30 degrees and fly a heading of 165 degrees until the ADF points to 190 degrees, then turn left to about 145 degrees to correct for wind drift.

    b. Turn right 30 degrees and fly a heading of 165 degrees until the ADF points to 150 degrees, then turn left to about 145 degrees to correct for wind drift.

    c. Turn left 30 degrees and fly a heading of 105 degrees until the ADF points to 190 degrees, then turn right to about 125 degrees to correct for wind drift.

    d. Turn left 30 degrees and fly a heading of 105 degrees until the needle points to 190 degrees, then turn right to about 125 degrees to correct for wind drift.

For the next questions refer to Fig. 22-3.

5. Four initial approach fixes are shown on the chart. They are:

    a. DIPPS, PLUMB, KRANE, OPANA.

    b. MPH, PLUMB, OPANA, MUNCY.

    c. Unnamed Intersection at the OGG 084-degree radial and the OGG 13 mile arc, MUNCY, OPANA, PLUMB.

    d. Unnamed intersection at the OGG 084-degree radial and the OGG 13 mile arc, OPANA, KRANE, PLUMB.

6. There are _____ ways to determine DIPPS intersection. They are;

    1. _____.

    2. _____.

    3. _____, and the

    4. _____.

7. When the control zone is not effective,

    a. The field has pilot controlled lighting.

    b. The procedure is not authorized unless you have approved weather service.

    c. You must use circling minimums instead of straight-in minimums.

    d. The IOGG Localizer is deactivated.

8. Both the initial approach altitude and the procedure turn altitude are 3,000 feet.
   True _____False _____

Answers are in the appendix.

23
The flight director

FLIGHT DIRECTORS AND LONG-RANGE (AREA) NAVIGATION WERE BARELY discussed when this book was first written because the average pilot could fly an entire career and never have an opportunity to see this equipment in action, let alone use it.

All of this changed in a short 20 years from the 1970s to the 1990s with the advent of the microcomputer industry and competition. A large number of general aviation aircraft are equipped with loran-C, flight director equipment, and GPS. For this reason, I am adding a few chapters to this edition of *The Art of Instrument Flying* to give you a quick overview of what you can expect to see and use as we approach a new century and millennium.

Although the antiquated transit satellite navigation is still available and is being used by some overwater ferry pilots, its use by the average pilot in the near future is probably not going to expand due to the fact that it is being phased out as the global positioning system (GPS) becomes fully operational. Not only that, but hand-held GPS units can be purchased for less than $700, and they work fine for extended overwater flights. Furthermore, the long acquisition time (up to 30 minutes) of the old transit satellite system makes it too slow for most flight operations.

This edition will hit the highlights of a few systems that are currently in use: flight director, loran-C, Omega, inertial navigation, and the newer kid on the block, GPS.

The industry thought that GPS would be fully operational by year 2025, but as I write these words, United Airlines just conducted studies with a fully-coupled autoland 747-400 during which the aircraft touched down on the same spot something like 179 out of 180 landings. GPS is here and should be fully operational now by 2000 or so.

Because there are many manufacturers of each type of system, and because each manufacturer has different models of these systems, I shall only talk about generalities. When the opportunity arises to operate an aircraft that uses one or more of these systems, the manufacturer will provide you with adequate documentation that will enable you to make use of all functions.

The flight director is an integral part of most area navigation systems, so we will talk about it in this chapter. The flight director can be turned off, and the aircraft can be hand flown like you're used to. A flight director can be turned on, and you can hand-fly the aircraft with reference to the commands on the instruments. Or the director can be turned on and interfaced with the autopilot. In addition, most units are made so that area navigation units can be interfaced.

TWO TYPES

Flight directors come in two basic configurations: single-cue and split-cue. Here we will discuss the Collins FD-109 flight director that utilizes a single cue.

Figure 23-1 is a black-and-white view of the attitude director indicator (ADI). In real life, this is a very colorful indicator, and we'll discuss these colors as we go along.

Not counting the computers required, the ADI is one of four units that will be on your instrument panel. It takes the place of your normal AI. The other three units are:

- The horizontal situation indicator (HSI), which takes the place of the OBI
- The flight mode controller indicator (FMI), which allows you to select the modes in which the flight director will operate
- The heading/course panel (HCP). (The FMI and HCP have no counterparts in nonflight-director panels.)

Figure 23-1 looks something like a standard AI with a few prominent additions. Rather than using a round ball as a horizon, the FD-109 ADI uses a flat tape that is easier to read. It is marked in 5-degree increments, both nose high and nose low.

Let's take a look at the outer bezel. You will see a series of markings along the upper portion. The markings are at 10-degree increments to 30 degrees, with a small tic mark at 45 degrees and a normal-sized mark again at 60 degrees. The center inverted triangle marking is orange, while the other markings are in white. These markings, in connection with the white, triangular-shaped index mark (that Collins calls the bank pointer) on the movable inner portion of the instrument, will indicate the angle of bank of the aircraft, and are fairly uniform in all flight directors.

At the 9 o'clock position of the outside bezel, you can see the glide path indicator. The movable indicia can be any color, but they are usually white, yellow, or orange.

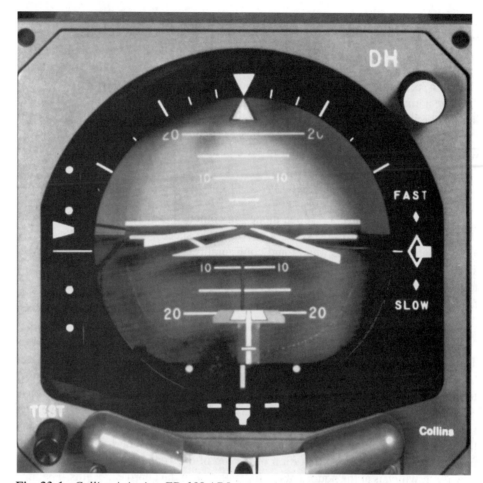

Fig. 23-1. *Collins Avionics, FD-109 ADI.* Collins Avionics, Division of Rockwell International

This indicator moves up and down with a range of two dots above and below the "on glide path" indication, which is the center marking. On most FDs, this indicator will be biased out of sight unless you have selected an ILS or VNAV (vertical navigation) mode, and it will also be out of view unless the aircraft is within about 2½ degrees of the glide path. If an ILS is selected but the glide slope transmitter or receiver is inoperative, or if you are too far from the station to receive an adequate signal, a red GS flag will appear instead of a pointer.

The Air Line Pilots Association worked hard for many years to standardize flight instruments so that a red flag would only appear if a specific function was selected but was inoperative or unusual. Many years ago some instruments would show a red flag anytime the specific function wasn't working, whether it was being selected or not. The problem with that was that pilots got so used to seeing red indicators that they didn't notice when a new red flag appeared that was really trying to warn them of something being amiss.

At the 3 o'clock position on the outer bezel, you can see the speed command indicator. This indicium is usually orange, and is designed to show you if you are fast or slow or a speed that you have dialed into the flight data computer.

The normal speed command will anticipate what you do with the controls, including the throttles, so you hardly have to take your eyes off the ADI and HSI during the entire ILS approach. If you use the elevators to fly the command bars and add or subtract power as necessary to keep the speed command centered, you'll be right on the money.

The placement of the glide path indicator and the speed command indicator will vary with the type and model of flight director you are using.

Many units will have an "alpha mode" in conjunction with the speed command. With this type of unit, if you select a speed in the speed command window that is slower than $1.3\ V_{S1}$ for the weight and configuration of the aircraft, or if your speed slows below that speed, an ALPHA flag will appear in the window. If you have autothrottles interfaced with the unit, the throttles will advance to prevent the aircraft from flying too slow.

BALL AND BARS

The three dashes at the 6 o'clock position are the rate of turn indicator (needle) and the ball below is the slip indicator. While many models of ADI will eliminate the rate of turn indicator, most of them retain the ball.

Moving into the face of the ADI, at the 6 o'clock position, you can see a vertical bar that has risen up to the 20-degree nose-down position. This is the runway indicator that comes into play during an ILS approach. Collins calls it the localizer deviation pointer (LDP). The horizontal portion of the top of the T-shaped indicator is the runway itself, which is at the bottom of the indicator when the approach begins. The indicator is white with green sides. As you get closer to the ground, the indicator will begin to rise to show you approaching the runway. It will also slide left and right to indicate your position left or right of centerline.

Two inverted Vs in the center of the instrument are the main parts of the flight director and are used during all modes of operation. The larger one in the center is orange in color. It is the fixed "airplane" symbol. The thinner bars above the airplane symbol are the yellow command bars.

In order to keep the aircraft operating in the flight mode you desire and have selected (climb, descent, course intercept, go-around, etc.), it is only necessary for you to "fly" the "airplane" symbol into the command bars.

If you want to turn left to a new heading, you would select the new heading with the heading select knob. The command bars would then bias in the direction that you have to bank to turn to that heading. You roll the aircraft to tuck the "airplane" symbol into the command bars. Once you have entered the proper bank, there is nothing else to do until the command bars bias in the other direction, telling you to roll out on the new course. By keeping the "airplane" symbol in a constant relationship with the command bars, you will automatically roll out at the proper time, and you will be right on course. In addition, in any of the NAV modes, the command bars will automatically apply any necessary wind correction angle.

When you're in a VNAV mode, the command bars will bias up or down to keep you on your desired climb or descent path.

If you've selected any of the LNAV (lateral navigation) modes, such as LOC (for localizer tracking), ILS, or NAV (for VOR or AREA NAV tracking), the command bars will bias at the proper time to give you the proper lead-in turns to perform picture- perfect captures of your desired courses.

As easy as all this seems to be, however, you will find that there are more buttons to push, knobs to turn, and do-dads to keep track of, so the actual manipulation of the flight controls will have to become more and more automatic.

I haven't mentioned the yellow light in the upper right-hand corner of the instrument. It is the decision height (DH) alert and will illuminate when the aircraft reaches the proper decision height as dialed into the radio altimeter if the aircraft is so equipped.

The tape portion of the instrument utilizes blue for the sky and white for the ground. With all indicators using different symbols and being color coded, it becomes second nature to read all of the information at one glance. This becomes more and more important as the speeds of the aircraft you fly increase.

HSI INFORMATION

The HSI is illustrated in Fig. 23-2. This specific HSI has a DME readout in the upper left corner, a course selection indicator in the upper right corner, a glide path indicator at the 9 o'clock position on the outer bezel, and a navigation mode indicator at the 3 o'clock position. These peripheral indicators change with the make and model of the HSI.

The face of the instrument combines the functions of instruments and visual aids:

- A movable azimuth that always indicates the heading of the aircraft at the 12 o'clock position.

- A course pointer, which is the large, long, segmented arrow that is pointing at 028 degrees.

- The OBI (usually white or yellow), which is the center portion of the course pointer indicating your relationship with the desired course.

- The airplane symbol (orange) in the center of the instrument, which shows at a glance your relationship to the desired course.

- A heading track symbol. The head of the heading track can be seen at about 079 degrees, and the tail is about 259 degrees. This is almost any color depending on the model and manufacturer. It is controlled by the heading selector knob on the heading/course panel (HCP).

Fig. 23-2. *Collins Avionics, FD-109 HSI.* Collins Avionics, Division of Rockwell International

Once you learn the various functions and control operation of the ADI and HSI, you won't know how you ever flew without a flight director before. It usually doesn't take much more than 2 or 3 hours to become completely familiar with all of the functions and idiosyncrasies of a unit, and many functions can be learned in simulator sessions.

Most of the flight directors on the market can be interfaced with all of the various navigation computers, as well as with the various autopilot and/or autothrottle combinations that you will encounter.

The split-cue, or dual-cue, ADI (not illustrated) looks something like a normal OBI, but with all of the other ADI features mentioned previously. Instead of the delta shapes for the aircraft and command symbols, the airplane symbol is usually just a partial horizontal indicator. The command bars look a lot like the glide path and OBI that you're already used to.

The difference here is that rather than the glide path indicator pivoting from the side of the instrument and the OBI pivoting along the bottom, both indicators are lineal, with the pitch command bar moving vertically up and down the face of the instrument and the course command bar moving horizontally left and right.

In use, if the pitch command bar moves up from the center, you ease back on the controls until the airplane symbol merges with the command bar. In actual practice, the command bar will move down to the airplane symbol.

If the course deviation indicator (CDI) moves to the left, you roll to the left until the bar centers. You will then hold this bank until the needle moves to the right, and by rolling to the right, attempting to keep the needle centered, you will roll out of the bank back to wings level.

As to which design works better, it's hard to say. Once again it seems to depend on which one you started with. In either case, they make controlling your aircraft a piece of cake.

Still and all, you should always learn where the OFF switches are located because if you program the unit incorrectly or if you have a failure, it's better to turn everything off and go back to flying by raw data until you can sort everything out again. Don't allow the aircraft to fly blindly through the sky while you're trying to figure out why it didn't do what you thought it was going to do.

24
Loran-C

THE EXPLOSION OF TECHNOLOGY IN THE PAST TWO DECADES HAS BEEN phenomenal. Many of these technological advances have directly or indirectly affected our industry. For the most part, these advances have been spin-offs of military/space research and the airline fleets.

Two areas of research that have given us so much are dovetailed in many ways: navigation and computers. Many of these improvements have been necessitated because of size and weight restrictions in space programs. These restrictions have forced major advances in miniaturization and such fantastic tools as the integrated circuit (IC) chips.

Competition in the free marketplace has brought the prices down to what we can afford in many general aviation aircraft.

I began with the flight director system in the last chapter. These next few chapters will look at additional instrumentation and navigational equipment that is ending up in the cockpits of more and more aircraft in the civil fleet. You will definitely be using some of these within the next few years of your aviation affiliations. As far as that's concerned, you might have been exposed to some of them already.

Closing chapters provide a brief look into loran navigation, Omega navigation, inertial navigation, and GPS. Because so many general aviation aircraft are already equipped with loran units, I shall discuss them first.

Discussions in the next few chapters describe the ARNAV FMS 5000 loran, the Litton LTN-211 Omega, the Litton LTN-92 INS, and the ARNAV STAR 5000 GPS. There are many other units on the market, and when you are ready to purchase your own, certainly look at everything the marketplace has to offer and get what you want depending on your own needs. The aforementioned units are used in these discussions because I either use them or have been provided with enough technical material on them to adequately describe their functions.

Webster's New World Dictionary describes loran: Lo(ng) Ra(nge) N(avigation), a system by which a ship or aircraft can determine its position by the difference in time between radio signals sent from two or more known stations. This is a good, simplified definition.

Loran is not new. It began in the early days of World War II as a secret project at the MIT Radiation Laboratory in 1940. Like all radio devices of those days, it was big, bulky, and subject to many failures due to its dependence on vacuum tubes. It was very complicated to use, requiring the operator to listen to and count the pulses of the radiated signals. Then, provided that he identified the signals correctly, he could determine the position with relative accuracy by locating that position with respect to hyperbolic curves drawn on large charts.

LORAN DEVELOPMENT

As time went on, loran improved in reliability and accuracy and during the late 1950s the present form of loran-C was developed. Due to the high cost (and military fears), it was used almost exclusively by the military. As the military released its hold on loran and private industry began competing for the use and sale of loran-C equipment, the prices came down so that it became available for the marine industry. More and more loran chains were installed, until now we have fairly good loran coverage across most of the Northern Hemisphere.

By the early 1980s the microchip industry really came into full bloom, driving down prices and weights, and improving the reliability of many items of everyday use that could make use of computers and quartz crystals. Loran-C and other navigational tools finally became available and affordable for the average pilot and boat owner. (In the rest of this chapter, "loran" means loran-C.)

To put this fantastic technological growth into perspective, back around 1975 or so I bought one of the first digital watches. It was a Pulsar that used an LED display. It was very accurate, but all it could do was tell the time (and it had to be shaded from sunlight to be seen), and it cost around $400. A few months ago I bought a World Timer watch to help me keep track of time in my international flying. It tells me the local time in every time zone in the world, as well as GMT. I can choose between a 12-hour and 24-hour display. I can change from daylight to standard time at will. The calendar function tells me the date (day, month, and year) and adjusts itself automatically for months of different lengths. In addition, it has four different alarm functions, a countdown timer, and a stopwatch function. The price is $35. So it is with loran. The price has come down dramatically, and what it can do for you has risen just as dramatically.

You don't have to listen to signals, count pulses, and laboriously work out your position on charts any longer. The new lorans calculate and display latitude and longitude. In addition, they are loaded with so many bells and whistles that it's almost impossible to list them all.

Unlike the very high frequency signals used by the VOR receivers that you are so familiar with, loran uses low frequency signals, down around 100,000 cycles per second. Whereas the VHF signals are line-of-sight, the loran signals wrap around the Earth for considerable distances, and although they do wander a bit when they cross shorelines, mountains, and the like, they are still extremely accurate.

The modern loran units can interface with autopilots and flight directors. By far, the most useful instrument in the newer loran units is the built-in data bank that can be updated periodically. The ARNAV FMS 5000 gets its update from Jeppesen. Jeppesen NavData Services is the world leader in computerized databases for flight navigation. The updated database cards come out every 28 days. Although it's not necessary to use the updated cards, much of the information in the database will be out of date if you do not do so, which will require a lot of double-checking on the user's part to assure accurate navigation.

The database contains 20,000 stored Jeppesen records that cover airports, VORs, and nondirectional beacons (NDBs), as well as enroute and terminal intersections. In addition, there is still room for a number of user-selected routes and waypoints.

The ARNAV FMS 5000 has a couple of desired features, such as a training mode that helps the new user become familiar with the operation of this complex unit. No matter how many times you read manuals on modern navigational instruments, you never really learn until you begin "hands on" usage. This training function allows you to do that at home. This is certainly a lot safer than trying to learn the system and fly an aircraft at the same time. The training mode also permits preprogramming and preflying the flight plan. You can load a long and complex flight plan into the user waypoint memory and then "fly" it at home to get used to it. By allowing you to program flight speeds up to 999 knots, you can prefly the routes without taking up too much time.

Another feature to look for in a loran is the unit's ability to tell you when you are receiving inaccurate signals. When this occurs, you can search for a better chain of stations. In the FMS 5000, if a chain cannot be reliably received, extended range operation utilizes radio-frequency skywaves that travel farther bouncing between the ionosphere and the Earth's surface.

TRANSMITTERS

Loran-C works like all other lorans, timing the signals that it receives. These signals are transmitted from a series of transmitters called a *chain*. Each chain has one master station and four secondary stations. The master station is identified with the letter M, and the secondaries are identified with the letters W, X, Y, and Z. Each chain operates on its own specific group repetition interval (GRI).

Although that all sounds confusing, the stations send out their signals in a series of pulses. The master sends out a group of nine pulses with a pause after the eighth. The time that elapses from the beginning of the first set of pulses to the beginning of the next set is the GRI. The time is measured in microseconds and each chain is identified by its own specific GRI. For example, the Great Lakes Chain is known as GRI 8970 because its GRI is 89,700 microseconds.

The secondary stations of each chain send out groups of eight pulses at the same GRI as the master. Each secondary sends out its pulses at a different time so that they don't overlap with each other or with the master. This delay is called the *emission delay*.

The airborne loran receiver times the arrival of these pulses. By starting its time with the arrival of the master signal and then determining the difference in the time between the master and a secondary, the unit can develop a *line of position* (LOP). By using more than one secondary, the unit can determine more than one LOP, and therefore "fix" the position of the aircraft. The FMS 5000 loran calculates a new position fix every half second.

Figure 24-1 illustrates how these fixes are determined.

From that basic method of determining position, the computer functions take over to provide you with the ability to track on a specific course, to proceed from one waypoint to another, to know the distance from point A to point B, and to figure the winds aloft. The computer will also calculate the wind correction angle, how far you are off the desired track, and even when to initiate a descent to arrive at a specific altitude at a specific point (vertical navigation, or VNAV). A good loran unit will inform you of the position accuracy by indicating the estimated position error (EPE). A good fix is within 0.1 nautical mile; a poor fix drifts off as far as 1.5 nautical miles.

The ARNAV FMS 5000 has a built-in MSA and MESA. This function does not take the place of IFR minimum enroute altitudes, but it's a good guide for IFR and is a great help for VFR flight. In the FMS 5000, the MSA (minimum safe altitude) and MESA (minimum enroute safe altitude) are predicated on what ARNAV calls the maximum elevation figure (MEF). The MEF is the highest elevation within a specific grid sector on your chart. A grid sector is a square that is ½ a degree (30 minutes) square. With this in mind, the MSA is predicated on any grid MEF within 5 nautical miles of your position, while the MESA is predicated on all grid sectors that fall within a 5-mile-wide buffer on each side of your route between waypoints. The MSA and MESA are 1,000 feet above the MEF if the MEF is less than 5,000 feet, and 2,000 feet if the MEF is more than 5,000 feet.

Most loran units also have built-in alerts to indicate when you are heading for controlled airspace, a restricted area, a prohibited area, a MOA, an alert area, or other similar area. These are important alerts and point out the value of having up-to-date data banks installed. In the case of the FMS 5000, this function is termed the special-use airspace (SUA) function. It will alert you about 10 minutes prior to entering and when entering any SUA.

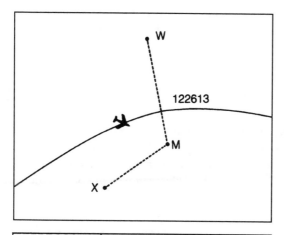

Fig. 24-1. *The arrival of signals from a Master transmitter and a secondary is timed at the loran receiver. The difference between the arrival times plus the emission delay gives a time difference which can be plotted to result in a hyperbolic loran Line of Position (LOP).*

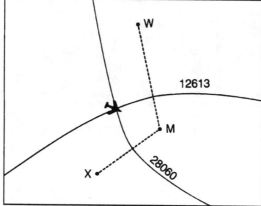

The intersection of LOPs from two secondaries provides a position fix.

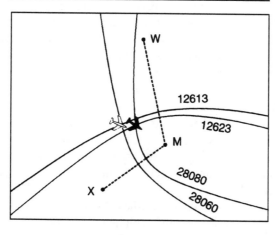

The R-50 calculates a new position fix every half second. LOP coordinates are then converted to latitude/longitude.
ARNAV Systems, Inc.

Another valuable feature of certain loran units is the airport search, which indicates the distance and bearing to the nearest airport in the event of an enroute emergency.

TYPICAL FEATURES

Every loran has its own arrangement of buttons, knobs, screen displays, and the like, but to give some idea of what you can expect, take a look at Fig. 24-2.

This is the front face of the ARNAV R-50. Although this model has been upgraded to the FMS 5000, with the exception of the model number, all of the details of the front face are the same. The ON/OFF switch is the pushbutton on the left. The slot in the upper left accepts the database card. There are eight rubberized pushbuttons on the unit, as well as a knob on the right side.

Fig. 24-2. *The ARNAV Systems R-50 loran receiver has the same face and controls as FMS-5000 and R-5000.* ARNAV Systems, Inc.

In addition to these controls, there are eight lights inside the display face. The four lights on the left side indicate which mode the unit is operating in (navigation, way-point, auxiliary, or flight plan); the lights on the right are warning or alert lights: airspace (Class B), warning (WRN), waypoint alert (WPA), and extended range (XR).

The MODE button is used to select the various modes. It is also used to cancel any data entry waypoint selection procedures. When it does this, it returns to the screen you were working on. Each mode has a number of pages. The home page is the first page that appears when a mode is selected.

The WRN (warning) button is selected when a warning alert flashes. The alert light will flash until the warning button is pushed, at which time the proper warning page will appear on the screen. Once you have digested the warning information, you push the warning button a second time and the unit will return to the mode and the page that you were using prior to the warning.

The TCA button is pushed when a TCA alert light flashes. As in the case of the warning button, the display will show the necessary information, and a second push of the button will return you to the page that was shown prior to the alert.

Three types of alerts are SUA, waypoint, and system. In the case of an SUA alert, the TCA indicator will flash. The WPA and WRN indicators will flash for a waypoint alert, and the WRN light will flash alone for a system alert. Once the alert has been acknowledged, the light will remain illuminated until the cause has been eliminated. If there are multiple alerts, each time the respective button is pushed, one of the alerts will be acknowledged.

The HOLD button is a very useful feature. When pushed, it will enter the aircraft's present position into the user waypoint memory. It will be given the name HOLDxx, where xx can be 00 through 99. The specific position can be renamed to open that hold position memory for future use.

The CLR (clear) button has a number of functions. If you have selected something for deletion, it will delete the object; if you are in a data-entry mode, it provides backspacing; and finally, it rejects any proposed actions that the unit suggests.

The ENT (enter) button is used to initiate data entry, to complete the data entry, to acknowledge specific alerts, and to accept proposed actions.

The APT (airport) button is pushed to initiate a search for the nearest 15 airports within 100 nm. The nearest airport will be at the top of the list.

The VOR button initiates a search for the nearest 15 VORs or intersections.

The knob on the right can be pushed in and rotated clockwise and counterclockwise. Using these movements, the knob, in conjunction with certain pushbuttons, is used to select pages within a specific mode, to enter alphanumeric characters during data-entry procedures, and to toggle between fields that have two possible selections.

All of this sounds very confusing, which is why the training mode is so useful. Take the unit home, hook it up to a 12-volt power source (available from ARNAV), and play with it to your heart's content. That way, when you put it into use for the first flight, you'll be able to concentrate on flying the aircraft.

Let's see what that specific screen is showing (Fig. 24-2). The large screen is two lines high with 20 characters per line permitting presentation of a lot of information on one page.

It is in the NAV mode, as indicated by the light in the upper left-hand corner. A TCA warning as indicated by the light in the upper right-hand corner.

The upper line indicates that you are on the 293-degree bearing to Seattle (SEA), and you are 16.0 nautical miles away. The symbol -V- indicates that you have preprogrammed the unit for vertical navigation.

The lower line is a built-in course deviation indicator that is showing left of the course selected (0 being on centerline). The arrow indicates that you have to correct toward the right to get back on course. Ground speed is 170 knots.

The airport page provides a lot of information on one screen, including the elevation, the length of the longest runway, whether the airport is lighted and has instrument approaches available, as well as the tower and ATIS frequencies.

Another interesting feature of the FMS 5000 is the turn cuing function. When you are approaching a specific waypoint, the unit will tell you when to turn to get on the next airway (as long as the turn is greater than 10 degrees and less than 120 degrees). At the proper time prior to reaching the intersection, the page will change to display LEFT (or RIGHT) TURN IN 10 SECONDS on the top line. The bottom line will display the CDI centered, followed by TO (and the new course). The seconds field will count down to zero, and the cursor will deflect two dots in the proper direction. As you line up the new course, the cursor will center, and after 5 seconds, the NAV mode home page will appear again.

Learn a loran unit well, and make use of all available features, but remember that just like anything else, you still have to keep your head up and your eyes out of the cockpit as much as possible.

25
Omega navigation

OMEGA NAVIGATION OPERATES ON EVEN LOWER FREQUENCIES THAN LORAN: very low frequency (VLF). These VLF signals travel around the Earth, seemingly captured between the Earth's surface and the atmosphere. Because of this, the signals travel for remarkable distances, upwards to 10,000 miles.

There are eight Omega and an additional nine VLF transmitters around the world, and because of this, Omega navigation is a worldwide system. Accuracy is very good for aeronautical use, being considered poor if the error exceeds 2 miles after a 2,500-mile flight.

Each Omega transmitter is identified by its number, and a letter, as well as its location:

1 (A) Norway
2 (B) Liberia
3 (C) Hawaii
4 (D) North Dakota
5 (E) La Reunion
6 (F) Argentina

7 (G) Australia

8 (H) Japan

The nine VLF transmitters are located at:

Norway
Rugby, England
Lualualei, Hawaii
Jim Creek, Washington
Annapolis, Maryland
Cutler, Maine
Northwest Cape, Australia
Yosami, Japan
Anthorne, England

Although some of the Omega and VLF transmitters are in the same country, they are not collocated.

Because the frequencies are so low, the antennas must be very long, exceeding 10,000 feet in length. The antenna in Norway, for example, actually stretches across one of the fjords.

Unlike loran, which transmits all of the signals on one frequency and changes the timing by transmitting in pulses, the Omega system transmits continuously but changes the frequencies at a constant rate. Frequencies used by Omega are 10.2, 11.05, 11.33, and 13.6 kHz. VLF signals utilize only one frequency.

The Omega signals form parallel lines around the Earth. The space within these lines is called a *lane*, and the Omega computer must know which lane it is in when it starts up, in order to compute which lane it is in after the vehicle begins moving. Once it knows which lane, the computer then calculates its exact position within that lane.

SYSTEM REVIEW

As in all other pieces of aircraft equipment, more than one manufacturer of airborne Omega receivers exists. Hawaiian Airlines elected to install Litton LTN-211 units in the Lockheed L-1011 fleet. I operated the LTN-211 and will use it to provide an overview of the Omega system.

The Litton LTN-211 Omega system is made up of three parts. The receiver processing unit (RPU) shown in Fig. 25-1 is the brains of the system. The RPU receives the station transmitter signals and airspeed and heading information from the aircraft computers and then processes and translates the information into usable displays and guidance signals for the flight director and/or autopilot.

The second unit, also shown in Fig. 25-1, is the control display unit (CDU), which is where the pilot/navigator inputs the necessary information to utilize the system, and where she reads desired information.

Fig. 25-1. *Litton Aero Products LTN-211.* Reproduced with permission of Litton Aero Products.

The third unit is the antenna coupler unit (ACU), which is not illustrated. It is a flat antenna that fits flush with the aircraft fuselage.

Take a look at the CDU on the left of Fig. 25-1. When you get into an aircraft, the unit will be switched off. To begin, you pull out the knob of the mode switch, located midway along the left side of the CDU, and rotate it to the left to the A (automatic) position.

You will be greeted by a number of lights in the upper window that are designed to show you that all of the LEDs are working properly. We will call this window the *numerical display window*. Because there are two display areas, left and right, for the remainder of this chapter I shall refer to the left display and the right display. There will also be two 8s in the lower left window: the *track window*. A number of abbreviated words in different colors are in the lower right window: the *annunciator window*.

These lights will be illuminated for a few seconds and then go out, giving you time to check that the displays are all operational. There will also be a few other system checks to make, depending upon the aircraft configuration.

The next step is to insert your present position. This is very important, as mentioned earlier. The unit must know where it is starting from in order to know where it is going.

To do this, you turn the display switch (the large knob on the lower left of the CDU) to POS, as shown in Fig. 25-1. The first thing you should note is that the lights in the left display indicate the unit number (211). The program number (in this case 40 for the basic program and –4 for the program update) should be in the right display.

You then enter the coordinates of your present position. Using those illustrated, you would push the N for north. The left display will be all blanks except for the N and the degrees, decimals, and minutes dots. The ENT (enter) button will be lit. Then you enter the latitude, from left to right. As you enter the numerals, they will appear to the right of the left display, moving to the left as each new numeral is entered. Once you have them all entered, you should check that they are in the proper position relative to the degrees, decimals, and minutes dots. If they are, press the enter button.

Then press W and repeat the above procedure to enter the longitude. If you make an error during the entry, you can press the green CLR (clear) button and begin again. If the error is not discovered until after pressing the enter button, you can correct it by pressing the W and doing it all over again.

After the present position has been entered, you will note that the enter button remains lit. It will remain lit until the GMT and the date are entered. There will also be an amber DR in the annunciator window.

Rotate the display switch to the GMT-DAT position. Press the GMT button, note that the left display blanks, and enter the Greenwich Mean Time. This time is entered as hours, minutes, and tenths of minutes. The time 10 hours, 14.2 minutes would be entered as 1,0,1,4,2. I find it easier to listen to a time signal from the HF radio, or wait until my watch signals the exact minute before pushing ENT. This way I only enter four digits, the hour and minutes of the minute coming up.

With the display switch still in the GMT-DAT position, press the DAT button, check that the right display goes blank, and enter the date: March 16, 1999, would be 3,1,6,9,9. When the date is correct, press ENT again. This time the DR will still be lit, but the light in the enter button will go out, signifying that the initialization is complete.

LIGHTS

The lights in the annunciator window are all color coded, and the letters are placed vertically. The six lights are (left to right) ALR, DR, VLF, AMB, MAN, and WRN.

ALR means alert. It is amber and will come on when the aircraft is 1.5 minutes from the TO waypoint (WPT). If the mode selector is in the A (automatic) position, the light will go out when the track leg change is made. If the mode selector is in the M (manual) mode, the light will begin flashing one-half minute before reaching the WPT as a signal that you must manually change the track leg. At ground speeds below 100 knots, the light will not come on.

The DR (dead reckoning) light is also amber. It comes on when you turn the system on and enter the present position. It will stay on until the system NAV status gets down to 01, which indicates that the unit is receiving sufficient signals for navigation. The DR comes on again when the system can no longer navigate using Omega or VLF signals, or when the system is "relaning."

The VLF light is another amber light. This comes on when the unit is receiving fewer than three suitable Omega stations and the unit has started using VLF stations as backups.

The MAN (manual) annunciator is amber. This illuminates whenever you have entered true airspeed, magnetic heading, or cross-track offset figures manually. The manual entries must be returned to zero before the light will go out.

The WRN (warning) annunciator is red. If it is steady, the system has failed. If it is flashing, a subassembly failure or insufficient input data by the operator is indicated. It will also be accompanied by a malfunction code in the right display. You'll also see the red WRN during initial data loading of the unit. If you wait too long before finishing all of the initialization process, the WRN light will flash at you. It will go out as soon as the initialization has been completed.

If there is more than one malfunction, you can view the various failure codes by holding the HLD button down. Once you have viewed all codes, you can look them up in the operator's manual to determine what part of the unit failed.

After the unit is initialized, it is time to enter the waypoints. All WPTs are entered as lat/long coordinates. The unit can hold up to nine WPTs. If the flight plan includes more than nine, you have to enter the additional WPTs as the flight progresses.

To enter the WPTs, first turn the display knob to the WPT position. Then rotate the thumbwheel on the left of the CDU, labeled WPT, to the desired WPT number. Then enter the coordinates in the same manner that you entered the present position. It is very important to double-check all of the entries prior to beginning the flight. A one-digit error of the minute-unit entry would put you 1 mile off course at that WPT. A one-digit error of the minute-10s entry would put you 10 miles off at that WPT, and a one-digit error of the degrees-unit entry would put you 60 miles off at that WPT. If you are off by one-digit in the 10s units of the degrees entry, you would be inputting a 600-mile error.

This is very possibly what caused Korean Air 007 to stray over Russian airspace many years ago. It is definitely the error that caused two United States flag carriers to miss each other by only 50 feet (horizontally) over the Atlantic a few years back. They were so close that the radar altimeter of the higher aircraft sounded an alarm.

Bottom line: Whenever you manually input lat/long coordinates, *CHECK AND DOUBLE-CHECK* because one button pushed in error could put you way off course.

TAXI AND TAKEOFF

Once you've entered all WPTs and double-checked them for accuracy, you're ready to go. If you have two Omegas on board, as in the airlines, you can crossfill the WPTs of one from the other. First, the second Omega must be properly initialized. Then you turn the mode selector to R and push TK CHG (for track change), 1,1, and ENT. Within seconds, all of the WPTs from the first Omega will be transferred to the second.

WPT 0 is always the present position. The unit determines its position from whatever appears in the displays when you select POS with the display switch. Because you have loaded the ramp position during initialization, the ramp position will be WPT 0.

After you've loaded the Omega properly and while still at the ramp, it is normal to set the display switch to DIS-TIME and press TK CHG, the 0, followed by 1. The track window will display 01, and the distance from the ramp to the first WPT will appear in the left display; the time to get there will be in the right display (with the aircraft stationary, this time will be computed at a speed of 480 knots).

Once airborne, you can make use of all the other goodies available from the display switch.

After ATC clears you direct to WPT 1, make sure that the mode selector is in A and that the display switch is in any position except WPT or AUX. You will normally have it in DIS-TIME. Then press TK CHG, 0 for present position, and 1 for WPT 1. Press ENT, and you're on your way. The HSI will point to the new course, and the autopilot (if engaged) will turn the aircraft to proceed directly to WPT 1. This is illustrated in Fig. 25-2. You take off, turn to the right, perhaps to comply with the SID, begin a radar vector to the left, and then proceed direct to WPT 1.

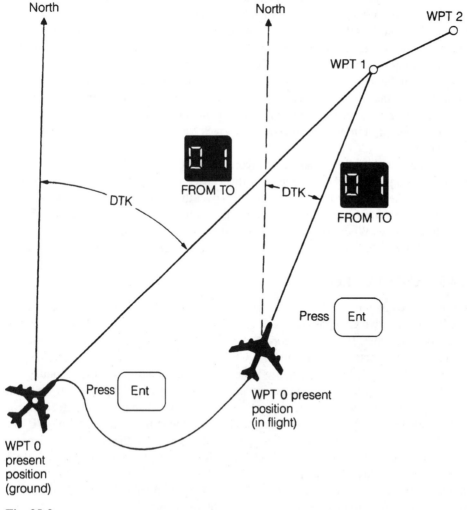

Fig. 25-2 Reproduced with permission of Litton Aero Products.

On the ground, the DTK (desired track) points from the ramp position to WPT 1. Once you're airborne and are cleared direct to WPT 1, you will have a different DTK because the present position 0 will have changed.

If the display switch is in the DIS-TIME position, the distance to WPT 1 will be in the left display, and the time to get there will be in the right display. If you want to know what time you will get to WPT 1, you can press the GMT button, and the time will change to read the GMT of arrival based on ground speed at that time.

Anytime you turn the display switch to POS, the present position will be displayed in the upper window. This position will keep changing as the aircraft moves. If you want to write the position (and the time) on your flight plan or give a position report, you will find it useful to press the green HLD button. This will freeze the position and the time (for display purposes only). Copy the position down, turn the display switch to GMT-DAT and copy the time down, then push the HLD button again. The green light will go out, and the displays will continue moving. The computer has been updating the time and position while the HLD button has been engaged.

While you are flying, the track window will be displaying the WPT you are flying from and the WPT you are flying toward. If for some reason you want to know how long it will take you to get to another WPT down the line or how far it is from where you are to another WPT, you can place the mode selector in R, the display switch in DIS-TIME, and then push TK CHG and enter the numbers corresponding to the WPTs you're interested in. For example, using Fig. 25-3, if you want to know how far it is from WPT 3, directly to WPT 5, and your present position is somewhere between 2 and 3, turn the mode selector to R, turn the display switch to DIS-TIME, push the TK CHG button, and then press 3 and 5; the distance will show up in the left display, and the time en route will show up in the right. The numbers in the track display will be flashing. Turning the mode selector knob back to A will cause the TO-FROM display to go back to the original 23.

ENROUTE OMEGA

You can use the same procedure to determine the distance from your present position to another position down the line by turning the mode selector to R and pressing the present position (0) and the WPT number you want.

If you are flying from WPT 1 to WPT 2 as shown in Fig. 25-4 and ATC clears you directly from present position to WPT 4, you would leave the mode selector in A, turn the display switch to any position except WPT or AUX, press the TK CHG button, then 0 for present position again, and 4 for where you want to go. Then press ENT. The track window will change to 04. The HSI will indicate the course change, and the autopilot will turn the aircraft to proceed directly to WPT 4. In Fig. 25-4, you can see the difference between the new and the original DTK.

If your flight plan had more than nine WPTs, you can start filling in the new WPTs once you are past WPT 2. You should never attempt to insert a new WPT into either the FROM or TO WPTs indicated in the track window.

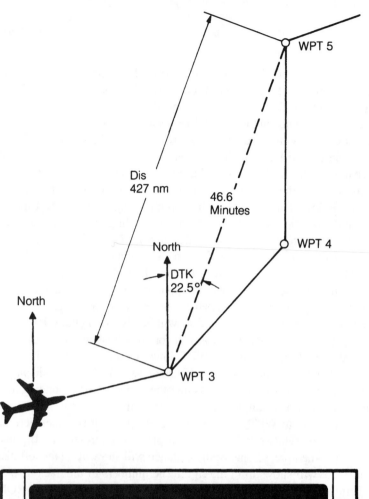

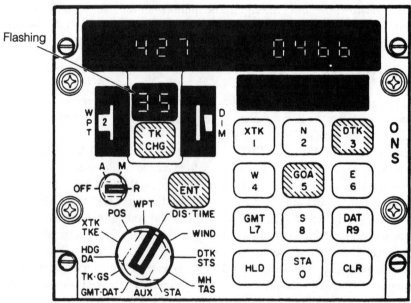

Fig. 25-3 Reproduced with permission of Litton Aero Products.

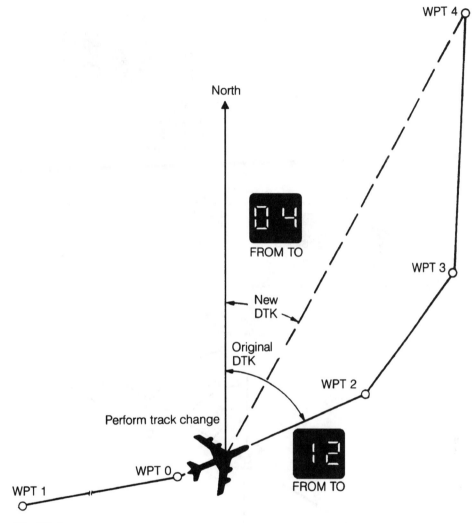

Fig. 25-4 Reproduced with permission of Litton Aero Products.

You can change the WPT coordinates of any WPT as long as those WPTs are not yet in the track display. As you can see in Fig. 25-5, the aircraft was flying from WPT 6 to WPT 7. They received a routing change, changing WPT 8. Because WPT 8 was not yet in the track window, the crew merely turned the display switch to WPT, turned the selector wheel to 8, and entered the new coordinates. Then the display switch was turned back to DIS-TIME and when the aircraft arrived at WPT 7, it automatically turned and flew to the new WPT 8.

You are on course and are proceeding from WPT 0 to WPT 1 (Fig. 25-6). You are at some point along the DTK shown as POS. You have a southeasterly wind component that requires you to crab into the wind, a little to the right of the DTK.

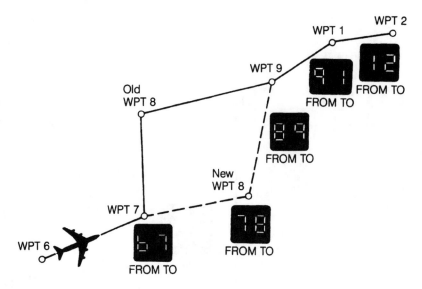

Fig. 25-5 Reproduced with permission of Litton Aero Products.

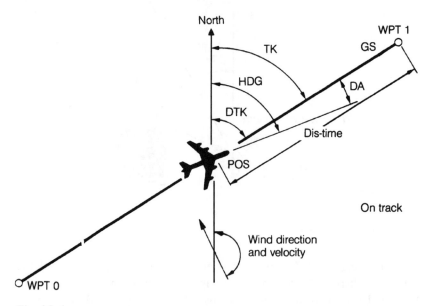

Fig. 25-6 Reproduced with permission of Litton Aero Products.

Now let's take a look at the rest of the information we can derive from the display switch positions. Start with the TK-GS (track angle-ground speed) position just above the GMT-DAT and work around the dial clockwise.

The reason this is called track angle rather than track is because the Omega can be installed to read out in either true or magnetic. Basically, the numerals in the left display indicate the ground track of the aircraft. The angle is measured clockwise from north through 359.9 degrees. The right display indicates the ground speed in knots. While you are on course, the DTK and TK are the same.

The next position on the dial is HDG/DA (heading drift angle). The heading can also be in either magnetic or true and is the actual longitudinal heading of the aircraft, also measured clockwise from north. The drift angle is the number of degrees that the aircraft's heading is to the track angle. This is shown as either left (L) or right (R) and can be a little confusing.

Let's say that the drift correction is 5 degrees to the right. The Omega would indicate the heading as referencing the aircraft's longitudinal axis. This might also be referenced as true or magnetic, depending on the configuration. The DA in this example would be shown as L 5.0 because the track angle is left of the heading.

Suppose that for some reason you are off course as seen in Fig. 25-7. Perhaps you took the autopilot off NAV and used the HDG control to deviate around a storm. Now you're using the HDG control to ease back up on the DTK.

In Fig. 25-7, you can see that the aircraft TK is not the same as the DTK. The aircraft has been turned to intercept the DTK.

The HDG is still right of the TK because the wind is still the same, and the DA is the same as pictured earlier for the same reason, the crosswind.

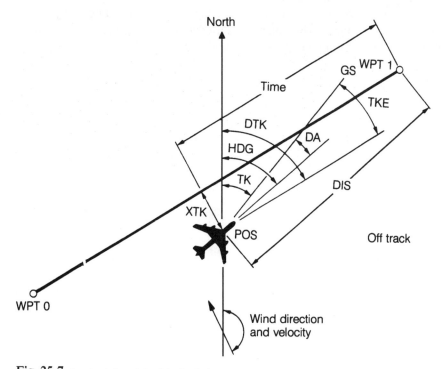

Fig. 25-7 Reproduced with permission of Litton Aero Products.

Turn the display switch to the XTK-TKE (cross-track distance and track-angle error) position.

The cross-track distance is the distance in nautical miles from the DTK to the aircraft position. As you can see in Fig. 25-6, it is measured perpendicularly.

The track-angle error is the angular difference between the DTK and the TK. This is helpful if you want to intercept the DTK at some desired angle, say 20 degrees.

If the aircraft is 5 miles right of the DTK, the left display would read R 5. To make a 20-degree intercept of the DTK, you know that you would have to turn somewhat to the left. How much? Until the TKE reads L 20. That will compensate for the DA as well.

In the WIND position, the left display will show the wind direction, and the right display will show the wind velocity, although the aircraft must have a TAS of more than 140 knots in order for the wind velocity to be displayed.

The DTK-SYS position will give you the DTK in the left display, and the system malfunction codes (if any) in the right display.

In the MH-TAS position, the left display will show the magnetic heading of the aircraft. This is useful if the configuration is for true. If it is for true, all indications mentioned earlier will be given in relation to true north, and this is the only magnetic north indication that you will have.

The right display will give you the true airspeed of the aircraft in knots.

The STA and AUX positions are used mostly to determine which signals are being received by the RPU, the quality of the signals, and a few other system checks.

Other functions are available to pilots using Omegas, including many manual insertions that can be made. This chapter has tried to review simpler automatic functions that are used to fly from point A to point B with Omega.

26
Inertial navigation

NAVIGATION WAS FAIRLY SIMPLE FOR THE EARLY CAVE DWELLERS. PLENTY of food and water was available. This gave them enough time to figure where they were, where they had come from, and where they were going.

As man ventured out to sea, he had to learn new ways to navigate: wind direction, wave direction, and birds sighted. The Polynesian and Micronesian navigators used relationships to various celestial bodies.

Centuries later the Europeans developed the basis of navigation. The early parallel sailing techniques worked satisfactorily for many centuries. The cumbersome lunar system of celestial navigation increased the accuracy somewhat.

This was further refined by John Hadley's octant in 1731, so a plumb bob was no longer needed. John Harrison's watch-machine helped solve the problem of longitude in the mid-1700s. The Sumner line of position was discovered by Captain Thomas E. Sumner on December 17, 1837. That and Nathaniel Bowditch's book *American Practical Navigator* simplified navigation still further. By that time, ships were able to navigate quite accurately and directly, if they could see the sky.

The advent of radar and consolan during World War II helped to improve the accuracy of navigation during all conditions. They were more than accurate enough for the speeds encountered. Loran-C works well in the areas where it is usable and sat/nav is useful around the world for surface vessels.

Long-range flight produced some new problems. During the recip days, celestial, DR, VOR, ADF, and consolan worked fine. Then came the advent of the jets. With their high speeds and fuel-hungry engines, the jets added a need for high speed navigation. True, these aircraft normally operate above 95 percent of the weather, but at 500-knot ground speeds the navigator must be fast and accurate.

Loran-C isn't useful in many parts of the world. At jet speeds, sat/nav fixes are too rare. Also, the accuracy of sat/nav is inversely proportional to the aircraft's speed. Omega works well, but it is subject to many problems that affect any type of radio transmission.

Enter *inertial navigation*, a navigation system that is completely self-contained, needing no link to any outside reference source.

HEAVYWEIGHT GUIDANCE

Scientists at the Massachusetts Institute of Technology (MIT) worked on and developed the first system back in the 1950s. At that time, it was extremely heavy. In fact, the first airborne system weighed in at 2,800 pounds. That might have been fine for the military, but that much weight is costly for civilian operators; it is the equivalent of 14 passengers.

The arrival of miniaturized computers and such inventions as Litton's ring laser gyro has helped bring the present weight of the system for civilian use down to 90 pounds. You can see the relative size of the entire package in Fig. 26-1. The versatility and accuracy of the system has improved, removing a lot of the potential for operator error. This has made it easier to use, especially in the aircraft cockpit, where navigation

Fig. 26-1. *Litton Aero Products LTN-92 INS.* Reproduced with permission of Litton Aero Products.

is only one of the tasks facing pilots. Additionally, its ability to interface with other navigation systems has increased its usability.

What, precisely, is inertial navigation? How does it operate? What problems were the scientists faced with, and how were they solved? I'll answer those questions as simply as possible.

Inertial navigation is based on Newton's second law of motion: Acceleration of a body is directly proportional to the forces acting on the body.

Remember your high school physics? Remember Newton's first law of motion? A body continues in a state of rest or uniform motion in a straight line unless acted upon by an external force. The "state of rest" was blown out the window by Einstein's theory of relativity. He proved that nothing is ever really "at rest." Everything is constantly moving. After all, the Earth never stops rotating, does it? This is just one of the problems that the INS scientists had to work with.

If it is possible to measure the velocity of a vehicle and then multiply that velocity by time, we would be on our way to determining its location. Isn't that one of the first steps in DR? The first step of all, of course, is to determine our starting point, but we'll get to that later.

What is velocity? How can we measure it absolutely, with no outside input? Simply stated, velocity is a time-rate-of-change of position. It doesn't matter what we're measuring. It could be a ship, a plane, or a person. It is still necessary to measure the velocity (feet-per-second) and multiply that by time to arrive at the distance covered.

Velocity remains constant without acceleration. The velocity will change depending on the amount of acceleration, and this can be positive or negative. Remember Newton's second law.

PROBLEM SOLVING

To measure the velocity, we have to start with an acceleration. To do this we use an accelerometer. In fact, in an inertial navigation system, we find three accelerometers. They are placed perpendicular to each other, one in each plane of motion. One is for roll, the second for pitch, and the third for yaw.

There are many types of accelerometers. For our explanation, we will look at a simple one. This is nothing more than a weight (mass), inside a cylinder. This weight is centered by a spring on each end. When the accelerometer (or the body it is attached to) is stationary or at a constant velocity, the mass is centered. If the accelerometer moves, the mass will try to remain stationary. In doing so, it will deflect a spring. The mass will continue to displace the spring until the acceleration stops and the accelerometer is once again at a constant velocity. When this occurs, the mass will once again be centered. The system operates somewhat like your inner ear.

If the springs are connected to an electrical pickup that is sensitive to various pressures, we can measure the acceleration. Once measured, the acceleration is sent through two integrators. The first integrator takes the acceleration in feet-per-second-per-second and multiplies it by time. The resulting figure is the velocity. The velocity is measured in feet-per-second. The second integrator multiplies the velocity by time, and the result is a distance. It can be in feet, or statute miles, or nautical miles, or any other distance measurement we wish to use.

If we measure the distance by two accelerometers, each one 90 degrees to the other, we can also determine the direction the body has moved. We call one of these accelerometers the *X axis*. The other is the *Y axis*. By telling the computer our starting position, it will then know where we are at any moment of time.

There are numerous other problems involved. If you are on a ship at anchor and the ship begins rolling in a ground swell, the accelerometers would sense movement. They would think that the ship was being displaced. The same holds true in an aircraft. When the aircraft rotates for liftoff, gravity pulls the accelerometer in the pitch plane. This gives it a false sense of acceleration.

To prevent these false signals, the accelerometers are set in *gimbals*. The platform that the accelerometers are on is the center of these gimbals, and this platform is kept level by gyroscopes. Like the accelerometers, the gyroscopes are mounted on the three axes of the platform. You know that gyroscopes want to remain upright. You used to play with tops when you were growing up; as long as they were spinning, they would remain upright. Likewise, once the gyroscopes are up to speed, they want to remain upright. When their case tries to move, a signal is generated, which is sent to a gimbal drive motor, which then forces the gimbal back to level to cancel the effects of gravity. As far as the INS knows, it is only moving laterally across the earth.

This would all be fine if the Earth were flat, or if the INS were heading into outer space. Unfortunately, the Earth is round, and the INS platform must be made to remain level with the Earth's surface. This is a function of the radius of the Earth, and even that is far from uniform. This correction is termed *transport rate compensation* and is part of the computer programming.

There is still another problem to be overcome, and that is the rate at which the Earth revolves. This rate of rotation is 15.04 degrees per hour. What we really want to compensate for, however, is the vertical and horizontal components of the earth's rotation. We are looking for the earth's *angular velocity vector*. The 15.04 degrees per hour is only felt at the equator. The rate reduces to zero as we travel toward either pole. Think about it for awhile. At the equator, the gyro platform is level with the Earth at one point of time. It will tilt, in relation to the Earth, as the Earth rotates. At the poles, however, even though the Earth is rotating, the gyro platform will always be horizontal.

Remember the integrators that come off the accelerometers? These signals are also used to make the compensations I have just mentioned. The computer takes the velocity of the body and divides it by the Earth's radius to arrive at the angular rate. The velocity is taken off the first integrator. The distance comes off the second integrator. The distance is applied to the starting position to determine the current latitude. This correction figure is the Earth rate multiplied by the cosine of the latitude.

The two correction figures are then combined to create a signal that is sent to the gyro, the *gyro torquing signal*. It is applied to a gyro torquer, which applies a torque to the gyro platform. This results in another signal being applied to the gimbal drive motor. This signal keeps the gimbal level in respect to the Earth's surface.

Two other corrections that must be made are for Coriolis effects and centrifugal effects.

It takes about 15 minutes for an aircraft INS system to align itself. The aircraft cannot be moved during this alignment process. The INS must first level itself and then align itself with true north. This latter phase is called *gyrocompassing*. In reality, it is a little more complicated than that. If the accelerometer is aligned to true north, it would tend to dip too much as the aircraft flew near the poles. Instead, it uses a system that is called *wander azimuth operation*.

In the wander angle system, the platform angle will change in relation to true north. This is due to the convergence and divergence of the lines of longitude. This means that the X and Y platforms of the INS are not actually pointed N-S and E-W.

The operator enters the present location while the INS is aligning itself. The more accurate the input of present location is, the more accurate the results will be. This is so important that each gate at an airport terminal has its own position.

So far we've seen the basis of a regular, heavy, internal navigation system. Of course, it's much more complex than that.

LIGHTWEIGHT GUIDANCE

The next task the manufacturers had was to make it lighter. One way was to eliminate the gimbals and mount the gyros and accelerometers directly to the frame, a *strap-down* INS system. First, though, digital computers had to be reduced in size. Another problem: A gyro had to be developed that could be operated in any plane of reference.

Litton solved the second problem by developing the ring laser gyro. The theory of the ring laser gyro was developed more than 60 years ago. It is two contrarotating co-linear light beams in a closed optical cavity. This is called a *sagnac interferometer*. It was used to measure the rotation of the Earth back in 1925. The only problem then was its size. A one-quarter wavelength device used a square interferometer that was 450 meters (about a quarter mile) on each side.

The theory of the sagnac interferometer is simple enough. A beam of light is introduced into the cavity. At the entry point, it goes through a beam splitter. One part of the beam goes clockwise. The other part goes counterclockwise. These beams are directed around the interior of the cavity by mirrors. Provided nothing has moved, both beams of light will arrive back at the starting point at the same moment. If the interferometer rotates at all, one beam will arrive before the other. The amount of motion can be determined by measuring that difference of time. Remember that the purpose of these gyros is to cancel the effects of gravity on the accelerometers.

To get a picture of how the sagnac interferometer works, imagine yourself looking down at a baseball diamond. Put a reflector at each of the bases with a beam splitter at home plate. If a beam of light is focused on the beam splitter from somewhere behind the plate, the splitter will be designed so that the light beam is split, sending one beam toward the reflector at third base, and the second toward the reflector at first base.

The beam going to third base will be reflected to second, then to first, and back to the beam splitter. The beam going to first base will do just the opposite, both meeting back at home plate if there was no rotation.

Back at the beam splitter at home plate, these arriving beams will be sent through a prism so that they arrived aimed directly at their own photodiodes. If there were any rotation, one beam would arrive at a different time than the other, thereby giving you the time/distance necessary to figure acceleration.

When scientists learned to work with lasers, it became possible to bring the size of the interferometer down to 28 centimeters per side. Three-ring laser gyros, their associated accelerometers, and their computers all fit in a box that weighs 57 pounds. The entire unit measures 10.12 inches wide, 8.62 inches high, and 19.98 inches long. In addition, its accuracy is within 0.4 degrees of true heading. It can present a ground speed within plus or minus 8 knots. That's in an aircraft that is flying at somewhere around 500 nautical miles per hour.

These facts are interesting by themselves. We are living in exciting times. Lasers and microchips have changed our world faster in 10 years, than science did in 100 years previously. If the civilians have this much, you wonder what the military must have to work with? What will we have 10 years from now when the TOP SECRET covers are removed?

OPERATION AND MANAGEMENT

By looking again at the CPU in Fig. 26-1, you can see that there are more buttons on the unit than on the Omega, but the switches have been removed. Also, instead of three annunciator windows, the INS has one larger window that displays five lines of information with 16 characters per line. There are four small, vertical annunciator windows, two on either side of the display.

Like the loran discussed in chapter 24, the INS memory has numerous pages that can be brought up on the display. Like both the loran and the Omega systems, the INS must have a proper initialization.

The INS is so accurate that it will read out the aircraft ground speed when taxiing. But that accuracy can also be a trap because with any computer the phrase "garbage in, garbage out" is true.

There are many times that the operator can input incorrect information, and if he or she does, incorrect navigational directions will occur.

Like Omega, the INS is designed for long-range overwater navigation where there are no landmarks below to check on the progress of the flight and the accuracy of the flight path; therefore, it is imperative that the inputs be made with extreme accuracy. A system of checks and double checks cannot be overemphasized.

It is always best to have two pilots perform these procedures. When entering waypoint information, one pilot will usually enter the information from the flight plan. The other pilot should be comparing the flight plan's waypoint coordinates to enroute charts and then double-checking that the coordinates have been entered correctly.

The reason the second pilot should do the double-checking is that if the pilot who installs the coordinates makes an error, it is human nature to misread the error as being the correct entry. If a second pilot is not available to do the double check, then the pilot who made the entries should go on with other tasks to clear his or her mind of waypoint coordinates and then do the double-checking after the mind clears.

I won't go into any actual operation because the INS does everything that Omega does, and more. There are 28 different menus to choose from, each of which has more than one page connected with it, and it would take a complete book to explain it all. For now I just want to give you an overview of what you might be working with as time goes on in your flying career.

27
GPS

THE SPACE AGE IS REALLY UPON US. THE *GLOBAL POSITIONING SYSTEM* (GPS) that was merely a dream a short time ago is now up and fully operational. In 1991, although the system was incomplete and would be inoperable for up to 4 hours a day, I was able to use a hand-held unit to navigate a yacht under the Golden Gate Bridge in fog so thick that the first my passenger and I saw of the bridge was the span itself, *when we were directly underneath it.*

The most senior FAA navigational inspector told me in the early 1990s that it would be a long time before the FAA would accept GPS as being safe for aviation use. Recall that an air carrier demonstrated the accuracy of GPS in 1994, 5 years ahead of schedule, by making more than 170 fully coupled (autoland) landings using GPS for both vertical and horizontal guidance, and each landing touched down within 10 feet of each other.

It is generally accepted that the rapid completion of the GPS constellation was caused by the necessity of accurate navigation in the desert during the Persian Gulf War. In any event, it's here, and it looks like it's here to stay. Not only is GPS here to stay, but it is generally believed that within 10 to 20 years, GPS will make all other types of navigation obsolete, and the other types will go the way of the lighted and Adcock ranges.

GPS APPROVAL

Since the middle of 1993, the FAA has allowed GPS to be used for enroute navigation as well as for "overlay" approaches to be flown using TSO C129 GPS avionics certified for nonprecision approaches, provided the procedure is retrievable from airborne navigation databases (such as the Jeppesen NavData Services). By the middle of 1994, the FAA had issued the first three "stand-alone" GPS approaches (Fig. 27-1). These approaches are completely new, and do not overlie existing approaches.

Figure 27-2 illustrates how Jeppesen identifies both a stand-alone and an overlay GPS approach. Another important illustration to notice is the way Jeppesen identifies its database identifiers (see the lower illustration in Fig. 27-2). Prior to October 1994, the identifiers were in italic type within parentheses. These have been changed to italic type with square brackets.

Figure 27-3 illustrates how GPS waypoints are incorporated into various portions of approaches. One thing to note is the Sensor FAF in the last two illustrations. An important fact here is that Jeppesen shows the distance from the Sensor FAF to the missed approach point.

GPS DEMYSTIFIED

With the foregoing in mind, just what is GPS, and how does it work? Basically, GPS is made up of a constellation of 24 satellites. Twenty-one of the satellites are required to provide three-dimensional navigational capability, 24 hours a day, anywhere in the world. The other three birds are used as spares. These satellites are in fixed orbits at about 10,900 miles high. Each satellite circles the Earth twice daily; this places each one over a monitoring station twice a day. The monitoring station will in turn update the positions of the satellites.

Because the satellites will know where they are all the time, they will then be able to tell us where we are after the onboard computer has four of them in range. I tend to compare getting a satellite fix to getting a three-star fix in celestial navigation. Perhaps a short introduction to celestial navigation will help you understand the concept. Too many pilots fly transoceanic with no real conception of latitude and longitude nor their relationship to each other. This short introduction into celestial navigation might help you to better understand these concepts.

GREAT CIRCLES

Look at Fig. 27-4. This is a circle representing a great circle of the Earth. It has no relationship to compass directions because *a "great circle" is any circle that cuts through the center of the Earth*, so for the time being, do not confuse yourself with thinking in terms of north, south, east, or west.

All lines of longitude are great circles. The only line of latitude that is a great circle is the equator. All other lines of latitude are parallel to the equator; thus, they are called "parallels." An unlimited number of great circles cut the lines of latitude and longitude at various angles. Remember, any line that cuts through the center of the Earth, *no matter what the orientation to the compass*, is a great circle.

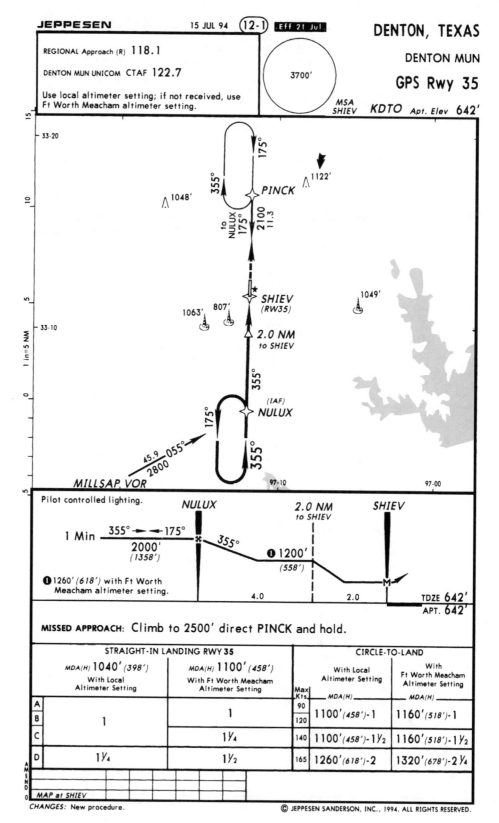

REGIONAL Approach (R) 118.1

DENTON MUN UNICOM CTAF 122.7

Use local altimeter setting; if not received, use
Ft Worth Meacham altimeter setting.

3700'

MSA
SHIEV   KDTO Apt. Elev 642'

175°

355°   175°

PINCK   1122'

1048'

to
NULUX   175°   2100
                 11.3

SHIEV
(RW35)

1063'   807'   1049'

2.0 NM
to SHIEV

355°

(IAF)

175°   NULUX

355°

45.9 055°
2800

MILLSAP VOR   97-10   97-00

Pilot controlled lighting.

NULUX   2.0 NM   SHIEV
               to SHIEV

1 Min   355° ⟶ ⟵ 175°
        2000'   355°
        (1358')   ❶ 1200'
                              (558')

❶ 1260' (618') with Ft Worth
  Meacham altimeter setting.   4.0   2.0

TDZE 642'
APT. 642'

MISSED APPROACH: Climb to 2500' direct PINCK and hold.

STRAIGHT-IN LANDING RWY 35		Max Kts	CIRCLE-TO-LAND	
MDA(H) 1040' (398') With Local Altimeter Setting	MDA(H) 1100' (458') With Ft Worth Meacham Altimeter Setting		With Local Altimeter Setting MDA(H)	With Ft Worth Meacham Altimeter Setting MDA(H)
A	1	90	1100'(458')-1	1160'(518')-1
B		120	1100'(458')-1	1160'(518')-1
C	1¼	140	1100'(458')-1½	1160'(518')-1½
D 1¼	1½	165	1260'(618')-2	1320'(678')-2¼

MAP at SHIEV

CHANGES: New procedure.

Fig. 27-1 Reproduced with permission of Jeppesen Sanderson, Inc. Not for use in navigation.

APPROACH CHART LEGEND
GPS APPROACH CHARTS

This GPS Approach Chart Legend supplements the standard approach chart legend beginning on Introduction Page 101. Equipment requirements, database requirements, and requirement or non-requirement for monitoring conventional navaids are not addressed in this legend-Refer to Jeppesen Air Traffic Control (ATC) pages for this information. [For the United States, refer to the Jeppesen Navigation Aids pages of the Airman's Information Manual.]

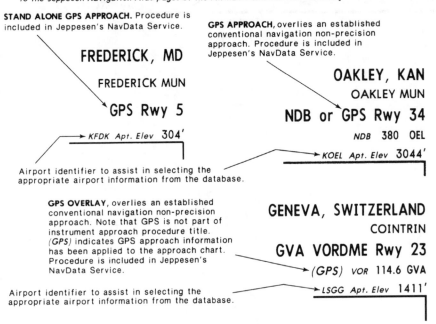

STAND ALONE GPS APPROACH. Procedure is included in Jeppesen's NavData Service.

FREDERICK, MD

FREDERICK MUN

GPS Rwy 5

KFDK *Apt. Elev* 304'

Airport identifier to assist in selecting the appropriate airport information from the database.

GPS APPROACH, overlies an established conventional navigation non-precision approach. Procedure is included in Jeppesen's NavData Service.

OAKLEY, KAN

OAKLEY MUN

NDB or GPS Rwy 34

NDB 380 OEL

KOEL *Apt. Elev* 3044'

GPS OVERLAY, overlies an established conventional navigation non-precision approach. Note that GPS is not part of instrument approach procedure title. *(GPS)* indicates GPS approach information has been applied to the approach chart. Procedure is included in Jeppesen's NavData Service.

Airport identifier to assist in selecting the appropriate airport information from the database.

GENEVA, SWITZERLAND

COINTRIN

GVA VORDME Rwy 23

(GPS) VOR 114.6 GVA

LSGG *Apt. Elev* 1411'

Jeppesen database identifiers are always shown in italic type. They are enclosed within square brackets, as [D255G], or prior to October 1994 within parentheses, as (D255G).

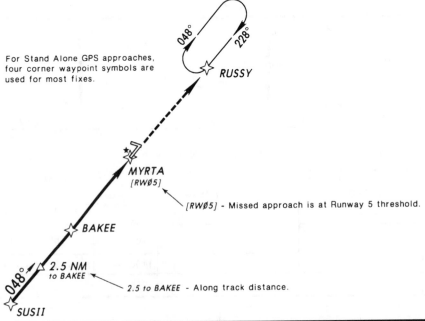

For Stand Alone GPS approaches, four corner waypoint symbols are used for most fixes.

RUSSY

048°   228°

MYRTA
[RW05]

[RW05] - Missed approach is at Runway 5 threshold.

BAKEE

048°   2.5 NM
to BAKEE

2.5 to BAKEE - Along track distance.

SUSII

Fig. 27-2

APPROACH CHART LEGEND
GPS APPROACH CHARTS (continued)

For "NDB or GPS" type approaches and for GPS overlays, waypoint symbol is used mostly for fixes that would otherwise be shown as position fixes with no triangle fix symbol or for added database fixes not part of the conventional non-precision navigation approach.

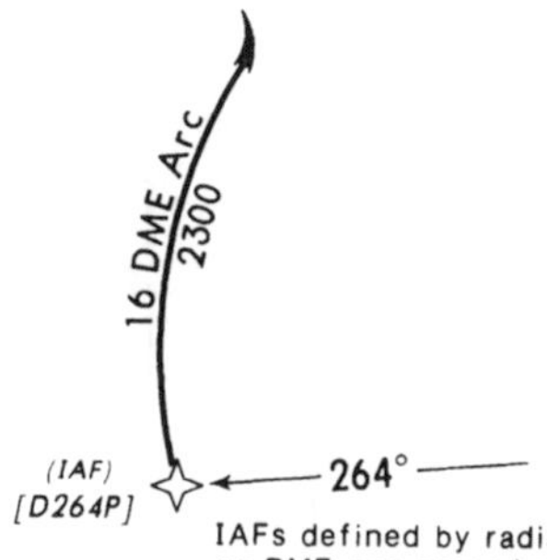

16 DME Arc
2300

(IAF)
[D264P]   ◇ ←──── 264° ────

IAFs defined by radials on DME arc procedures.

Turn points where headings or courses intersect courses between IAF and FAF.

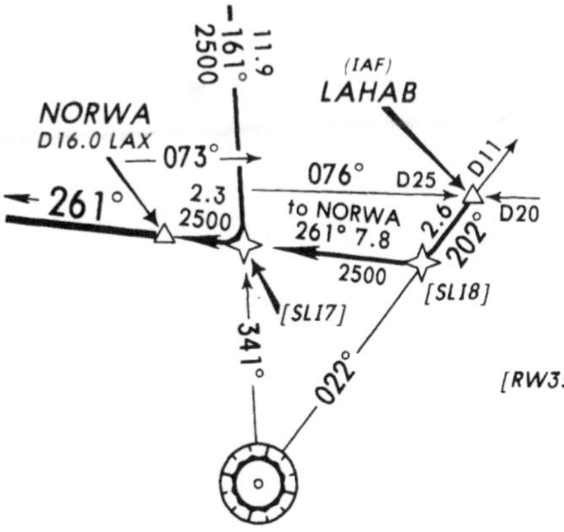

11.9
161°
2500

(IAF)
LAHAB

NORWA
D16.0 LAX   073°   076°   D25   D11

──── 261°   2.3   to NORWA   2.6   D20
              2500   261° 7.8   202°
              2500

[SL17]   [SL18]

341°

022°

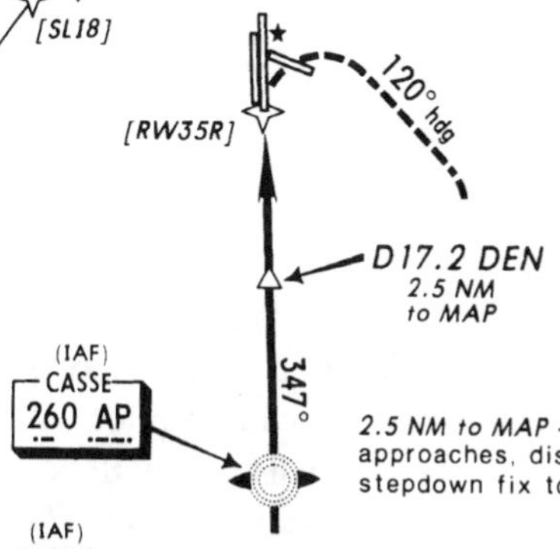

[RW35R]   120° hdg

D17.2 DEN
2.5 NM
to MAP

347°

(IAF)
┌─CASSE─┐
│ 260 AP │
└────────┘

2.5 NM to MAP - For timed approaches, distance from stepdown fix to MAP is included.

(IAF)
┌─RAPIDS─┐
│ 407 RZZ │
└─────────┘

Sensor FAFs ❶ on No-FAF procedures.

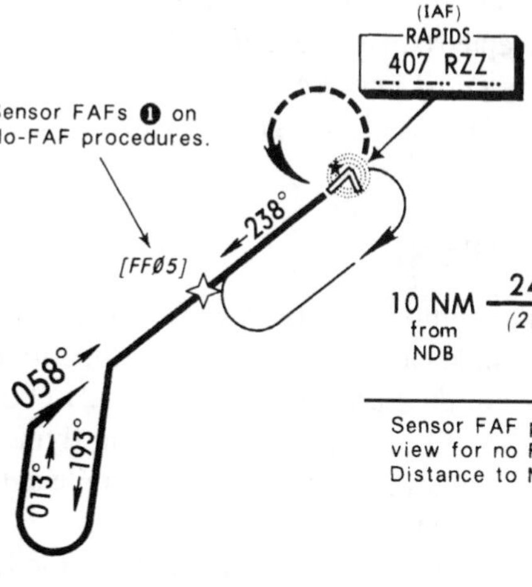

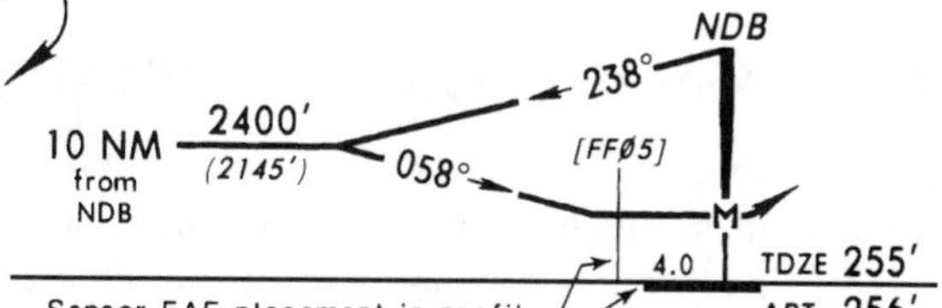

238°

[FF05]

NDB

10 NM   2400'   238°
from   (2145')   058°   [FF05]
NDB

058°   M

013°   193°   4.0   TDZE 255'
                                APT. 256'

Sensor FAF placement in profile view for no FAF procedures. Distance to MAP is included.

❶ Definition: A Sensor FAF is a final approach waypoint created and added to the database sequence of waypoints to support GPS navigation of a published, no FAF, non-precision approach. The Sensor FAF is included in Jeppesen's NavData waypoint sequence and included in the plan and profile views of no FAF non-precision approach charts. In some cases, a step down fix, recognized by a charted database identifier, may serve as the Sensor FAF.

Fig. 27-3 Reproduced with permission of Jeppesen Sanderson, Inc. Not for use in navigation.

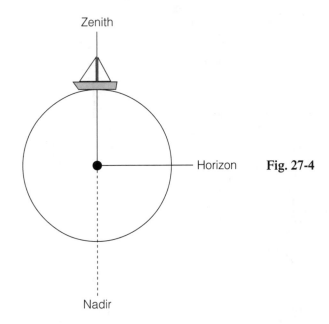

Fig. 27-4

A great circle is the shortest route between two points on the Earth, and most long-range navigation systems will provide a pilot with great-circle routes. The nearer a route is to east and west, the more distance will be saved by flying a great-circle route. Until now, all of your flying has been between VORs, which has been flown at a constant compass heading (wind correction excepted). In a great circle, the compass heading is constantly changing, although for practical purposes, great-circle flight plans usually update headings at regular intervals such as each degree, 5 degrees, or 10 degrees, depending on aircraft speed.

RELATIONSHIP OF ARC TO DISTANCE

A circle, as in Fig. 27-4, is 360 degrees in circumference. Each degree of arc is made up of 60 minutes, which means that a full circle can be converted to 21,600 minutes. Give or take a few miles, the circumference of the Earth at the equator is 21,600 nautical miles. Recall that a statute mile is 5,280 feet in length. In instrument flying, you will be using the nautical mile, which is 1.15 times longer than a statute mile at 6,076 feet. For simplicity, we round that down to 6,000 feet.

One degree of arc along the equator (or along any other great circle on the Earth) is equal to 60 nautical miles; therefore, 1 minute of a degree of arc on a great circle equals 1 nautical mile. One minute of a degree on a line of latitude will vary in length from 1 nautical mile at the equator to zero at the North or South Pole where all of the lines of longitude converge. If you are flying along a great-circle route, you can calculate the distance in your head. If you are not on a great-circle route, you will have to use the conversion scale on the chart.

PRIMER OF CELESTIAL NAVIGATION

Refer to Fig. 27-4 again. In order to determine a position on the Earth using celestial navigation, it is first necessary to determine the height of a celestial body above the horizon: Sun, Moon, Venus, Mars, Saturn, Jupiter, or any of 76 navigational stars. From any point on Earth (in this case, the boat in Fig. 27-4), the point directly overhead is called the *zenith* (Z). The point on the opposite side of the Earth is called the *nadir*. The horizon is where the Earth and sky join, which is 90 degrees from the zenith; this is applicable to all in all directions. The arc of this 90-degree circle is 5,400 nautical miles in length (90 × 60).

Examine Fig. 27-5. Let's use a sextant to determine that the height of a star is 30 degrees above the horizon. The illustration indicates that the angle is being measured from the center of the Earth because the distance to any celestial body is so much greater than the radius of the Earth that for all intents and purposes the center of the Earth can be assumed for our position. Corrections are made for this and other anomalies when the sights are reduced.

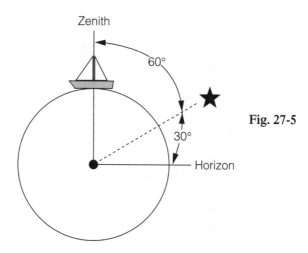

Fig. 27-5

The point on the Earth directly underneath the celestial body is termed the *geographical position* (GP).

Subtracting the height of the body (30 degrees) from the 90-degree arc between the zenith and the horizon will result in the *zenith distance* (ZD). In this case, the ZD is 60 degrees of arc, which equals 3,600 miles (if converted into distance), which will be the distance from the GP to the boat.

The GP of the body at the exact second the shot was taken can be determined from the *Nautical Almanac*. If you had a long enough string, by knowing the exact latitude/longitude of the GP, you could pin one end of the string to the GP and scribe a circle. This circle would be called a *circle of equal altitudes* (COEA) because no matter where you were on that circle, the altitude of the body would be the same (30 degrees).

The circle is also called a *circle of equal radius* (COER). The term used would depend on whether it is referring to the altitude of the body or the distance from the GP on the Earth. The boat, therefore, would have to be somewhere on that circle. The circle could also be referred to as a *circle of position* (COP), and if we were to transcribe a small portion of a circle of that magnitude onto a chart, the result would be a straight line, which would be called a *line of position* (LOP).

If this procedure were repeated using two celestial objects, two COEAs would result, as can be seen in Fig. 27-6. Note that these circles will cross at two points: A and B. Obviously, if the boat had to be somewhere on the first COEA, it would also have to be somewhere on the second, which means that it will have to be at either point A or point B, and because these points will usually be many miles apart, the navigator would know which point the boat was on.

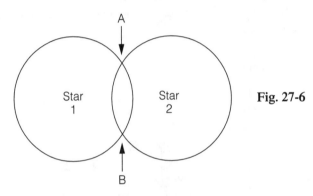

Fig. 27-6

A number of factors can affect the accuracy of that position. So to attain the greatest accuracy, the navigator will take a third shot on another object, which is called a *three-star fix* (Fig. 27-7).

Theoretically, these three COERs would all cross at one position, which, if the bodies shot were properly chosen, would cancel out all errors, resulting in a perfect fix.

This is rarely the case, however, and the navigator usually ends up with what is called a "cocked hat," as in Fig. 27-8. The navigator then applies rules of logic and her own experience to determine a more precise position.

TIMING IS CRUCIAL

Just as the navigator knows the GP of the various bodies from the tables in the *Nautical Almanac*, the GPS receiver knows where the satellites are because the receiver's computer "builds an almanac" from information received from the satellites themselves, which you recall are updated from the master ground stations twice daily.

By measuring the length of time it takes the satellite signal to reach the receiver, the receiver's computer knows how far away it is from each satellite. By knowing the distance from the satellite and knowing where the satellite is from the information in

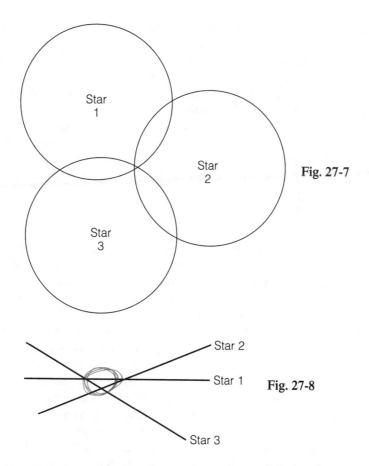

Fig. 27-7

Fig. 27-8

the "almanac," the computer "draws" a COER around the GP of the satellite. This is exactly the same thing the navigator does when she draws a LOP of a celestial shot.

It gets a little more complicated than that though. In order for the receiver to know how long the signal took to get down from the satellite, it has to know exactly when the signal was sent. After all, the signals travel at the speed of light, which is 186,000 miles per second, so we're speaking in terms of short time periods here. (Understanding time periods in nanoseconds is about like trying to really comprehend the size of the United States's deficit. Still and all, it's duck soup for the computers.)

The satellites have very expensive atomic clocks onboard to assure the proper timing of the signals. If the same expensive clocks were put in the receivers, only the government could afford them. For this reason, quartz clocks are used in the receivers, which requires adding one extra satellite to the equation to compensate for the difference in time measurements that the receiver's clock might end up with.

The way it works: If the receiver gets a signal from two satellites, it will figure out two LOPs, just as celestial navigators do from two stars. In the case of the navigator, if her watch or clock has a 10-second error in it when she "shoots the stars," she will be more than 3 miles away from where the LOPs cross. This would occur because the Earth rotates at a rate of about 1 mile every 4 seconds. This error can be reduced by taking a three-star fix as previously mentioned.

The same thing is true of the satellites. To correct for the time error, the GPS receiver will use three satellites in the two-dimensional mode and four satellites in the three-dimensional mode. To simplify it, in the 2-D mode (latitude and longitude only), if there is an error in the clocks, the three LOPs won't cross in one spot. They'll end up with some sort of cocked hat. The receiver's computer then begins adjusting the times (by use of algebraic equations) until the LOPs do cross in one spot, which is the exact position. In the 3-D mode (which pilots are more interested in), the addition of a fourth satellite provides altitude information.

GPS ERRORS

Other factors will affect the accuracy of GPS receivers. One of these is that the speed of light varies as it goes through the atmosphere. This might result in a receiver error of up to 12 feet. The clock error alone might add up to 2 feet. Built-in receiver errors might come to another 4 feet, the worst-case satellite-selection errors might add another 25 feet, and the ephemeris error will result in 2 more feet. All of this adds up to somewhere between 10 and 30 feet of error. One other error has until recently prevented GPS from being used for precision IFR approaches: *selective availability* (SA).

Two frequencies are used by the satellites. The *precision code* (P-code) is used by the military, and the *course acquisition code* (C/A-code) is used by the public. The military can arbitrarily induce an error into the C/A-code, which can impart an error of up to 300 feet without the user being aware of it. Naturally, an error of this magnitude would prevent the pilot from using GPS for a precision approach.

To overcome this, ground stations are being provided that "know" their position precisely. This ground station will then derive its own GPS position, recognize any error, and then transmit that difference to the user's receiver so that the receiver's computer will then be able to give a precise location with repeatable accuracy of within 3–10 meters (roughly 10–30 feet). This is called *differential GPS* (DGPS). It is this precision that is enabling aircraft to make fully-coupled autopilot landings, and which, someday, will make all other types of navigation obsolete.

ARNAV Systems, Inc. has two types of GPS receivers available. The first type uses a separate receiver (GPS-506) that interfaces with the FMS-5000 or R-5000 receiver. This combination will provide the pilot with either a loran or GPS position, whichever signal is deemed most accurate. The pilot can also manually select either mode of navigation. The three-dimensional accuracy in the GPS mode (without SA) is within 15 meters horizontally and 90 feet vertically.

The second GPS available from ARNAV is the pure GPS receiver, the STAR 5000 (Fig. 27-9). The only physical difference between this receiver and the FMS-5000 is apparently the name on the lower right-hand side, the letters "GPS" on the upper left-hand side, and the absence of the "XR" light on the STAR 5000. The operation of the STAR 5000 is basically the same as mentioned in chapter 24.

Fig. 27-9. *ARNAV Systems Inc., STAR 5000 GPS Receiver.* ARNAV Systems, Inc.

EXCITING FUTURE

Instrument flying and navigation came a long way in the 32 years that I was associated with flying, from the Adcock ranges to the hand-cranked (coffee grinder) VOR receivers, through INS, OMEGA, loran, and now GPS systems. Cockpits have evolved from hands-on flying to heading-only autopilots to fully coupled autoland systems to fully coupled flight management systems that will control the aircraft from shortly after takeoff through the landing and turning off the runway (on properly equipped aircraft and airports). Many of these ramifications are already finding their way into general aviation.

It boggles the mind to even begin to think of what the future holds. It almost makes me wish that I could begin my career anew, but then I think of the joke told by a late-night TV-show host. Cockpits of next-generation aircraft will have only one pilot and one dog. The job of the pilot will be to feed the dog. The job of the dog will be to bite the hand of the pilot if he or she tries to touch anything.

Whatever happens, enjoy what comes, but above all, *do it safely*, so that in another 30 years you too will be able to reminisce about your career and wonder what the future will hold.

Dos and don'ts

THAT'S ABOUT IT. WE'VE COVERED INSTRUMENT FLYING FROM THE BASIC principles through practically every type of approach and even looked at some of the more advanced navigational equipment you might eventually be working with.

To wrap it all up, let's review some of the more important dos and don'ts as they relate to instrument flying.

DOs

* Do learn to fly the basic maneuvers well before thinking about approaches.

* Do thoroughly study every current approach chart for every airport you will be using as a destination or alternate. Use a highlighter to mark salient features such as the minimums for your category of aircraft, the missed approach procedures, and other important data.

* Do check all current NOTAMs.

* Do keep abreast of all changes that might occur in the symbols used on the charts.

* Do complete the descent checklist before initiating the approach. It would be very embarrassing to have your engine quit inside the outer marker because your mixture was still leaned out.

* Do get the latest weather before initiating an approach to ascertain whether or not the airport is above your minimums. It will also give you an idea of what to expect when you break out.

* Do identify every navaid you use. Make it standard practice to leave the speaker turned up on your primary navigational radio. If at anytime you stop hearing the maddening identifier, you'll know that you've got problems.

* Do work to improve the speed of your instrument scan. The more effective and rapid your scan becomes, the more accurate your approach will be.

* Do have the proper approach plate handy. As you've seen, some airports have many different approaches, and sometimes the approach names sound similar.

* Do lower the landing gear and perform the prelanding checklist when you cross the final approach fix inbound.

* Do use every bit of functioning navigational equipment you have on board. It won't do you a bit of good if you suddenly need it and it has be turned on and tuned.

* Do be sure to check, understand, and respect the weather. Remember that your instrument ticket has been issued to you not only because you have proven that you know how to fly on the gauges, but also because you have shown that you can exercise common sense and that you know that there is some weather out there that you really shouldn't be fooling around with. You don't have to get anywhere so badly that you should take unnecessary risks. No appointment is so valuable that it's worth dying over.

* Do practice instrument procedures and instrument flying at every opportunity. The more you practice, the better you become, but you become very rusty very quickly when you don't use your skills. Maintain your currency according to regulations.

* Do be very careful when loading information into any navigational equipment, but especially when inserting latitude and longitude coordinates into any area navigation unit. Check and double-check everything you enter.

DON'TS

* Don't chase the needles on any approach, especially on the localizer or glide slope.

* Don't be afraid to make a missed approach. In fact, just as you program your thinking to the possibility of an abort on each takeoff, you should program your thinking for a missed approach on each approach. You don't have to wait until you get all the way to your MDA before you pull up. If at any time you feel that you're getting confused or behind your aircraft, pull up. Get some altitude under you where you'll be safe until you get your thinking and confidence back. Then and only then should you consider initiating a new approach. You'll only be taking an extra 15 minutes or so, but at least you'll still be alive.

* Don't duck under the glide slope after you break out. Maintain a constant rate of descent to your normal flare-out altitude.

* Don't use obsolete charts—ever.

* Don't expect the autopilot with all of its couplers to work properly for you all the time. You might end up being just a computer monitor in an up-to-date cockpit, but computers fail from time to time and don't work as expected. Most of these failures are due to improper input, but there are other failures due to spurious electronics. If the autopilot or flight director doesn't do what it was programmed to do, or what you thought you had it programmed to do, hit the OFF button and fly manually until you find time to safely correct the problem. Don't wait for the computer to correct itself. It won't happen.

* Don't descend below the MDA or DH unless you actually see the runway or approach lights and are in a position to make a normal landing. And naturally, as in all instrument work . . .

* Don't get so involved watching all of your newfangled navigational equipment that you forget to *look outside your cockpit*. This is especially true when you are running in and out of clouds. A VFR pilot might be "scud running" in your part of the sky.

* Do have faith in the basic flight instruments, not all of the computerized equipment.

I've tried to keep the tone general enough for most aircraft and most situations. Certain aircraft might operate a little differently, so check the pilot's operating handbook or aircraft manual carefully to be sure that you are operating within the proper guidelines.

I'm sure that once you've successfully completed your first actual IFR flight to a minimums landing, you'll feel even better than you did on your first solo flight.

HAPPY LANDINGS

Glossary

T HE FOLLOWING GLOSSARY OF INSTRUMENT FLIGHT TERMS HAS BEEN compiled from the Jeppesen chart glossary and the FAA's *Pilot/Controller Glossary*. It is specifically directed to terms used during instrument flight as the author feels that the IFR student is already familiar with terms used in VFR flight. The list is by no means complete. Those terms most frequently used in pilot/controller communications are italicized.

abbreviated IFR flight plans—An authorization by ATC requiring pilots to submit only that information needed for the purpose of ATC. It includes only a small portion of the usual IFR flight plan information. In certain instances, this may be only aircraft identification, location, and pilot request. Other information may be requested if needed by ATC for separation/control purposes. It is frequently used by aircraft which are airborne and desire an instrument approach, or by aircraft on the ground that desire a climb to VFR-on-top.

Accelerate Stop Distance Available (ASDA)—The length of the takeoff run available plus the length of the stopway, if provided.

adequate VIS REF (adequate visual reference)—Runway markings or runway lighting that provides the pilot with adequate visual reference to continuously identify the takeoff surface and maintain directional control throughout the takeoff run.

advise intentions—Tell me what you plan to do.

aircraft approach category—A grouping of aircraft based on a speed of 1.3 times the stall speed in the landing configuration at maximum gross landing weight. An aircraft shall fit in only one category. If it is necessary to maneuver at speeds in excess of the upper limit of a speed range for a category, the minimum for the next higher category should be used. For example, an aircraft which falls in Category A, but is circling to land at a speed in excess of 91 knots, should use the approach Category B minimums when circling to land. The categories are as follows:

1. Category A—speed less than 91 knots.
2. Category B—speed 91 knots or more, or less than 121 knots.
3. Category C—speed 121 knots or more, but less than 141 knots.
4. Category D—speed 141 knots or more but less than 166 knots.
5. Category E—speed 166 knots or more.

aircraft classes—For the purposes of wake turbulence separation minima, ATC classifies aircraft as heavy, large, and small as follows:

1. Heavy—Aircraft capable of takeoff weights of 300,000 pounds or more whether or not they are operating at this weight during a particular phase of flight.
2. Large—Aircraft of more then 12,500 pounds, maximum certificated takeoff weight, up to 300,000 pounds.
3. Small—Aircraft of 12,500 pounds or less maximum certificated takeoff weight.

Air Defense Identification Zone (ADIZ)—The area of airspace over land or water, extending upward from the surface, with which the ready identification, the location, and the control of aircraft are required in the interest of national security.

AIRman's METeorological information (AIRMET)—Inflight weather advisories issued only to amend the area forecast concerning weather phenomena which are of operational interest to all aircraft and potentially hazardous to aircraft having limited capability because of lack of equipment, instrumentation, or pilot qualifications. AIRMETs concern weather of less severity than that covered by SIGMETs or Convective SIGMETs. AIRMETs cover moderate icing, moderate turbulence, sustained winds of 30 knots or more at the surface, widespread areas of ceilings less than 1,000 feet and/or visibility less than 3 miles, and extensive mountain obscurement.

airport elevation/field elevation—The highest point of an airport's usable runways measured in feet from mean sea level.

Airport Reference Point (ARP)—A point on the airport designated as the official airport location.

Air Route Traffic Control Center (ARTCC)—A facility established to provide air traffic control service to aircraft operating on IFR flight plans within controlled airspace and principally during the enroute phase of flight.

Air Traffic Control (ATC)—A service provided by appropriate authority to promote the safe, orderly, and expeditious flow of air traffic.

airspeed—The speed of an aircraft relative to its surrounding air mass. The unqualified term airspeed means one of the following:

1. Indicated Airspeed—The speed shown on the aircraft airspeed indicator. This is the speed used in pilot/controller communications under the general term airspeed.
2. True Airspeed—The airspeed of an aircraft relative to undisturbed air. Used primarily in flight planning and enroute portion of flight. When used in pilot/controller communications, it is referred to as true airspeed and not shortened to airspeed.

airway—A Class E airspace area established in the form of a corridor, the centerline of which is defined by radio navigational aids.

alternate airport—An airport at which an aircraft may land if a landing at the intended airport becomes inadvisable.

altitude restrictions are canceled—Adherence to previously imposed altitude restrictions is no longer required during a climb or descent.

approach clearance—Authorization by ATC for a pilot to conduct an instrument approach. The type of instrument approach for which a clearance and other pertinent information is provided in the approach clearance when required.

approach gate—An imaginary point used within ATC as a basis for vectoring aircraft to the final approach course. The gate will be established along the final approach course 1 mile from the outer marker (or the fix used in lieu of the outer marker) on the side away from the airport for precision approaches and 1 mile from the final approach fix on the side away from the airport for nonprecision approaches. In either case when measured along the final approach course, the gate will be no closer than 5 miles from the landing threshold.

approach speed—The recommended speed contained in aircraft manuals used by pilots when making an approach to landing. This speed will vary for different segments of an approach as well as for aircraft weight and configuration.

arc—The curved track over the ground of an aircraft flying at a constant distance from a navigational aid by reference to the distance measuring equipment (DME).

Area Minimum Altitude (AMA)—This is an altitude derived by Jeppesen. The AMA is designed to provide reference point clearance within AMA Envelopes shown on Area Charts. It represents the upper limit of all reference points adjusted upward for vertical clearance. AMA values clear all reference points by 1,000 feet in areas where the highest reference points are 5,000 feet MSL or lower. AMA values clear all reference points by 2,000 feet in areas where the highest reference points are 5,001 feet MSL or higher.

Area Minimum Altitude (AMA) envelope—AMA Envelopes are generalized contour lines that enclose all known reference points above a specified elevation, omitting small valleys. An AMA Envelope portrays the general layout of terrain in comparison to the detailed layout represented by terrain contour lines.

area navigation/RNAV—A method of navigation that permits aircraft operation on any desired course within the coverage of station-referenced navigation signals or within the limits of a self-contained system capability. Random Area Navigation routes are direct routes, based on area navigation capability, between waypoints defined in terms of latitude/longitude coordinates, degree/distance fixes, or offsets from published or established routes/airways at a specified distance and direction. The major types of equipment are:

1. VORTAC referenced or Course Line Computer (CLC) systems, which account for the greatest number of RNAV units in use. To function, the CLC must be within the service range of a VORTAC.
2. OMEGA/VLF, although two separate systems, can be considered as one operationally. A long-range navigation system based upon Very Low Frequency radio signals transmitted from a total of 17 stations worldwide.
3. Inertial (INS) systems, which are totally self-contained and require no information from external references. They provide aircraft position and navigation information in response to signals resulting from inertial effects on components within the system.
4. MLS area navigation (MLS/RNAV), which provides area navigation with reference to an MLS ground facility.
5. Loran-C is a long-range radio navigation system that uses ground waves transmitted at low frequency to provide user information at ranges of up to 600 to 1,200 nautical miles at both enroute and approach altitudes. The usable signal coverage areas are determined by the signal-to-noise ratio, the envelope-to-cycle difference, and the geometric relationship between the positions of the user and the transmitting stations.
6. GPS is a space-based radio positioning, navigation, and time-transfer system. The system provides highly accurate position and velocity information, and precise time, on a continuous global basis, to an unlimited number of properly equipped users. The system is unaffected by weather and provides a worldwide common grid reference system.

automatic direction finder—An aircraft radio navigation system which senses and indicates the direction to an L/MF nondirectional radio beacon (NDB) ground transmitter. Direction is indicated to the pilot as a magnetic bearing or as a relative bearing to the longitudinal axis of the aircraft depending on the type of indicator installed in the aircraft. In certain applications, such as military, ADF operations may be based on airborne and ground transmitters in the VHF/UHF frequency spectrum.

bearing—The horizontal direction to or from any point, usually measured clockwise from true north, magnetic north or some other reference point, through 360 degrees.

below minimums—Weather conditions below the minimums prescribed by regulation for the particular action involved; e.g., landing minimums, takeoff minimums.

braking action (good, fair, poor, or nil)—A report of conditions on the airport movement area providing a pilot with a degree/quality of braking that he might expect. Braking action is reported in terms of good, fair, poor, or nil.

braking action advisories—When tower controllers have received runway braking action reports which include the term poor or nil, or whenever weather conditions are conducive to deteriorating or rapidly changing runway braking conditions, the tower will include on the ATIS broadcast the statement, "BRAKING ACTION ADVISORIES ARE IN EFFECT." During the time Braking Action Advisories are in effect, ATC will issue the latest braking action report for the runway in use to each arriving and departing aircraft. Pilots should be prepared for deteriorating braking conditions and should request current runway condition information if not volunteered by controllers. Pilots should also be prepared to provide a descriptive runway condition report to controllers after landing.

ceiling—The heights above the earth's surface of the lowest layer of clouds or obscuring phenomena that is reported as broken, overcast, or obscuration, and not classified as thin or partial.

charted visual flight procedure approach—An approach conducted on an instrument flight rules (IFR) flight plan which authorizes the pilot of an aircraft under radar control to proceed visually and clear of clouds to the airport via visual landmarks and other information depicted on a charted visual flight procedure. This approach must be authorized and under the control of the appropriate air traffic control facility. Weather minimums required are depicted on the chart.

circle-to-land maneuver/circling maneuver—A maneuver initiated by the pilot to align the aircraft with a runway for landing when a straight-in landing from an instrument approach is not possible or is not desirable. This maneuver is made only after ATC authorization has been obtained and the pilot has established required visual reference to the airport.

circle to runway (runway numbered)—Used by ATC to inform the pilot that he must circle to land because the runway in use is other than the runway aligned with the instrument approach procedure. When the direction of the circling maneuver in relation to the airport/runway is required, the controller will state the direction (eight cardinal compass points) and specify a left or right downwind or base leg as appropriate. . . .

clearance limit—The fix, point, or location to which an aircraft is cleared when issued an air traffic clearance.

clearance void if not off by (time)—Used by ATC to advise an aircraft that the departure clearance is automatically canceled if takeoff is not made prior to a specified time. The pilot must obtain a new clearance or cancel his IFR flight plan if not off by the specified time.

cleared as filed—Means the aircraft is cleared to proceed in accordance with the route of flight filed in the flight plan. This clearance does not include the altitude, SID, or SID transition.

cleared approach—ATC authorization for an aircraft to execute any standard or special instrument approach procedure for that airport. Normally, an aircraft will be cleared for a specific instrument approach procedure.

cleared (type of) approach—ATC authorization for an aircraft to execute a specific instrument approach procedure to an airport. . . .

climb to VFR—ATC authorization for an aircraft to climb to VFR conditions within Class B, C, D, and E surface areas when the only weather limitation is restricted visibility. The aircraft must remain clear of clouds while climbing to VFR.

common traffic advisory frequency—A frequency designed for the purpose of carrying out airport advisory practices while operating to or from an airport without an operating control tower. The CTAF may be a UNICOM, Multicom, FSS, or tower frequency and is identified in appropriate aeronautical publications.

compass locator—A low power, low or medium frequency (L/MF) radio beacon installed at the site of the outer or middle marker of an instrument landing system (ILS). It can be used for navigation at distances of approximately 15 miles or as authorized in the approach procedure. . . .

compulsory reporting points—Reporting points which must be reported to ATC. They are designated on aeronautical charts by solid triangles or filed in a flight plan as fixes selected to define direct routes. These points are geographical locations which are defined by navigational aids/fixes. Pilots should discontinue position reporting . . . when informed by ATC that their aircraft is in radar contact.

contact approach—An approach wherein an aircraft on an IFR flight plan, having an air traffic control authorization, operating clear of clouds with at least 1 mile flight visibility and a reasonable expectation of continuing to the destination airport in those conditions, may deviate from the instrument approach procedure and proceed to the destination airport by visual reference to the surface. This approach will only be authorized when requested by the pilot and the reported ground visibility at the destination airport is at least 1 statute mile.

Convective SIGnificant METeorological information (Convective SIGMET)—A weather advisory concerning convective weather significant to the safety of all aircraft. Convective SIGMETs are issued for tornadoes, lines of thunderstorms, embedded thunderstorms of any intensity level, areas of thunderstorms greater than or equal to VIP level 4 with an area coverage of $\frac{4}{10}$ (40 percent) or more, and hail ¾ inch or greater.

cross (fix) at (altitude)—Used by ATC when a specific altitude restriction at a specific fix is required.

cross (fix) at or above (altitude)—Used by ATC when an altitude restriction at a specified fix is required. It does not prohibit the aircraft from crossing the fix at a higher altitude than specified; however, the higher altitude may not be one that will violate a succeeding altitude restriction or altitude assignment.

cross (fix) at or below (altitude)—Used by ATC when a maximum altitude at a specific fix is required. It does not prohibit the aircraft from crossing the fix at a lower altitude; however, it must be at or above the minimum IFR altitude.

cruise—Used in an ATC clearance to authorize a pilot to conduct a flight at any altitude from the minimum IFR altitude up to and including the altitude specified in the clearance. The pilot may level off at any intermediate altitude within this block of airspace. Climb/descent within the block is to be made at the discretion of the pilot. However, once the pilot starts descent and verbally reports leaving an altitude in the block, he may not return to that altitude without additional ATC clearance. Further, it is approval for the pilot to proceed to and make an approach at destination airport and can be used in conjunction with:

1. An airport clearance limit at locations with a standard/special instrument approach procedure. The FARs require that if an instrument letdown to an airport is necessary the pilot shall make the letdown in accordance with a standard/special instrument approach procedure for that airport, or
2. An airport clearance limit at locations that are within/below/outside controlled airspace and without a standard/special instrument approach procedure. Such a clearance is NOT AUTHORIZATION for the pilot to descend under IFR conditions below the applicable minimum IFR altitude nor does it imply that ATC is exercising control over aircraft in uncontrolled airspace; however, it provides a means for the aircraft to proceed to destination airport, descend, and land in accordance with applicable FARs governing VFR flight operations. Also, this provides search and rescue protection until such time as the IFR flight plan is closed.

cruising altitude/level—An altitude or flight level maintained during enroute level flight. This is a constant altitude and should not be confused with a cruise clearance.

Decision Height (DH) (USA)—With respect to the operation of aircraft, means the height at which a decision must be made during an ILS, MLS, or PAR instrument approach to either continue the approach or to execute a missed approach.

NOTE: Jeppesen approach charts use the abbreviation DA(H). The decision altitude "DA" is referenced to mean sea level (MSL) and the parenthetical decision height (DH) is referenced to the TDZE or threshold elevation. A DA(H) of 1,440' (200') is a Decision Altitude of 1,440' and a Decision Height of 200'.

descent below MDA or DH—No person may operate an aircraft below the prescribed minimum descent altitude or continue an approach below the decision height unless—

1. The aircraft is in a position from which a normal approach to the runway of intended landing can be made; and
2. The approach threshold of that runway, or approach lights or other marking identification with the approach end of that runway, are clearly visible to the pilot.

If upon arrival at the missed approach point or decision height, or at any time thereafter, any of the above requirements are not met, the pilot shall immediately execute the appropriate missed approach procedure.

direct—Straight-line flight between two navigational aids, fixes, points, or any combination thereof. When used by pilots in describing off-airway routes, points defining direct route segments become compulsory reporting points unless the aircraft is under radar contact.

displaced threshold—A threshold that is located at a point on the runway other than the designated beginning of the runway.

Distance Measuring Equipment (DME)—Equipment (airborne and ground) used to measure, in nautical miles, the slant range distance of an aircraft from the DME navigational aid.

DME fix—A geographical position determined by reference to a navigational aid which provides distance and azimuth information. It is defined by a specific distance in nautical miles and a radial, azimuth, or course (i.e., localizer) in degrees magnetic from that aid.

downburst—A strong downdraft which induces an outburst of damaging winds on or near the ground. Damaging winds, either straight or curved, are highly divergent. The sizes of downbursts vary from ½ mile or less to more than 10 miles. An intense downburst often causes widespread damage. Damaging winds, lasting 5 to 30 minutes, could reach speeds as high as 120 knots.

execute missed approach—Instructions issued to a pilot making an instrument approach which means continue inbound to the missed approach point and execute the missed approach procedure as described on the Instrument Approach Procedure Chart or as previously assigned by ATC. The pilot may climb immediately to the altitude specified in the missed approach procedure upon making a missed approach. No turns should be initiated prior to reaching the missed approach point. When conducting an ASR or PAR approach, execute the assigned missed approach procedure immediately upon receiving instructions to "execute missed approach."

expect (altitude) at (time) or (fix)—Used under certain conditions to provide a pilot with an altitude to be used in the event of two-way communications failure. It also provides altitude information to assist the pilot in planning.

expect further clearance (time)—The time a pilot can expect to receive clearance beyond a clearance limit.

feeder route—Routes depicted on instrument approach procedure charts to designate routes for aircraft to proceed from the enroute structure to the initial approach fix (IAF).

final approach course—A published MLS course, a straight-line extension of a localizer, a final approach radial/bearing, or a runway centerline, all without regard to distance.

Final Approach Fix (FAF)—The fix from which the final approach (IFR) to an airport is executed and which identifies the beginning of the final approach segment. It is designated in the profile view of Jeppesen Terminal charts by the Maltese Cross symbol for nonprecision approaches and by the glide slope/path intercept point on precision approaches. The glide slope/path symbol starts at the FAF. When ATC directs a lower-than-published Glide slope/path Intercept Altitude, it is the resultant actual point of the glide slope/path intercept.

final approach (IFR) (USA)—The flight path of an aircraft which is inbound to an airport on a final instrument approach course, beginning at the final approach fix or point and extending to the airport or the point where a circle-to-land maneuver or a missed approach is executed.

final approach point—The point, applicable only to a nonprecision approach with no designated FAF (such as an on-airport VOR), where the aircraft is established inbound on the final approach course from the procedure turn and where the final approach descent may be commenced. The FAP serves as the FAF and identifies the beginning of the final approach segment.

fix—A geographical position determined by visual reference to the surface, by reference to one or more radio NAVAIDs, by celestial plotting, or by another navigational device.

flight level—A level of constant atmospheric pressure related to a reference datum of 29.92 inches of mercury . . . stated in three digits that represents hundreds of feet. For example, flight level 250 represents a barometric altimeter indication of 25,000 feet; flight level 255, an indication of 25,500 feet.

flight path—A line, course, or track along which an aircraft is flying or intended to be flown.

gate hold procedures—Procedures at selected airports to hold aircraft at the gate or other ground location whenever departure delays exceed or are anticipated to exceed 15 minutes. The sequence for departure will be maintained in accordance with initial call-up unless modified by flow control restrictions. Pilots should monitor the ground control/clearance delivery frequency for engine start/taxi advisories or new proposed time if the delay changes.

glide slope—Provides vertical guidance for aircraft during approach and landing. The glide slope/glide path is based on the following:
1. Electronic components emitting signals which provide vertical guidance by reference to airborne instruments during instrument approaches such as ILS/MLS, or
2. Visual ground aids, such as VASI, which provide vertical guidance for a VFR approach or for the visual portion of an instrument approach and landing.
3. PAR. Used by ATC to inform an aircraft making a PAR approach of its vertical position (elevation) relative to the descent profile.

glide slope/glide path intercept altitude—The minimum altitude to intercept the glide slope/path on a precision approach. The intersection of the published intercept altitude with the glide slope/path, designated on Jeppesen Terminal charts by the start of the glide slope/path symbol, is the precision FAF; however, when ATC directs a lower altitude, the resultant lower intercept position is then the FAF.

global positioning system—A space-based radio positioning, navigation, and time-transfer system. The system provides highly accurate position and velocity information, and precise time, on a continuous global basis, to an unlimited number of properly equipped users. The system is unaffected by weather, and provides a worldwide common grid reference system. The GPS concept is predicated upon accurate and continuous knowledge of the spatial position of each satellite in the system with respect to time and distance from a transmitting satellite to the user. The GPS receiver automatically selects appropriate signals from the satellites in view and translates these into three-dimensional position, velocity, and time. System accuracy for civil users is normally 100 meters horizontally.

Height Above Airport (HAA)—The height of the minimum descent altitude above the published airport elevation. This is published in conjunction with circling minimums.

Height Above Touchdown (HAT)—The height of the decision height or minimum descent altitude above the highest runway elevation in the touchdown zone (first

3,000 feet of the runway). HAT is published on instrument approach charts in conjunction with all straight-in-minimums.

hold/holding procedure—A predetermined maneuver which keeps aircraft within a specified airspace while awaiting further clearance from air traffic control. Also used during ground operations to keep aircraft within a specified area or at a specified point while awaiting further clearance from air traffic control. The standard holding time is one minute at or below 14,000 feet or FL140 and 1½ minutes above.

holding fix—A specified fix identifiable to a pilot by NAVAIDs or visual reference to the ground used as a reference point in establishing and maintaining the position of an aircraft while holding.

if no transmission received for (time) —Used by ATC in radar approaches to prefix procedures which should be followed by the pilot in event of lost communications.

IFR conditions—Weather conditions below the minimum for flight under visual flight rules.

IFR takeoff minimums and departure procedures—Standard takeoff rules are prescribed for certain civil users. At some airports, obstructions or other factors require the establishment of nonstandard takeoff minimums, departure procedures, or both, to assist pilots in avoiding obstacles during climb to the minimum enroute altitude. When departing IFR from such airports, or from any airports where there are no departure procedures, SIDs, or ATC facilities available, pilots should advise ATC of any departure limitations. Controllers may query a pilot to determine acceptable departure directions, turns, or heading after takeoff. Pilots should be familiar with the departure procedures and must assure that their aircraft can meet or exceed any specified climb gradients.

ILS categories (FAA)—

1. ILS Category I—An ILS approach procedure which provides for approach to a height above touchdown of not less than 200 feet and with runway visual range of not less than 1,800 feet.
2. ILS Category II (Special authorization required)—An ILS approach procedure which provides for approach to a height above touchdown of not less than 100 feet and with runway visual range of not less than 1,200 feet.
3. ILS Category III (Special authorization required)—
   a. IIIA—An ILS approach procedure which provides for approach without a decision height minimum and with runway visual range of not less than 700 feet.
   b. IIIB—An ILS approach procedure which provides for approach without a decision height minimum and with runway visual range of not less than 150 feet.
   c. IIIC—An ILS approach procedure which provides for approach without a decision height minimum and without runway visual range minimum.

immediately—Used by ATC when such action compliance is required to avoid an imminent situation.

Initial Approach Fix (IAF)—The fix(s) depicted on instrument approach procedure charts that identifies the beginning of the initial approach segment(s).

Inner Marker (IM)/inner marker beacon—A marker beacon used with an ILS (CAT II) precision approach located between the middle marker and the end of the ILS runway, transmitting a radiation pattern keyed at six dots per second and indicating to the pilot, both aurally and visually, that he is at the designated decision height (DH), normally 100 feet above the touchdown zone elevation, on the ILS CAT II approach. It also marks progress during a CAT III approach.

Instrument Approach Procedure (IAP)/instrument approach—A series of predetermined maneuvers for the orderly transfer of an aircraft under instrument flight conditions, from the beginning of the initial approach to a landing, or to a point from which a landing may be made visually. It is prescribed and approved for a specific airport by a competent authority. . . .

Instrument Flight Rules (IFR)—Rules governing the procedures for conducting instrument flight. Also a term used by pilots and controllers to indicate type of flight plan.

Instrument Landing System (ILS)—A precision instrument approach system which normally consists of the following electronic components and visual aids:

1. Localizer
2. Glide slope
3. Outer Marker
4. Middle Marker
5. Approach Lights

Instrument Meteorological Conditions (IMC)—Meteorological conditions expressed in terms of visibility, distance from cloud, and ceiling less than the minimums specified for visual meteorological conditions.

instrument runway—A runway equipped with electronic and visual navigation aids for which a precision or nonprecision approach procedure having straight-in landing minimums has been approved.

Landing Distance Available (LDA)—The length of runway which is declared available and suitable for the ground run of an airplane landing.

landing minimums/IFR landing minimums—The minimum visibility prescribed for landing a civil aircraft while using an instrument approach procedure. The minimum applies with other limitations set forth in FAR Part 91 with respect to the Minimum Descent Altitude (MDA) or Decision Height (DH) prescribed in the instrument approach procedures as follows:

1. Straight-in landing minimums—A statement of MDA and visibility, or DH and visibility, required for a straight-in landing on a specified runway, or
2. Circling minimums—A statement of MDA and visibility required for the circle-to-land maneuver.

Descent below the established MDA or DH is not authorized during an approach unless the aircraft is in a position from which a normal approach to the runway of intended landing can be made and adequate visual reference to required visual cues is maintained.

localizer—The component of an ILS which provides course guidance to the runway.

Localizer type Directional Aid (LDA)—A NAVAID used for nonprecision instrument approaches with utility and accuracy comparable to a localizer but which is not a part of a complete ILS and is not aligned with the runway.

Loran—An electronic navigational system by which hyperbolic lines of position are determined by measuring the difference in the time of reception of synchronized pulse signals from two fixed transmitters. Loran A operates in the 1,750–1,950-kHz frequency band. Loran C and D operate in the 100–110-kHz frequency band.

Maintain—

1. Concerning altitude/flight level, the term means to remain at the altitude/flight level specified. The phrase "climb and" or "descend and" normally precedes "maintain" and the altitude assignment;. . . e.g., "maintain 5000."

2. Concerning other ATC instructions, the term is used in its literal sense; e.g., maintain VFR.

mandatory altitude—An altitude depicted on an instrument approach procedure chart requiring the aircraft to maintain altitude at the depicted value.

marker beacon—An electronic navigation facility transmitting a 75-MHz vertical fan or boneshaped radiation pattern. Marker beacons are identified by their modulation frequency and keying code, and when received by compatible airborne equipment, indicate to the pilot, both aurally and visually, that he is passing over the facility.

Maximum Authorized Altitude (MAA)—A published altitude representing the maximum usable altitude or flight level for an airspace structure or route segment.

microburst—A small downburst with outbursts of damaging winds extending 2.5 miles or less. In spite of its small horizontal scale, an intense microburst could induce wind speeds as high as 150 knots.

Middle Marker (MM)—A marker beacon that defines a point along the glide slope of an ILS normally located at or near the point of decision height.

Minimum Crossing Altitude (MCA)—The lowest altitude at certain fixes at which an aircraft must cross when proceeding in the direction of a higher minimum enroute IFR altitude (MEA).

Minimum Descent Altitude (MDA) (USA)—The lowest altitude, expressed in feet above mean sea level, to which descent is authorized on final approach or during circle-to-land maneuvering in execution of a standard instrument approach procedure where no electronic glide slope is provided.

minimum enroute IFR altitude—The lowest published altitude between radio fixes which assures acceptable navigational signal coverage and meets obstacle clearance requirements between those fixes. The MEA prescribed for a Federal airway or segment thereof, area navigation low or high route, or other direct route applies to the entire width of the airway, segment, or route between the radio fixes defining the airway, segment, or route.

minimum fuel—Indicates that an aircraft's fuel supply has reached a state where, upon reaching the destination, it can accept little or no delay. This is not an emergency situation but merely indicates an emergency situation is possible should any undue delay occur.

Minimum Holding Altitude (MHA)—The lowest altitude prescribed for a holding pattern which assures navigational signal coverage, communications, and meets obstacle clearance requirements.

minimum IFR altitude—Minimum altitudes for IFR operations as prescribed in FAR Part 91. These altitudes are published on aeronautical charts and prescribed in FAR Part 95 for airways and routes, and in FAR Part 97 for standard instrument approach procedures. If no applicable minimum altitude is prescribed in FAR Parts 95 or 97, the following minimum IFR altitude applies:

1. In designated mountainous areas, 2,000 feet above the highest obstacle within a horizontal distance of 5 statute miles from the course to be flown; or
2. Other than mountainous areas, 1,000 feet above the highest obstacle within a horizontal distance of 5 statute miles from the course to be flown; or
3. As otherwise authorized by the Administrator or assigned by ATC.

Minimum Obstruction Clearance Altitude (MOCA)—The lowest published altitude in effect between radio fixes on VOR airways, off-airway routes, or route segments which meets obstacle clearance requirements for the entire route segment and which assures acceptable navigational signal coverage only within 25 statute (22 nautical) miles of a VOR.

Minimum Off-Route Altitude (MORA)—This is an altitude derived by Jeppesen. The MORA provides reference point clearance within 10 nm of the route centerline (regardless of route width) and end fixes. A grid MORA altitude provides reference point clearance within the section outlined by latitude and longitude lines. MORA values clear all reference points by 1,000 feet in areas where the highest reference points are 5,000 feet MSL or lower. MORA values clear all reference points by 2,000 feet in areas where the reference points are 5,001 feet MSL or higher. When a MORA is shown along a route as "unknown" or within a grid as "unsurveyed" a MORA is not shown due to incomplete or insufficient information.

Minimum Reception Altitude (MRA)—The lowest altitude at which an intersection can be determined.

minimum safe altitude—

1. The minimum altitude specified in FAR Part 91 for various aircraft operations.
2. Altitudes depicted on approach charts which provide for at least 1,000 feet of obstacle clearance for emergency use within a specified distance from the navigational facility upon which a procedure is predicated. These altitudes will be identified as Minimum Sector Altitudes or Emergency Safe Altitudes and are established as follows:
   a. Minimum Sector Altitudes—Altitudes depicted on approach charts which provide at least 1,000 feet of obstacle clearance within a 25-mile radius of the navigation facility upon which the procedure is predicated. Sectors depicted on approach charts must be at least 90 degrees in scope. These alti-

tudes are for emergency use only and do not necessarily assure acceptable navigational signal coverage.

    b. Emergency Safe Altitudes—Altitudes depicted on approach charts which provide at least 1,000 feet of obstacle clearance in nonmountainous areas and 2,000 feet of obstacle clearance in designated mountainous areas within a 100-mile radius of the navigation facility upon which the procedure is predicated and normally used only in military procedures. These altitudes are identified on published procedures as "Emergency Safe Altitudes."

Minimum Vectoring Altitude (MVA)—The lowest MSL altitude at which an IFR aircraft will be vectored by a radar controller, except as otherwise authorized for radar approaches, departures and missed approaches. The altitude meets IFR obstacle clearance criteria. It may be lower than the published MEA along an airway or J-route segment. It may be utilized for radar vectoring only upon the controller's determination that an adequate radar return is being received from the aircraft being controlled. Charts depicting minimum vectoring altitudes are normally available only to the controller not to pilots.

minimums/minima—Weather condition requirements established for a particular operation or type of operation; e.g., IFR takeoff or landing, alternate airport for IFR flight plans, VFR flight.

missed approach—

    1. A maneuver conducted by a pilot when an instrument approach cannot be completed to a landing. The route of flight and altitude are shown on instrument approach procedure charts. A pilot executing a missed approach prior to the Missed Approach Point (MAP) must continue along the final approach to the MAP. The pilot may climb immediately to the altitude specified in the missed approach procedure.

    2. A term used by the pilot to inform ATC that he is executing the missed approach.

    3. At locations where ATC radar service is provided, the pilot should conform to radar vectors when provided by ATC in lieu of the published missed approach procedure.

missed approach point—A point prescribed in each instrument approach procedure at which a missed approach procedure shall be executed if the required visual reference does not exist.

nautical mile—A geographical or sea mile, 1.15 statute miles, 6076.1 feet, or 1852 meters.

negative—"No" or "permission not granted" or "that is not correct."

negative contact—Used by pilots to inform ATC that:

    1. Previously issued traffic is not in sight. It may be followed by the pilot's request for the controller to provide assistance in avoiding the traffic.

    2. They were unable to contact ATC on a particular frequency.

no gyro approach—A radar approach/vector provided in case of a malfunctioning gyro-compass or directional gyro. Instead of providing the pilot with headings to be flown, the controller observes the radar track and issues control instructions "turn right/left" or "stop turn" as appropriate.

nondirectional beacon—An L/MF or UHF radio beacon transmitting nondirectional signals whereby the pilot of an aircraft equipped with direction finding equipment can determine his bearing to or from the radio beacon and "home" on, or track to or from, the station. When the radio beacon is installed in conjunction with the Instrument Landing System marker, it is normally called a Compass Locator.

nonprecision approach procedure/nonprecision approach—A standard instrument approach procedure in which no electronic glide slope is provided; e.g., VOR, TACAN, NDB, LOC, ASR, LDA, or SDF approaches.

No Procedure Turn (NoPT)—No procedure turn is required nor authorized without ATC clearance.

outer marker—A marker beacon at or near the glide slope intercept altitude of an ILS approach. It is keyed to transmit two dashes per second on a 400-Hz tone, which is received aurally and visually by compatible airborne equipment. The OM is normally located four to seven miles from the runway threshold on the extended centerline of the runway.

pilot's discretion—When used in conjunction with altitude assignments, means that ATC has offered the pilot the option of starting climb or descent whenever he wishes and conducting the climb or descent at any rate he wishes. He may temporarily level off at any intermediate altitude. However, once he has vacated an altitude, he may not return to that altitude.

precision approach procedure—A standard instrument approach procedure in which an electronic glide slope/glide path is provided; e.g., ILS/MLS and PAR.

Precision Approach Path Indicator (PAPI)—Is a development of the Visual Approach Slope Indicator system (VASI) and uses the same principle, giving red and white visual signals for guidance in maintaining the required approach angle. "Sharp transition" equipment is used in which the pink sector between the red and white signal, which is a characteristic of VASI, is virtually eliminated. The essential differences between the two aids are the number and arrangement of light units and the way in which their indications are interpreted.

The basic PAPI display comprises 4 units mounted in a wing bar on the left side of the runway adjacent to the touchdown point. The outermost unit is set ½ degree lower than the required approach angle, with progressive increments of ⅓ degree setting angle for each unit inboard, the fourth being set ½ degree higher than the approach angle. The correct approach slope is indicated by a + 10 minute tolerance by two red and two white lights. A high degree of accuracy can be achieved at the threshold since the required approach slope is defined by a channel approximately 2 meters (6 feet) in vertical extent at the threshold. . . .

procedure turn—The maneuver prescribed when it is necessary to reverse direction to establish an aircraft on the intermediate approach segment or final approach course. The outbound course, direction of turn, distance within which the turn must be completed, and minimum altitude are specified in the procedure. However, unless otherwise restricted, the point at which the turn may be commenced and the type and rate of turn are left to the discretion of the pilot.

procedure turn inbound—That point of a procedure turn maneuver where course reversal has been completed and an aircraft is established inbound on the intermediate approach segment or final approach course. A report of "procedure turn inbound" is normally used by ATC as a position report for separation purposes.

profile descent—An uninterrupted descent (except where level flight is required for speed adjustment; e.g., 250 knots at 10,000 feet MSL) from cruising altitude/level to interception of a glide slope or to a minimum altitude specified for the initial or intermediate approach segment of a nonprecision instrument approach. The profile descent normally terminates at the approach gate or where the glide slope or other appropriate minimum altitude is intercepted.

QFE—Height above airport elevation (or runway threshold elevation) based on local station pressure.

QNE—Altimeter setting 29.92 inches of mercury, 1013.2 hectopascals or 1013.2 millibars.

QNH—Altitude above mean sea level based on local station pressure.

radar approach—An instrument approach procedure which utilizes Precision Approach Radar (PAR) or Airport Surveillance Radar (ASR).

radar contact—

1. Used by ATC to inform an aircraft that it is identified on the radar display and radar flight following will be provided until radar identification is terminated. Radar service may also be provided within the limits of necessity and capability. When a pilot is informed of "radar contact," he automatically discontinues reporting over compulsory reporting points.
2. The term used to inform the controller that the aircraft is identified and approval is granted for the aircraft to enter the receiving controller's airspace.

radar contact lost—Used by ATC to inform a pilot that radar data used to determine the aircraft's position is no longer being received, or is no longer reliable and radar service is no longer being provided. The loss may be attributed to several factors including the aircraft merging with weather or ground clutter, the aircraft operating below radar line of sight, the aircraft entering an area of poor radar return, failure of the aircraft transponder, or failure of the ground radar equipment.

radar service terminated—Used by ATC to inform a pilot that he will no longer be provided any of the services that could be received while in radar contact. Radar service is automatically terminated, and the pilot is not advised in the following cases:

1. An aircraft cancels its IFR flight plan, except within Class B airspace, Class C airspace, a TRSA, or where Basic Radar service is provided.
2. An aircraft conducting an instrument, visual, or contact approach has landed or has been instructed to change to advisory frequency.
3. An arriving VFR aircraft, receiving radar service to a tower-controlled airport within Class B airspace, Class C airspace, a TRSA, or where sequencing ser-

vice is provided, has landed; or to all other airports, is instructed to change to tower or advisory frequency.

4. An aircraft completes a radar approach.

radio altimeter/radar altimeter—Aircraft equipment which makes use of the reflection of radio waves from the ground to determine the height of the aircraft above the surface.

reference point—A natural (Peak, Knoll, Hill, etc.) or man-made (Tower, Stack, Tank, Building, etc.) object.

release time—A departure time restriction issued to a pilot by ATC (either directly or through an authorized relay) when necessary to separate a departing aircraft from other traffic.

reporting point—A geographical location in relation to which the position of an aircraft is reported.

request full route clearance—Used by pilots to request that the entire route of flight be read verbatim in an ATC clearance. Such request should be made to preclude receiving an ATC clearance based on the original filed flight plan when a filed IFR flight plan has been revised by the pilot, company, or operations prior to departure.

resume own navigation—Used by ATC to advise a pilot to resume his own navigational responsibility. It is issued after completion of a radar vector or when radar contact is lost while the aircraft is being radar vectored.

roger—I have received all of your last transmission. It should not be used to answer a question requiring a yes or no answer.

runway edge lights (USA)—Lights used to outline the edges of runways during periods of darkness or restricted visibility conditions. The light systems are classified according to the intensity or brightness they are capable of producing: they are the High Intensity Runway Lights (HIRL), Medium Intensity Runway Lights (MIRL), and the Low Intensity Runway Lights (RL). The HIRL and MIRL systems have variable intensity controls, where the RLs normally have one intensity setting.

a. The runway edge lights are white, except on instrument runways amber replaces white on the last 2,000 feet or half the runway length, whichever is less, to form a caution zone for landings.

b. The lights marking the ends of the runway emit red light toward the runway to indicate the end of runway to a departing aircraft and emit green outward from the runway end to indicate the threshold to landing aircraft.

runway profile descent—An instrument flight rules (IFR) air traffic control arrival procedure to a runway published for pilot use in graphic and/or textual form and may be associated with a STAR. RUNWAY PROFILE DESCENTs provide routing, and may depict crossing altitudes, speed restrictions, and headings to be flown from the enroute structure to the point where the pilot will receive clearance for and execute an instrument approach procedure. A RUNWAY PROFILE DESCENT may apply to more than one runway if so stated on the chart.

safety alert—A safety alert issued by ATC to aircraft under their control if ATC is aware the aircraft is at an altitude which, in the controller's judgment, places the aircraft in unsafe proximity to terrain, obstructions, or other aircraft. The controller may discontinue the issuance of further alerts if the pilot advises that he is taking action to correct the situation or has the other aircraft in sight.

1. Terrain/Obstruction Alert—A safety alert issued by ATC to aircraft under their control if ATC is aware the aircraft is at an altitude which, in the controller's judgment, places the aircraft in unsafe proximity to terrain/obstructions; e.g., "Low Altitude Alert, check your altitude immediately."

2. Aircraft Conflict Alert—A safety alert issued by ATC to aircraft under their control if ATC is aware of an aircraft that is not under their control at an altitude which, in the controller's judgment, places both aircraft in unsafe proximity to each other. With the alert, ATC will offer the pilot an alternate course of action when feasible; e.g., "Traffic Alert, advise you turn right heading zero niner zero or climb to eight thousand immediately."

The issuance of a safety alert is contingent upon the capability of the controller to have an awareness of an unsafe condition. The course of action provided will be predicated on other traffic under ATC control. Once the alert is issued, it is solely the pilot's prerogative to determine what course of action, if any, he will take.

segments of an instrument approach procedure—An instrument approach procedure may have as many as four separate segments depending on how the approach procedure is structured.

1. Initial Approach. The segment between the initial approach fix and the intermediate fix or the point where the aircraft is established on the intermediate course or final approach course.

2. Intermediate Approach. The segment between the intermediate fix or point and the final approach fix.

3. Final Approach. The segment between the final approach fix or point and the runway, airport, or missed approach point.

4. Missed Approach. The segment between the missed approach point or point of arrival at decision height and the missed approach fix at the prescribed altitude.

short range clearance—A clearance issued to a departing IFR flight which authorizes IFR flight to a specific fix short of the destination while air traffic control facilities are coordinating and obtaining the complete clearance.

sidestep maneuver—A visual maneuver accomplished by a pilot at the completion of an instrument approach to permit a straight-in landing on a parallel runway not more than 1,200 feet to either side of the runway to which the instrument approach was conducted.

sigmet—A weather advisory issued concerning weather significant to the safety of all aircraft. SIGMET advisories cover severe and extreme turbulence, severe icing, and widespread dust or sandstorms that reduce visibility to less than 3 miles.

simplified directional facility—A NAVAID used for nonprecision instrument approaches. The final approach course is similar to that of an ILS localizer except that the SDF course may be offset from the runway, generally not more than 3 degrees, and the course may be wider than the localizer, resulting in a lower degree of accuracy.

simultaneous ILS approaches—An approach system permitting simultaneous ILS approaches to airports having parallel runways separated by at least 4,300 feet between centerlines. Integral parts of a total system are ILS, Radar, Communications, ATC procedures, and appropriate airborne equipment.

speed adjustment—An ATC procedure used to request pilots to adjust aircraft speed to a specific value for the purpose of providing desired spacing. Pilots are expected to maintain a speed of plus or minus 10 knots or 0.02 Mach number of the specified speed.

Standard Instrument Departure (SID)—A preplanned instrument flight rule (IFR) air traffic control departure procedure printed for pilot use in graphic and/or textual form. SIDs provide transition from the terminal to the appropriate enroute structure.

standard rate turn—A turn of three degrees per second.

Standard Terminal Arrival Route (STAR)—A preplanned instrument flight rule (IFR) air traffic control arrival route published for pilot use in graphic and/or textual form. STARs provide transition from the enroute structure to a fix or point from which an approach can be made.

stand by—Means the controller or pilot must pause a few seconds, usually to attend to other duties of a higher priority. Also means to wait as in "stand by for clearance." The caller should reestablish contact if a delay is lengthy. "Stand by" is not an approval or denial.

stepdown fix—A fix permitting additional descent within a segment of an instrument approach procedure by identifying a point at which a controlling obstacle has been safely overflown.

straight-in approach (IFR)—An instrument approach wherein final approach is begun without first having executed a procedure turn, not necessarily completed with a straight-in landing or made to straight-in landing minimums.

straight-in landing—A landing made on a runway aligned within 30 degrees of the final approach course following completion of an instrument approach.

surveillance approach—An instrument approach wherein the air traffic controller issues instructions, for pilot compliance, based on aircraft position in relation to the final approach course (azimuth), and the distance (range) from the end of the runway as displayed on the controller's radar scope. The controller will provide recommended altitudes on final approach if requested by the pilots.

TakeOff Distance Available (TODA)—The length of the takeoff run available plus the length of the clearway, if provided.

TakeOff Run Available (TORA)—The length of runway declared available and suitable for the ground run of an airplane taking off.

threshold—The beginning of that portion of the runway usable for landing.

Threshold Crossing Height (TCH)—The theoretical height above the runway threshold at which the aircraft's glide slope antenna would be if the aircraft maintains the trajectory established by the mean ILS glide path.

touchdown zone—The first 3,000 feet of the runway beginning at the threshold. The area is used for determination of Touchdown Zone Elevation . . .

TouchDown Zone Elevation (TDZE)—The highest elevation in the first 3,000 feet of the landing surface. TDZE is indicated on the instrument approach procedure chart when straight-in landing minimums are authorized.

transition—

1. The general term that describes the change from one phase of flight or flight condition to another; e.g., a transition from enroute flight to the approach or a transition from instrument flight to visual flight.
2. A published procedure (SID transition) used to connect the basic SID to one of several enroute airways/jet routes, or a published procedure (STAR Transition) used to connect one of several enroute airways/jet routes to the basic STAR.

transition altitude (QNH)—The altitude in the vicinity of an airport at or below which the vertical position of an aircraft is controlled by reference to altitudes (MSL).

transition height (QFE)—The height in the vicinity of an airport at or below which the vertical position of an aircraft is expressed in height above the airport reference datum.

transition level (QNH)—The lowest flight level available for use above the transition altitude.

transmissometer—An apparatus used to determine visibility by measuring the transmission of light through the atmosphere. It is the measurement source for determining runway visual range (RVR) and runway visibility value (RVV).

verify—Request confirmation of information; e.g., "verify assigned altitude."

verify specific direction of takeoff (or turns after takeoff)—Used by ATC to ascertain an aircraft's direction of takeoff and/or direction of turn after takeoff. It is normally used for IFR departures from an airport not having a control tower. When direct communications with the pilot is not possible, the request and information may be relayed through an FSS, dispatcher, or by other means.

Vertical NAVigation (VNAV)—That function of RNAV equipment which provides guidance in the vertical plane.

VFR-on-top—ATC authorization for an IFR aircraft to operate in VFR conditions at any appropriate VFR altitude (as specified in FAR and as restricted by ATC). A pilot receiving this authorization must comply with VFR visibility, distance from cloud criteria, and the minimum IFR altitudes specified in FAR Part 91. The use of this term does not relieve controllers of their responsibility to separate aircraft in Class B and Class C airspace or TRSAs as required by FAA Handbook 7110.65.

visibility—The ability, as determined by atmospheric conditions and expressed in units of distance, to see and identify prominent unlighted objects by day and prominent lighted objects by night. Visibility is reported as statute or nautical miles, hundreds of feet, or meters.

1. Flight Visibility—The average forward horizontal distance, from the cockpit of an aircraft in flight, at which prominent unlighted objects may be seen and identified by day and prominent lighted objects may be seen and identified by night.

2. Ground Visibility—Prevailing horizontal visibility near the earth's surface as reported by the United States National Weather Service or an accredited observer.

3. Prevailing Visibility—The greatest horizontal visibility equaled or exceeded throughout at least half the horizon circle which need not necessarily be continuous.

4. Runway Visibility Value (RVV)—The visibility determined for a particular runway by a transmissometer. A meter provides a continuous indication of the visibility (reported in miles or fractions of miles) for the runway. RVV is used in lieu of prevailing visibility in determining minimums for a particular runway.

5. Runway Visual Range (RVR)—An instrumentally derived value, based on standard calibrations, that represents the horizontal distance a pilot will see down the runway from the approach end. It is based on the sighting of either high intensity runway lights or on the visual contrast of other targets whichever yields the greatest visual range. RVR, in contrast to prevailing or runway visibility, is based on what a pilot in a moving aircraft should see looking down the runway. RVR is horizontal visual range, not slant visual range. It is based on the measurement of a transmissometer made near the touchdown point of the instrument runway and is reported in hundreds of feet. RVR is used in lieu of RVV and/or prevailing visibility in determining minimums for a particular runway.

   a. Touchdown RVR—The RVR visibility readout values obtained from RVR equipment serving the runway touchdown zone.

   b. Mid-RVR—The RVR readout values obtained from RVR equipment located midfield of the runway.

   c. Rollout RVR—The RVR readout values obtained from RVR equipment located nearest the rollout end of the runway.

visual approach (FAA)—An approach wherein an aircraft on an IFR flight plan, operating in VFR conditions under the control of an air traffic control facility and having an air traffic control authorization, may proceed to the airport of destination in VFR conditions.

Visual Approach Slope Indicator (VASI)—A visual guidance system for aircraft used to ensure proper obstruction clearance and to provide a runway aiming point. It provides a fixed light path to be utilized for descent guidance during approach. . . .

Visual Descent Point (VDP)—A defined point on the final approach course of a nonprecision straight-in approach procedure from which normal descent from the MDA to the runway touchdown point may be commenced, provided the approach threshold of that runway, or approach lights, or other markings identifiable with the approach end of that runway are clearly visible to the pilot.

waypoint (RNAV)—A predetermined geographical position, used for route or approach definition or progress reporting purposes. Two waypoints define a route segment.

wind shear—A change in wind speed and/or wind direction in a short distance resulting in a tearing or shearing effect. It can exist in a horizontal or vertical direction and occasionally in both.

Appendix
Chapter quiz answers

Chapter 1

1. **False.** The aircraft doesn't know the difference between day and night, or between IFR or VFR flight conditions.

2. In order to set the elevator trim properly, first **fly the aircraft at the desired attitude using the elevators,** then **remove the pressure from the controls with the trim tab, and finally let go of the controls to be sure that the aircraft will continue flying at the proper attitude.**

3. **d. any of the above.** The attitude indicator, like the aircraft itself, can assume any pitch attitude in level flight, depending on airspeed, gusts, and the like. The attitude indicator is also subject to gyro precession.

4. **False.** Due to the effects of gyro precession, the attitude indicator does not always indicate the actual attitude of the aircraft.

5. The two steps to take to correct an unwanted flight path are:
   1. stop the unwanted trend.
   2. begin a correction toward the desired trend.

6. **c.** The attitude indicator, being a gyro driven instrument, has the least lag.

7. **b.** If the aircraft has been trimmed properly for level flight, when the thrust is reduced slightly, drag will be more than thrust. This will cause the aircraft to decelerate, but because it has been trimmed for a certain speed, the nose attitude will drop slightly in an attempt to maintain the speed the aircraft has been trimmed for.

8. **d.** Lift. The aileron banks the aircraft. The rudder controls the aileron yaw, the thrust will maintain the airspeed, but the lift, now vectored partially to the inside of the turn, will lift the aircraft through the turn.

9. When the aircraft is banked into the turn, part of the lift that was merely overcoming gravity will now be used to lift the aircraft through the turn. The excess gravity will then try to pull the aircraft down. This will be overcome with an increased angle of attack through the elevators that increased the drag. The increased drag will try to slow the aircraft, unless additional thrust is provided to maintain the equilibrium.

Chapter 2

1. Flicker vertigo **is disorientation caused by strobe lights or rotating beacons flickering on the aircraft or the canopy. It can also be caused by the lights or the aircraft shadow flickering on clouds.**

2. You can overcome the effects of flicker vertigo by **going on the gauges immediately. If at night, or under instrument conditions, turn off the rotating beacon and/or the strobe lights, until the sensations pass.**

3. In order for the postural senses to detect velocity, either **acceleration** or **deceleration** must be present.

4. The reservoir within the inner ear is called the **common sac.**

5. The other parts of the inner ear are the **semicircular canals** and the **sensory hairs.**

6. Sudden, jerky control inputs during instrument flight can lead to **vertigo.**

Chapter 3

1. **e. Any of the above.** If you don't know the effects of a certain medication, even over-the-counter drugs, ask someone who does know. If you can't find anyone, don't fly for at least 24 hours.

2. If you take muscle relaxants, definitely call in sick because they cause weakness as well as sleepiness and vertigo.

3. Alcohol interferes with the normal use of oxygen by the tissues. It also takes the place of oxygen in the bloodstream.

4. The substance that transports oxygen through the bloodstream is **hemoglobin.**

5. **True.** In fact, hemoglobin can absorb carbon monoxide 200 times easier than oxygen.

6. **False.** It is almost impossible to tell that you are beginning to suffer from hypoxia because the symptoms can easily be attributed to other causes.

7. Hyperventilation brings about many of the symptoms of **hypoxia.** It is caused by breathing **deeply** and **heavily.**

8. The use of cocaine can bring about sudden heart attacks by **constricting** the blood vessels. This decreases the **oxygen** supply to the heart and **makes the heart work harder.**

Chapter 4

1. **True.**

2. By resetting the directional gyro to the magnetic compass on a regular basis. For the most accuracy, it is necessary for the aircraft to be flying straight-and-level and at a constant airspeed when the compass reading and gyro adjustment are made.

3. **False.**

4. For all practical purposes you cannot compensate for the attitude indicator precession. You must take the precession into consideration, however, and realize that the apparent attitude indicated on the AI will change gradually after a prolonged climb, descent, or turn.

5. Northerly turning error of the magnetic compass is caused by the **needle trying to align itself with the magnetic lines of flux of the earth**. It becomes greater **nearer the poles**.

6. The acronym ANDS stands for **Accelerate North Decelerate South**.

7. By taking the **northerly turning error** and **acceleration error** into consideration, a pilot can consistently make accurate turns to specific headings using the **magnetic compass**.

8. Timed turns to specific headings can be accomplished with great accuracy by using a clock, the **turn coordinator**, and/or the **attitude indicator**.

9. To accomplish both questions 7 and 8, it is necessary to have a **consistent roll rate** and **smooth control inputs**.

10. The smoothest climb is accomplished by not **applying climb power** until the airspeed is within **5 knots of climb speed**.

Chapter 5

1. The **power** controls the speed when power is variable and available.

2. When power is variable and available, the **elevator** controls the altitude or rate of altitude change.

3. The **elevator** controls the altitude or rate of altitude change when power is fixed or unavailable.

4. The **elevator** controls the airspeed when the power is fixed or unavailable. This basic question has been repeated because it is very important to be aware of this basic fact. When power is fixed, as in a climb, or unavailable, as in a descent or during an engine failure, the elevator is your only pitch/speed control.

5. If recovery from a power-on spiral under instruments were broken down into steps, the first thing you would do would be to **reduce power**.

6. The next two steps in question 5 would be **roll recovery** and **pitch recovery**.

7. The three steps in recovering from a stall while on instruments are:
   a. **max power,**
   b. **lower the nose,** and
   c. **roll wings level.**

8. When recovering from either a power-on spiral or a stall, you know you are in level attitude for that specific airspeed when there is a **definite change** in the **trend** of the **airspeed indicator**.

9. **False.** Any gyro instrument is likely to tumble during unusual attitudes. You should base the recovery on the partial panel instruments until you can ascertain the status of the gyros.

10. When lifting off during an instrument takeoff, the attitude indicator has a tendency to **read nose high**.

Chapter 6

1. The inbound course will be 035 degrees. The reciprocal of the 215-degree radial.

2. You should turn to a 125-degree heading. You are southwest of the station. You want to head southeast to cross a northeast inbound course.

3. The first course you would want to enter into the OBI would be 035 degrees.

4. This is the inbound course. By setting it in the OBI at this time, you will assure yourself that you have not yet passed through the inbound course.

5. The OBI needle should be to the right of the OBI, indicating that you have not yet made the course intercept.

6. The next course to set in the OBI is 055 degrees.

7. You have to time through 10 degrees to determine the time from the station when turning inbound. In order to do this, and still have time to plan the turn, you should set the OBI 20 degrees before the inbound course, and then time it until 10 degrees before the inbound course.

8. The OBI needle should still be to the right if you are going to be able to use it to time yourself through 10 degrees. If it were to the left you would be somewhere between that course and the desired course inbound, without enough time to figure out how close you are to the station.

9. The next course to set in the OBI would be 045 degrees. You will time yourself through the 10 degrees between 055 degrees and 045 degrees, and still have 10 degrees left to figure out what you want to do.

10. If the needle centers itself in 65 seconds, you will be six and a half minutes from the station when you turn inbound. You find this by multiplying the time (65 seconds) by 10 percent, or by simply moving the decimal point in one number from the right.

11. At a cruise speed of 90 knots, you would be just about 10 miles from the station when you intercept the inbound course. At a speed of 90 knots in a no-wind condition, you would be making one and a half miles per minute. In 6 minutes you would fly 9 miles. In the other half minute you would fly ¾ of a mile, or close to 10 miles.

12. You should turn inbound when intercepting the 035-degree radial.

13. If the time in question 10 were only 20 seconds, you would turn outbound when intercepting the course.

14. If you were to turn inbound, you would only be 2 minutes from the station, not enough time to get the inbound course that well established. Therefore you would turn outbound, and the first outbound heading would be 185 degrees, which is 30 degrees from the reciprocal of the inbound course.

15. After 1½ minutes you should turn to the **right** to a heading of **005 degrees**.

16. It should take you approximately 6½ minutes to cross the station after first crossing the inbound course.

17. The outbound turn should take just under half a minute. You will then fly for 1½ minutes outbound and turn 180 degrees, which will take another minute. From that point it should take approximately one more minute to intercept the inbound course, another half a minute to get back to the point at which you initially crossed the inbound course, and finally the 2 minutes from there to the station.

Chapter 7

1. **f. All of the above.** Flight planning for an instrument flight requires much more planning than for a VFR flight.

2. **False.** Sectional charts are a required part of an instrument flight kit. They are especially needed to check for heights of obstacles should you decide to file an "off airway flight plan."

3. To be usable for IFR flight, VOR equipment must be checked within every **30** days.

4. **False.** It is not necessary to have a qualified technician perform the VOR accuracy tests. You, as the pilot, can do it yourself, however, you must remember to make the proper entry in the aircraft log book.

5. **False.** Unfortunately, the regulations prohibiting flight with snow, ice, or frost adhering to an aircraft, or from flying into forecast moderate icing conditions during IFR flight, are written in FAR 91.527, which applies to large and turbine-powered aircraft. Common sense would dictate that the pilot of a small general aviation aircraft would pay attention to these regulations anyway.

6. Clear ice usually forms in the temperature range of from **10 to 32°F (–10 to 0°C)**.

7. Carburetor ice can form in any outside air temperature from **14 to 70°F.**

8. The difference between MEA, MOCA, and MRA is that the MEA gives the pilot obstacle clearance for the entire route segment, as well as adequate navigational signal coverage for the entire route (or segment). The MOCA provides the necessary obstacle clearance, but the navigational signal performance is only guaranteed to be acceptable within 25 statute miles of the VOR being used. The MRA is the lowest altitude at which an intersection can be determined, but it says nothing about obstacle clearances.

9. The basic fuel requirements for IFR are: enough fuel to land at the destination airport, plus enough fuel to fly from there to an alternate airport, plus enough fuel to fly for an additional **45** minutes at normal cruise speed.

10. The alternate airport (and its fuel requirements) mentioned in question 9 is not required, provided that the destination airport has a standard instrument approach procedure, and that for a period of **1 hour before and 1 hour after** the estimated time of arrival at the airport, the weather reports or forecasts, or any combination of them, indicate that the ceiling will be at least **2,000 feet above the airport elevation**, and the visibility will be **at least 3 miles**.

11. The basic alternate airport minimums for an airport with a published instrument approach procedure are a ceiling of **600 feet** and visibility of **2 statute miles** for a precision approach and a ceiling of **800 feet** and visibility of **2 statute miles** for a nonprecision approach.

12. **False.** Part 91.169 explains that if no instrument approach procedures have been published for an airport, that airport can still be used as an alternate provided that the ceiling and visibility will allow you to descend from the MEA, make your approach, and land, under basic VFR conditions.

Chapter 8

1. **False.** Regulations regarding SIDs say that you must possess **at least** the textual description of the SID. Although the graphic picture helps, it is not a requirement.

2. The basic IFR obstacle clearance climb requires an aircraft to climb at a rate of **200** feet per **nautical mile**, crossing the end of the runway at **35 feet** AGL, and climbing to **400 feet** above the airport elevation before turning, unless otherwise specified in the procedure.

3. If no climb gradient is specified in the SID, the pilot is expected to climb at a rate of at least **200 feet per mile** to the **MEA** unless required to level off by a crossing restriction.

4. The proper computer code to use to file a DUMBARTON FIVE DEPARTURE with a Red Bluff Transition, is DUMB5.RBL.

5. 1,000 feet per minute. Actually, if you closely examine the chart, notice that the 1,000-foot-per-minute rate of climb is for an aircraft with a ground speed of 125 knots, so to truly interpolate to the "nth" degree, the answer would be 960 feet per minute, but it's always best to err on the safe side, and it's rather hard to read 960 feet per minute on the vertical velocity indicator.

6. **True.** Altitude is not part of a "cleared as filed" clearance. Neither is the SID for that matter. If filing a flight plan that included a SID, you would receive a readback such as Hawaiian Flight 11 gets when flying from San Francisco to Honolulu, which is usually: "Hawaiian 11 Heavy is cleared to the Honolulu Airport via the San Francisco Three Departure, NORMM Transition, radar vectors to BEBOP, as filed, maintain one zero thousand, expect three three zero 10 minutes after departure, departure frequency is one three five decimal one, squawk two six seven seven, do not exceed two five zero knots until advised." The "cleared as filed" portion is for the enroute section, and does not include the SID, nor the altitude. In fact, if you look at the clearance again, Hawaiian 11 is only cleared to 10,000 feet initially, and is told to *expect* the final enroute altitude 10 minutes after departure. This is a normal high altitude clearance.

7. **b.** After takeoff you enter the clouds and intercept the course, then lose air-to-ground communications. You should **fly the ATC clearance as you received it.**

8. Gyro instruments will require at least **5 minutes** to stabilize after starting the engines.

9. **False.** Watch the gyro instruments during taxi to make sure that they are all operating properly and turn in the proper direction.

Chapter 9

1. You should tell the new controller who you're calling, who you are, what your altitude is (what altitude you're climbing or descending to and your final altitude), and any headings you may have been given by the previous controller.

2. If the previously estimated time to a required reporting point changes by more than **3** minutes, you are required to give a revised estimated time of arrival to that reporting point.

3. You should refigure ground speed whenever time permits.

4. Three good reasons to keep the volume up on the VOR receiver are:

1. **To know that the station's still on the air;**
2. **To get the latest weather reports; and**
3. **As a backup in the event you lose your communications radio.**

5. If the barometric pressure lowers, and/or if the temperature lowers, the altimeter will read higher than the actual aircraft altitude. The aircraft will be lower than you think.

6. Always check previous weather reports in order to determine the trend of the weather. In addition to using the past trend to plan the flight, with the past trend in mind, you can readjust your thinking if conditions change more rapidly than you anticipated.

7. If the weather conditions at the destination airport are changing for the worse faster than forecast, you should consider **diverting to your alternate.**

8. **False.** Always fly on the route centerline.

9. Climb or descend as fast as practicable until within 1,000 feet of the assigned altitude. Then attempt to maintain a climb or descent of 500 feet per minute.

10. Specific changeover points are indicated on enroute charts whenever the distance between navigational facilities exceeds 45 miles.

Chapter 10

1. **d.** A compulsory reporting point is indicated on the charts by **a solid triangle.**

2. When giving a position report in a nonradar environment, two times are necessary. These times are:
   1. **the time you crossed the compulsory reporting point**; and
   2. **the estimated time to the next compulsory reporting point**.

3. **True**.

4. **False**.

5. **True**. When you miss an approach you will be asked what your intentions are, so be ready to answer that question.

6. **False**. If you are in VFR conditions, remain in VFR conditions and land as soon as practicable. Once on the ground notify ATC as soon as possible.

7. The altitude you must fly will be the highest of, **the altitude last assigned by ATC**, **the altitude ATC has advised you to expect in a later clearance**, or **the minimum enroute altitude for each segment of the route.**

8. The proper transponder code for a two-way communications failure is to squawk code 7600 for the remainder of the flight.

9. The length of the inbound leg in a timed holding pattern should be **one minute** below **14,000** feet and **one-and-one-half minutes** above **14,000** feet.

10. **True**. The requirements are the same as for using a SID. While the graphical depiction will help the pilot visualize the procedure, all that is really necessary is the textual description.

Chapter 11

1. A pilot can be assured of terrain and obstruction clearance as well as runway or airport alignment by adhering to the altitudes, flight paths, and weather minimums depicted on the instrument approach procedure chart, or vectors and altitudes issued by the radar controller.

2. The father of our modern day instrument approach charts was Captain Elroy B. "Jepp" Jeppesen.

3. The main difference between a precision and a nonprecision approach is that the precision approach uses an electronic glide slope.

4. The DH is the lowest possible altitude on a precision approach: an absolute go-no-go point. If specific parts of the runway environment are not seen at the DH, a pilot must execute a missed approach immediately. The MDA is the lowest possible altitude on a nonprecision approach; plan to be at the MDA prior to reaching the actual missed approach point. Fly at the MDA until reaching the MAP and if the runway environment is not seen, execute the missed approach.

5. The aircraft approach category is a grouping of aircraft based on a speed of **1.3** times **the stall speed** in the **landing configuration** at **maximum gross landing weight**.

6. **Yes**. If the circling speed of an aircraft, that is executing a circling approach, exceeds the highest speed for the category that it normally falls into, it must use the next higher category minimums.

7. The three main conditions that must be met in order for a pilot to descend below the DH or MDA are:
   1. The aircraft is continuously in a position from which a descent to a landing on the intended runway can be made at a normal rate of descent using normal maneuvers;
   2. The flight visibility is not less than the visibility prescribed in the standard instrument approach procedure being used; and

3. At least one of the FAA-specified visual references for the intended runway is distinctly visible and identifiable to the pilot.

8. If you lose sight of the landing runway environment while executing a circling approach, you must immediately execute a missed approach unless **the inability to see an identifiable part of the airport results only from a normal bank of the aircraft**.

Chapter 12

1. The two methods used to determine visibility are:
   1. The human eye (prevailing visibility), and
   2. Transmissometers (RVV and RVR).

2. **False**. Once the pilot has been cleared for a visual approach—and accepts it—he is responsible for his own separation.

3. The three conditions that a pilot must meet in order to ask for a contact approach are:
   1. That he must be clear of clouds
   2. He must have at least 1 mile flight visibility, and
   3. He must reasonably expect to continue to the airport in those conditions.

4. The main advantage of a contact approach over a visual approach is that on a contact approach the pilot is still considered as operating IFR and ATC must provide him with aircraft separation.

5. The two things a contact approach is not intended to do is to be used by a pilot on **an IFR flight clearance to operate to an airport not having an authorized IAP**, nor **to conduct an instrument approach to one airport and then, when "in the clear," to discontinue that approach and proceed to another airport**.

6. During a contact approach, although ATC is still providing separation between your aircraft and other IFR and special VFR traffic, you are still responsible for **obstruction clearance**.

7. A straight-in approach to an airport will not be furnished if the normal rate of descent or the runway alignment factor of 30 degrees is exceeded.

8. A pilot is expected to make a straight-in landing if he has the runway in sight in sufficient time to make a normal approach for landing. In those conditions he is not expected to circle even though only circling minimums are published.

9. **False**. You are not authorized to descend below the MDA until you are in a position to make a normal, safe approach to a landing. You are provided with no obstruction clearance protection unless you remain at the MDA throughout the circling maneuver.

10. If you lose sight of the airport while circling, you execute a missed approach by turning toward the landing runway. You must continue the turn until you are established on the proper missed approach procedure. Nothing in the foregoing prohibits you from beginning a climb at any time throughout this procedure.

Chapter 13

1. **True.** That is why it is very important to check the scale of each chart.

2. Two numerals separated by a period over a communications block indicate the VHF frequency used minus the first two numerals. In the example, 2.2 would indicate a frequency of 122.2 MHz.

3. When an airport name is printed in all uppercase letters it signifies that there is a Jeppesen (instrument) approach chart published for that airport, and that the chart is indexed under that name. When the airport name is in uppercase and lowercase letters, it means that the instrument approach chart is indexed under the location that is printed above it in all uppercase letters.

4. A compulsory reporting point is indicated by a **solid triangle.**

5. In our example, the V-5 8500 SE, means that the minimum enroute altitude is 8,500 feet along the section of V-5 that runs southeast from the intersection. MRA 6000 indicates that the minimum reception altitude for that intersection is 6,000 feet.

6. The numerals 25/38 inside a holding pattern figure indicate that the holding pattern is a DME pattern, that the holding fix is 25 DME from the respective facility and that the outbound leg ends at 38 DME from the facility.

7. The MEA assures both acceptable navigational signal coverage between the radio fixes and obstacle clearance between those fixes.

8. The MOCA meets the obstacle clearance requirements along the route, but only assures acceptable navigational signal coverage within 25 statute (22 nautical) miles of a VOR.

Chapter 14

1. AMAs are shown on area charts. They act like MORAs to provide terrain clearance information but they depict **contour lines** rather than **latitude and longitude grids.**

2. **True.** You are not allowed to descend below the floor of the TCA.

3. The pilot will always be provided with radar vectors to a fix or route intercept on a vector SID. He will intend to provide his own navigation on a pilot nav SID, although even then he might receive some radar vectors.

4. A profile descent is an uninterrupted descent from cruising altitude to initial approach.

5. On an instrument departure, you are expected to be at least **35** feet above the runway at the departure end, to climb to at least **400** feet AGL before turning unless instructed otherwise, and to maintain a rate of climb of at least **200** feet per nautical mile to remain above the standard obstruction clearance slope of **152** feet per nautical mile unless a greater rate of climb is indicated on the procedure.

6. **False.** The MEA is shown for information and emergency use only. You cannot descend below the altitudes shown as crossing altitudes unless instructed by ATC.

7. **False.** If ATC gives you a heading or altitude change during a profile descent, the clearance will cancel the profile descent and ATC will provide you with heading, altitude, and speeds. But, if ATC simply changes the speed, they will provide speed restrictions only. You must still comply with the headings and altitudes depicted on the profile descent chart. If you cannot comply because of the speed changes made by ATC, you must advise ATC.

8. **False.** You are not allowed to leave the final altitude depicted on the profile descent unless cleared to a lower altitude or for an instrument approach procedure by ATC.

Chapter 15

1. **False.** The approach charts are only effective when you receive them if they do not show an effective date. If they show an effective date, they are not to be used before that date.

2. The three sources that provide the information for chart updates are:
   1. **letters of transmittal** from the *Federal Register,*
   2. the daily *National Flight Digest,* and
   3. **NOTAMs.**

3. The only difference is that there are two airports in the same area and the first number is to differentiate one from another. As these are arbitrary numbers only, neither is more important.

4. The second numeral indicates the type of approach: 1 is for ILS, 3 is for VOR.

5. The MSA is designed to provide the pilot with **1,000-foot obstacle clearance within 25 nautical miles from a specific navigational facility.**

6. **True.** The MSA altitudes are for emergency use only and do not necessarily provide NAVAID reception.

7. A letter suffix on an approach chart indicates that it is a circling approach.

8. **False.** You are never allowed to make a course reversal when NoPT appears on the chart without permission from ATC.

9. **False.** Only the racetrack and teardrop patterns must be flown as illustrated. The normal course reversal and the 80/260 are for guidance only and any course reversal can be used provided you stay within the protected airspace and don't go below the minimum altitude.

Chapter 16

1. The profile view is officially the **vertical cross section of the plan view** and depicts **the aircraft's altitude above the surface.**

2. **True.** They are oriented in the same direction as the profile is depicted.

3. The numbers near the procedure turn symbols **represent,** and **define** the limits of, the procedure turn.

4. On the profile views, large numbers indicate **minimum altitudes,** while small numbers in parentheses depict the **height** in feet above the **TDZE**, the **runway end**, or the **airport**.

5. The nonprecision FAF is depicted on the profile view by a **Maltese cross**, while the precision approach FAF is **at the glide path intercept point**.

6. **False.** If the runway environment is not in sight when reaching the DH, you must initiate a missed approach immediately. You can only fly out the time when reaching the MDA on a nonprecision approach.

7. The letters TCH on a precision approach stand for **threshold crossing height** and indicate the **height at which the glide slope crosses the threshold**.

8. You will find the missed approach instructions on the (plan/profile) view, located just **below the profile view** and **above the landing minimums**.

9. The time/speed table is useful in a precision approach to determine the approximate **rate of descent**. Many times this will be a first indication of **wind shear**.

Chapter 17

1. The initials ARP stand for **airport reference point**, and is the spot at which the **latitude and longitude** of the airport are determined.

2. A white bar across a runway on an airport plan view indicates a **displaced threshold.**

3. While runways are identified **numerically**, taxiways are designated **alphabetically**.

4. CL (30W, 20R & W, 20R) in the additional runway information means that the runway is equipped with centerline lights, and that the first 3,000 feet are white, the next 2,000 feet are alternating red and white, and the last 2,000 feet are red.

5. The runway takeoff length is usually the entire runway length. The displaced threshold usually only applies to landing aircraft.

6. **True.** There are no takeoff minimums for general aviation aircraft, but common sense must prevail.

7. **False.** There are times when obstructions in the takeoff clearance plane will require higher takeoff minimums than landing minimums as the landing aircraft will already be at a higher altitude and will be accelerating from a higher speed than the aircraft parked on the runway.

Chapter 18

1. NOS charts are updated every **56** days with a change notice issued every **28** days.

2. The NOS chart reference circle is usually **10** nm in radius.

3. On a NOS chart, straight-in approaches are indicated by an **"S" in front of the runway numeral** in the **minima table**.

4. **False.** This information is found in the tabulated data for airports in the front of the booklet.

5. **False.** This information is also found in the front of the booklet.

6. Pilot controlled lighting is indicated by **printing the symbols in reverse type**.

7. A lightning bolt symbol on a profile view of a NOS chart indicates the **glide slope intercept point**.

Chapter 19

1. **False.** You should always keep the volume of the navigational radio high enough to hear the identifier in order to ascertain that it is still on the air as well as serving as a back-up receiver in case communications radios are lost without knowing it.

2. **True.** Tune and identify every piece of navigational equipment on board. That way if something happens to the primary navigational tool, a back-up is ready and waiting.

3. **a, b, and d are correct.** Although you should always be ready to execute a missed approach, and should have some course of action in mind, ATC is too busy to handle IFR routings that might never be used. If you have to execute a missed approach, ATC will fit you back into the system in an expeditious manner. As far as the up-to-date weather is concerned, I always get the latest from ATC because ATIS is usually behind quite a bit. As for reviewing the approach chart and checking the missed approach procedures, you should always plan on a missed approach. An instrument approach is never completed until the aircraft is stopped on the runway.

4. **c. LOKIE is not an IAF.** It is a convenient fix, but all IAFs are identified by the letters (IAF) in quotation marks at the fixes that are applicable.

5. **b. These are part-time frequencies.**

6. **c.** Although it does point to the FAF (which is the MKK VOR), and the MKK VOR is the facility that the approach is predicated on, these are consequential facts. The heavy arrow on a plan view always points to the highest obstacle on the chart.

7. **b.** The tower is not always operational, and when it is not, arriving and departing pilots use the tower frequency as the common traffic advisory frequency. As the note in the additional runway information block tells us, it is also the frequency for the pilot-controlled lighting after 1830, which is when the tower shuts down.

8. **e. All of the above.** The course reversal is shown on the north side of the course, the minimum altitude is 2,500 feet, the 10 nm in the profile view shows us that the turn must be completed within 10 nautical miles of the VOR to remain in protected airspace, and the only holding patterns that must be flown as depicted are holding patterns and teardrops.

Chapter 20

1. **False.** The "x" simply indicates a dogleg turn to final. The "x" itself is where you would change from one track to another. The only symbol for a final approach fix is the Maltese cross on the profile view.

2. **b.** An approach transition that is coincidental with the approach procedure flight track is charted offset from the flight track for clarity.

3. **c.** These flag symbols indicate the placement of wind indicators. Due to changing wind conditions at MUE there is one located at each end of the runway.

4. **False.** JASON is never an initial approach fix. If it were, it would be identified by the symbol IAF.

5. **b.** Although the pilot controlled lighting usually functions off the control tower frequency when the tower is closed, the only way to know for sure is to check the notes on the airport chart under additional runway information.

6. **False.** If radar could be used it would be noted at the fix on the plan view.

7. **d.** If you look at the Category D minimums, you will see that the vertical line separates both the RAIL and ALS from the "all working" section.

8. **c.** While ATC might provide an arrival route based on the other choices, as far as the approach chart is concerned, the thin lines and small arrows simply indicate cross radials used to help identify the intersections.

Chapter 21

1. **d.** The 3,100-foot minimum altitude on the DME has absolutely no bearing on the straight-in NoPT approach. Get down to FAF altitude as soon as possible, and that is when you pass SELIC.

2. **c.** The MDA for all category aircraft on a LOC (GS out) approach is 460 feet. The only thing that will change will be the visibility requirements.

3. **d.** The aircraft category is determined during certification as 1.3 V_{SO} (stalling speed) in the landing configuration based on the maximum gross weight of the aircraft. The category might become higher if circling at a higher speed, or lower if operating specifications allow circling at a slower speed, but for straight-in approaches the aircraft category never changes.

4. **b.** If you normally fly an approach at 110 knots, and there is a headwind component of about 10 knots, the ground speed should be about 100 knots, and you can look up the time directly from the tables.

5. **The D6.7 at EWABE is based on the distance from the HNL VOR, which is located about midfield alongside Runway 8R. The distance from EWABE to the**

0 point can be found by adding the distance between the fixes, 5.4 miles, to the distance from the 0 point to the MM, .5 miles. The total distance then from EWABE to the 0 point is 5.9 miles.

6. It is important that you confirm the runway you have been cleared to because **as the CAUTION note says: "Due to tower location, controllers unable to determine whether aircraft are on correct final approach to Rwys 4L/R and 22L/R."**

Chapter 22

1. **b.** The ADF needle always reads the bearing of the station from the aircraft.

2. **b.** Remember what I said earlier. The sum of the DG, and the relative bearing on the ADF (if less than 360 degrees) is the magnetic bearing to the station. If the sum exceeds 360 degrees, subtract 360 from the sum. Going along with the same thinking, if you wanted to know the magnetic bearing from the station (an incorrect term that is coming more and more into use), you would add or subtract 180 degrees to the magnetic bearing. In this case the aircraft would be on the 220-degree bearing from the station.

3. **a and c are both correct,** although if the aircraft is too close to the station when you begin the procedure, the aircraft might be almost over the station when procedure C is used. Procedure A would provide a positive intercept and also allow you to compute the time and distance away from the station.

4. **b.** Let's put this down on paper and try to figure out what all is happening. First of all, the heading is 135 degrees, which is also the track you want to be flying. When on the track in a zero wind condition, the DG would read 135 degrees and the ADF needle would be pointing behind you, to 180 degrees. Because the DG is 135 degrees, and the ADF is pointing to the right of the tail (170 degrees), it would appear that a wind component from the south has drifted the aircraft northward by 10 degrees. Reestablish the proper track with a turn to the right toward the wind component. A 30-degree turn would provide a positive wind correction angle. At the moment of the completion of the turn, the DG would read 165 degrees and the ADF would read 140 degrees. Recall that it is sometimes easier to think of pulling the tail of the ADF needle, so if you want to think of it that way, when the head of the ADF is pointing at 140 degrees, the tail is on the reciprocal, or 320 degrees. You want to make a 10-degree correction to get back on course, so you would "pull the tail" of the needle 10 degrees, until it was on 330 degrees (or the head is on the reciprocal of 150 degrees). At that moment the aircraft would be crossing the 135-degree track. How do we know? Recall that the magnetic heading, plus the relative bearing, equals the magnetic bearing to the station. The magnetic bearing to the station is the reciprocal of the 135-degree track, or 135 degrees + 180 degrees = 315 de-

grees. If you add the DG 165 degrees, to the relative bearing 150 degrees, it also adds up to 315 degrees. If you turned back to the original heading of 135 degrees, the southerly wind component would soon drift the aircraft off course again, so add about 10 degrees to the right as a wind correction angle. This would result in a heading of 145 degrees.

5. **c.** Neither KRANE nor DIPPS are initial approach fixes. DIPPS is the holding fix, and KRANE is merely the intersection of the inbound course and the 13 DME.

6. There are **four** ways to determine DIPPS intersection. They are;
   1. 22 DME on the LNY 090-degree radial,
   2. the LNY 090-degree radial and the OGG 204-degree radial,
   3. 14.7 DME on the OGG 204-degree radial, and the
   4. LNY 090-degree radial and the IOGG localizer.

7. **a and b are correct.**

8. **False.** The statement is almost true, except for the 13 DME arc segment from the unnamed intersection at the OGG 084-degree intersection to OPANA, where the minimum altitude is 5,500 feet.

Resources

Information regarding the products and services mentioned in this book is available from:

Air Chart Systems
13368 Beach Ave.
Venice, CA 90292-5622
For brochures and information
(310) 822-1996
For VISA, Mastercard,
or American Express orders
(800) 338-7221
Contact Howie Keefe, Pres.

ARNAV Systems, Inc.
16923 Meridian East
P.O. Box 73730
Puyallup, WA 98373
Phone (206) 848-6060
Fax   (206) 848-3555
Contact Susan M. Hamner,
Vice-President—Marketing

Raytheon Aircraft Corp.
P.O. Box 85
Wichita, KS 67201-0085
(316) 676-7111

Collins Avionics
A Division of Rockwell International
400 Collins Rd. N.E.
Cedar Rapids, IA 52498
(319) 395-5772
Contact Karen Tripp
Corporate Communications

Jeppesen/Sanderson
55 Inverness Drive East
Englewood, CO 80112-5498
(303) 799-9090
(800)-621-5377
Contact Georgia Wolf
Corporate Communications Department

Aero Products Division
Litton Systems Inc.
21050 Burbank Blvd.
Woodland Hills, CA 91367
(818) 226-2000
Contact Gale James

RESOURCES

Department of Human Resources
NOAA Distribution Branch
N/CG33
National Ocean Service
Distribution Branch
Riverdale, MD 20737
General Information and one-time sales
(301) 436-6990
Subscriptions
(301) 436-6993

Index

About the author

J.R. Williams was born in the hard coal region of northeastern Pennsylvania in 1934. He graduated from the General Motors Institute in Flint, Michigan, in 1955. He spent 15 years in the automobile industry as garage and service station owner, Chrysler service manager, and automobile damage appraiser. During this time, he also drove professional race cars: midgets, sprint cars, and stock cars.

He learned to fly at Smith's Flying Service at the Wyoming Valley Airport in Forty-Fort, Pennsylvania, and worked in the area as a charter pilot and flight instructor until he went to work for Northeast Flying Service at Washington National Airport flying DC-3s before joining Hawaiian Airlines in May 1964.

At HAL, he flew DC-3s, Convair 340/440s, Convair 640s, Nihon YS-11s, DC-9 series 10, 30, 50 and Super 80 models, Lockheed L-1011 Tri-stars, and was flying DC-10s when he retired in December of 1994. From 1985 until his retirement, he was a Lockheed L-1011 and DC-10 Captain based in SFO where he was flying between SFO and HNL as well as internationally to London, Paris, Jamaica, American and Western Samoa, Tahiti, Guam, Manila, Rarotonga, and Tonga.

Because Hawaiian Airlines is part of CRAF (civil reserve air fleet), he spent part of 1991 flying troops in and out of the Persian Gulf in support of Desert Shield and Desert Storm. These flights took him to Prestwick, Scotland; Shannon, Ireland; Frankfurt, Germany; Rota, Spain; Rome, Italy; Athens, Greece; Bahrain; and Dhahran and Jubail in Saudi Arabia. He first checked out as captain in 1972, and retired with more than 20,000 hours of flight time.

Williams was a contributing editor to *Private Pilot* magazine for seven years and has written for *AOPA Pilot* and *Air Line Pilot* magazines, as well. He has sold more than 150 articles on flying, motorcycles, sailing, health, and travel. His first novel was published in 1981.

P 56 :-40 F=-40 c?
182-5/8 fig 16-2

920. 265.01-3